Welcome

The potential the iPad gives us for work and play is quite immense. From playing music, to checking your emails wherever you are, streaming videos and much, much more, the possibilities are endless. But with the staggering amount the iPad can do, often users aren't quite getting everything out of it that they could.

With the iPad Book no area is left uncovered as we take you through these possibilities with in-depth guides. The Getting Started section introduces you to all the apps that come bundled with your new device, offering you all the essential hints and tips. The Lifestyle, Productivity and Entertainment tutorials have all the need-to-know functions covered, and the Essential apps section introduces you to all the apps you simply must have. The iPad Book is the ultimate guide to Apple's tablet, helping you get the very best out of this revolutionary device.

Enjoy the book.

The iPad Book

The iPad Book

Imagine Publishing Ltd
Richmond House
33 Richmond Hill
Bournemouth
Dorset BH2 6EZ
☎ +44 (0) 1202 586200
Website: www.imagine-publishing.co.uk

Editor in Chief
Aaron Asadi

Production Editor
Amy Squibb

Design
Charles Goddard

Photo Studio
Studio equipment courtesy of Lastolite (www.lastolite.co.uk)

Printed by
William Gibbons, 26 Planetary Road, Willenhall, West Midlands, WV13 3XT

Distributed in the UK & Eire by
Imagine Publishing Ltd, www.imagineshop.co.uk. Tel 01202 586200

Distributed in Australia by
Gordon & Gotch, Equinox Centre, 18 Rodborough Road, Frenchs Forest, NSW 2086. Tel + 61 2 9972 8800

Distributed in the Rest of the World by
Marketforce, Blue Fin Building, 110 Southwark Street, London, SE1 0SU.

ISBN 978-1-908222 0 60

IMAGINE PUBLISHING

The iPad Book

Contents

Getting started

Lifestyle

Productivity

08: Complete Guide to the iPad
Everything you need to know to get the most from your device

See page 174 for unmissable subscription deals!

Entertainment

Essential Apps

iPad
9:41 AM
Thursday
27
Calendar
Contacts
Notes
280
Maps
Videos
YouTube
iTunes
App Store
Game Center
FaceTime
Camera
Photo Booth
Settings
7
Safari
Mail
Photos
iPod

Complete guide to the iPad

Apple calls the iPad its third post-PC device – the first two being the iPod and iPhone – a new class of computers that enable anyone to browse the web, create content and enjoy media without the restriction of a desktop, mouse and keyboard. But what exactly is a post-PC device?

Well, it certainly isn't a replacement for your trusted desktop computer. After all, the iPad needs to be activated using a computer before it can be fully unlocked and used. A post-PC device should be seen as the next generation of computing, one that's highly portable, far more personal than a PC, devoid of desktop traditions such as an on-screen pointer, file menus and folder hierarchy, but still able to carry out the everyday tasks that we expect to achieve. The iPad fits the bill perfectly, with intuitive touch controls, ease-of-use, and apps for consuming media, creating content and communicating like never before.

The iPad has an absolutely been a phenomenal part of Apple's history, selling 15 million units in its first year of sale alone. Not only this, but it has ushered in a new era of computing; introducing millions of first-time computer users to email, the web, video communication, word processing and even home movie-making. There has never been a better time to jump on board the touch-computing revolution…

Lifestyle

There's an app for every part of your life

Perhaps the biggest draw of the iPad is its lifestyle enhancements. Using the iPad to access Facebook, view photos, finger-paint or chat with friends is more engaging and easier than ever before, thanks to the large touch screen and the sheer number of apps.

With the built-in cameras on the iPad 2, it's now possible to video call anyone in the world. It's as simple as tapping on the FaceTime app icon, then selecting a contact from the list on the right side of the screen. As long as the recipient has an iPad 2, iPhone 4 or Mac, they'll be able to accept the call and engage in a video conversation with smooth video and clear, digital audio. Thanks to the clever accelerometer built into the iPad 2, when you rotate the device the video will automatically swap orientation so both you and the other user stay the right way up. You can also flip between the front and back camera with just the tap of finger, enabling you to show friends and family objects and environments behind the iPad.

At the time of writing there's no official Facebook app for the iPad, but there's practically no need thanks to Safari's ability to display Facebook in full on your iPad's screen. It's possible to view photos and videos, leave messages on friends' walls, send private message and like posts. If, however, you'd prefer to use a dedicated app for accessing Facebook, then both Friendly Plus for Facebook and Facebook for iPad will enable you to access the website.

Using your iPad to view photos is one of the most engaging ways to relive memories and share images with friends. The large, 9.7-inch display is the perfect size for displaying snaps, possessing a sharp and colourful image. Using Multi-Touch gestures it's possible to zoom in and out of photos with a pinch of two fingers, or jump to another shot with the swipe of your hand.

Viewing photos on your iPad is a great experience, but it's also possible to create your own digital paintings using apps. ArtRage is one of our favourites, with the ability to paint using realistic brushes such as a watercolour brush, pencil, palette knife and airbrush. Another popular painting app is SketchBook Pro, with support for layers, high-quality brushes and a professional-grade painting engine. With it's 4:3 ratio screen, painting on the iPad is like painting onto your very own mini-canvas; one that can undo mistakes, zoom in on areas and share paintings with friends.

"Using the iPad to access Facebook, view photos, finger-paint or chat with friends is more engaging and easier"

If you enjoy reading the latest Twitter posts from friends and celebrities, then you'll find an abundance of Twitter apps available in the App Store. The official Twitter app is perhaps the best of these, with a futuristic interface that slides content and tweets into view. Using the iPad, it's also possible to blog your own thoughts and experiences on the web by using the official WordPress app.

The iPad provides a number of amazing ways to enhance your lifestyle, but it does so much more. We've detailed even more abilities across the page for you to discover…

5 ways to improve your everyday life

1 Start shopping from your iPad

The iPad offers you many ways to make purchases online. You can use Safari, or plenty of dedicated shopping apps. eBay is our preferred way to find items. It has a wonderful interface, listings appear in a floating window, so you'll never need to tap back a page, and it's even possible to pay for items via PayPal through the app. It makes the full website on your desktop computer look clumsy and rather old fashioned.

2 Use your iPad as a picture frame

If you'd like to use your iPad as a digital photo frame, simply open the Settings app, tap on Picture Frame, and toggle the on/off button. The iPad will now fade or animate between photos when you tap the flower icon on the lock screen. You can also tell the iPad to zoom in on the faces in photos enabling the Zoom in on Faces button, and choose whether to display all photos or just the images from a specific album.

3 Instant message your friends

The iPad doesn't have a Messages app for sending SMS and MMS messages, but that doesn't mean you can't instantly message your friends. IM+ Pro is perhaps the most feature-packed app, with support for every major chat program available, including GTalk, MSN/Live, AIM/iChat, ICQ, MySpace, Twitter, Facebook and Skype. Messages are free, and the app supports push notifications. IM+ Pro even includes a built-in browser for viewing links. It's not free, however, priced £5.99/$9.99.

4 Get cooking with your iPad

There are a plethora of recipe apps on the App Store, including great additions from celebrity chefs such as Gordon Ramsay Cook With Me HD. You'll never run out of dinner ideas, however, with the free iPad app 170,000+ Recipes: Big Oven. As the name suggests, more than 170,000 recipes can be found, most with lengthy instructions. Big Oven also enables you to post your own recipes, create a favourites list, create a groceries list and more.

5 Update Facebook from anywhere

Whether you're sat on the couch, lying in bed or sunbathing on the beach, you can update your Facebook status at any time using the iPad. Simply open Safari, log into your Facebook account, and away you go. It's also possible to upload photos to Facebook using third-party apps such as Facebook for iPad. This popular app can also download photos to your iPad photo album, and even enable you to chat to friends in real time.

Complete guide

Productivity

Make your daily tasks much easier with the iPad's extensive functionality

With its 9.7-inch Multi-Touch display and groundbreaking interface, the iPad makes being productive far easier than using a desktop computer. Take checking your email. By tapping the Mail icon, your inbox will instantly spring to life. When used in landscape mode, your messages can be found on the left side of the screen, with selected messages viewed in full on the right. On-screen controls make sending emails, forwarding messages, saving to inboxes and attaching files easier than ever before. With instant access to your email account, you'll always have your messages by your side.

But what about more intensive productivity tasks, such as word processing? By using Apple's Pages app, you can quickly create things such as a resume, letter, thank-you card and more by using the templates. Apple also supplies apps for creating presentations and spreadsheets (see 'Make iWork docs' in the sidebar). Additional apps – of which there are more than 65,000 – include Dropbox, a free service that enables you to store documents on the web and access them at any time using an iPad, iPhone or desktop computer. Then there's Evernote, a free note-taking app that stores anything you write on the internet for you to access anywhere on any device. The list of productivity apps is nearly endless, and is growing by the day.

Of course, apps are not the only way of being productive on your iPad. It's possible to print wirelessly using Apple's AirPrint technology, enabling you to print movie tickets, emails, word documents and much more at just the tap of a finger. At the time of writing, only AirPrint-enabled HP printers are supported, but further models are expected to be added in the near future. The iPad also has extensive support for common file types, so opening a PDF in Mail takes just one tap of a finger, and it renders almost instantly. It's also possible to open Microsoft Office files such as Word documents and Excel spreadsheets without installing any third-party apps.

Where the iPad's true strengths really lie, though, is in its sheer portability. Its size and weight make it easy to carry around, and unlike traditional laptops and notebooks, iPads don't need to be opened and rested on a table before they can be used. They don't emit any heat (so no burned thighs), have on-screen keyboards that with practice can be as efficient as physical keyboards, and some models have built-in 3G support so you're never unable to access the web and be out of contact. And now, with the release of the iPad 2, being productive is even more efficient than ever before. The iPad 2 can automatically and instantly turn on as you peel back the Smart Cover (purchased separately), and has two cameras for making video calls and conferences anywhere in the world. At first glance the iPad is easy to underestimate, but it truly is a productive device that anyone can use.

"With its 9.7-inch Multi-Touch display and groundbreaking user interface, it is easy to be productive with an iPad"

5 top iPad tips for your daily tasks

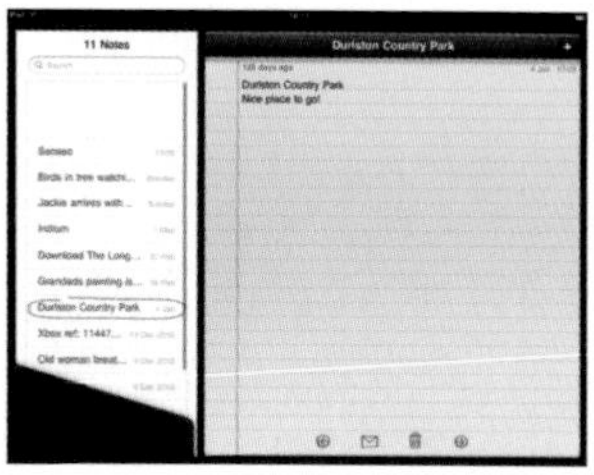

1 Make notes on your iPad

The Notes app makes it simple to write and store notes. Its interface takes the appearance of a leather book, storing notes in a sleeve. You can sync notes to your desktop, and apps such as Evernote enable you to store them in the cloud, so you can access them from any device.

2 Email friends and family

With the iPad, you're never far from your email. Mail is perfect for email-related tasks, and includes every function you'd expect, such as the ability to send attachments, forward messages and view images. Mail supports POP, IMAP, Microsoft Exchange, MobileMe, Gmail, Yahoo, AOL and Hotmail, so anyone can quickly set up an account.

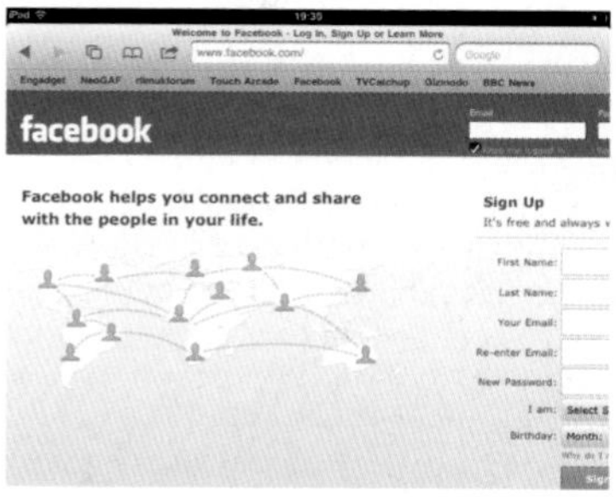

3 Surf the internet with Safari

Browsing the web on the iPad is an amazing way to read the news, chat with friends and watch media. That's because of the sheer rendering speed and ease of use of Safari, the iPad's app for accessing the internet.
Safari is a portable version of its desktop iteration, and supports the very latest web standards including HTML 5. As a result, you can access the web whenever and wherever on your iPad.

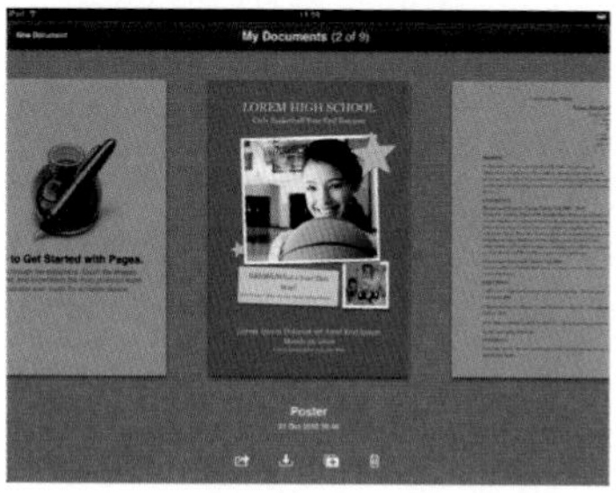

4 Print wirelessly from your iPad

Apple's AirPrint technology automatically looks for printers on the same Wi-Fi network as your iPad. You'll need a HP printer to take advantage of this, however (see **www.apple.com/ipad/features/airprint.html** for the full list). For those without a HP printer, third-party apps like PrintCentral will help you, but these apps are not free.

5 Make iWork docs

With Pages, it's possible to format text and images, spell-check, email documents and print via AirPrint. The Numbers app is the perfect way to create and edit spreadsheets, with more than 250 functions for creating formulas, calculations and more, and Keynote can create amazing presentations.

Entertainment

Get more from the ultimate multimedia device

One of the attractions of owning an iPad is the ability to enjoy movies, books, music, TV shows and games anywhere and at any time. The large screen combined with a slim profile and light weight makes the iPad the perfect companion for long trips, laying on the sofa or sitting in a coffee shop. No longer will you need to carry a hefty laptop or squint at a tiny mobile phone screen.

Launched alongside a brand new iBookstore in April 2010, the iPad is great for reading books. Its vibrant, colourful screen is perfect for viewing embedded photos and videos, and the on-screen controls enable you to change the text size, font, screen brightness, access a dictionary and bookmark pages. In portrait mode, a single page fills the screen, but turn the iPad on its side, and you'll be greeted by two-pages. Buying books is easy, thanks to the built-in iBookstore that enables you to purchase and download eBooks with just the tap of a finger.

With it's 4:3 ratio screen, the iPad makes for a great video player too. Its Videos app displays a multitude of information about movies, including a description, cast list, date and poster. It's possible to jump between chapters, and it automatically saves where you pause, so the next time you open it the film will carry on playing where you left it. By tapping the iTunes app, you can purchase films from the iTunes store, plus your favourite TV shows. The iPad also includes a YouTube app for viewing videos. You can view a video's info, comments and related videos – even while one is playing. You can also choose favourite videos for viewing at a later date.

It might be several times larger than an iPod, but the iPad makes for a great music player. For this it has its own dedicated app, which takes full advantage of the 9.7-inch display to show album art and full track listings. In many ways the iPod app mimics the desktop computer iteration of iTunes, with a sidebar in landscape mode for jumping between music, podcasts and audiobooks. You can also add more music by purchasing tracks and albums from the iTunes app, which is included with the iPad.

What really makes the iPad stand out from its competitors are the sheer number of apps available to download, however. Some of the most popular are games, and there are literately thousands of great titles to download and enjoy. The racing genre is packed with first-class titles such as *Real Racing 2* and *Need For Speed: Shift*. Both use the accelerometer for steering – turning the iPad into a gigantic steering wheel. Other popular genres include strategy games, which take full advantage of the Multi-Touch display to make ordering units quicker than any other games console. Puzzle games such as *Angry Birds* and *Fruit Ninja* also have addictive iPad versions, with high-resolution graphics too.

5 ways to have fun with your iPad

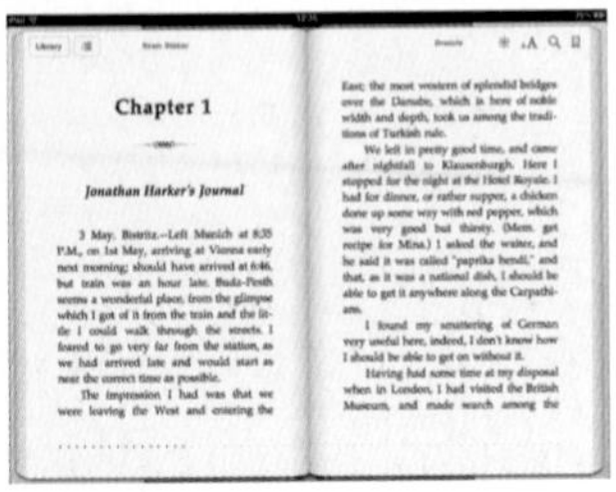

1 Buy and read digital books

iBooks is perfect for reading eBooks, but there are others like Kindle, which allows you to buy eBooks and sync between devices. WHSmith eBooks also has a built-in reader with a virtual bookshelf and Waterstone's lets you buy books and find the nearest store to reserve physical copies.

2 Use a big screen

The iPad 2 has a clever ability that makes it a powerful tool for entertainment and education purposes – HDMI mirroring. By purchasing the Digital AV Adapter (sold separately), you can plug your iPad 2 into a HDTV and mirror its display in full. That means you can watch movies on your big screen, play games such as *Real Racing 2* in 1080p, and mirror keynotes and educational apps on a large screen.

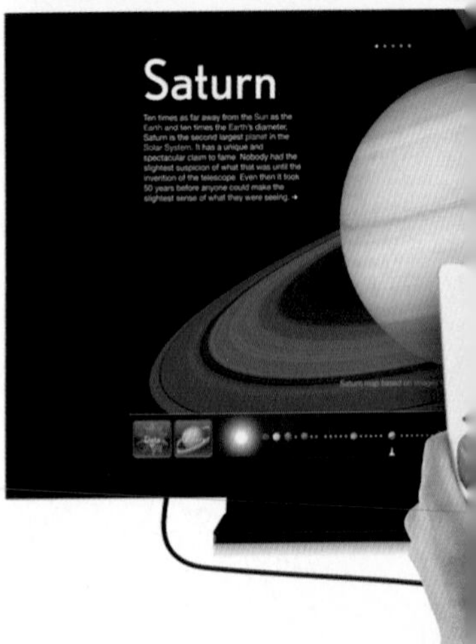

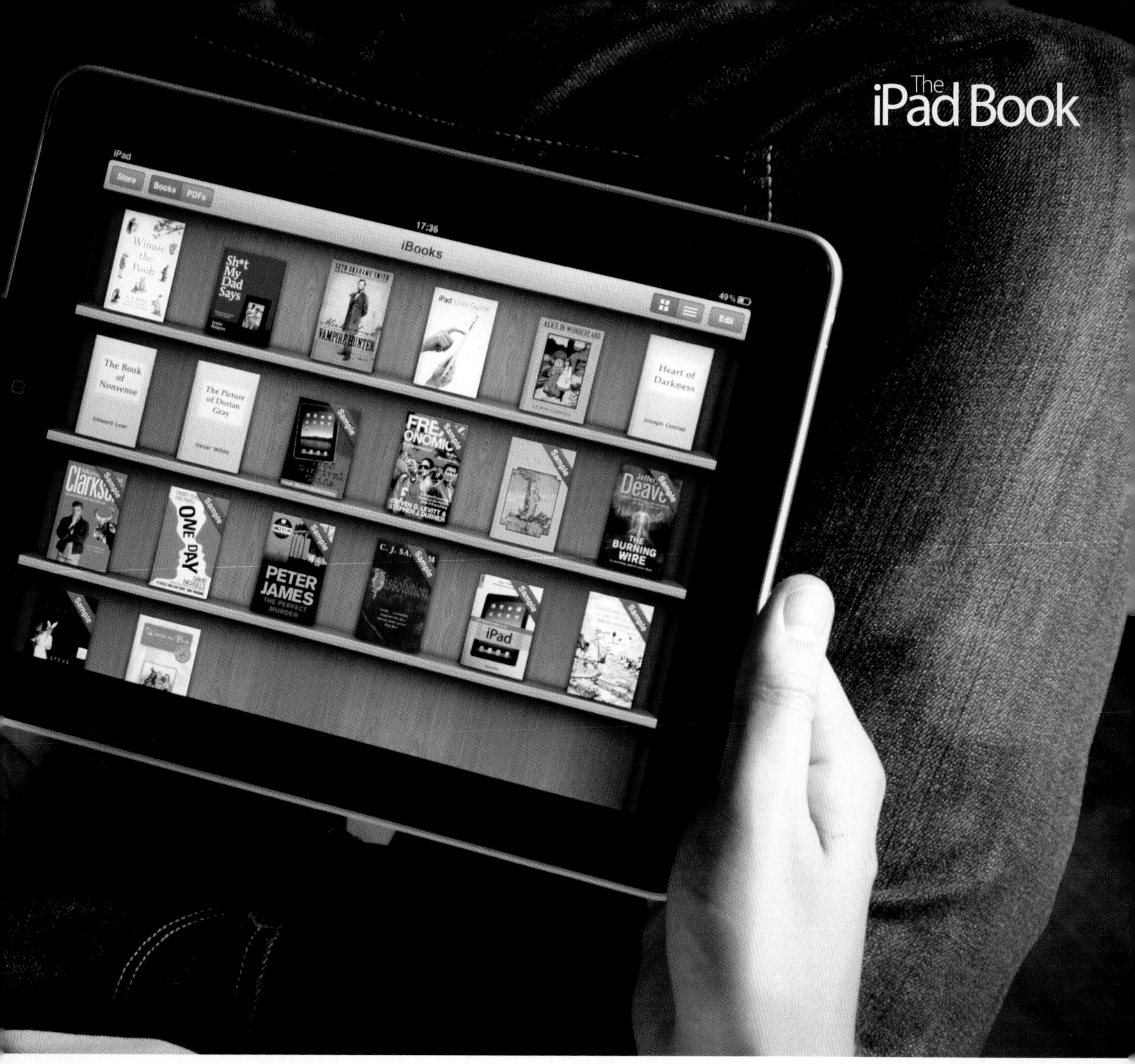

3 Use the video capabilities

It's easy to watch movies and TV shows on your iPad, but by downloading a handful of third-party apps you can really turn your iPad into a powerful video entertainment system. Air Video enables you to stream videos from your Mac and PC – without converting and syncing them via iTunes, and Air Display turns your iPad's screen into a second monitor for your desktop computer. This is handy if you need extra space for a program such as iTunes.

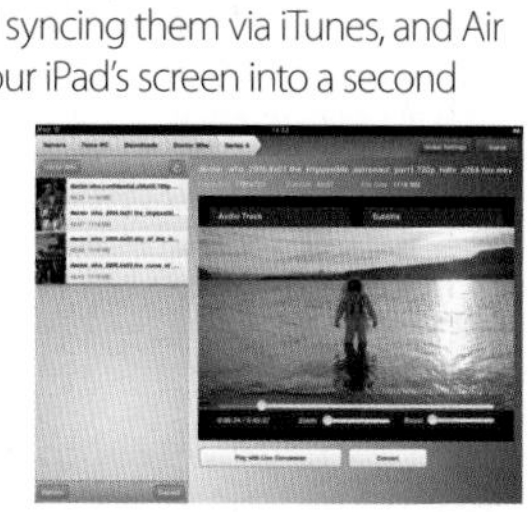

4 Read magazines and newspapers

The iPad doesn't only display books, it can also display your favourite magazines and newspapers. Magazine titles such as *How It Works*, *games*™ and *Apps Magazine* have their very own apps that enable you to buy individual issues and subscribe. Newspapers such as *The Times* and *The Sun* have apps that display the day's newspaper in full, although these typically require a subscription.

5 Enjoy your iPad's music wirelessly

The iPad has a headphone socket at the top for quickly plugging in a set of headphones for music, films and games, but it's not exactly the most convenient place for a dangly wire to be protruding. Thankfully, the iPad fully supports wireless Bluetooth headphones, such as the Sennheiser MM 100. Sync these via the Settings app, and you'll be able to enjoy wireless audio that's crystal clear, bassy and in sync with the content on-screen.

Getting Started

Your ultimate guide to the iPad's default apps

When you first get your new iPad, it can be a bit daunting, as there is simply plethora of things to do with it. Getting Started is here to show you all the key features of the apps that come bundled with your device, as well as giving you a quick tip for each application to get you going. We will take you through the App Store and its essential functions, how to get the most out of surfing with Safari, using the Mail app to its best and much more. No default app is left unexplored in our essential guides. Once you've been introduced to all the iPad has to offer you'll be better equipped to get stuck in and making the most of these staple apps and the amazing functions they deliver to you.

018 Get to grips with the iPad's most important and useful settings.

034 Navigate your way around the ultimate location resource – the Map app.

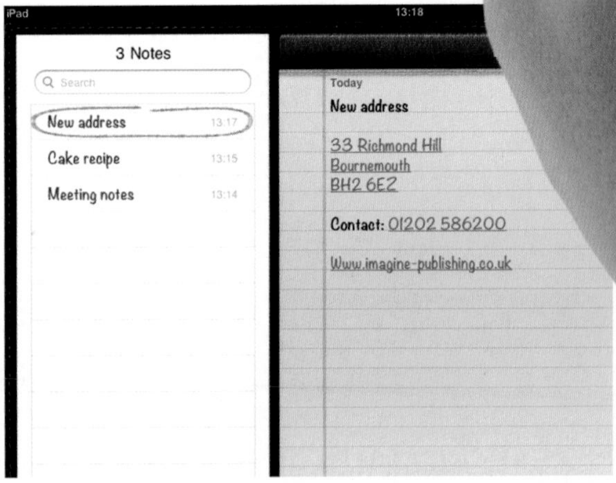

032 Learn how to always keep track of your ideas with the Notes app.

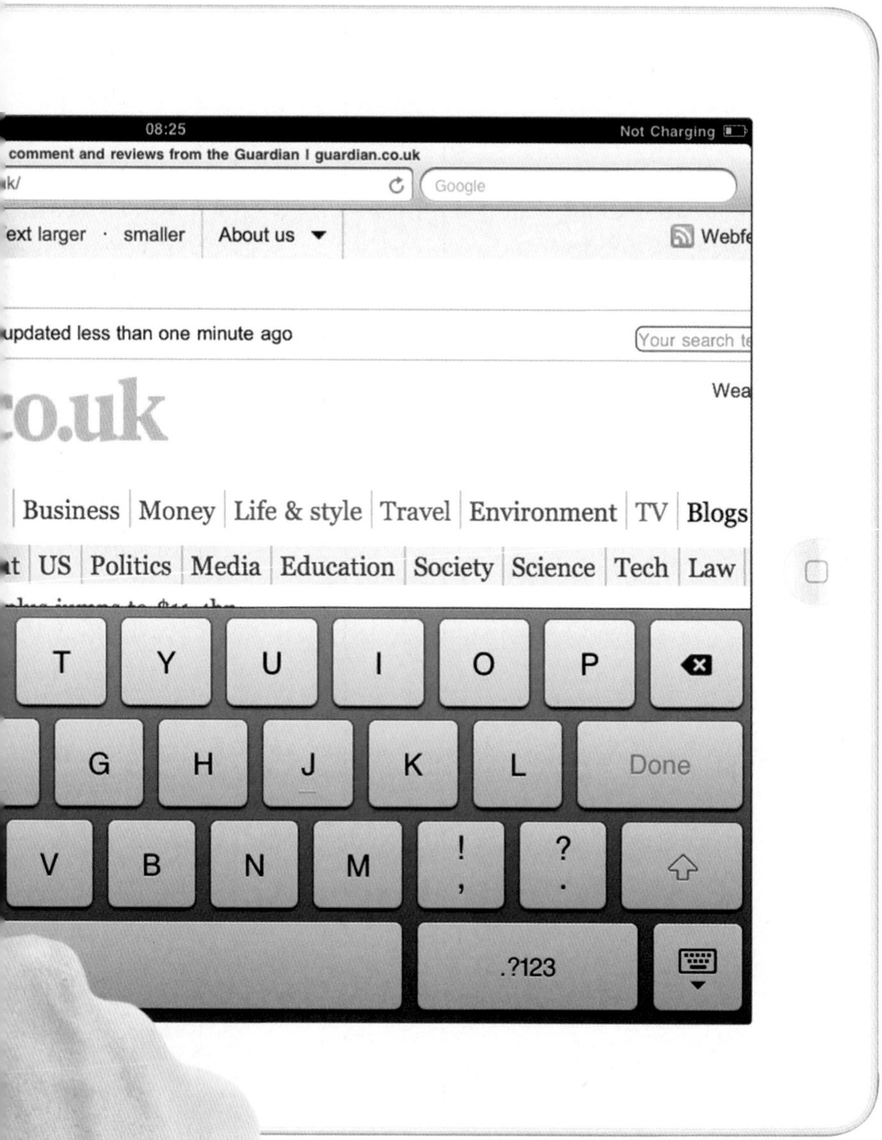

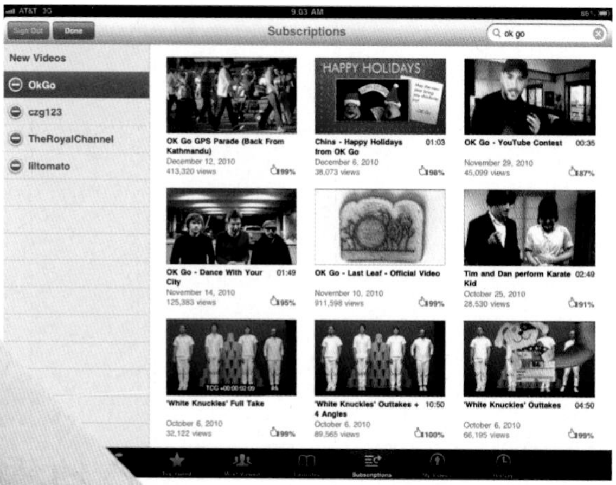

048 Take control of YouTube with this fantastic videos app for iPad.

Understanding Settings

A guide to using the iPad's Settings panel

The Settings app is, as you'd expect, where you can tweak and personalise the inner workings of your iPad. Click on the cog icon and you'll be transported to a control panel listing topics from wallpapers to Wi-Fi and everything else in between.

'General' houses the most commonly accessed and vital functions. Here you can add and remove Wi-Fi networks, apply a password, amend the date and time, change the language, plus more.

Elsewhere, each header will directly relate to the app in its title – so selecting the Safari header, for example, will give you the chance to customise settings for web browsing, such as blocking pop-ups, clearing the history, and opting for your preferred internet search engine. Meanwhile, 'iPod' offers you the chance to apply a volume limit or implement home sharing through your Apple ID.

If you want to change your email signature, your screen brightness or the iPad's wallpaper, you can do it all in the Settings app.

"Click on the cog icon and you'll be transported to a control panel with topics from wallpapers to Wi-Fi"

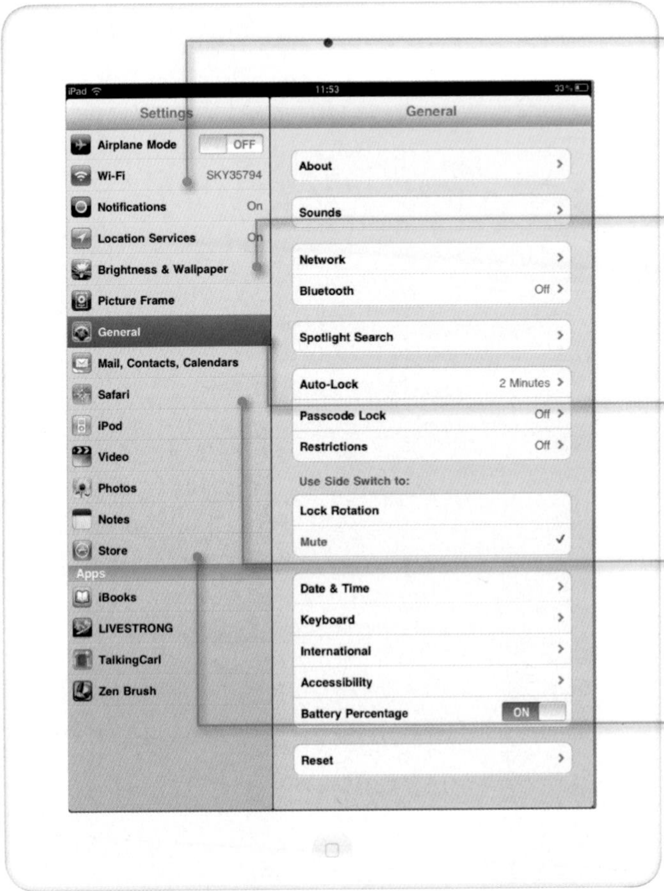

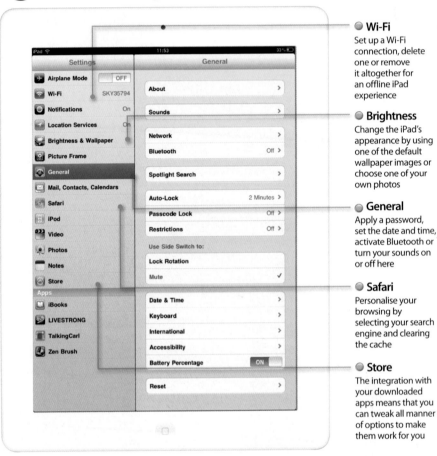

Wi-Fi
Set up a Wi-Fi connection, delete one or remove it altogether for an offline iPad experience

Brightness
Change the iPad's appearance by using one of the default wallpaper images or choose one of your own photos

General
Apply a password, set the date and time, activate Bluetooth or turn your sounds on or off here

Safari
Personalise your browsing by selecting your search engine and clearing the cache

Store
The integration with your downloaded apps means that you can tweak all manner of options to make them work for you

QUICK TIP

Enable restrictions

Take control of your iPad

If there's more than one person that will be using your iPad – especially if it is a child or teenager – you might like to consider enabling restrictions to certain apps or functions for security purposes. It's incredibly easy to do and provides peace of mind while your newly purchased iPad is in the hands of someone else.

If you would like to restrict certain privileges, selecting General>Restrictions in the Settings app will present a page of the most popular apps with settings to restrict. In the first instance you will be asked to set a four-digit Passcode and, once that's done, you'll be able to browse through the list of apps and select On/Off accordingly.

Possibly one of the most important areas for parents of young children is the prevention of in-app purchases, and just a simple slide from On to Off in the Restrictions menu could prevent a hefty iTunes bill after a child's gaming session. Additionally, you can set ratings that are relevant for the country that you're living in to prevent unsuitable apps, games, music, films or television shows being purchased by children or teenagers via the iTunes Store.

However, perhaps one of the best features of the Restrictions section is the ability to approve multiplayer games or adding friends – a vital feature for parents of children of all ages, we're sure you'll agree.

A passcode is needed to set restrictions – make sure no one else knows it!

Key features

What you can do within this app

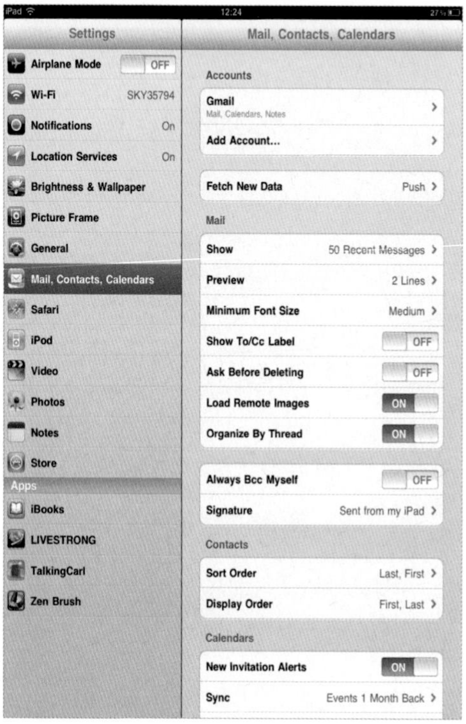

Customise email settings

It's possible to have more than one email account accessible from your iPad, which is great if you're running your own business or working from home. To add or delete these go to the 'Mail, Contacts and Calendar' section. While you're here you can tweak how many recent messages you can view, whether you'd like to preview a line or two of these when they're displayed in a list, and also change the font. For those that would prefer to attach a signature, sync events in your iCal or sort the order of your contacts, this is also doable from within the Mail section.

Personalise browsing

Select Safari in order to change your internet settings. Choose from three of the most popular search engines listed to pick your preferred option, activate AutoFill to save typing time and show/hide the Bookmarks bar. Within Safari's security section you can choose to block pop-up adverts, receive a warning if you were to stumble onto a dodgy site, or simply clear your history at the click of a button. These options ensure you're afforded full control over how you access the web.

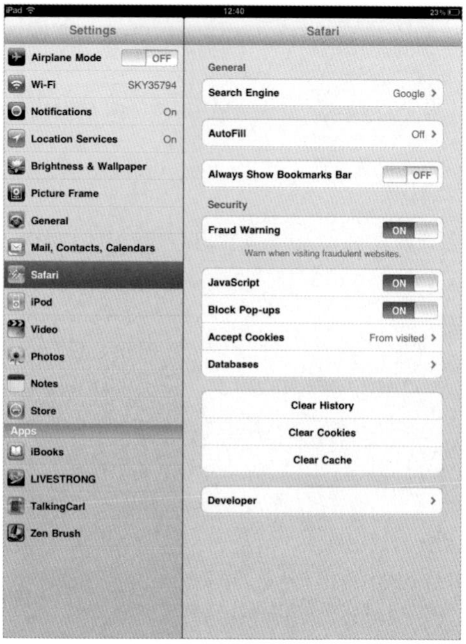

Change wallpaper

If want to alter the iPad screen's appearance then Brightness & Wallpaper houses the options to do this. The Auto-Brightness is controllable on a sliding scale function, which you can just press and drag left or right to suit. Meanwhile, the wallpaper image can be selected from the range of default pictures already stored on the iPad. Alternatively, you can simply pick one of your saved photos to form the backdrop.

Networking

As you'd expect, the Wi-Fi tab houses your internet network options. Your current network – if you're hooked up to it – will be displayed in blue text with a tick to the left-hand side of it. However, if you'd like to add another network simply click on Other and you'll have the option to input the new details and password. It's great if you're out and about with your iPad and you've been given permission to use another connection.

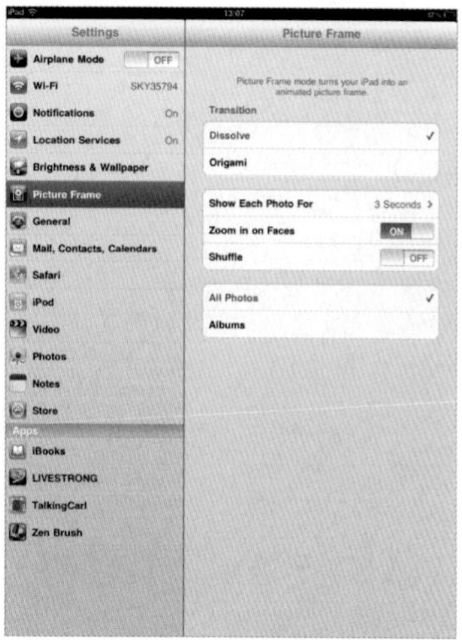

Animated picture frame

Digital photos have become the way of the world now, but that means the shots often stay stashed on a computer hard drive. Fortunately the Picture Frame tab enables you to display your pics by using your iPad as an animated picture frame. You're gifted full control of which albums it selects, how long each shot is shown for, whether it zooms in on faces and even if you would like it to shuffle them up.

Introducing iTunes

Learning more about your very own music and media store

iTunes is an app that houses a whole range of music, films, television programmes, podcasts and audiobooks. If it's a particular artist or author you're looking for, you can find them via the Search bar – simply type the name in, and you're good to go. Additionally, the Featured and Top Charts tabs enable you to see the newly released singles, albums, films and TV shows.

The great thing about this app is that even if you're feeling a little uninspired musically or otherwise, you can activate the Genius function through your home Mac or PC, and it will offer recommendations based on your past selections and history.

Not only that, whether you're on a budget or have cash to splash, you're sure to find something here that will suit your wallet. Podcasts are very often free, and are searchable by category, 'new and noteworthy', or simply by you knowing what or who you're looking for.

"iTunes houses a whole range of music, films, TV programmes, podcasts and audiobooks"

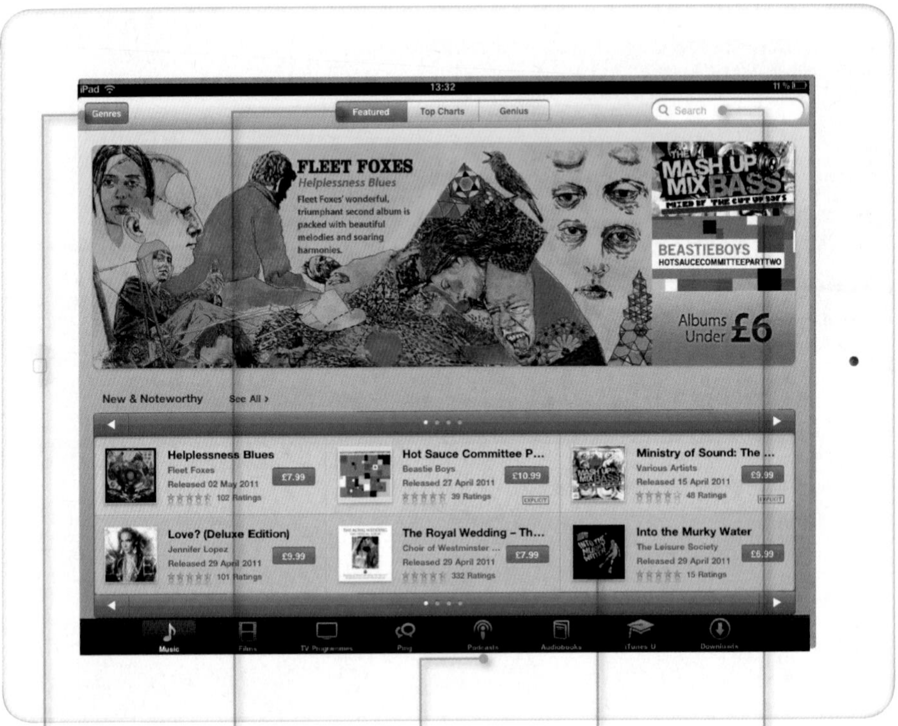

Genres
If nothing is taking your fancy, narrow your search with the Genres button on the top left

Tabs
The most popular and latest tracks and films are on the Featured and Top Chart tabs

Categories
Content is organised into categories, and are viewable as icons at the bottom

View
Tap the thumbnail to take a closer look – you can buy from within this screen too

Search
The intelligent search bar ensures you're able to look for what you want when you need it

QUICK TIP

iTunes U Click. Sync. Learn

A rather excellent addition to this app is the iTunes U – learning resources searchable either by subject or educational institution. This collection – or, rather, library – of discussions and more enables individuals to start or continue their education via their iPad. Many of them are free, and could be of use whether you're studying or just eager to expand your knowledge on a new topic.

The Featured tab offers a hot pick of the latest resources uploaded; meanwhile, as you would expect, the Top Charts provide a snapshot of the most popular files. With highly regarded institutions such as Oxford University, Stanford and more providing content, it's an excellent opportunity to indulge in some higher learning.

Learn how to build a business, and tackle iPhone Application Development, or Astronomy. If that doesn't take your fancy, then search for a topic that does – the choice is yours. Meanwhile, clicking on Beyond Campus will take you to a drop-down list of institutions such as museums, theatres and organisations like the British Council offering advice and expertise on a range of topics. And the best thing about it? You don't have to be a student to partake in this. What are you waiting for?

With a plethora of free content available on iTunes U, it is an excellent resource.

Key features

Heading beyond the interface

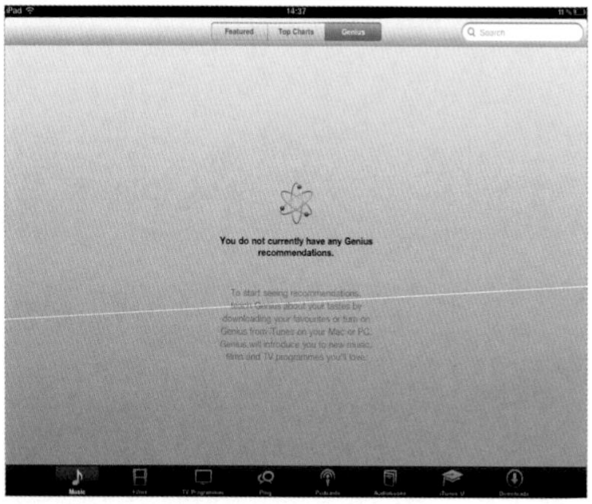

Recommendations

iTunes' Genius function recommends new music, films, television shows and more based on existing and previous purchases and downloads. While it requires activation via your home Mac or PC, once you've done this there will be a whole range of new media to choose from. It's ideal if you're looking to expand your tastes and explore new avenues of entertainment.

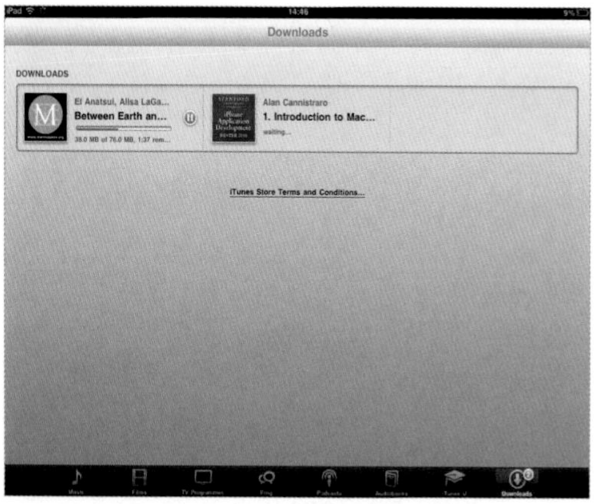

View downloads

Pressing the Downloads tab along the bottom of the iTunes window will take you to the track, album, movie or more that you're currently downloading, or content that's queued up for download. The latest version of the iTunes Store's Terms and Conditions is also viewable here – click on it, and you'll be transported to a page full of each country's relevant Ts and Cs in case you need to refer to them at any point.

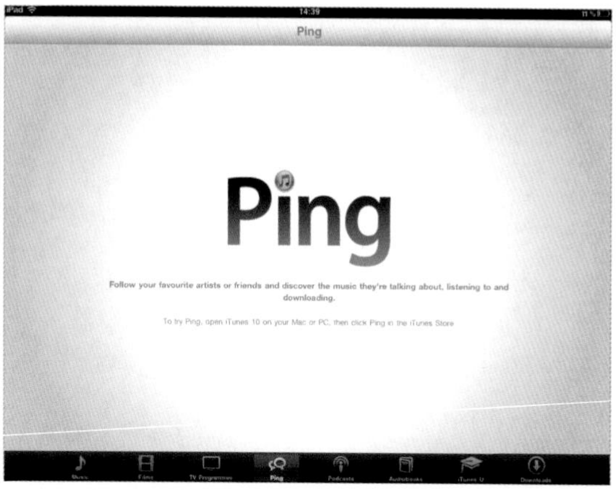

Discover new music with Ping

The Ping function is another great way to find out about new music. It enables you to follow your favourite artist or friends to find out what they're listening to or downloading. While you'll need to activate it within iTunes 10 on your Mac or PC, once that's done the button on your iPad will ensure its functionality is, quite literally, at your fingertips.

> "The Ping Function is another great way to find out about new music on the iPad"

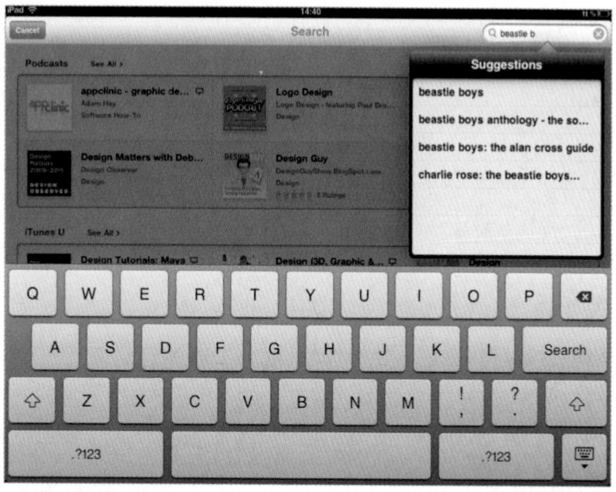

Intelligent searching

If you know exactly what you're looking for, then simply typing in the first letter or two of the author's or artist's name will present a drop-down list of content matching your search term. This way, there is no need to waste time typing in the the whole name, and you are spared the lengthy loading times that are sometimes associated with other search software.

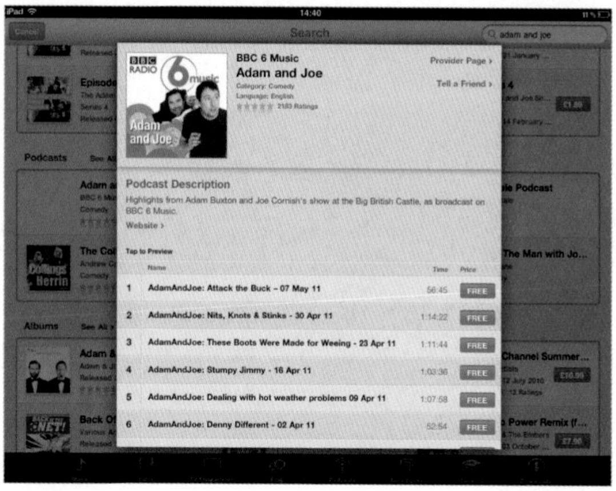

Get the best bits

Podcasts are a great way to listen to your favourite comedians and radio shows. The majority of them are free, which means you can stock up on content without having to worry about your bank account. If there's something you've particularly enjoyed, you can also subscribe to this podcast so that future recordings will be lined up ready for you to listen to.

The App Store guide

A closer look at this interactive storefront

The App Store is a separate storefront where you can stock up on fun, informative or entertaining applications for your iPad. Much like the iTunes Store, you can search by newly released apps or popular recommendations from other users. Additionally, by setting up the Genius function with the app, you'll be presented choices tailored to your previous downloads or purchases.

These apps can range from the bizarre to the downright useful, but the price varies on each. While there are a large number of free apps, other paid-for programmes can offer free trials or 'lite' versions for you to enjoy. The rating system is also another way to research how good a product is before you potentially waste your hard drive space or, worse, hard-earned cash on it. You can also view any updates that are relevant to apps you've purchased in the past here too.

New
Browse through the apps by release date, 'what's hot', or the new ones on offer

Genius
The Genius button introduces you to new apps that you'll love, judging by past downloads

Search bar
Know what you're looking for? Type the name in the Search bar to access it quickly

Updates
Click on the Updates icon to see if any glitches in your apps have now been fixed

Rating stars
If you're not sure whether the app is worth the cash then check out the average rating

> "These apps can range from the bizarre to the downright useful"

Key features

The features on offer to you

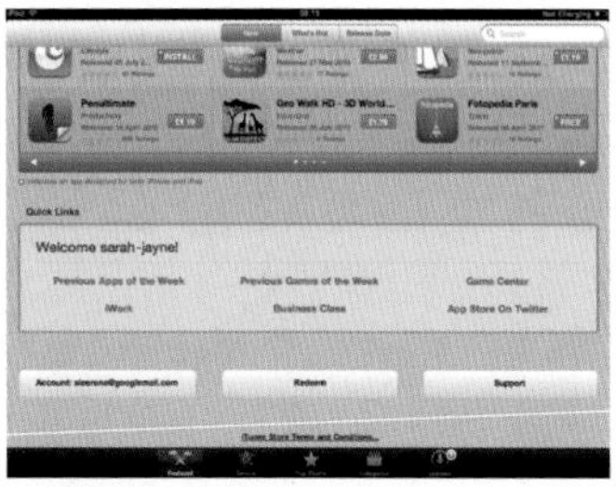

Redeem your voucher

If you've purchased or have been given an iTunes voucher as a gift then you're able to redeem it through the App Store interface. Don't worry if you'd like to spread it across music and app purchases, as the money will be credited to your iTunes account so you can spend the cash as you see fit. Simply click on 'Redeem' and type the code in from the back of the card or email.

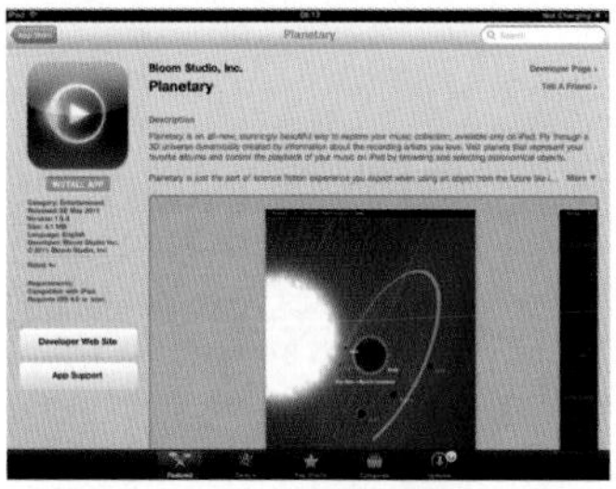

Purchase apps

As you would expect, the App Store enables you to purchase and download products that you like the look of. You can search by name, if you know it, with the bar on the top-right of the screen, or browse through the hot picks, newly released or Genius selections – there's a whole wealth of content out there just waiting to be downloaded and used.

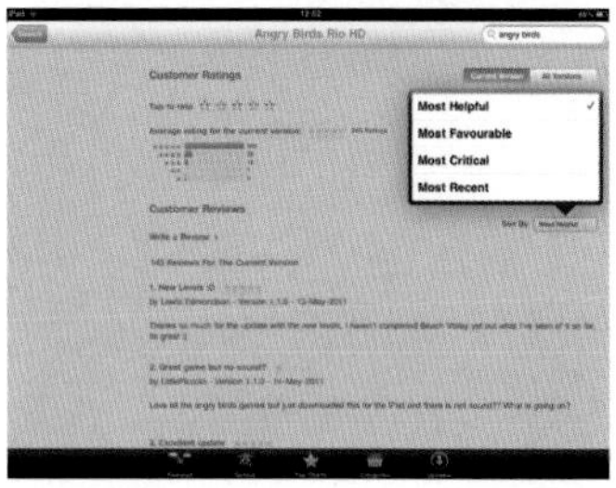

Leave and read comments

It can be hard to know just by looking at an app's blurb whether it is worth its asking price, so before you buy you can read user comments. These can be sorted by Most Favourable, Most Critical or Most Recent, and you can leave comments of your own by tapping on 'Write A Review'. These provide a quick way to get feedback to inform your purchase decisions.

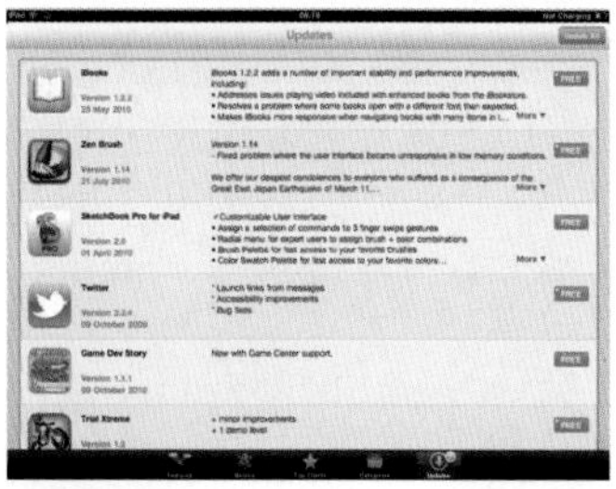

Update existing apps

From time to time, the developers of the apps you've bought or downloaded will update their apps to fix glitches or offer new content, and you can download the latest version of the app from the Store. You'll be alerted to the fact you have updates by a number in a red circle on the Downloads icon. You can scroll through the list, read the amendments, then update as you wish.

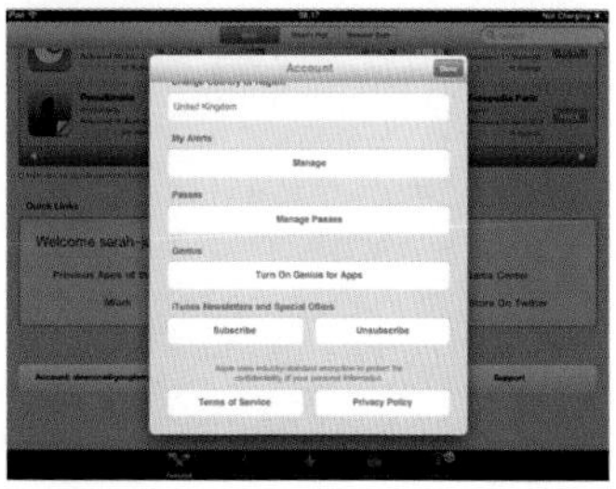

Access your iTunes account

You can look at and amend your account details as you see fit. If you need to change your debit card details or email address, it can all be done here. Additionally, if you want to log out of your account – and it might be an idea to do so if you're handing your iPad over to keep other, less-responsible hands entertained – you can also do this at the touch of a digit.

QUICK TIP

Customer service

Get a little extra help when you need it

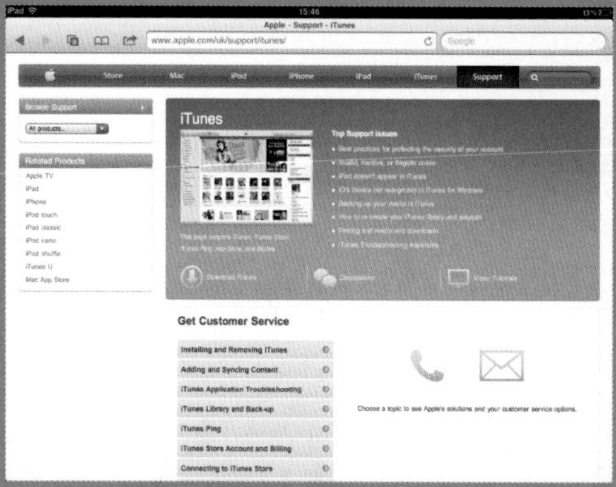

Most of the time we've no doubt that your App Store experience will be enjoyable and problem-free; however, it's always best to be prepared in case something unforeseen crops up. Luckily for us Apple customers, its support centre is packed full of helpful information, including discussion forums, video tutorials and lists of popular topics that you can access by clicking on the Support button at the bottom of the main screen.

So, for example, if you have tried to redeem an iTunes voucher code that's turned out to be invalid, if you need to find your lost tracks or downloaded shows, or you just have a couple of questions about your iTunes bill then have a look through this large selection of troubleshooting tips.

Alternatively, if you still can't find the answer that you're looking for, simply email Apple and you should receive a response to your question within 24 hours.

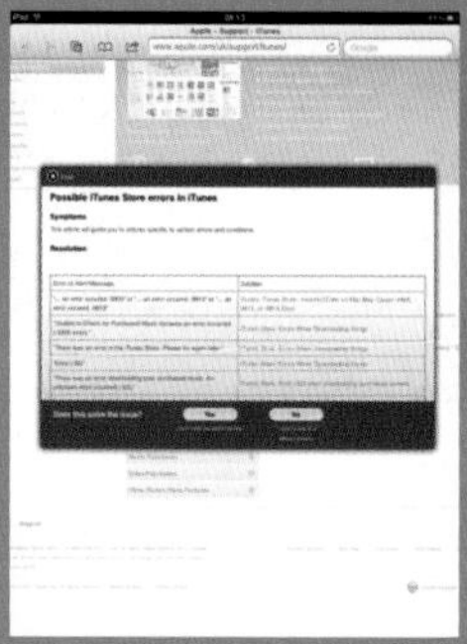

Search
Use the Search bar, top-right of the page, to look for the website or topic you have in mind. It can be hooked up to one of three major internet search engines

Web URL
If you know exactly which website you are looking for, then simply type the URL/web address into the middle bar, and click on Go

Tabs
Favourite websites, or ones which you view regularly, can be stored on your iPad's Home screen to make it quicker and easier to access

Print
If you see a site that you like, or a page of particular relevance, you have the option to print it via the Arrow icon near the URL bar

Bookmarks
Bookmarks can be accessed or edited by pressing the button located to the left of the URL bar. This makes accessing your chosen sites a lot easier

> "Safari is your window to the worldwide web. You have the internet at your fingertips"

Exploring Safari

Your guide to web browsing on the iPad

The Safari app is your window to the worldwide web. Here, you've got the internet at your fingertips – scroll through your chosen webpages with your digits, or zoom with the same gestures that you'd apply to your iPhone and iPod Touch – it's up to you.

Another great thing is, much like Firefox's tabbed browsing, you too can have multiple windows open at the same time, which is great for switching to chosen sites whenever you need to. If you click on a site's image with a zoom function, it will often open into a new window by default, so as not to overcomplicate or clutter your iPad's browsing abilities.

In the same way that you'd bookmark your favourite sites or pages of note, you can do that too, or add it to your Safari homepage to ensure you can access these pages in a flash whenever you need to.

Key features The functions of this browsing app

Visit websites

As you'd expect, this internet-browsing app enables you to check out webpages at your leisure. While sites with Flash functionality won't work on here – iPads don't support Flash, unfortunately – overall, it shouldn't affect your browsing experience too much.

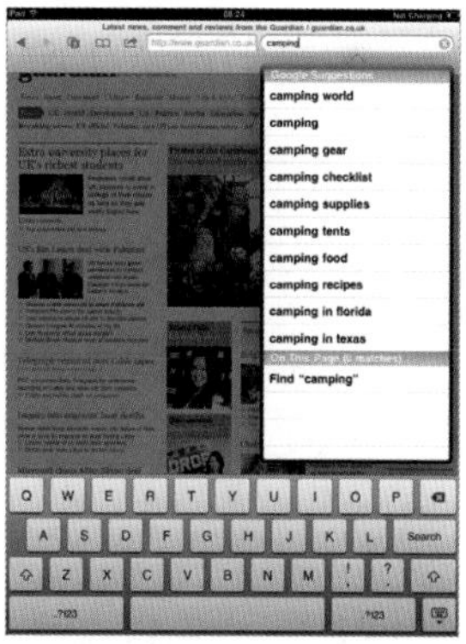

Search and go

The bar on the top-right of the screen enables you to search for a topic or website by typing it in. You can use one of three of the major search engine providers – this can be changed within the Safari tab when you click on Settings – it's set to Google by default. It'll make suggestions as soon as you type the first letter; it will also list more recent searches in case they're relevant too.

Bookmarks

In the same way that your favourite sites can be bookmarked for future use, the Safari app lets you do this too. If you click on the open book symbol along the top bar of the screen, you'll be presented with a drop-down list. Within that list you can edit and organise your bookmarked pages, or add new ones to it. See the Quick Tip boxout for more.

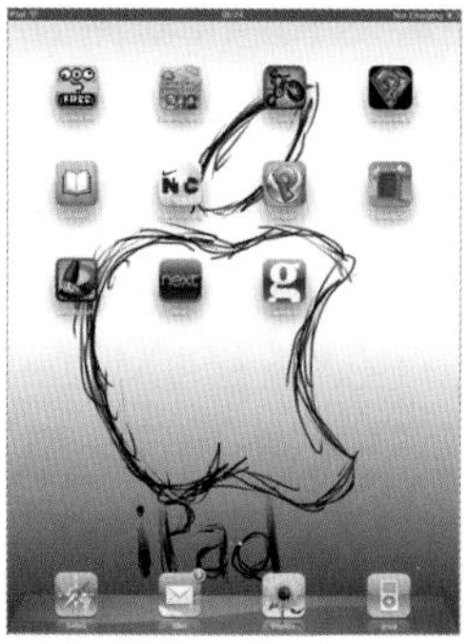

Short cuts

If you use a site regularly, there's something even more convenient than a bookmark that you can utilise. While you're on a site, if you click on the arrow coming out a box, you'll have the chance to add it as a bookmark to the Home screen. Much like the apps you've bought from the App Store, this logo from the site will sit alongside it for you to press when you need it.

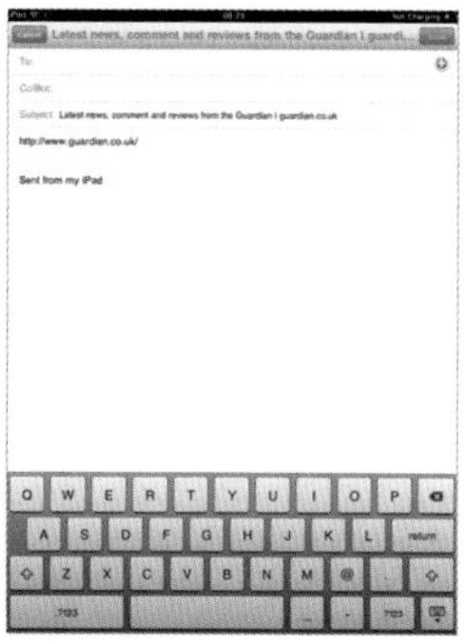

Mail a link

Sometimes links are too good not to share – whether it's talking cats, recipes, or a gift idea. Luckily, Safari lets you email these links. In the same way that you would bookmark a page, click on the arrow to the side of the URL bar, and select Mail Link to this Page. It will hook up directly with your email, so all you have to do is fill in the recipient's details, and you're good to go.

QUICK TIP

Bookmarks

Organise your favourite sites

The internet has a whole variety of uses for us in our day-to-day and working lives, so it's understandable that bookmarking a few of those is a great way to save time in the future. However, having a whole load of bookmarked sites can eventually get out of hand.

To prevent this situation, it's wise to implement a systematic approach to bookmarking in the first instance. By creating folders with recognisable names, you can access those handy pages when you really need them, rather than trawling through a long list of confusing URLs that you've long-since forgotten.

If you click on the open book icon along the top of the Safari browser window, you'll be presented with a Bookmarks bar, which you can either use to select Bookmarks, or Edit. By clicking on Edit, you can then form lots of different folders with helpful names, such as News, Gift Ideas, Cool Exhibitions and so on. Then when you come to bookmark your sites (Press the arrow logo and select from the drop-down list when you're on your site of choice), you can select the destination folder that it should sit in.

Mail on the iPad

All your emails on one handy app

Mail on the iPad is a simple way to access your emails without having to always face a login screen and enter a password. Once it's set up you can view all your mailboxes in one place at just a press of a button from the home screen.

Your inbox is displayed in one long clickable column down the side on the left; meanwhile, when you click on a message it'll appear in a screen on the right. Editing your collections is easy – just select the Edit button and you can tick off which messages to archive or move into folders. One of the other great things about Mail is that your number of new messages is viewable from the number in the red circle on the Home screen icon. Additionally, to refresh the inbox, select the curved arrow symbol at the bottom of the inbox column. Simple and effective.

"You can view your mailboxes at just a press of a button"

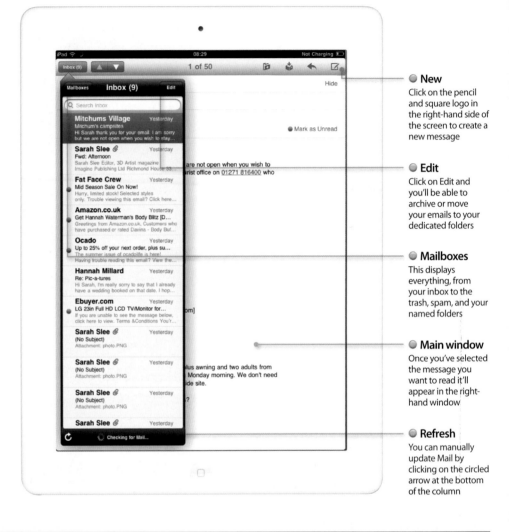

New
Click on the pencil and square logo in the right-hand side of the screen to create a new message

Edit
Click on Edit and you'll be able to archive or move your emails to your dedicated folders

Mailboxes
This displays everything, from your inbox to the trash, spam, and your named folders

Main window
Once you've selected the message you want to read it'll appear in the right-hand window

Refresh
You can manually update Mail by clicking on the circled arrow at the bottom of the column

QUICK TIP

Clear out your inbox

Take charge of all those emails with the Edit function

An unruly inbox is commonplace, but it does make it extremely difficult to spot the important messages from the spam and nonsense. Don't worry, though, there are ways to cut it down to size. One way is to select the Edit function within the mailbox you want to organise – we decided to tackle the inbox. Once you've done that you'll have a circle appear down the left-hand side of your message column – ditching some of the spam in bulk will clear the space a lot quicker.

As soon as you select the message it'll have a red tick by the side of it and they'll start forming a little pile in the right-hand panel. Keep going as many times as necessary and then press the blue 'Move' button. Select Trash and away they go. To keep the messages down in the future, you could also file some in the Spam folder.

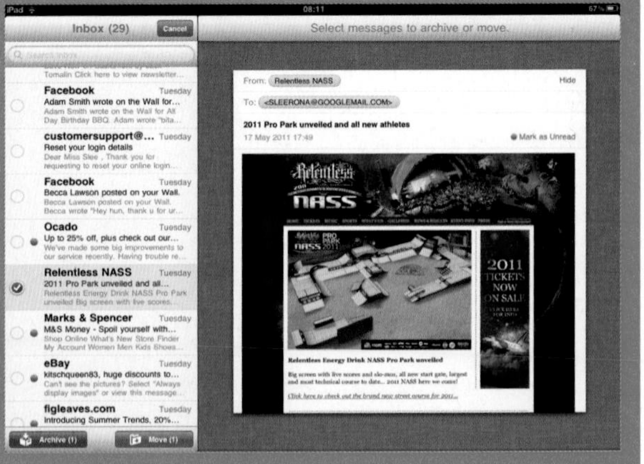

Make sure you 'Move' to Trash rather than 'Archive'.

Key features

Five things the Mail app does

Receive mail

You can link up any of your existing email addresses to the Mail app via the iPad's Settings app (see below for more information on this process). You'll need all the relevant details, including passwords and so on to do this, but once it's all set up you'll be able to view it from the icon on the Home screen. There are other things to change in the Mail, Contacts, Calendars section, including your email signature (set to 'Sent from my iPad by default) and the number of messages shown.

Set up an account

If you click on the Settings icon from the Homescreen, then select Mail, Contacts, Calendars, you'll see the header 'Accounts' at the top of the screen. Simply select the type of email account it is – Gmail, Yahoo!, AOL, plus others – and input the correct details. If you have more than one account, you'll be able to view both within this app too – it's perfect for those who prefer to keep professional and personal business tied to two different email addresses.

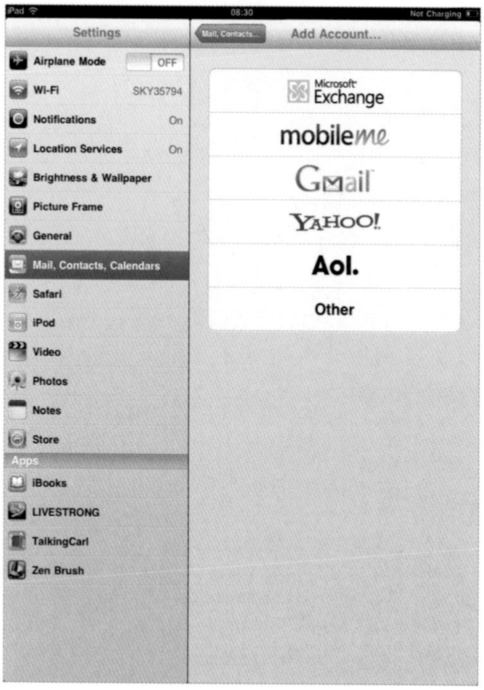

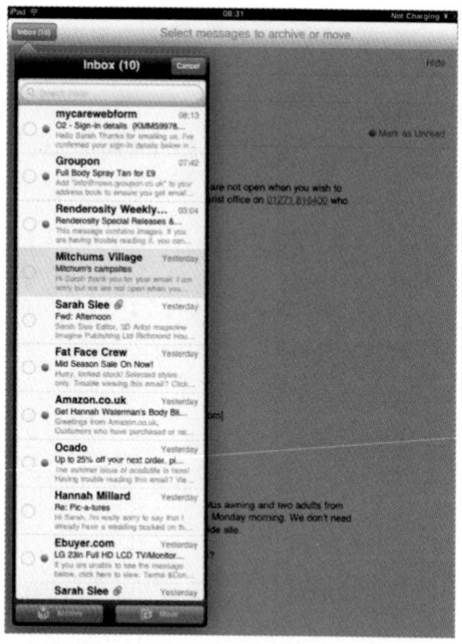

Edit mailbox

Just like the online mailbox functions you use through your chosen internet browser, you can edit your various mailboxes – inbox, junk, sent and so on – as you wish. Whether you use these mailboxes for deleting your unwanted messages or archiving them for future use, it's all doable here. It's something to consider if you want to keep your inboxes organised and under control.

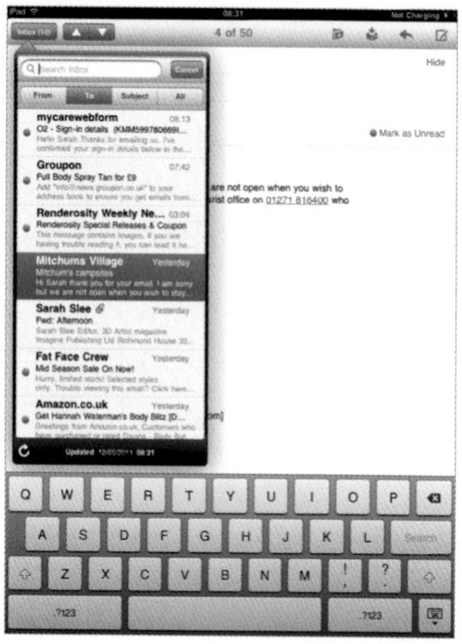

Search mail

If you haven't yet got round to filing your emails into their respective folders (don't worry, it's a job we put off too!) then the Search function will definitely come in handy. Just type in your keyword or name into the Search bar and the app will do the rest for you. If it doesn't find what it's looking for in the downloaded messages, you also have the option of checking on the mail server too.

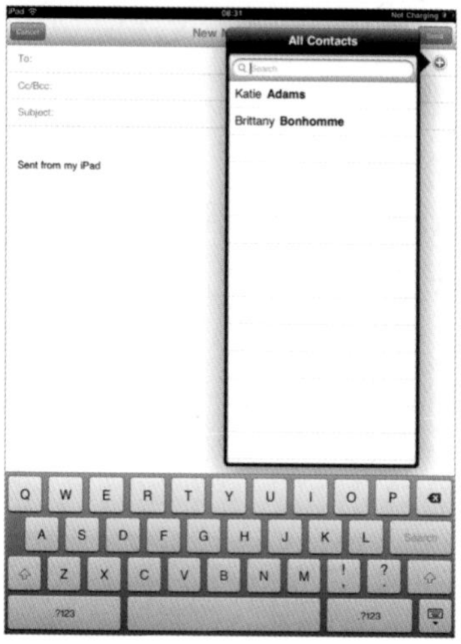

Contacts, contacts

There are a couple of ways that you can input your recipient's details into an email – the first way is to just type it, but if you simply type the first letter you'll be presented with a drop-down list of contacts that could match who you're after. It's one of the many time-saving features included in Mail. Alternatively, you can press on the '+' symbol in the top-right corner and then choose from your saved contacts.

Understanding the Calendar

Your all-in-one organisational tool

Calendar is one of those apps that if you put a bit of time into sorting it out, you will find it completely invaluable. This is because it acts as a planner, scheduler, reminder and diary all in one. Its features enable you to view it in a variety of formats, each allowing for more and more detail to be added. So if you like to have your days planned to perfection, hour by hour, then this is definitely for you. On the flipside, for those with a bad memory for dates, pop in all your anniversaries and birthdays (which are picked up from Contacts anyway), and set them to repeat and alert annually, meaning you have no excuses. The Calendar can be synced with all your portable devices and with other non-Apple organisers too, so you only need to keep one up to date, and the rest will have the information at the next sync.

Today
The Today tab lets you switch back to the current day in an instant

Landscape
In landscape orientation, you can view both the current day and a list of upcoming events

View
Hit these tabs along the top to choose your Calendar view

Months
Scroll through the months using this bar along the bottom

Add Event
Click the '+' button to add a new event to the Calendar

> "Put some time into it, and you will find Calendar invaluable"

Key features

How to use to the app to its best ability to organise your life

Planner

In Month view, your Calendar serves as the essential monthly planner, with all of your plans shown by day. You can add different calendars for keeping your personal and work engagements separate, and any birthday dates that you have stored in your Contacts listings have their own Calendar, so you don't need to input these again. Click any event to see more information about it, such as times and locations.

Add new event

It's easy to add a new event to your Calendar. First, hit the '+' button to bring up the New Event dialogue. Here, you can add the start and end times, the location, whether it repeats or not (say for anniversaries and the like), meaning that you only have to input it once. There is also a Notes section that enables you to add further information about an event.

Search for events

As with all the built-in System apps, there is a Search field. By typing in here, you will be presented with a list of all the events that match your search in any of their fields. These are presented in chronological order, and you can simply tap an event to go to that day and see more information. If you have a lot of dates, using the Notes field will help to narrow things down should you need to search for a specific event.

Alert me!

When there are a lot of events it can get be difficult to remember to check in with your Calendar to see what's coming up in the next week or so. Luckily, you can set an Alert either when you create the event or by editing it afterwards, which will remind you any time from 5 minutes before up to 2 days before, so you know what's happening when with plenty of warning.

Birthdays

Birthdays have their own calendar in the app, and this is synced from your Contacts database. In Contacts, choose to 'Add field' when you are editing a contact, and you can input that person's birthday. That will automatically now show up in Calendar to save you having to retype all those details again. These can then be synced with all your devices via iTunes as long as you have Calendar checked in the sync options.

QUICK TIP

In-depth views

See your Calendar four different ways

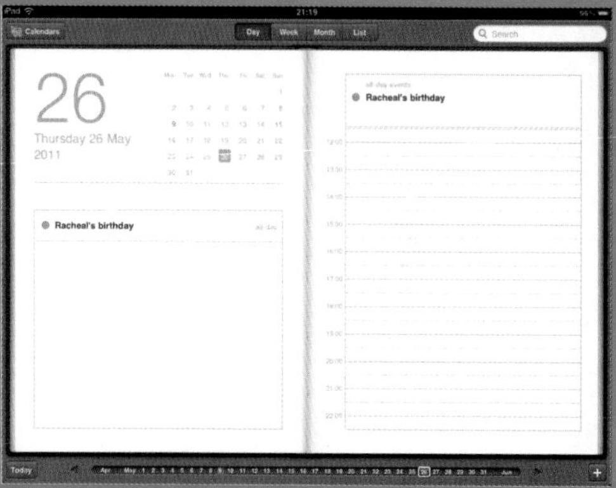

There are four view options on the iPad's Calendar selected from the menu along the top. The Month view gives you the entire month to view, as you would expect for a calendar. This is great for seeing what you have coming up over a long period of time and spotting free space. The Week view helps you break down your events in time slots, so that you have an accurate view of what you have to do each week. For work-based tasks, this really comes into its own. The Day view is the most like your standard diary, so you can write in personal notes and thoughts for each day as required. The final view is List, which gives you a full list of upcoming events to scroll through. This works best in landscape orientation, as you can view both the list and the current day in one go for the ultimate in multi-tasking. Using Calendar is most productive when using all of these views, as you can ditch the paper diary completely, plus it syncs with all the other system apps in a way that's ultra-intuitive.

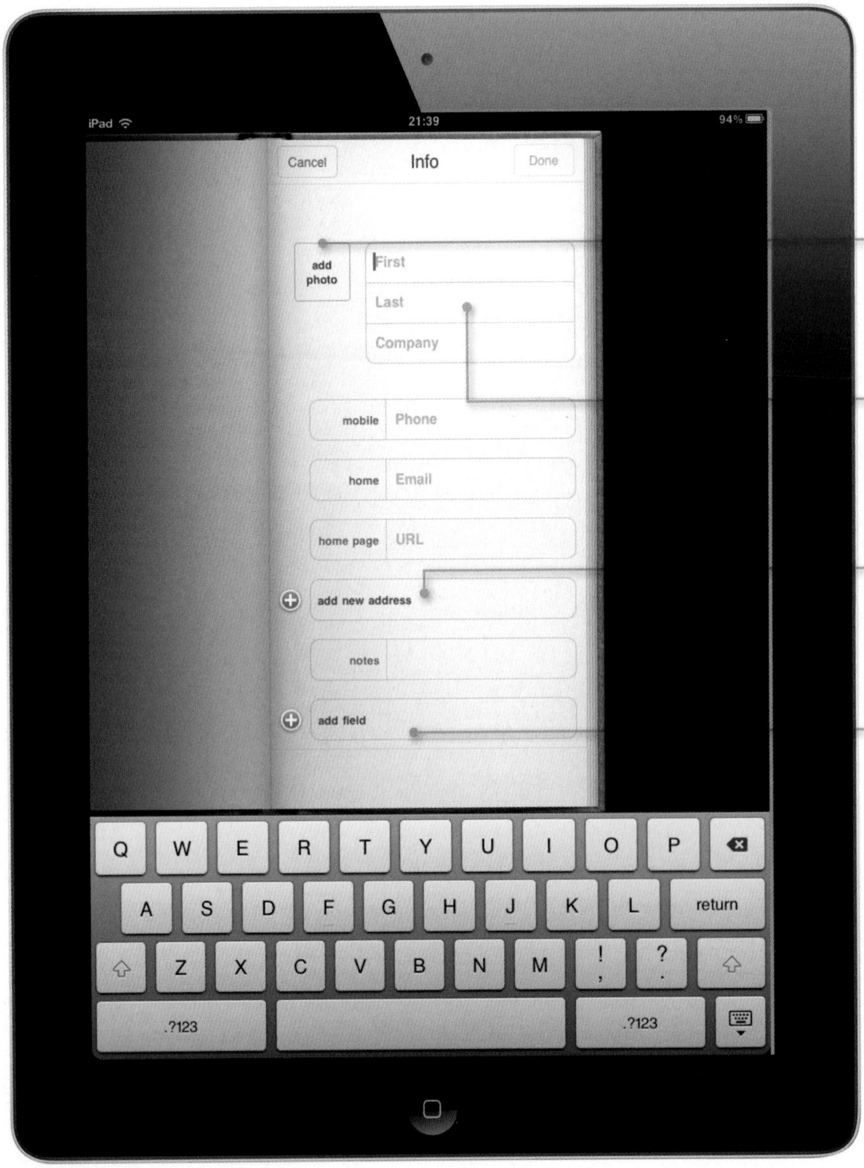

New Contact
Hit the '+' icon on the left side of the screen in order to create a new contact listing. Then, fill in the relevant details

Add Photo
Click Add Photo to access your iPad's photo albums. Here, you can pick a photo to add to the contact

Details
The main details are added into the fields shown. You don't have to fill them all in, although it helps

Address
Hit an address to get directions to that location in Maps instantly, saving you looking it up

Add Field
The Add Field option gives you more fields that can be added to a contact. Which field that may be is your choice

"Contacts helps you stay up to date and in touch wherever you are"

Introducing Contacts

Have all your essential contact details at a tap

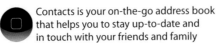

Contacts is your on-the-go address book that helps you to stay up-to-date and in touch with your friends and family wherever you are. It looks like a standard print address book, with lettered tabs down the left-hand side, and a full list of all your contacts. When you select a contact, you see all of that person's details in full on the right. As well as storing the usual phone numbers and addresses, Contacts enables you to add photos, notes, multiple addresses, websites, email addresses and much more. All your contacts can be grouped, so that your personal and work contacts, for example, can be kept separately. There's plenty of additional fields that you can add too, such as birthday, job title, IM address, middle names and so on, so it's perfect for use as a networking tool.

Key features

It's more than just an address book

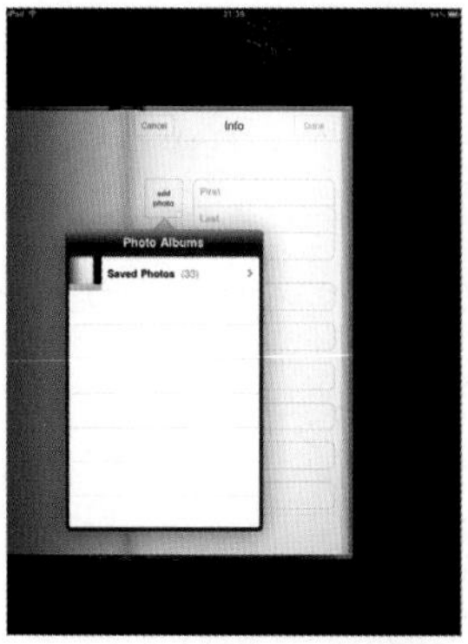

Put a face to a name

You can easily add a photo to a contact using the Add Photo command when you open a contact for editing. This will default to the photo albums stored on your iPad. If you have an iPhone, you can sync your contacts from here, which enables you to use the iPhone's camera. Or if you have an iPad 2 you can use the in-built camera. This makes it much easier to place a face to the right name.

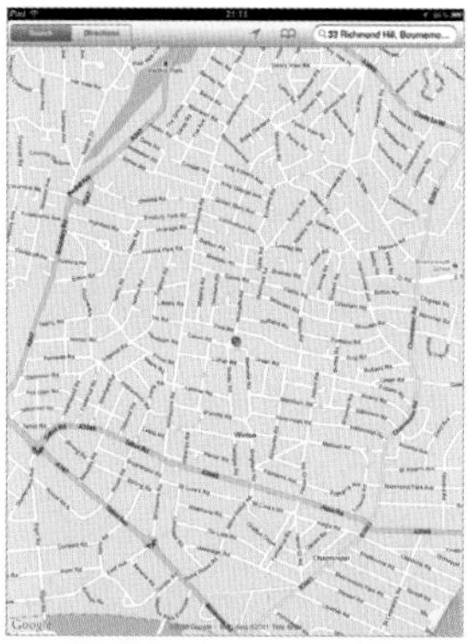

Get directions

With so many addresses in one place, it can be easy to get lost. With Contacts, you can tap an address to be taken to the Maps application, from which you can see the address, get directions, and figure out how long it will take you to get there. It works in both directions too, so if you find a service in Maps, for example, then you can add it directly to your Contacts.

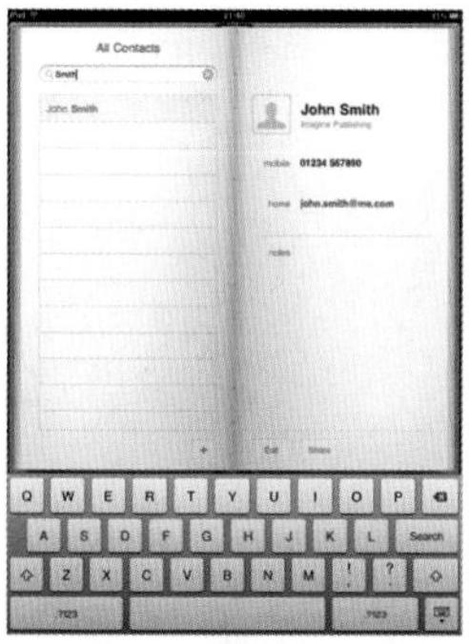

Search contacts

There is a dedicated Search engine at the top of your contacts list on the left side of the page, which you can use to find people without having to manually flick through – which is essential if your number of contacts is getting unwieldy. Start typing any part of the contact's name, and a list of matches will pop up for you to select from.

Attach notes

You can add notes to contact details, which are displayed on the main contact page. This is perfect for giving yourself reminders that relate to that person, such as a brief overview of when you met them and where. Or you can write in details of a meeting you have scheduled with a person, which can be added to your Calendar, and have a reminder set.

Extra fields

The Add Fields option brings up a long list of additional items that can be added to a contact. This includes their company and job title details, IM address, their birthday, and much more. This makes Contacts more than just an address book – more a complete guide to all of your friends and family – so no excuses for forgetting your spouse's birthday ever again!

QUICK TIP

Customising contacts

Set up contacts your way

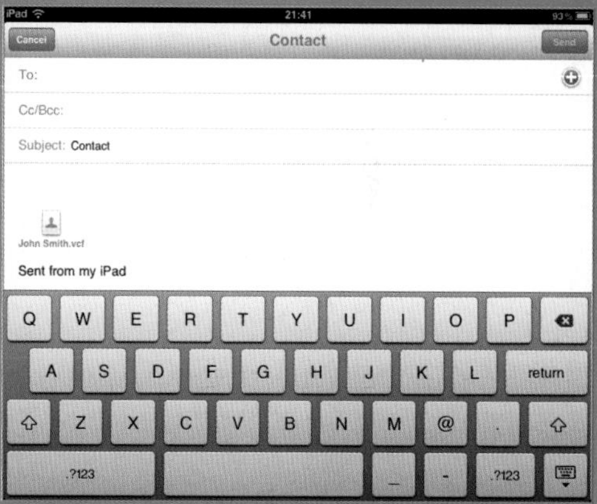

One of the great things about Contacts on the iPad is that it's easy to add loads of supplementary detail about a person, making it a complete organiser. We've already mentioned that you can add photos to profiles, which can be any photo you have on your iPad. You can also list a person's iPhone number on the iPad 2 so that you can make the most of the FaceTime feature. There are fields for all the usual essential details, like address and email, but to really make the most of this app, make sure that you use the additional fields too. This lets you add a birthday for your contact, which you can be reminded of via the Calendar. You can also add things like nicknames or job titles, which help you to remember more about them – perfect for networking. When you have a detailed contact, you can also choose to share it with others by hitting the Share button underneath any contact. This will attach a VCF file to an email so that it can be sent to anyone who might need it.

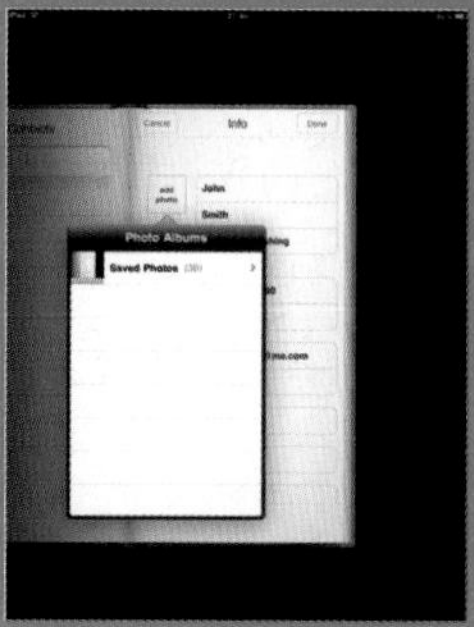

Using the Notes app

Get the most out of the iPad's note-taking app

Notes is a simple application that is all-too-often overlooked in favour of one of the many premium organiser tools available on the App Store. But Notes is an invaluable resource. Its premise is simple, working on the concept of a journal with large lined pages ready to be filled with thoughts and information.

In portrait orientation you're presented with a full-screen blank page, perfect for when you want to type away without distractions. To browse through all your notes, you can use the Previous and Next arrows at the bottom of the screen, or hit the Notes menu. You can also delete notes, as well as email them directly.

In landscape, the application is perfect for heavy note-takers who need multiple pages for each day. You are presented with a split-screen view, with the note that you're using on the left, and the list of all your notes on the right with the current note circled.

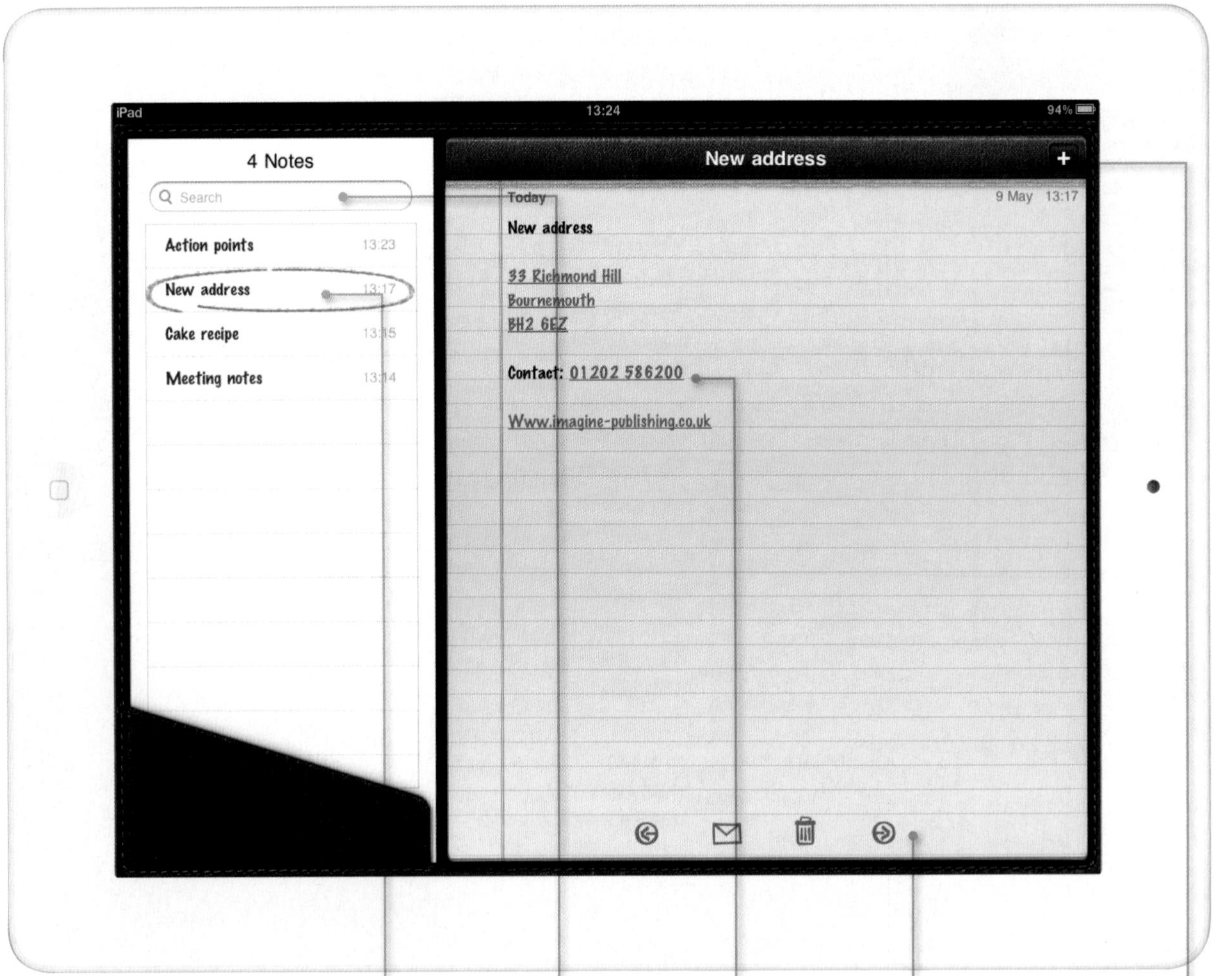

List
The Notes list shows you all your notes with the current one highlighted

Search field
The handy Search field enables you to quickly find your notes based on a keyword

Links
Phone numbers and addresses can be viewed instantly in Maps or Contacts

Icons
Use the icons at the bottom of the screen to flick through notes, email or delete

New page
If you need a fresh start, hit the '+' icon in the top-right of the screen to open a new, blank note

"Perfect for heavy note-takers who need multiple pages for each day"

Key features

Stay organised on the move

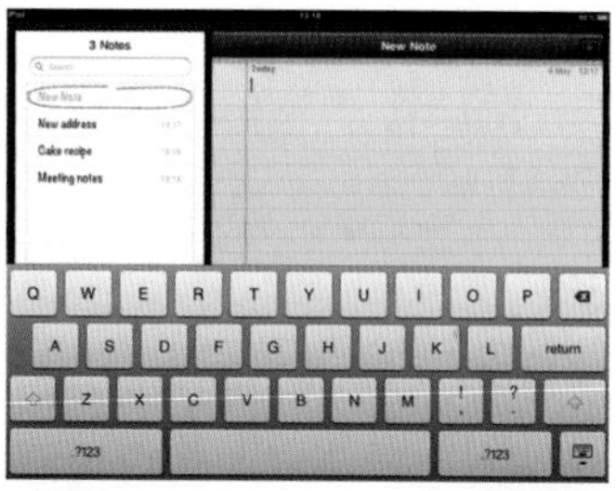

New note

You can create a new note in either orientation by simply hitting the '+' sign in the top right-hand corner of the screen. This presents you with a new blank page, which is date-stamped so you can easily find it again. The note is titled by your first sentence or first few words, so it's best to always put a header that will make it easy to locate in the future.

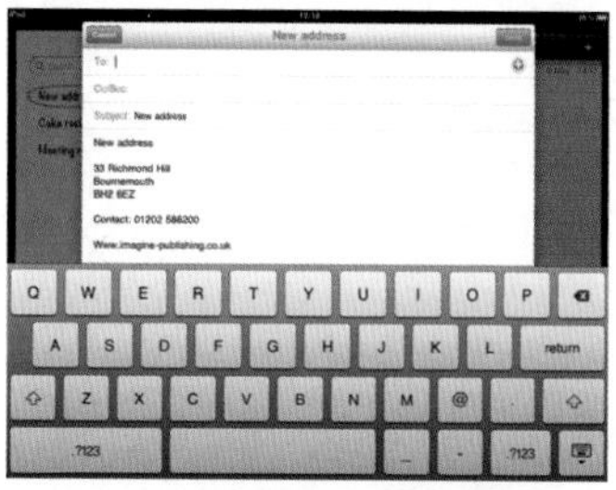

Email your thoughts

One of the best things about all of the built-in apps on the iPad is the way that each of the applications work with each other seamlessly. One of the easiest examples of this is the fact that you can email your notes directly from the icon at the bottom of each note. This places your note text as the main body of an email, with the Subject line the same as the header.

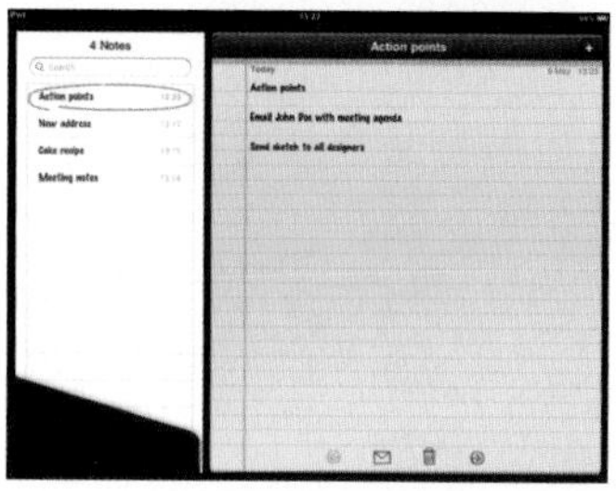

Note list

A list of all your notes is presented on the left-hand side in landscape, or as a drop-down menu when in portrait. This always has the current note that you're viewing circled in red, with the header of the notes and the day that they were created. If you create multiple notes one after another, then the time is listed on that day too while you are working on the same day.

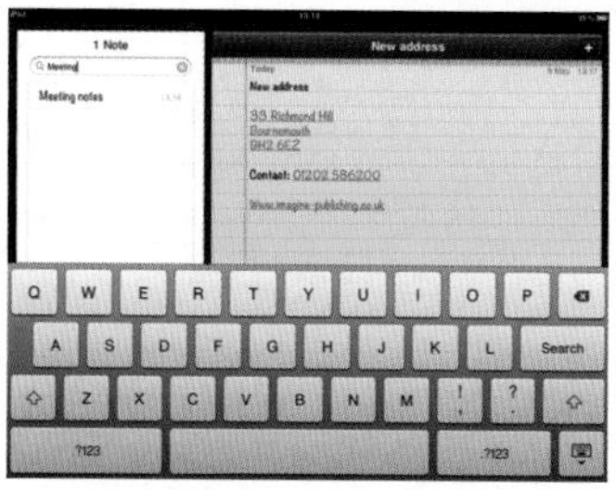

Search notes

If you are prone to having a lot of notes on your iPad, then it is essential that you can easily find the one that you need. In this case, you use the Search field at the top of the note list. Here you can search for anything, such as name, date and keywords, to see all of the notes that match your search. It saves you the hassle of flicking through them all.

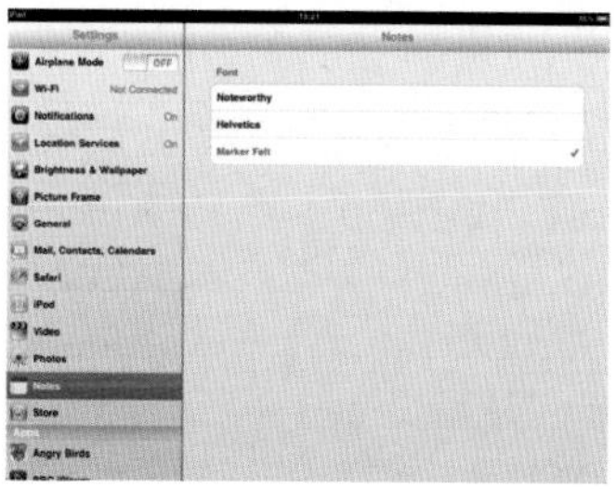

Settings

To be honest, there isn't really a great deal that you can do to customise your notes or the app itself, but if you take a trip to the Settings app, then you can pick from one of three fonts to use to suit your preferences. The default font used is Noteworthy, but you can go for the more classic Helvetica or the charming, relatively underused Marker Felt as well.

QUICK TIP

Make the most of Notes compatibility

Tailor your notes to work with other built-in iPad apps

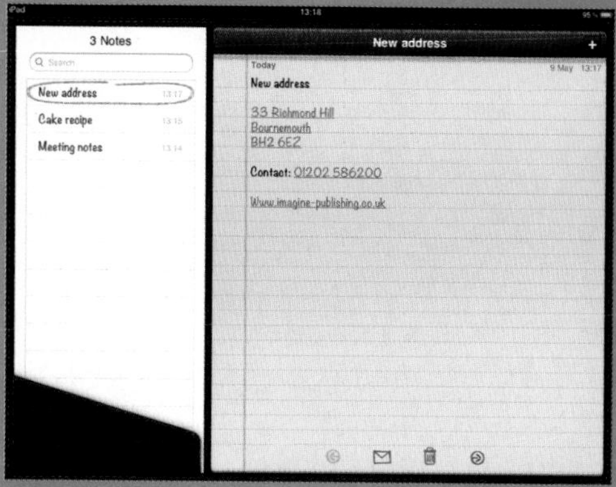

One of the best things about all iPad apps is the fact that all of the built-in programs are designed to work with each other with no hiccups. Notes is certainly no exception to this rule. Therefore, it pays to ensure that when you are creating new notes, you include information that can be picked up by the other apps.

If you list a name, you can instantly access that person's details via Contacts with a quick tap, so make sure that you list the full name of a person as listed in your Contacts. Similarly, addresses can be viewed in Maps, so include full addresses that make it easier for Maps to give accurate data. URLs will automatically become links so that you can view them with a tap in Safari.

To get the real power out of Notes, make sure that these sorts of details are included and you will thank yourself for the effort when you go back and view notes at a later date.

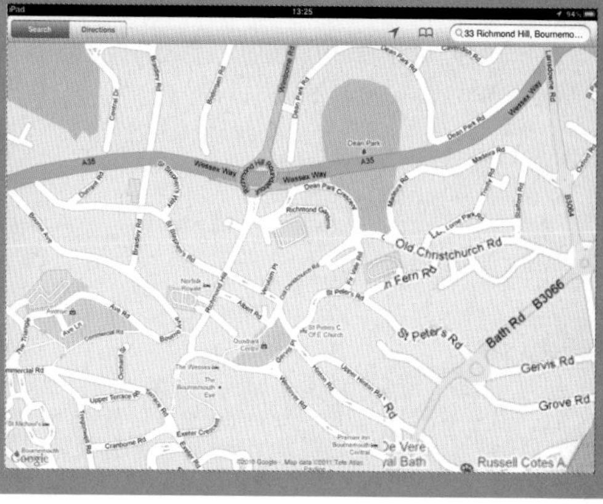

Make the most of Maps

It's your essential navigation guide

Gone are the days of having to carry an A-Z around with you – your iPad does the same job, but better. The Maps function works with the iPad's Assisted-GPS (AGPS) to plot your current location. Bear in mind that this is not the same as 'true' GPS, which uses a GPS receiver to locate a device using satellites. AGPS requires you to have a connection to the internet, through which your location can be determined. This means that if you don't have a 3G iPad, then you are limited to finding a Wi-Fi signal. Plot your routes in advance if you're planning to go into the great unknown! However, it is still an essential app to get to grips with, and is perfect for identifying driving and walking routes, or checking the location of a point of interest.

> "Gone are the days of having to carry an A-Z around with you"

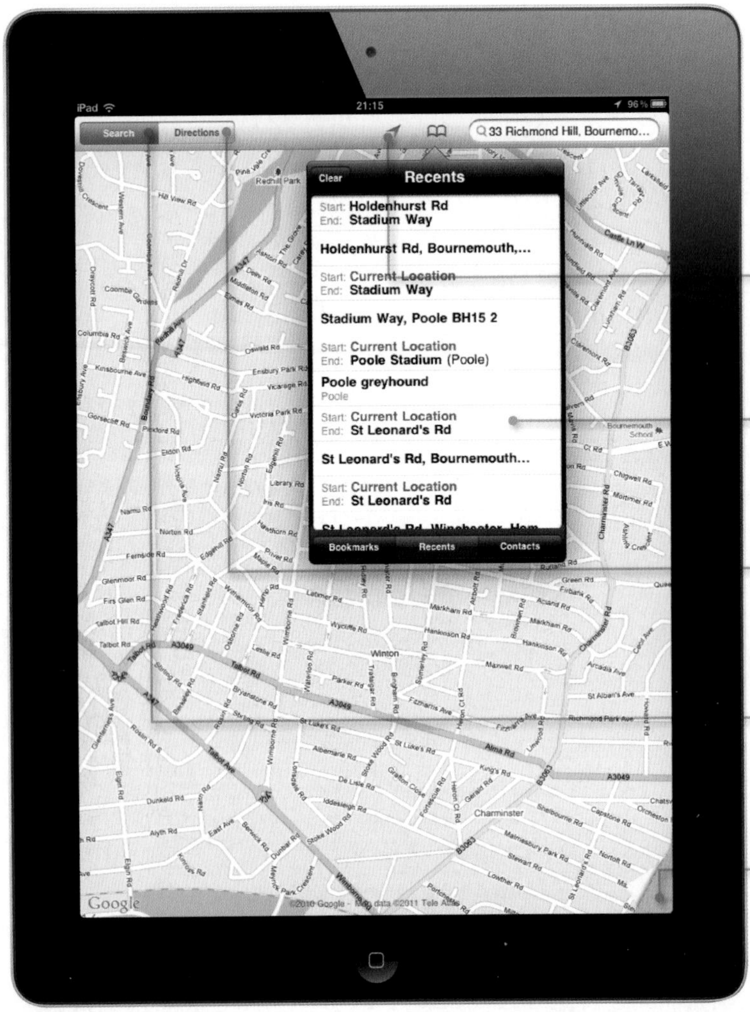

Compass
This compass arrow can be pressed to find your current location

Bookmarks
The bookmarks icon gives you a list of bookmarked, recent or Contacts locations

Directions
Switch to the Directions screen to enter start and end points of a journey

Search
The Search screen has a search window in the top right to input location details

Menu
The menu options are found by turning the bottom right of the map over

QUICK TIP

Map views

Get detailed location information

The map can be viewed in four different views. The first, Classic, is the default setting, and this is the one that you will use the majority of the time, as it's best for navigating without any distractions. Satellite is perfect for pinpointing a certain building on a road, for example, as this gives you a photographic view of the area. It provides endless fun checking out your home address, but is also a practical feature. The third option is Hybrid, which is the same as the Satellite view, but with road markings from the Classic view over the top, allowing you to navigate easily, with the ability to zoom in and look in more detail when you get close. The final option is Terrain, which is reminiscent of Ordnance Survey maps, with elevation of land marked. This is best for walkers who need to plot a route around (or over!) large hills or mountains. You'll likely find that you'll leave the map in Classic mode and never really use the other options, but it is worth experimenting to find the best view for each task you need to undertake.

The Satellite view is handy for pinpointing a certain building or road.

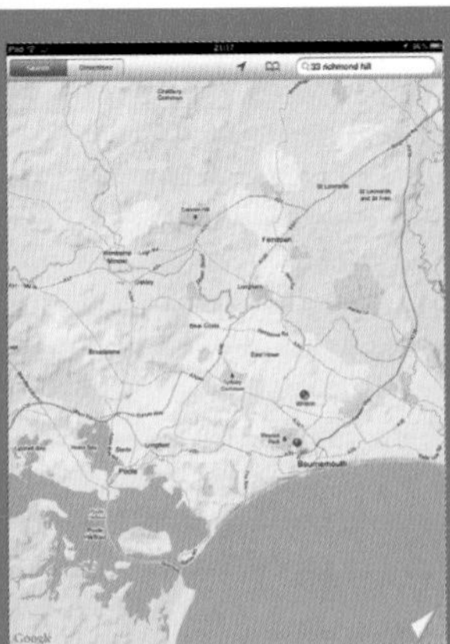

The Terrain view shades the land according to the distance above sea level.

Key features

Inside the Maps app

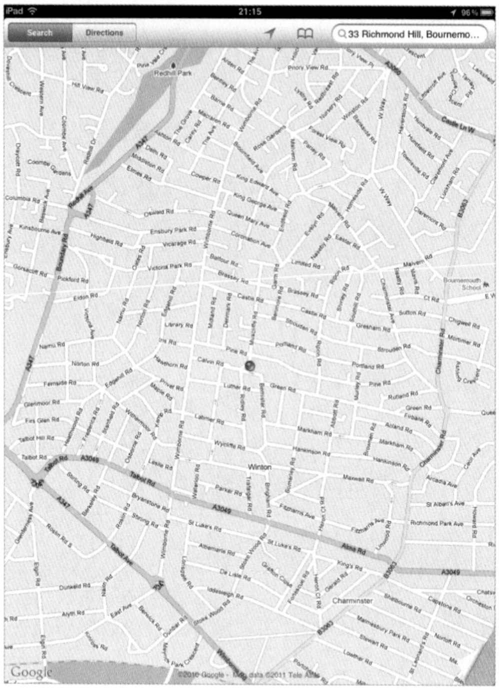

Locate yourself

At the top of the map screen, there are various icons that are present. The compass arrow can be used to accurately locate yourself through your iPad. Tap on it once, and a pin will appear at your present location, which can then be used to get directions to another place. Or, if you're a bit lost, getting the 'You are here' location can be invaluable. You will need an internet connection to use this feature.

Place your pins

If you visit a place more than once, you might want to give it a pin so that you can easily locate the same place in the future. It is worth placing a pin in all your common locations, such as home, work and the gym. That way, it is easy to get directions from one point to another. To add a custom pin, navigate to the area you want to highlight, then swipe along the screen to reveal the hidden menu underneath, where you can select to place a pin.

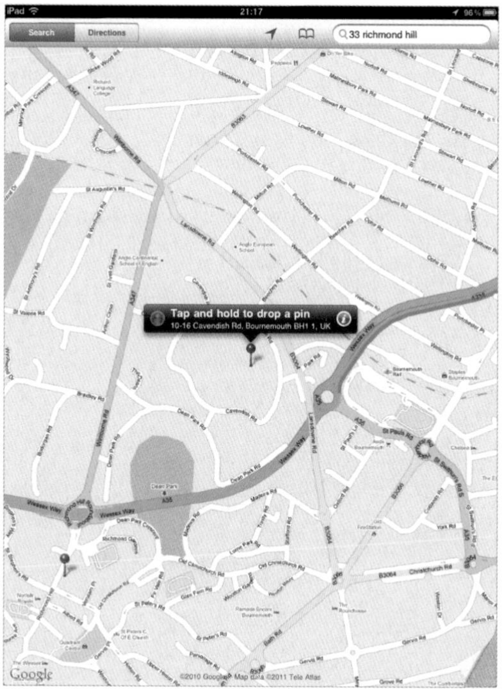

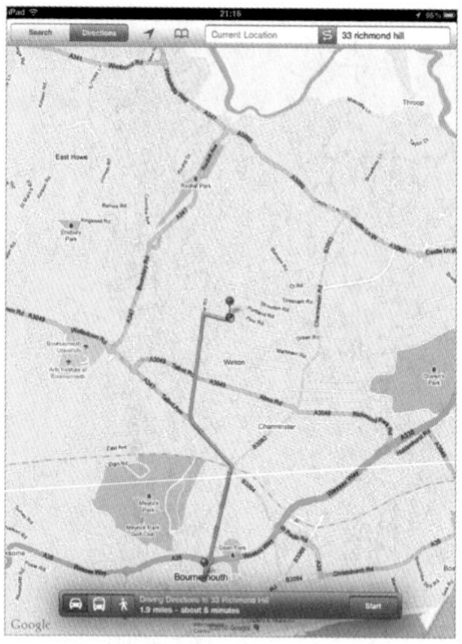

Get directions

By hitting Directions and choosing a start and end point, you can get accurate travel plans to go from one point to the other. By default, these will be driving directions, but you can choose to switch to walking instead. There is also an option to reveal public transport solutions, but this won't always be available in every area. When you have directions, you can hit Start to follow your route step by step.

Finding places

In order to help you find particular places more easily, you have the Search box in the top-right corner of the screen. Start typing here, and your iPad will begin looking for possible matches. It keeps a history of your Recent Searches, so any matches from what you type in will be automatically listed. You can list a town, road name, full address or point of interest, and if it's in the database, then you'll find it.

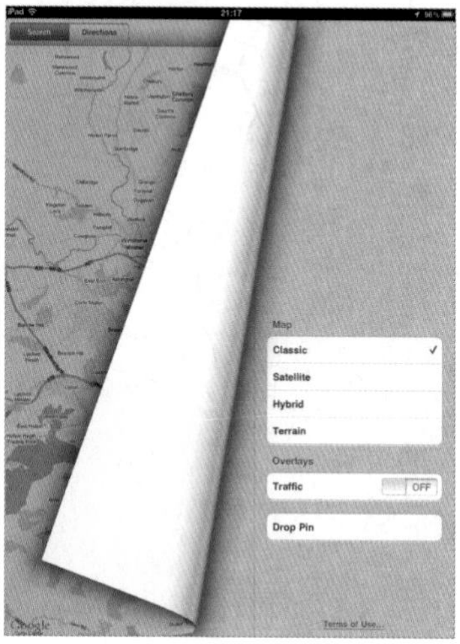

Menu options

We have already mentioned that there is a hidden menu in the Maps screen, which you can find by swiping along the screen. The map rolls up from the bottom right-hand corner to reveal a selection of options, including map views, placing pins and having a Traffic Overlay added so that you can avoid congestion in busy areas. Bear in mind that having this on slows the app down a bit.

Get to know FaceTime

Chat with anyone on a Mac, iPhone, iPod touch or iPad 2

There must be very few people in the technological world who haven't heard or used Skype to make video calls with friends, family and colleagues. But despite how amazing it is to see someone on the other side of the world (or town), setting up an account to be able to use the service in the first place is a bit of a chore – especially when you have to find a username which no one has thought of yet.

This is where Apple's FaceTime comes into its own. You can use either someone's iPhone number or their email address and you're good to go – no setup is necessary. As long as the person's online or by their phone, your call will get through. It finally takes the geekiness out of video calls and brings them into the hands of regular users.

"Use either someone's iPhone number or their email address and you're good to go"

No 3G
Currently, FaceTime only works over Wi-Fi, not the 3G mobile network

Mute button
This stops you from being heard. Tap on it again to reactivate the microphone

End button
Terminating the FaceTime call is a simple matter of tapping on this button

Swap
Tap this button to switch to the rear camera and back again, if you need to use it

You!
This little window of yourself can be moved around to any corner of the screen

QUICK TIP

Using multiple accounts

When more than one person needs to use FaceTime from the same iPad

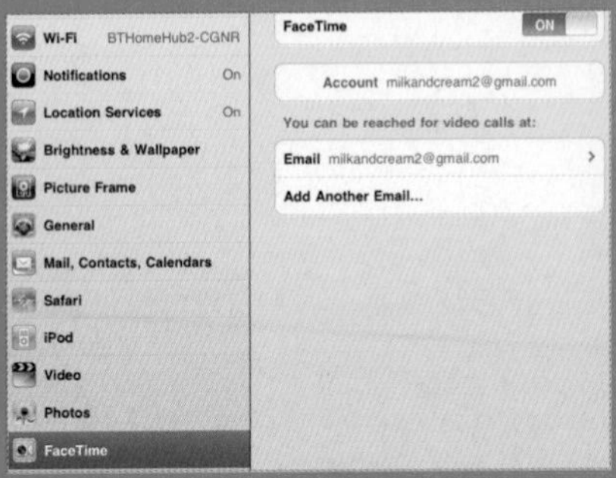

FaceTime options can be found in the 'FaceTime' tab in the Settings app.

Once you've entered your Apple ID and chosen your preferred email address to be contacted through, FaceTime will run without any more setup on your part. But what if you share your iPad with other people who would rather communicate using their own FaceTime username and password? There doesn't appear to be any way to log out and sign in with another ID from the app itself.

This is because the app's main preferences reside elsewhere – in the Settings application, to be exact. Select it and scroll down the sidebar to the bottom of the default options – beneath them is a section which contains the preferences of many of the third-party programs you've purchased and installed on your iPad.

You'll find the FaceTime settings sandwiched between the Photos and Notes options. From here you can switch FaceTime off, add other emails you can be contacted through and see which account is currently being used. Tap on that account's name to bring up a floating window that you can use to sign out. Once you've done this, you can then log in using a different account.

Key features

Use your iPad to see your friends and family

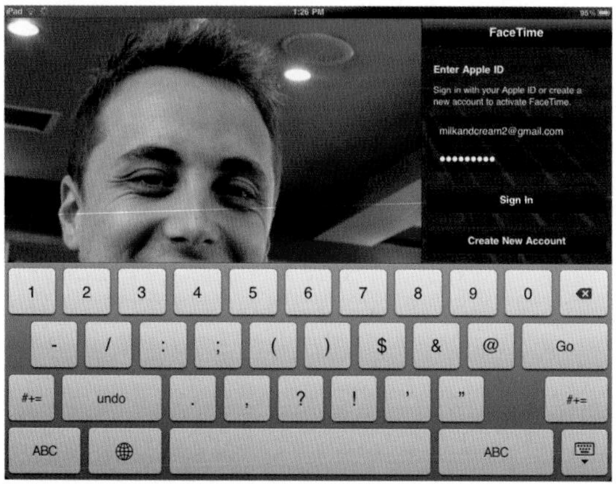

Your contacts

Once logged in, you'll be asked to give the email address you would like people to contact you through. Most Apple IDs are email addresses and will be chosen by default, but if you want to use another, just type it in. Once done, you'll be able to access your entire address book, although you won't be able to see who's online and available. You can also add people to your Favourites list to make them easier to find.

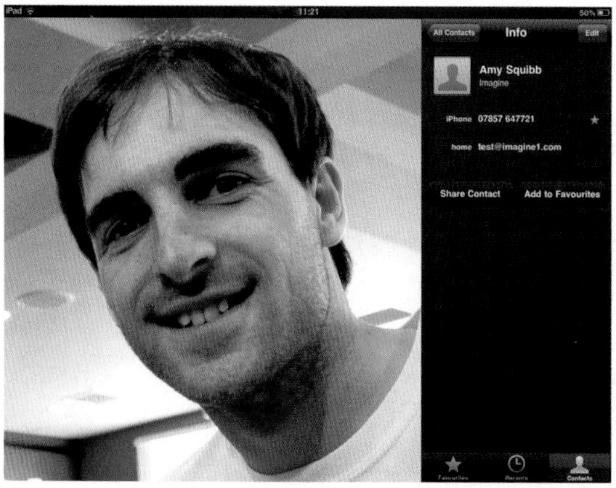

Making calls

To call someone, tap on their mobile phone number (to reach them through their iPhone) or their email address (if they only have an iPod touch or iPad 2). You must make sure that you are tapping the correct number or address as your iPad will attempt to connect regardless. If your contact is in the Favourites section, tap on their name to initiate the call.

Recent

The Recent icon lets you see who you've been in contact with, or who tried to initiate a FaceTime session but failed. These unsuccessful sessions show up in red. At the top-right of the screen are two buttons, All and Missed. The former is selected by default. Select the other to only see those calls you didn't answer. You can also delete the list by tapping on 'Clear'.

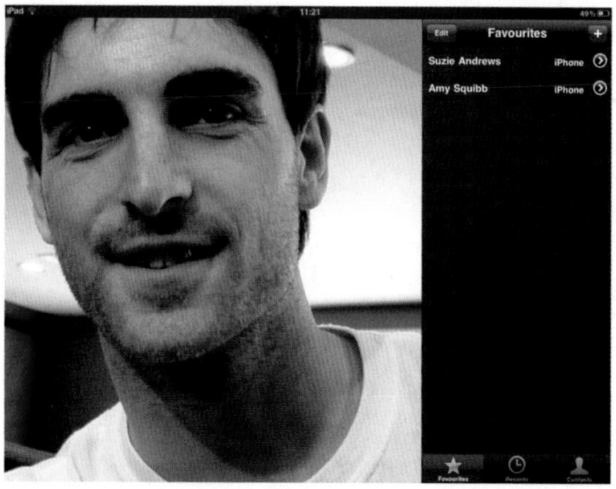

Organising Favourites

Adding people to your Favourites list is done either via their contact details or by tapping on the '+' button at the top-right of the screen and choosing the right number or address from your contact. Once in the list, you can further customise it by tapping on the 'Edit' button. You can delete them or reorder them so the most important ones are always at the top of your list.

> "You can take advantage of the back camera to show people what you can see around you"

Use the back camera

You don't just have to use the forward-facing camera to make video calls; you can take advantage of the back camera to show people what you can see around you. This can have many advantages, such as showing someone the location you're in, filming someone else who may be with you and much more. It opens up the flexibility of your video calling.

Using the iPod app

Get the latest music and access your tunes on the go

Chances are you have a portable music player already, so why would you want to turn your iPad into one? Well, for one, bigger really is better in this case. You can see full-screen cover artwork, flip through your collection with ease and see more of your library in one go. You can directly control the music that you want to hear on screen, and download music any time you have a connection.

Tunes that you download on the go will be synced with your main computer's iTunes and vice versa, keeping all your music devices up to date. You can create playlists in the same way that you would on an iPod/iPod touch, and these are also synced between devices. The iPod app is also the place to store and watch video clips, which is where that large HD screen really comes into its own.

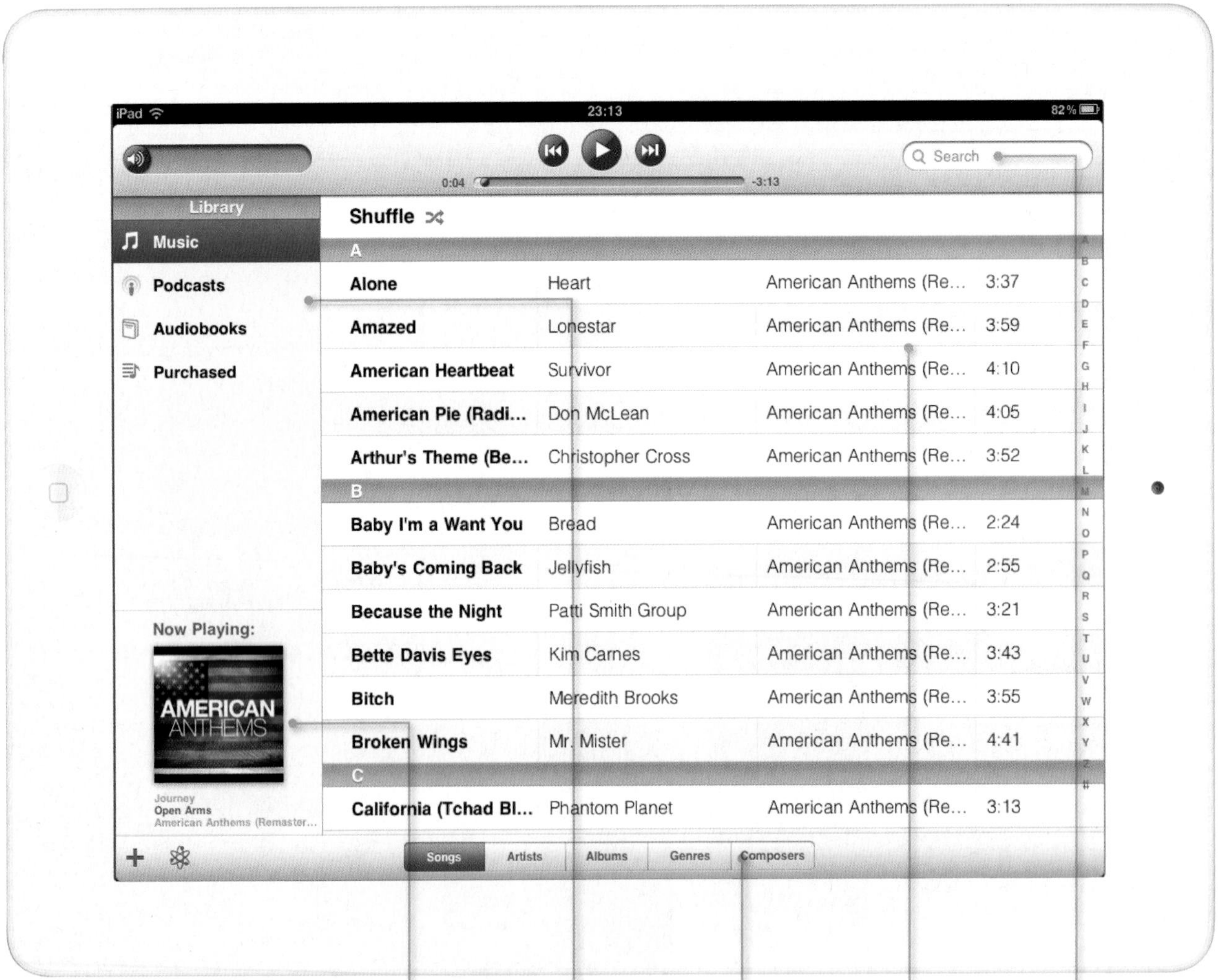

"You can create playlists in the same way that you would on an iPod"

Now Playing
Album artwork of the selected track is displayed in the bottom left

Library
Down the left of the screen is where your library and playlists live

Tabs
The tabs along the bottom offer different ways of viewing content

Songs
Songs are listed alphabetically by song title in the main window

Search
Use the Search bar to find particular songs or artists in your library

Key features

Get the most out of the iPod app

Full-screen images

When you are listening to your tracks, you can view the album cover full screen. There is an info bar at the top, with which you can see the artist, album and song title, as well as repeat and shuffle tracks. However, this can be hidden with a tap of the screen, so you can enjoy your artwork uncovered. A great display for when using the iPad as a music player around the house.

Album info

During playback in the full-screen mode, you can choose to see album listing information by hitting the menu icon in the bottom-right of the screen. This enables you to see what songs you have coming up next. You can hit any track to start a new song if you see something you fancy hearing sooner. The arrow takes you back to the playlist again.

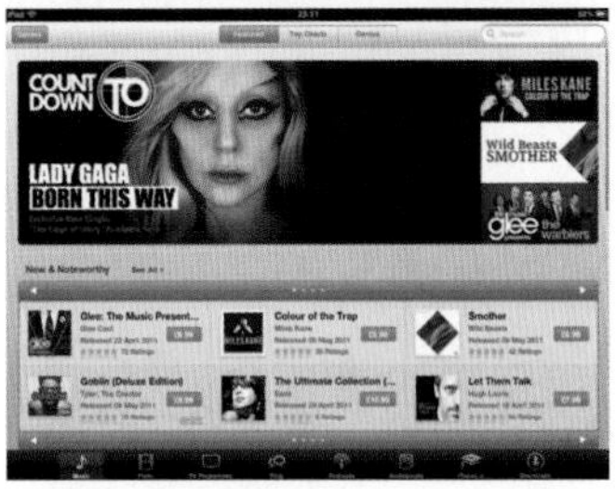

Purchase from iTunes

You can buy audiobooks, podcasts, music, films and TV shows from the iTunes Store, which you can link to directly from within the iPod interface. Simply browse until you find something you like, hit the Buy button and wait for it to download. When it's finished it'll be ready and waiting for you in your iPod app. You can also sync music and other files through iTunes on your computer.

Playlists

Creating your own custom playlist is the best way to hear the tunes that you want, whatever the occasion. Hit the '+' button in the bottom-right of the screen to create a brand new playlist. Here you can give it a handy title, then you can start populating it by choosing the tracks you want to include from the library listing that comes up automatically.

Search options

There is a Search bar at the top of the screen, which is great if you know exactly what you want. The iPad will start filtering content as you type to find you a match. If you'd rather just browse, then you can use the tabs along the bottom of the screen to filter your library results into categories: Songs, Artists, Albums, Genres and Composers.

QUICK TIP

Genius music selections

Let your iPad do the hard work of finding you tunes you'll love

Genius is an Apple feature that you will find on all the latest iDevices, as well as the newest versions of iTunes on your Mac or PC. When you're listening to music and you come across a song that you really like, then you can hit the Genius button. The iPad then goes through the tunes that you have on your device and creates a custom playlist of songs that it believes will go well together.

You can then choose to play the Genius playlist and save it for the future, or start over again with another song that you love. Genius is the perfect alternative to a simple shuffle as you can tailor the sort of songs that come up to suit your mood, depending on the type of track initially chosen.

You may already have seen Genius pop up on some of your other devices, as it is also available when browsing for new songs on iTunes, by recommending bands and albums that you might like to download, based on the sort of songs that you already own.

The App Store has a Genius category on the iPad too, which works in much the same way as the iTunes version does. It recommends apps that you might want based on those you have previously bought and downloaded.

Introducing the Camera

The iPad 2 finally has an eye on the world

Many critics bemoaned the fact that the original iPad didn't have a camera, but in fairness, anyone who's held this device for any extended length of time is probably grateful that a camera didn't come with it, as it was clearly too heavy and bulky to hold comfortably, or accurately take pictures or videos.

The thinner and lighter iPad 2 removes many photo-taking hurdles, and with the huge success of FaceTime, Apple's video chat application, it was inevitable that the world's most successful tablet would end up incorporating this feature this time round.

If you have used to the Camera app on your iPhone or iPod Touch in the past, then the chances are that you'll feel right at home with the iPad version, but if you're new to this technology, read on to find out everything you need to know about taking photos and videos with a tablet device.

> "The thinner and lighter iPad removes many photo-taking hurdles"

Camera
To swap from the rear to the front camera and back again, tap on this icon

Preview
The entire iPad screen offers you a giant preview of what you're shooting

Browse
All the photos you've taken can be browsed by tapping on this button

Record
When you're making a video, this record button pulsates from red to dark red

Slider
You can take a photo or shoot a video. Make your choice by moving this slider

QUICK TIP

Trimming your clips

Basic editing is but a tap away

Recording video is far from an easy process, and more often than not you can end up with parts you don't need, especially at the start and end of your recording. Considering the fact that storage on your iPad is somewhat limited, and how space-hungry HD video can be, it's a good idea to get rid of those unwanted sections. Thankfully, you don't need to have access to a video editing program like iMovie to do this: you can perform this action straight from the Camera app itself.

Once you've finish taking your video, go to the Camera Roll and select the shot you wish to work with. You'll notice that as the clip plays out, a small playhead moves at the top of your screen over thumbnails of your video. Either side of this row of thumbnails are handles. Drag one inwards to turn them yellow, and start the trimming process. You can drag either handle as often as you want until you're happy with your selection. Once done, tap on the yellow Trim button on the top right. You can then choose to delete the unwanted parts or save your selection as a new clip.

Key features

The essential functions of the Camera app that help you dive into digital photography with your iPad

Two cameras, one device

If this is the first time that you have launched this application, then the back camera will be switched on by default, effectively letting you use the entire screen as a giant viewfinder. If you'd rather take a picture using the front camera (bear in mind though that it's of a much lower resolution than the back one), then all you have to do it tap on the switch icon, which is located on the top right of your iPad's screen.

Orientation-aware

Your iPad uses its accelerometer to determine which way is up. In your Camera app, it is used to making sure that your photos are saved in the correct orientation. When filming, though, you need to make sure the correct orientation is set prior to tapping on the record button. Once the iPad's started recording, it won't change orientation even if you physically rotate the device. If you're not careful, then you could end up inadvertently recording a scene sideways because of this.

Stills and motion

Both the front and back cameras are capable of recording stills and videos. You can switch over to the other one by swiping the icon on the right of the screen. Aside from this icon, there aren't any visible signs to tell you which mode the app's in aside from a timer once recording has started. Also, whichever mode the application was in when you left it is the one you'll find when you go back into it.

Camera Roll

Once you've taken a photo or recorded a scene, it's immediately saved to your Camera Roll – a section of the Photos app where all images taken with your iPad are stored. To get to it, tap on the icon, lower left of the screen. When a shot's taken, you'll see it shrink and travel to that icon. You can browse through them, and even focus your search solely on either Photos or Videos.

Roll options

You can share your images directly from the Camera Roll without even going to the dedicated Photos application. To do this, tap on the share icon (a rectangle with an curved arrow coming out of it) on the top right of the screen. This brings up a series of options. With them, you can select which items you'd like to email, and copy for use in another program, or simply print. You can also delete them straight from there as well.

Explore the Photos app

Where all your stills and videos are stored

If you've got a Mac, you're undoubtedly using iPhoto to store and catalogue your digital photos. The Photos application serves this purpose on the iPad. In fact, although it has the same name as the one that exists on the iPhone or iPod touch, it offers a lot of additional features not available on its smaller counterparts – an excellent example of the differences a bigger screen provides to the apps that are designed to work natively with any Apple device.

With Photos, you'll not only be able to browse through any images you transferred from your computer, but this is also the place where any photos or videos you took with your iPad 2 will be stored – be it with the Camera, Photo Booth or any other third-party app. Here we'll show you how you can work with your photos.

"It's where any photos or videos you took with your iPad 2 will be stored"

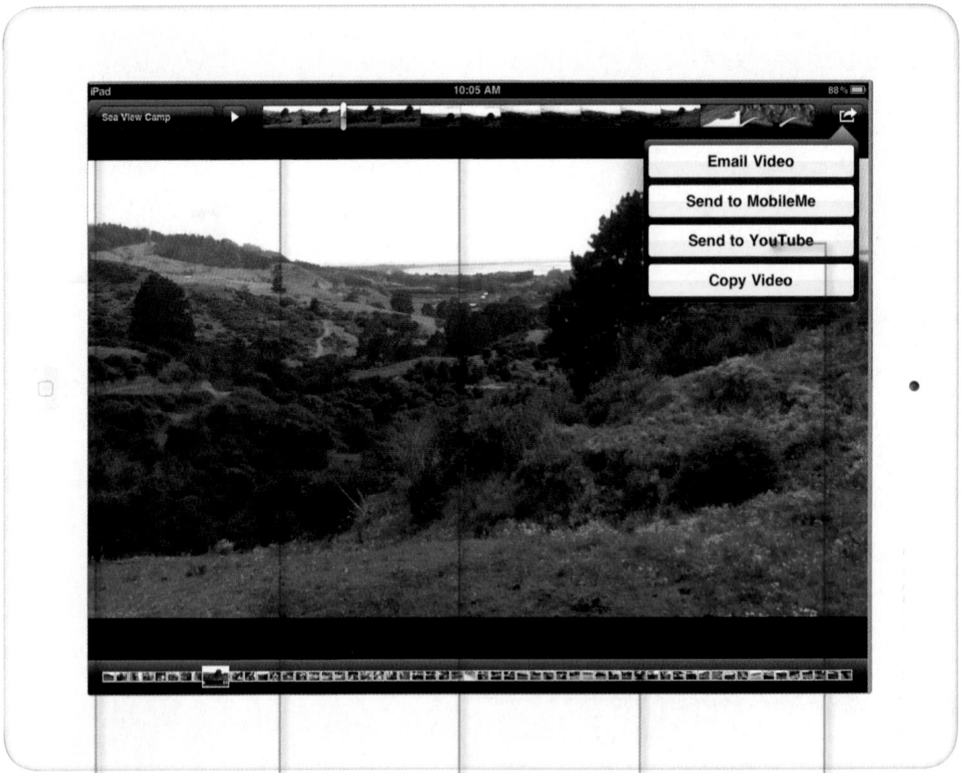

Back
To go back to your album (or all your photos), simply tap on this button

Play
If you can't use the Play button on the clip, you can use this one instead

Scrub
You can scrub through your video by dragging this thick playhead

Thumbnails
All photos/videos in the album can be accessed from these thumbnails

Share
You can send your clip directly to YouTube from the Share menu

QUICK TIP

A selected slideshow

Choose an album and enjoy the show

Your iPad can make a great picture frame. It's such an obvious part of the design that there's even a slideshow option right on your Lock Screen. However, this feature draws from your entire library of images by default which may not suit your purposes. If you want to be more selective, choose an album from the Photos application (or event, face or place – it's entirely up to you) and tap on the Slideshow button, top-right of the interface.

You are given three basic options: select the type of transition you'd like to use (out of a possible five – Origami is the most interesting one), whether or not to have music and, if so, which track to choose from your music library.

When you're ready, tap on 'Start Slideshow' and enjoy the results. If videos are part of your album, these will be played as well, but not in Origami mode – instead, only the first frame will be shown.

You can get out of your slideshow at any time by tapping on the screen or by swiping left or right to go to the previous or next image on the list.

As you would expect, the photos will auto-rotate when the iPad is itself rotated.

Key features

You can touch your digital photographs

Finger action

At the top of the screen are a series of tabs, including 'Photos', 'Events' and 'Places'. Tap on the 'Album' one. There's a simple yet smart way to take a peek inside one of these albums: put two fingers over one of them and move them away from one another. Let go and the album opens fully. To get back to your list, you can either tap on the 'Albums' button to the top-left, or bring two fingers closer together on your iPad's screen.

Zoom In

Tap on a photo for it to zoom in and fill the screen (if you see black borders on either side of it, rotate your iPad to change its orientation). You can also zoom into your photo to see greater detail: just place two fingers on the screen and move them away from each other. Bring them closer to zoom out. This also works with video clips stored in your photo library.

Sharing

You'll find the Share menu acts differently depending on which part of the interface you find yourself in. When you see multiple thumbnails, you can select more than one to email, copy, print or delete. However, focus on a single image and you can assign it to a contact, use as a wallpaper, or even send it to MobileMe.

The Dock

When you're looking at a single image, you'll probably notice a row of tiny thumbnails at the bottom of the screen. This is known as 'The Dock'. These images represent all the other photos that you have in your currently selected photo album. Tap one of them to see it full screen. You can also swipe your finger to the left or right on the main photo to see the previous or next image in the list.

Organisational limitations

To the right of the 'Photos' and 'Albums' tabs are 'Events', 'Faces' and 'Places'. You can't assign photos in your library to these tabs; this can only be done from your computer. If you use iPhoto, all your organisational work will be preserved and available. You just won't be able to make any changes to them from your iPad – at least not with version 4.3.3 of the operating system.

Get to know the Photo Booth app

The most fun time waster on the iPad

Photo Booth's been available on the Mac for a while – since the introduction of Mac OS X version 1.4, in fact – and has been used for years by children and adults alike to waste a few minutes by having a lot of fun with all the bundled video effects.

This program's obviously very popular on Apple's campus, since no sooner did the iPad 2 gain a couple of cameras, a version for this new device was released. You can't apply as many effects with it as you can with the Mac version, but this drawback is compensated by the fact that you can play with Photo Booth anywhere as opposed to being tethered to a cumbersome computer – even the MacBook Air isn't as easy to hold with one hand as the iPad. To sweeten the deal, there's also a trick you can achieve that isn't possible with the Mac version. Read on to find out more…

"Photo Booth is loved by adults and children alike"

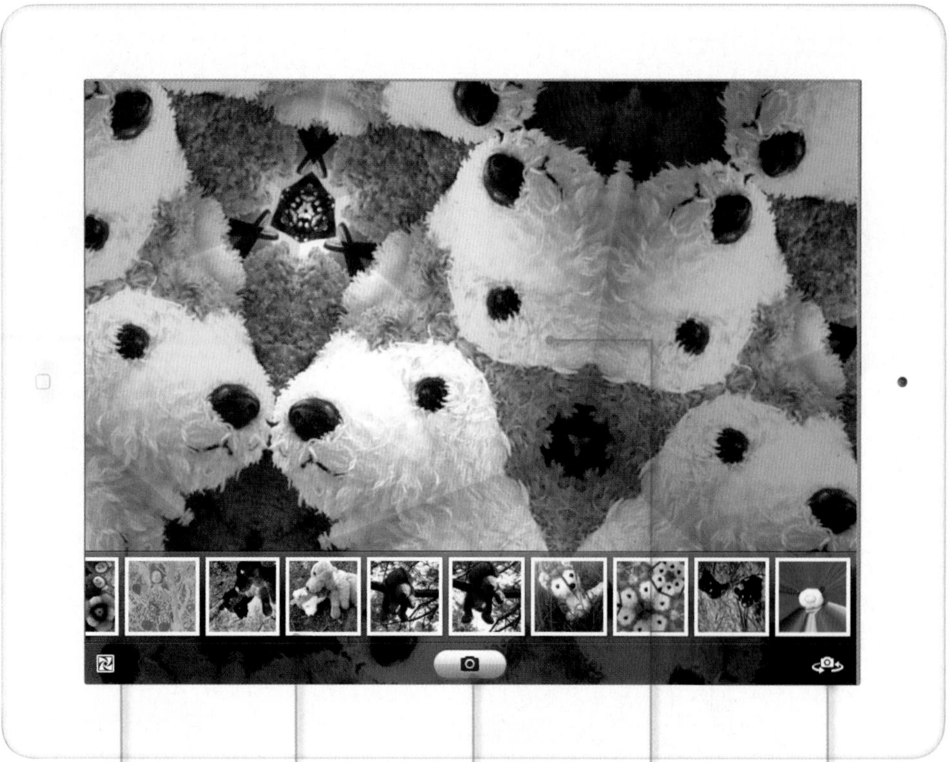

Undo
If you change your mind, you can go back to all your effects with this button here

Fullscreen
Click on any of your previous photographs for it to take over the entire screen

Photo
Take a shot by tapping on this button (this allows you to take stills only, no video)

Screen
Like the Camera app, your entire screen acts as a giant view of the shot you're taking

Switch
Tap on this button here to switch between your iPad's front and back cameras

QUICK TIP

Share your work

Email, Copy or Delete… all from Photo Booth

Any photo taken with Photo Booth will then appear in your iPad's camera roll, which means that it can be accessed by other programs if they've been designed to do so. You can also see them all by going to the Photos app, but if you just want to email one or more photos, then you can actually do this directly from the Photo Booth app itself.

Select one of your previously taken images, and you will see the usual Share button on the lower right-hand side of the screen. Tap on it, and you will bring up three options: Email, Copy and Delete, none of which are currently tappable. You have to select at least one photo from the thumbnail section (not necessarily the one you have selected to activate this feature).

You can choose as many photos as you like. All the selected ones get a blue tick on the bottom right of their thumbnails. Once you're ready, you can choose from your three options, or tap on Cancel should you subsequently change your mind. Deleting a photo is such a permanent decision that you have to confirm this choice should you happen to have tapped that button by mistake.

If you want to assign a photo to a contact or use it as a wallpaper, you have to access it via the Photos app instead.

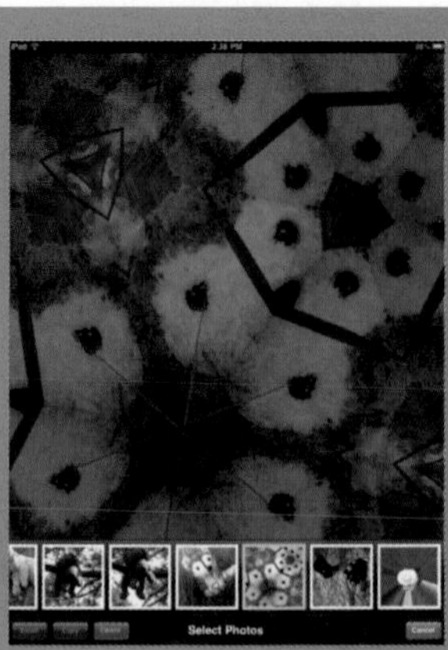

Any photo taken with the *Photo Booth* app will appear in your camera roll.

Key features

Have fun with the iPad's powerful graphic engine

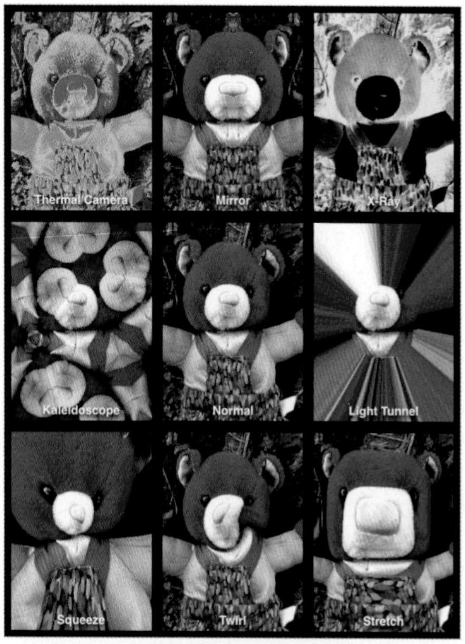

Multiple effects

Launch Photo Booth, and once the digital red curtain is pulled back, you'll be graced with nine images of your subject, each showing a different effect applied to it, all updating in real time. Each preview is also clearly labelled, helping you understand what is happening to your subject. It must be noted that Thermal and X-ray are obviously special visual effects: your iPad doesn't have thermal imaging, nor does it emit radiation!

Either camera

Unlike the Camera app, Photo Booth triggers the front camera by default. You can use it to take fun shots of yourself or anyone near you facing your iPad – just like you can with Photo Booth on your Mac. However, you can also use the rear camera. To do this, select an effect, and you'll notice the Camera Switch icon on the lower right of the screen. Tap on it to see what the rear camera sees.

Effect drag

By default, the effect is focused on the centre of your screen. You can, however, do something that would be impossible if this wasn't a touchscreen interface: select an effect, then drag your finger across the screen. The effect follows your finger, so you can choose the distortion.

The Gallery

Select an effect, and not only will you see a full-scale version of it, but you'll also be able to browse any other Photo Booth shot that you've taken in the past. They are all available at the bottom of the screen in a row of thumbnails. You can select one to see it fullscreen, and when it's chosen a small 'x' appears on the top left of its thumbnail should you wish to delete it.

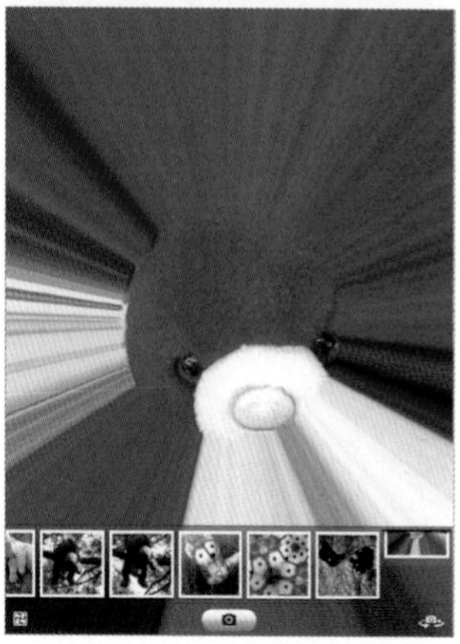

No delay

Unlike a computer – designed to rest on a desk – keeping your iPad still isn't exactly easy. As a result, there is a major difference between the Mac and iPad version of Photo Booth: with the former, you have a three-second delay; and with the latter, the photo is snapped as you tap on the app's camera button, which is located at the bottom of the chosen effect's screen.

Introducing Videos

How to find, purchase, and view Videos

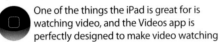

One of the things the iPad is great for is watching video, and the Videos app is perfectly designed to make video watching effortless and enjoyable. When you rent or purchase videos from the iTunes Store, they are automatically downloaded to the built-in Videos app where you can watch them. The Videos app displays all your downloaded, rented and purchased television shows and movies. Your movies and shows are displayed by category when you start Videos. To watch something, simply tap it, and it begins playing. Watch in widescreen by turning your iPad on its side. Tap once to show or hide the controls. Switch between widescreen and full screen views by double tapping. You can also pause, rewind, fast forward, and navigate through chapters. Drag the timeline for high speed scrubbing. If you stop watching midway through, the app keeps track of exactly where you are in your show.

TV Shows
The TV Shows button returns you to the display of your TV shows

Episodes
If you want to play a different episode in your list, tap the thumbnail for it

Store
This opens the iTunes Store, where you can buy new episodes

Play
Tap the Play button in order to begin viewing the video

Info
Tap this icon to get some more information about this episode

> "The Videos app makes video watching effortless and enjoyable"

Key features

Getting around the Videos app

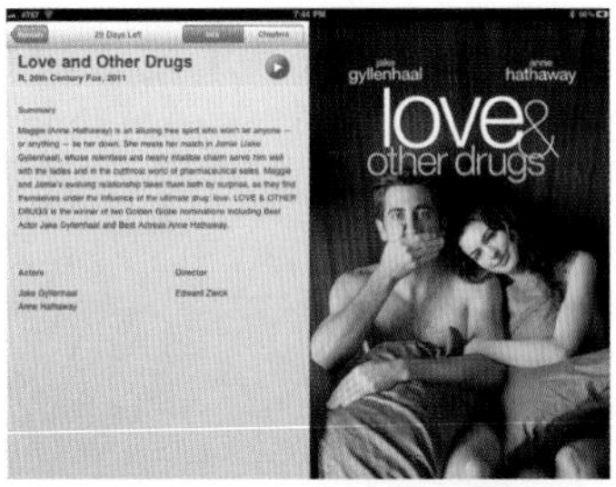

Rentals

When you rent movies from the iTunes Store, a Rentals button appears. Tapping this displays the screen listing your current rentals. This displays how many days of your rental period you have remaining. Once you begin watching, you have 24 hours to finish watching. To rent movies, open iTunes and tap on Movies. Find a movie you want to rent, and tap it to see the rental price.

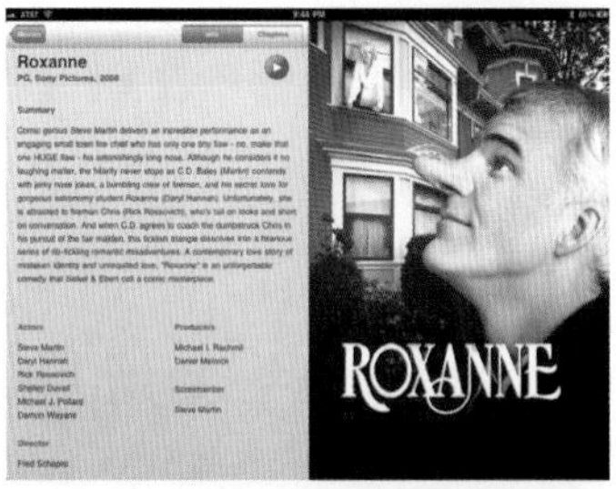

Movies

Movies you purchase from the iTunes Store show up when you tap the Movies button. All your movies show up here. Tap a thumbnail to see details about the movie. Tap the Chapters button to see the movie broken into chapters and to navigate through them. To purchase movies, open iTunes and tap on Movies. Tap each movie to see its purchase price.

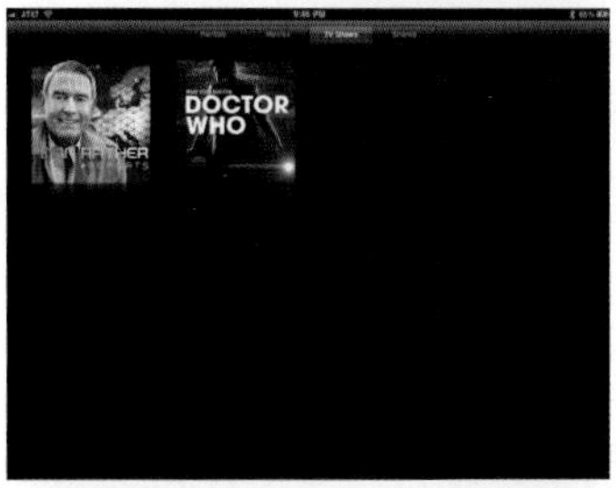

TV Shows

The TV Shows screen displays thumbnails for all TV series from which you have downloaded at least one show. Each season has its own thumbnail – tap one to see details about the series, season, and episodes. When you purchase episodes for the same series and season, they appear here. Tap Get More Episodes to go straight to this in the iTunes Store.

Playing videos

To play any type of video, tap its thumbnail, and then the Play button. If your iPad is on its side, the video will play in full screen mode. Tap once to show the controls. You can change the volume by sliding the bar on the bottom of the screen. To scrub through the video, slide the bar on the top of the screen. To return to the detail screen for the current video, tap Done.

Shared

The Shared button and screen only appear when you've activated Home Sharing. Turn on Home Sharing to display videos you can play from your computer on the same network as your iPad. Home Sharing allows you to view videos on your iPad that are already purchased, and downloaded to iTunes on your PC or Mac. Videos will automatically appear on this screen.

QUICK TIP

Free Videos

Find free TV shows and features on iTunes

When you first open the Videos app, the first thing you see is a blank screen with no videos installed. To make videos appear, you have to get them from the iTunes Store. If you don't want to pay money, you're out of luck when it comes to movies. But there are many free TV shows and features available.

To find them, tap the iTunes app on your iPad. Tap TV Shows, scroll down to the bottom of the screen, and then tap Free TV Episodes. Browse the available shows, and tap the View button next to one. Don't be alarmed if you see a button with a price!

Scroll down the page, and you'll find the free listings. Choose one, and then tap Free Episode (or Free HD Episode). The button turns green. Tap it again to begin downloading it. You are now prompted to enter your Apple ID Password, but you won't be charged. Tap the Downloads button on the bottom right to view the progress of your video's download. You must have a Wi-Fi connection for downloading to work. Downloading the episode may take some time, but when it is complete, you will see the episode installed when you next start up the Videos app.

There are many free TV shows and other videos available.

Using YouTube

Getting the best YouTube experience

Odds are that you've visited YouTube in the last few weeks to see the latest viral video. The YouTube app allows you to watch YouTube videos in full screen and HD when available. The app takes advantage of the touchscreen technology, allowing you to view and control video viewing with just a few taps. You can view videos in widescreen mode by turning your iPad on its side. It allows you to easily browse featured, related, most viewed, and top rated videos. You can also use the search feature to locate videos by keyword. You can log in with your YouTube account, and stay logged in so you can bookmark your favourite videos. While logged in, you can also comment on and rate videos. The app also remembers your viewing history so you can locate videos you've recently watched to watch again.

"The YouTube app lets you watch videos in full screen and HD"

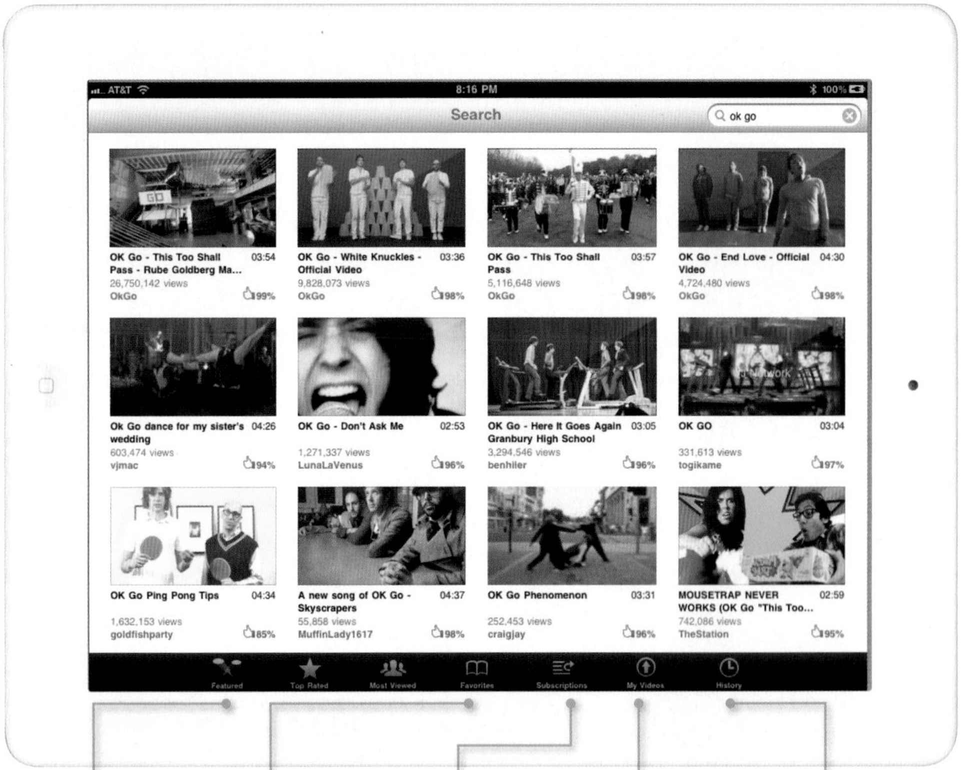

Featured
Featured, Top Rated and Most Viewed display the popular and highly rated videos

Favorites
Tap here to see any videos that you've previously designated as Favorites

Subscriptions
Subscriptions displays videos of authors whose streams you have subscribed to

Uploads
Videos you've uploaded under your current username appear here

History
History keeps track of the videos you've viewed. Tap clear to remove your history

QUICK TIP

Using Subscriptions

Keep track of your favourite video creators with Subscriptions

Use Subscriptions to keep tabs on your favourite artists.

Say, for example, that you really like Ok Go's wacky music videos, and you watch them again and again. You want to keep track of the current videos, and know when new ones are added. The YouTube app lets you keep track of everything an author has published to YouTube using Subscriptions. To add a subscription, view one of the videos by the author in small screen view. Tap on the More From button. At the top of the list, tap the Subscribe button. View your new subscription by tapping the Subscriptions button on the bottom of the screen. The Subscriptions screen shows you a list of your current subscriptions. Tap on each to see all videos that are currently on YouTube for that author, in order from most recent up to the oldest. As new videos from these authors are added, they will automatically appear in your lists. There are two ways to unsubscribe. From the Subscriptions screen, tap the Edit button, and then tap the name of the subscription that you want to delete, and then tap Done. To unsubscribe in small screen mode, view one of the videos from the author. Tap on More From, and then tap the Unsubscribe button.

Key features

Finding your way around the YouTube app

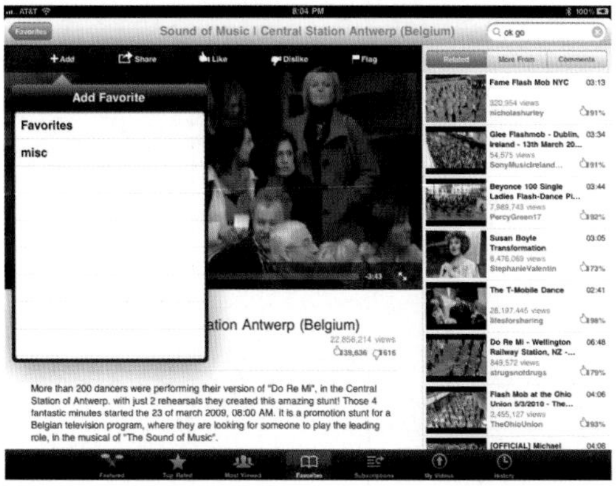

Add favourites

When viewing a video in the small screen mode, click on the Add button on the upper right to save the current video as a favourite. This opens the Add Favorite panel. Tap on the word Favourite to save this video in your favourites list. Your saved favourites show up when you tap the Favorites button on the bottom of the screen. On this screen, you can tap the edit button to remove previously saved favourites from your list.

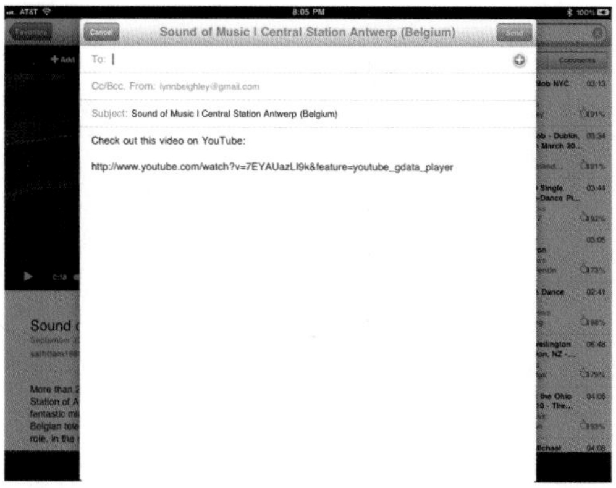

Share

In small screen mode, tap the Share button to send a link for the video to a friend. This button opens an email window. Type in the email address where you want to send the link to the video. The subject of the message will be the video title. You can change this by typing over the current subject. The body of the message is also editable. Customise it, and tap Send when you're done.

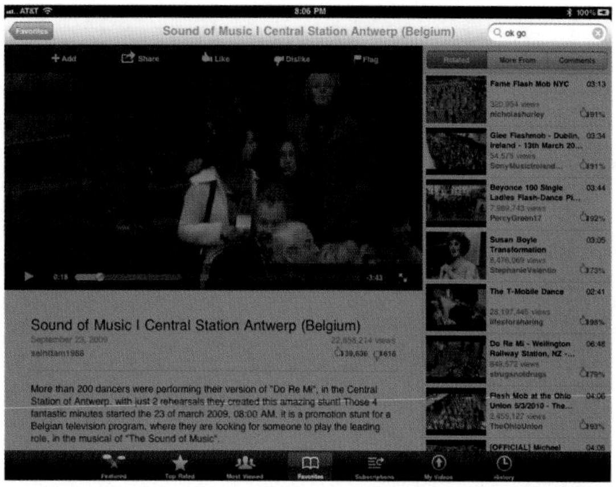

Search

On the top right of all of the screens (except the full screen view), there's a search box in the upper right. Type in all of the video's title, keywords from the title, or the name of the author of the video. Press Search to see thumbnails for the matches. You may need to scroll down to see them all. In general, you'll get better results when you search for video title keywords rather than author names.

> "You will get better search results when you type in video title keywords rather than author names"

View full screen

You can view full screen videos by turning your iPad on its side. Tap the video you wish to view. If it's still in small screen mode, tap the expand icon on the bottom right of the small video display – two tiny outward pointing diagonal arrows. When in full screen mode, return to small screen by tapping the contract icon (two inward pointing arrows), which is on the bottom right of the screen.

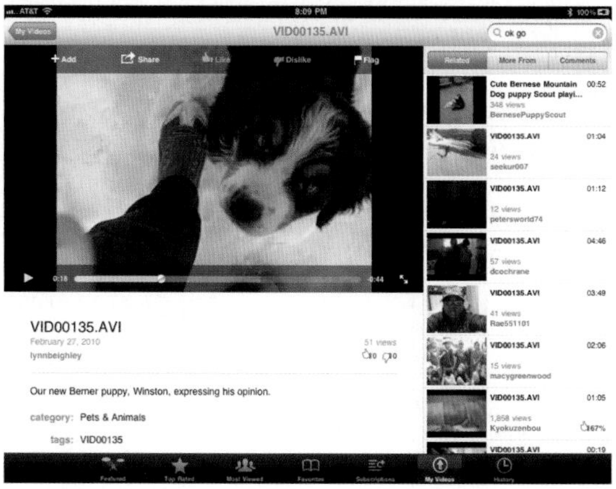

Related, More From, and Comments

In small screen mode, you will see three buttons labelled Related, More From, and Comments. When your iPad is horizontal, they're on the right-hand side, and when it's vertical they appear below. Related videos are similar to the one you're viewing. More From shows ones from the same author. Comments display comments about the current video.

Playing with Game Center

Get started playing games with your friends on Apple's Game Center

Game Center is the app that lets you keep track of the games you've played, the games your friends have played and how you stack up against them. It even enables you to compete against people you don't know in multiplayer games.

Use Game Center to invite friends using their nickname or email address, and once you're connected you can see what games your friends are playing, their status, and how they're doing.

To begin, start Game Center and sign in with your Apple ID. You only have to do this once, as when you log in, you will stay logged in until you choose to log out. You can type in a status message that will be visible to your friends, or you can begin playing by clicking on the Games link and choosing one of your installed Game Center-compatible games. Game Center will keep track of your high scores and achievements and display them on your friends' Center.

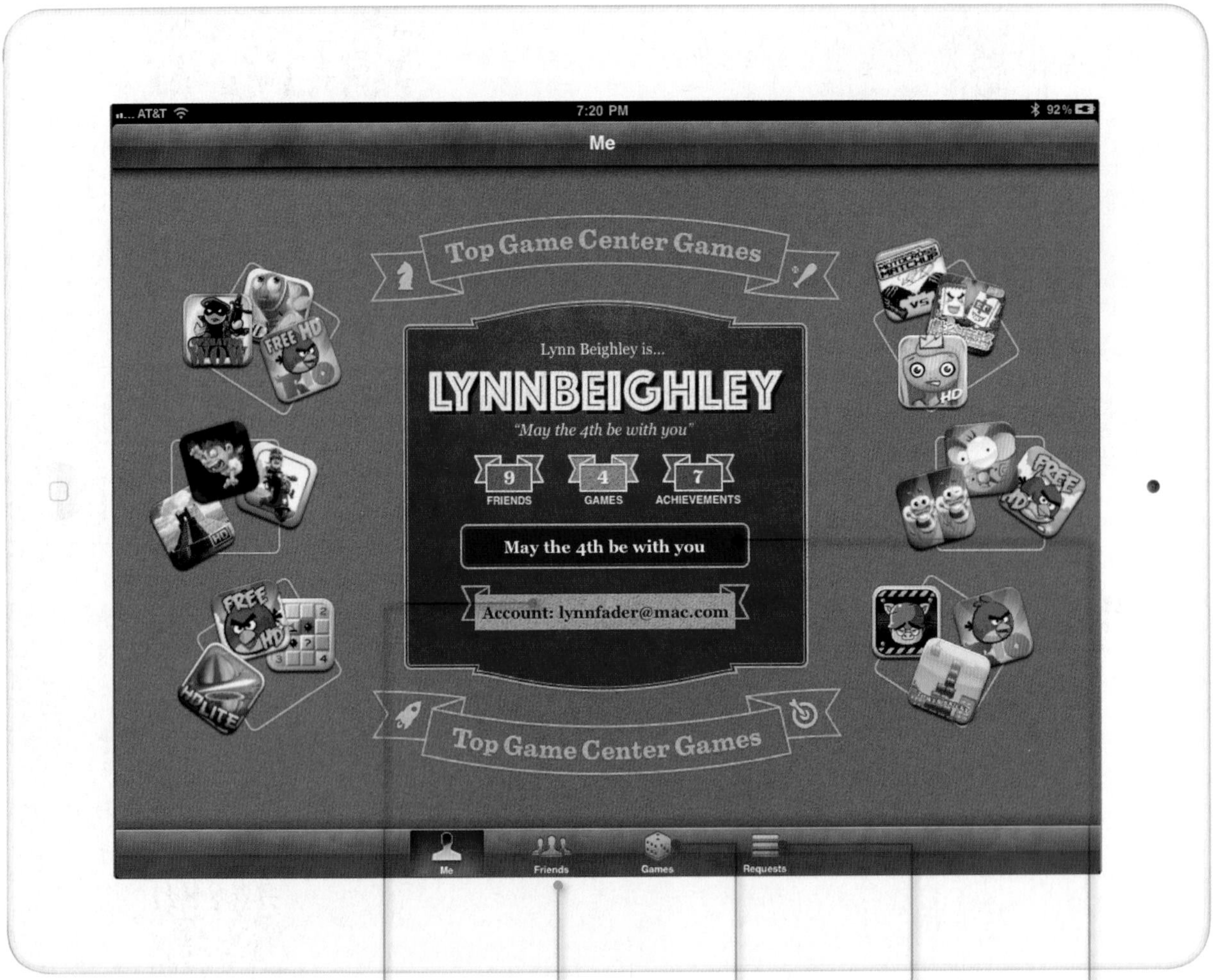

"You can see what games your friends are playing and how they're doing"

Account
Tapping the Account banner opens your Game Center settings

Friends
See all your current friends and the games that they're playing

Games
Tap to open the Games screen with links to the games you've purchased

Requests
View your pending friend requests when you tap the Requests button

Status
Type a current status in this box to share it with your friends

Key features

Getting to know the parts of Game Center

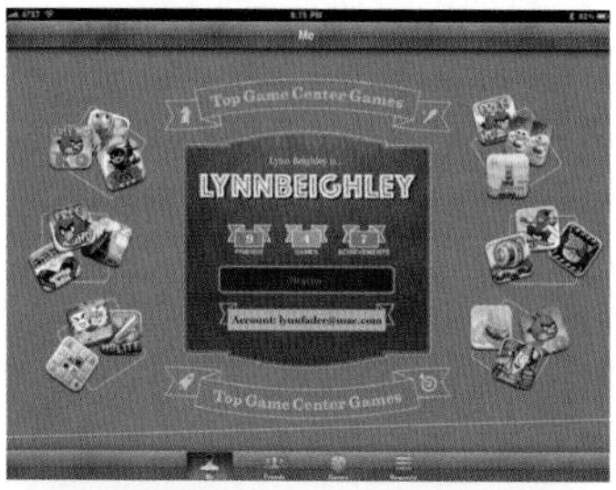

Me

This is the main page of the Game Center app. From here you can set your status, choose popular games to install and play, and modify your account settings. To choose one of the featured games, tap on the icons scattered around the screen. If it's a game you have installed, you'll go right to it. If not, the App Store opens and you can choose to purchase it.

Friends

The Friends screen displays all your Game Center friends. Tapping on each friend's name on the left opens his or her details. You see how many friends your friend has and how many different games your friend's played. Drag down on the list of friends on the left to see a search box that lets you search your friends and games they've recently played.

Games

Tap the Games button to open the Games screen. Here you see the Game Center games you have installed. This screen also displays when you install each game. Next to each game is your current score, number of achievements and your rank. Tap on a game to begin playing. You can find, purchase and install new games by tapping the Find Game Center Games banner.

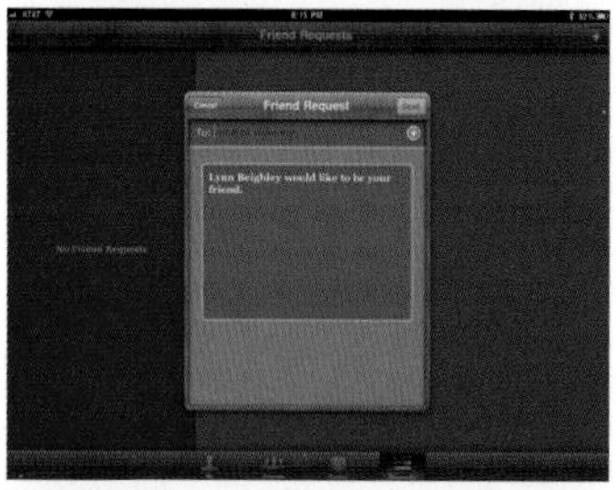

Friend requests

Send a request to a friend with Game Center by using the Friend Request screen. To get to this screen, either tap the Friends or Requests button. Click on the plus sign on the upper right of the screen. Begin typing your friend's Game Center name or email address. Customise the body of the message if you wish, or use the default text. When you're done, tap Send.

Account settings

To get to your Game Center account settings, tap on the Me button. Tap the yellow banner that says Account, followed by your email address. Tap on View Account. Use this screen to control whether you allow other people to send you invites, choose if other users can find you by using your email account and add another email so you can be found with that as well.

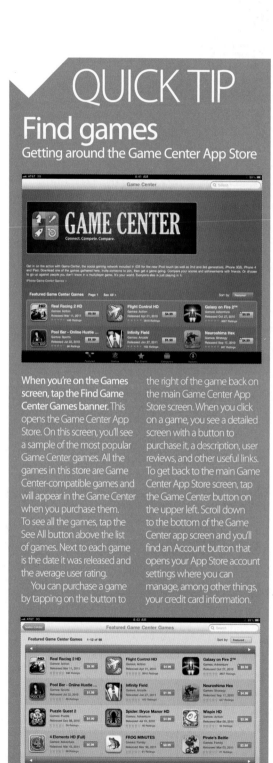

QUICK TIP

Find games

Getting around the Game Center App Store

When you're on the Games screen, tap the Find Game Center Games banner. This opens the Game Center App Store. On this screen, you'll see a sample of the most popular Game Center games. All the games in this store are Game Center-compatible games and will appear in the Game Center when you purchase them. To see all the games, tap the See All button above the list of games. Next to each game is the date it was released and the average user rating.

You can purchase a game by tapping on the button to the right of the game back on the main Game Center App Store screen. When you click on a game, you see a detailed screen with a button to purchase it, a description, user reviews, and other useful links. To get back to the main Game Center App Store screen, tap the Game Center button on the upper left. Scroll down to the bottom of the Game Center app screen and you'll find an Account button that opens your App Store account settings where you can manage, among other things, your credit card information.

Reading with iBooks

Major features of the iBooks app that enhance your reading experience

The iBooks app is Apple's answer to the Kindle. You can purchase and download titles from the iBookstore, then view and organise your titles on your virtual bookshelf. Read your books and adjust screen brightness, font size, and font face for more readability. Search for words, characters, or phrases anywhere in your books. Change the page colour to white or sepia, and change the text layout to left or fully justified. As you're reading, highlight text and add notes, and the page navigator on the bottom of each page helps you keep track of where you are. If you need to stop reading, create a bookmark so you can come back later. iBooks allows you to read ePub and PDF formatted books and documents. In addition to purchasing books from the iBookstore, you can add PDF documents from the Mail app and both PDF and ePub documents by adding them to iTunes and syncing your iPad.

> "Purchase and download titles, then organise them on your virtual bookshelf"

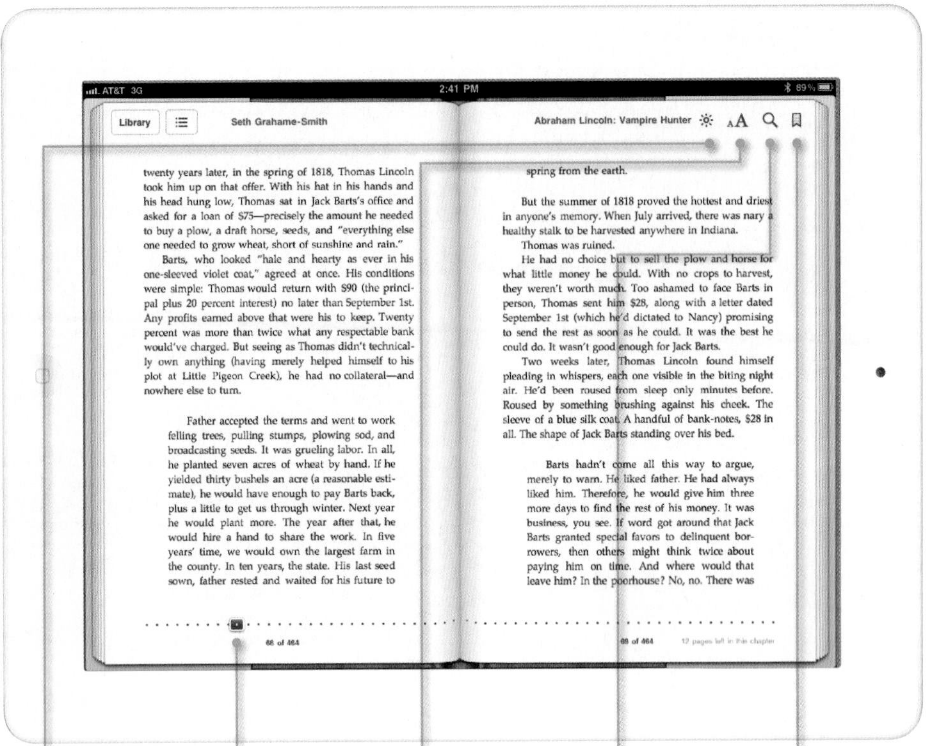

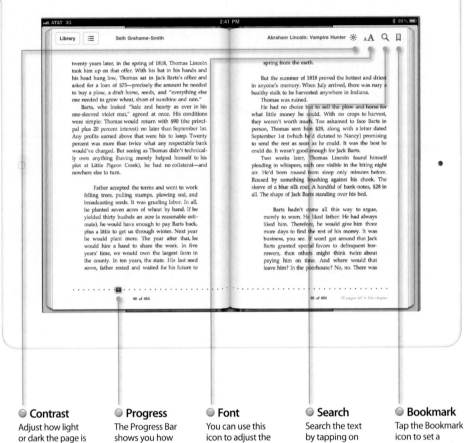

Contrast
Adjust how light or dark the page is by tapping on the Contrast icon

Progress
The Progress Bar shows you how far along you are in the book

Font
You can use this icon to adjust the font according to your preferences

Search
Search the text by tapping on the magnifying glass icon

Bookmark
Tap the Bookmark icon to set a bookmark on the current page

QUICK TIP

Books in the iBookstore

Viewing details on individual books in the iBookstore

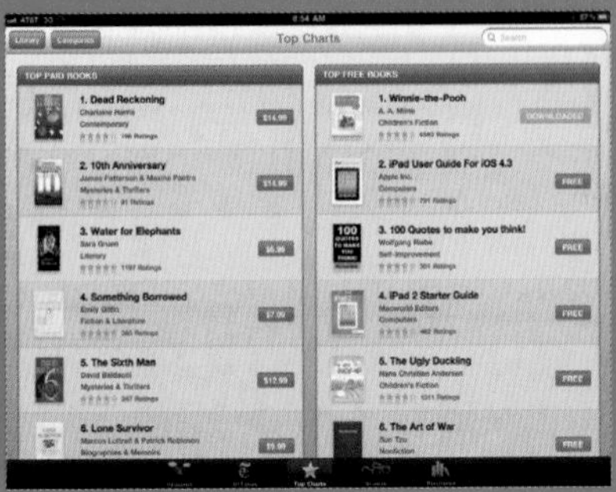

The book detail screen is full of helpful tools and information.

When you locate a book in the iBookstore, tapping on it opens up the detail screen. This screen is full of helpful tools and information. On the top right is the Author Page link, and just beneath it is the Alert Me link. Whenever this author has a new publication released, you'll receive an alert. You can also send an email to a friend with information on this book. The basic information about the book is displayed to the right of the cover image, as well as a button to purchase the book. If you want to read a few pages of the book before buying, then tap the Get Sample button. A sample will be automatically added to your bookshelf. If you scroll down the detail screen, you will see a graphical summary of customer ratings. Scroll further down to read any customer reviews. You can rate the book yourself by tapping on the star icons just under the Customer Ratings section. Finally, you can see other, similar books that customers who bought this book also bought. Tap on the cover of one of these to see its detail page. When you're done viewing the detail page, tap on the shaded portion of the display.

Key features

Major features of the iBooks app that enhance your reading experience

iBookstore

The iBookstore is where you shop for books to add to iBooks. Open the store by tapping the button on the upper left of your screen. Once there, you can view featured titles, search by title or author, and see bestsellers. Tapping an individual title gives you more information, including a description and reviews. Your purchases are automatically transferred to the app, and appear on your shelf.

Collections

After you've used iBooks for a while, you'll probably have a number of books. To keep them organised, you can group them into Collections. By default, you begin with two collections: Books and PDFs. Titles are automatically placed in the appropriate collection. Tap the Collections button on the top right to see existing Collections. Tap the Edit button, and then the book you wish to move to a Collection.

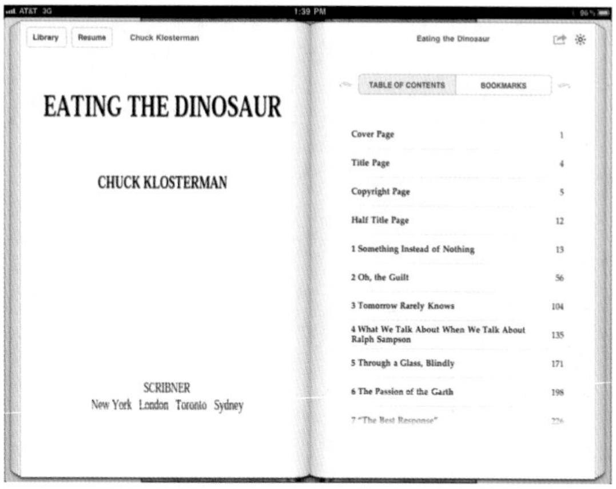

Table of Contents

Each book includes a table of contents. It allows you to see at a glance the chapter titles, and gives you a quick way to access chapters by tapping on the chapter title. To get to the Table of Contents, tap a book to open it, and then tap on the button on the upper left next to the Library button. When you are done viewing the Table of Contents, tap the Resume button.

"The iBookstore is where you shop for books to add to your collection. Your purchases appear on your shelf"

Search the Bookshelf

You can search your bookshelf by title or author. In Bookshelf view, the search box is hidden. To reveal it, drag down on the Bookshelf. As you type, the books with titles or authors that match the search remain visible. It searches both first and last names, and all words in the title. To clear the results and display all of your titles, tap the small X in the search box.

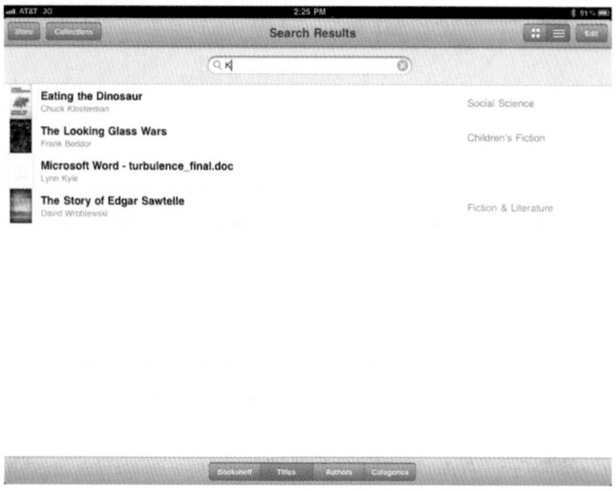

Change the listing style

When you first open iBooks, your books are displayed on a virtual shelf. You can move them around to organise the display. You can also arrange your titles in a list view by tapping the button with three horizontal lines on the top left of your display next to the Edit button. To return to the shelf display, tap the button to the left that has an icon of four small squares.

The iPad Lifestyle Guide

In-depth tutorials on apps to enhance your life

The iPad can be many different things, but one of its biggest appeals is how easily it can be slotted into every aspect of your day-to-day life. From acting as a portal to your social network, to allowing you to take and edit photos, it can be a great help in many different ways. The Ultimate Lifestyle Guide delves into the photographic potential of the device, as well as showing how to make the most of videocalling through FaceTime on the iPad 2, before we go on to explore Facebook, Twitter and much more. We even show you how to use your iPad as a creative sketchbook with Adobe Ideas, proving the sheer diversity of this machine for delivering you solutions to everyday activities. The potential is astounding.

074 Find your way around the Facebook app on your iPad.

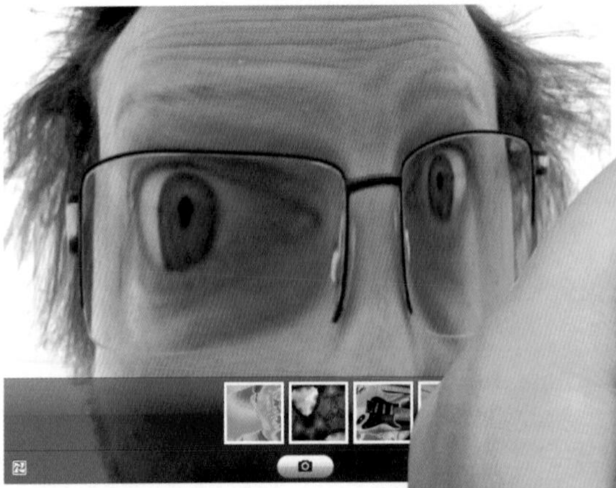

064 Learn how to add interesting effects to your photos with Photo Booth.

062 Take photos using the new front and rear-facing cameras on the iPad 2.

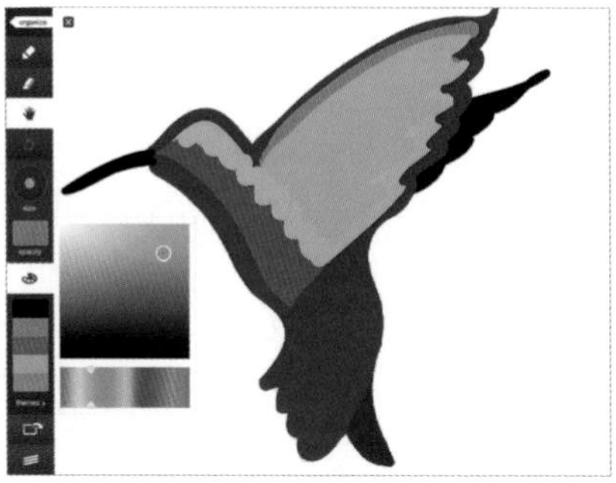

072 Learn how to easily sketch on your iPad with Adobe Ideas and its fantastic features.

Tutorial: Manage your contacts in FaceTime

If you want to make a call you have to know how to access your contacts. Here's how to add new details and delete others while managing your FaceTime contacts

Task: To add new contacts and remove old ones

Difficulty: Beginner

Time needed: 10 minutes

The first time you use FaceTime it might be surprising to see that the Contacts section is fully populated. It's because FaceTime uses the details in the Contacts app and this in turn can import all the contacts that you have in Outlook or Address Book. Each time there's a sync with iTunes, the contacts are synchronised across all the apps. If you don't use Outlook or Address Book then, of course, the people in the Contacts folder will just be the ones you've added. It isn't necessary to add or delete anything using FaceTime; you can do it in the Contacts app. As soon as anything is changed here it is reflected in the FaceTime app. Any changes will then be propagated back to the desktop program you are syncing contacts with to ensure conformity across all the software. Equally, any change to a contact in FaceTime is reflected in Contacts and then transferred back when syncing. In this tutorial though, we're going to import contacts from Outlook and manage them in FaceTime.

Step-by-step | FaceTime, Outlook Managing your contacts

1: Import contacts

Go to iTunes and plug in your iPad. Click on your device in the pane on the left side. Click Info on the menu above the main screen. Now put a tick in the box that says 'Sync Contacts with' and select Outlook.

2: Delete old contacts

Perform a sync to add your Outlook contacts to Contacts and FaceTime. Tap on FaceTime and then Contacts. To delete a contact, tap on the name of it, then Edit. Scroll to the bottom and tap Delete Contact.

Managing the details

Add images, input details or delete old contacts entirely

Remove details

To change the entry for a field just tap on it and edit it. However, to remove it completely without editing or replacement, tap on the red dash by the side on any entry

Information on calls

To see who has called you and who you have called, tap on the Recents entry. This contains complete details of the length of the calls and the date when they were made. Important contacts can be added to Favorites or shared

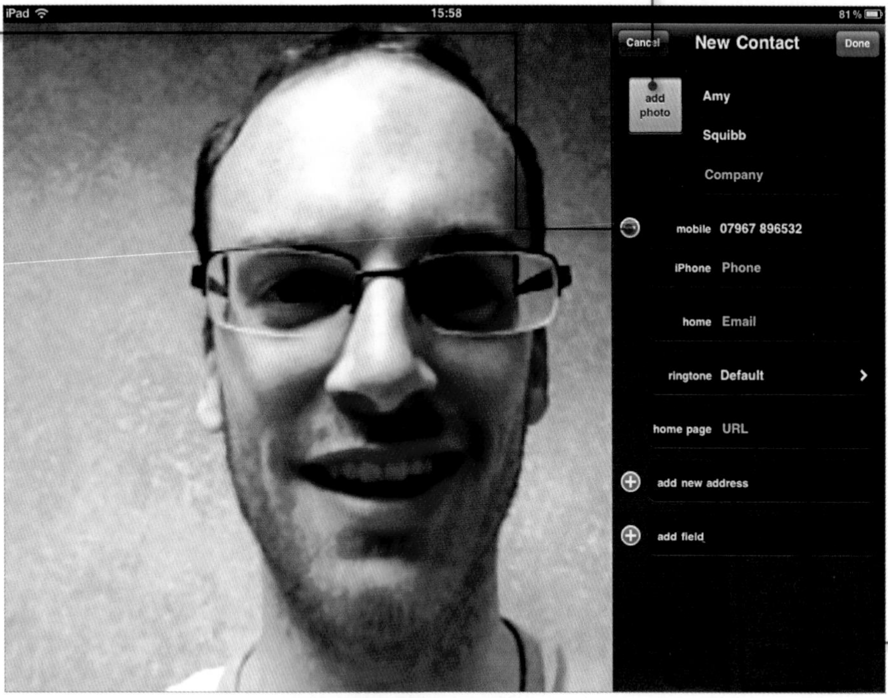

Add an image

To give your contacts a more visual look tap on the Add Photo button and either use the camera to take a picture or browse the Photo Library for one. You can scale the image to fit the square.

Knowledge base

Adding favourites

If you have a lot of contacts and most of them aren't on FaceTime then it makes sense to sort them out using the Favorites button. Either add people to Favorites when looking at their details, or, if looking at the Favorites list, tap on the Plus sign and scroll through the contacts list.

Change the tune

By default, all contacts will ring you with the same built-in ringtone which is the Strum noise. However, you can change this to any of the alarm noises by tapping on Ringtone.

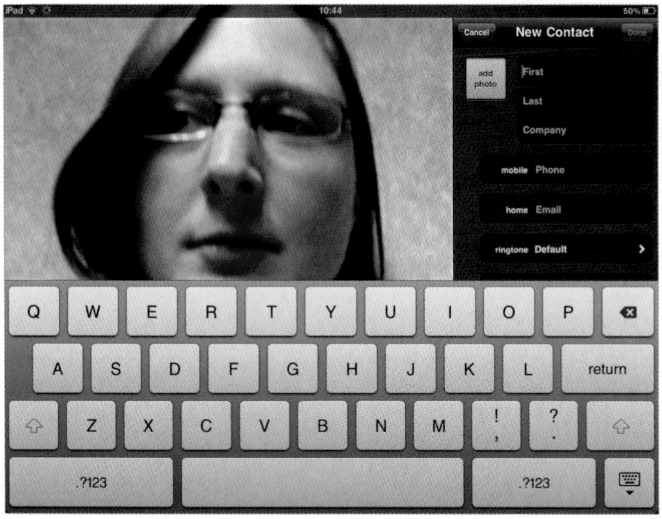

3: Add new contacts

To add a new contact tap on the Plus symbol, top right. Enter all the details you have then click on Add Photo. Select to either take a photo or choose one from the Library. Click on Done.

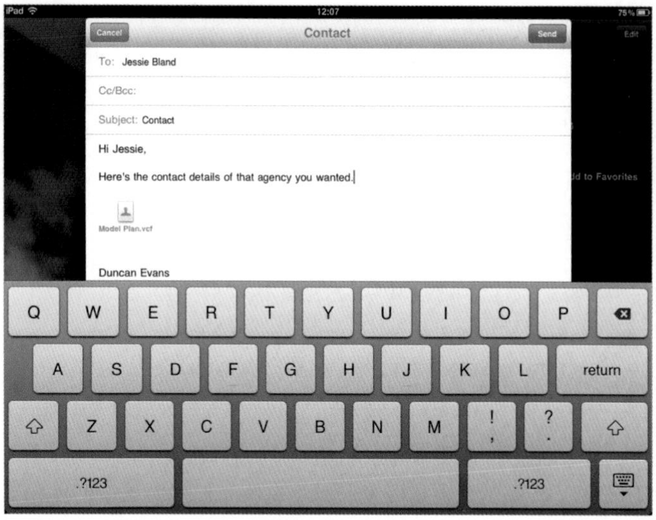

4: Share your contacts

To share a contact with someone else, select the contact in question and then tap on Share Contact. Type in the email address of the person to share the contact with, write your message and click on Send.

Tutorial: Make calls using FaceTime

It's the most exciting new feature of the iPad 2, the ability to make video calls. Here's how you sign up and then call someone for a video conversation

Task: What you need to do to be able to make a call with FaceTime

Difficulty: Beginner

Time needed: 10 minutes

The addition of dual cameras to the iPad 2 was one of the worst kept secrets yet most anticipated features of the new device's launch. Not so much for the ability to go out and take pictures with your iPad, but for video calling and video capture and transmission. Yes, FaceTime has arrived on the iPad 2 and it has its own app. If you're used to an iPhone where FaceTime is built in to the phone app then this is slightly different. The cameras are the same resolution, so if you think your main screen image looks soft, it's because it's being displayed at the huge iPad size, not a tiny iPod touch screen size. The first thing you need to have in place before any calls are made is to register FaceTime using your Apple ID. This is the ID that is used by Apple and the App Store for purchases. Once the Apple ID is set up for the FaceTime account then an email address needs to be assigned to it. This is the one that you will use to call other people and that they will use to call you.

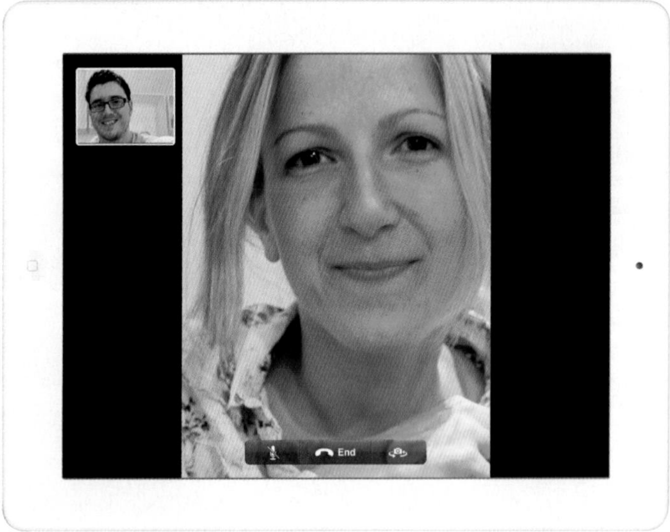

Step-by-step | FaceTime **Register FaceTime and make calls**

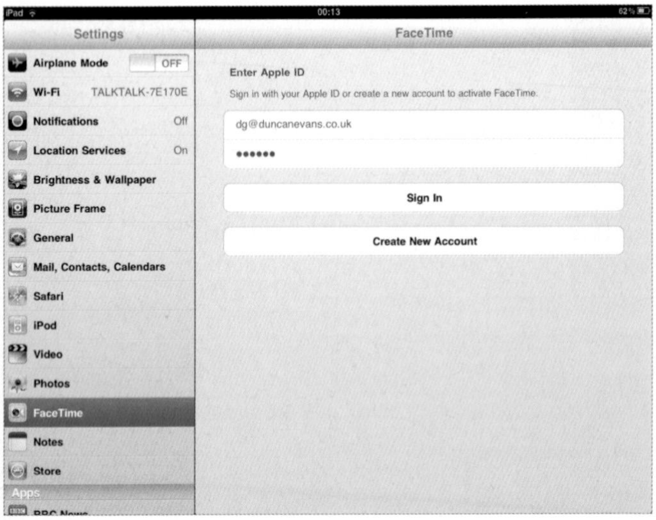

1: Register your details

Tap on the Settings app and scroll down the list of built-in apps until you get to FaceTime. Tap on this and toggle FaceTime On. You will need to enter your Apple ID. Enter the email and password and tap on Sign In.

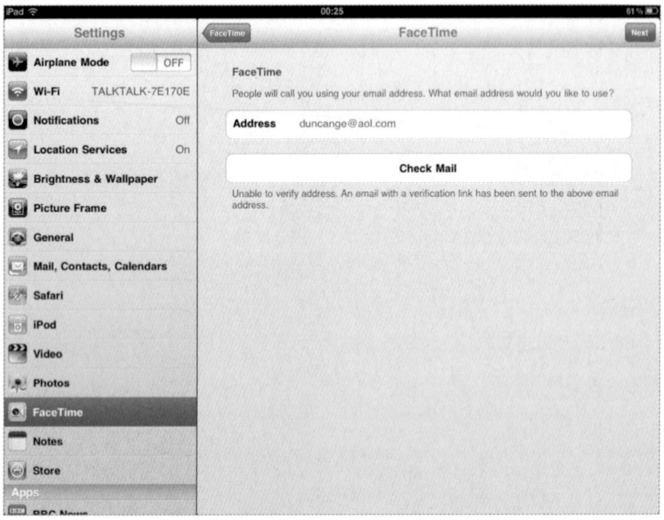

2: Select an address

FaceTime can use different email addresses. Enter which one you want to use for calls. If it's the same as your Apple ID account it will be verified immediately. If it's different it will send a verification link to that address.

Making a call

It's easy as pie to make FaceTime calls. Just find your contacts who actually use it and call away

Making contact

The names in this list aren't ones you've logged as FaceTime users, it's everyone in your Contacts database. Tap on a name to see if they have a FaceTime email you can use

People in touch

The list of Recent calls covers both those ringing you and you ringing them. If it's a frequent contact you want to call, it's quicker to tap here than scroll through the entire contacts list for someone's details

Cameras in use

When activating FaceTime for a call, the first thing you see is yourself. When FaceTime connects the call, this window shrinks to a postage size so you can still see yourself and this main window fills with the video from the contact

Knowledge base

Dual cameras

The real advantage of having front and rear-facing cameras in a FaceTime call is that either the person calling or the one receiving, or both, can turn the other camera on and show the other person something that is going on in front of them. All you need to do is tap the camera symbol with the rotating arms to switch your camera from front facing to rear facing.

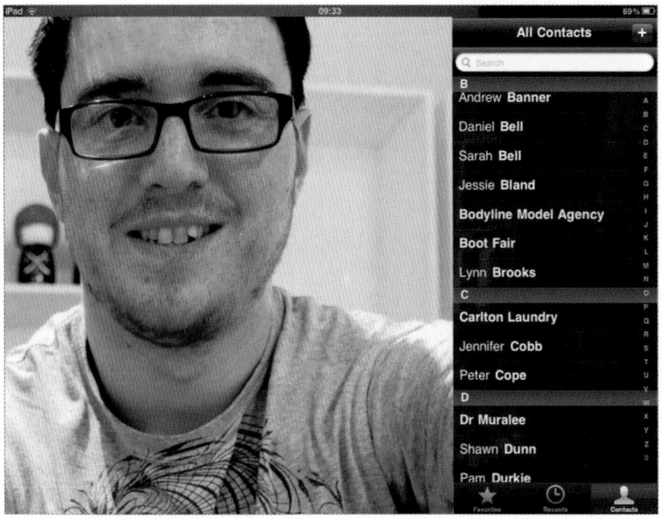

3: Get into FaceTime

Once verified, your details will be displayed and FaceTime will be on. Exit Settings and tap on the FaceTime app. This shows the display from the front facing camera. Tap on the Contacts box at the bottom to list them.

4: Make a call

Tap on the person to call. If they have a FaceTime account the email address will be shown with a blue video camera next to it. Tap on the email address to make the call. This will then ring the contact.

Tutorial: Take photos and videos with the Camera

The iPad 2 finally has a camera – in fact it has two, and they're more than just a token addition…

Task: Use the iPad's cameras to record videos and take photos

Difficulty: Beginner

Time needed: 10 minutes

It was always clear that the iPad was going to get a camera at some point, even though some people questioned whether it would be as much use as having one in the much smaller and lighter iPhone and iPod models. In the event, it is really handy, not just because it lets you use FaceTime but also because it opens up the world of camera-based apps to iPad users for the first time. Things like augmented reality and barcode scanners need a camera to work, and now you get one. The cameras in the iPad are different, and the front-facing one allows you to record video and take still pictures at VGA quality, which is not the largest frame size in the world, but does the job. The rear facing camera on the other hand captures at 720p and so is HD resolution, perfect for making home movies. Both cameras record at 30 frames per second and also capture audio. With the iPad's innovative interface you can tap to control focusing and exposure, and photos will also be geotagged over Wi-Fi so you can see where they were taken.

Step-by-step | Camera Take video and stills with the iPad's camera

1: Fire it up

Open the Camera app and at the bottom right of the screen, make sure the slider is set to still camera. Tap on the screen to focus on a particular element.

2: Take a still picture

Tap on the camera icon at the bottom and the iPad will take the picture. Click on the photo icon at the bottom left to be taken to the Camera Roll.

3: Zoom in

Remaining in photo mode, tap the screen to focus again and you will call up the zoom slider. Drag this with your finger to zoom in.

The camera interface

The camera is very simple and easy to understand. Here are the main features…

Knowledge base

Share videos

When watching a video in the Camera Roll, there's a Share icon at the top. Click on this and you can choose to email the video from the iPad, to send it to YouTube, or to copy it. If you choose to send it, it will be compressed using settings appropriate to the destination. This is because native video files are huge – far too big for email. Apple's compression reduces file size while maintaining quality.

Camera chooser
Flip between the front-facing and rear-facing cameras. The front-facing one is lower resolution but the rear-facing one records in higher quality. Both can record stills, video and sound

Capture button
This really couldn't be any simpler – press it to take a snap in camera mode, or to start and stop recording in video mode

Capture type
Use this button to switch the cameras between taking still images and recording video. In either mode you can tap to focus and adjust exposure. The still camera mode also has a zoom function

Camera Roll
Stills and videos that you take are placed into the iPad's Camera Roll. Tap here to quickly jump to it and preview the images you have taken

4: Flip the camera

Hit the swap icon in the top right-hand corner to switch to the iPad's front-facing camera. This is lower resolution, but it's good for taking self portraits.

5: Change to video

Flip back to the rear-facing camera and use the slider at the bottom right to switch to video mode. Press the red button to record and again to stop.

6: Play your video

Recorded videos are placed into the Camera Roll as well, so if you select one you can play it back. Use the timeline at the top to scroll through the video.

Tutorial: Take photos with Photo Booth

Photo Booth is capable of applying weird and wonderful camera effects and using both the front and rear-facing cameras on your iPad 2. It's a bit crazy, but also tremendous fun…

Task: Create wacky snapshots with Photo Booth

Difficulty: Beginner

Time needed: 5 minutes

Photo Booth made its debut on the Mac some years ago, when built-in iSight cameras became standard across most models of Apple computers. Now thanks to the cameras on the iPad 2, it has made its way to the device and it's a fun way to take snapshots of yourself and your friends, or just to take strange looking photos of anything you can point a camera at. The app itself is a little more limited on the iPad for some reason, with fewer effects and without the ability to record video with effects, but it's still great fun to play with. The touch screen interface means that when effects have a focus point, which is to say that they distort the image based on a certain area of the screen, you can use your finger to change the position and so edit the effect. Some of the others are just on or off – they can't be edited. Of course you are also able to use either the front or rear-facing cameras depending on whether you're photographing yourself or someone else.

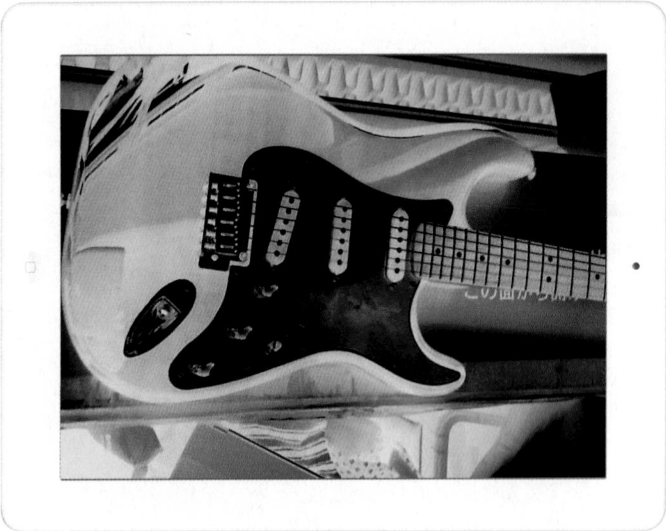

Step-by-step | Photo Booth **Take pictures in Photo Booth**

1: Fire it up

Open Photo Booth and it should default to using the front-facing camera. You'll see a range of different crazy effects and if you tap on one, you will get to see that effect in full screen.

2: Light Tunnel

This is the Light Tunnel effect and if you drag with your finger, you will be able to position the centre of the effect over any part of the screen. This applies to other effects that distort the image.

Using Photo Booth

Use Photo Booth's wacky effects to create fun and outlandish pictures to share or use on social networking sites…

The image
The weird and wonderful results of Photo Booth's effects can be seen on the main screen. This is a thermographic effect

Take a picture
Press the shutter button to take a snapshot and the image will be saved to a special camera roll inside Photo Booth. Form there, pictures can be deleted, viewed or emailed

Effects
To return to the effects list, click the effects icon. You will be able to choose from the built-in effects such as pinch, twirl, X-ray, mirror and a host of other strange ones

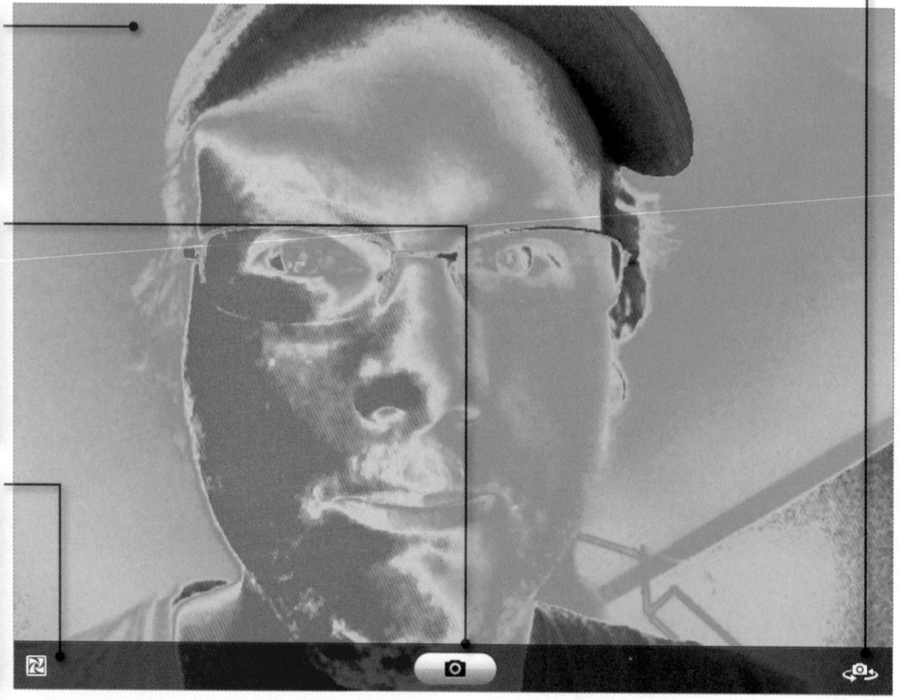

Camera flip
The iPad 2 has both front and rear-facing cameras and you can flip between them by using this icon. The effects all work the same way through both of the cameras

Knowledge base

Hardware requirements

The kinds of real-time image processing performed by Photo Booth actually place quite a strain on hardware, though the reason it isn't included on the iPad 1 is because it doesn't have any cameras. You're not able at present to apply Photo Booth effects to video on the iPad, though this may be something that Apple chooses to unlock with a software update at some point in the future.

3: View your pictures

Pictures that you take are shown along the bottom. Scroll around and load up any one to view it full screen. Click the camera chooser to flip to the rear camera, or the effect icon to choose a different effect.

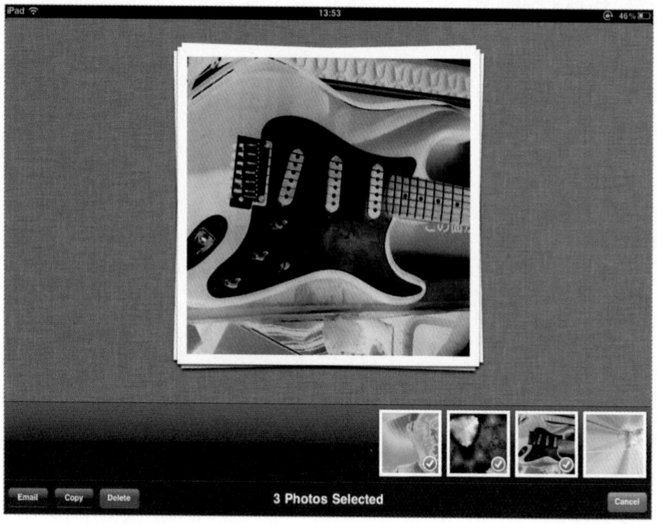

4: Share pictures

Click on the Share button and you can choose a number of pictures to either place in an email, copy, or delete. They are shown in a helpful stack view. If you deselect a picture it 'slides' out of the stack.

Tutorial: Use creative effects in Photo Booth

Photo Booth is great fun to play around with on your iPad, and you can create some weird and wonderful snapshots. Here's a selection of the effects available to you…

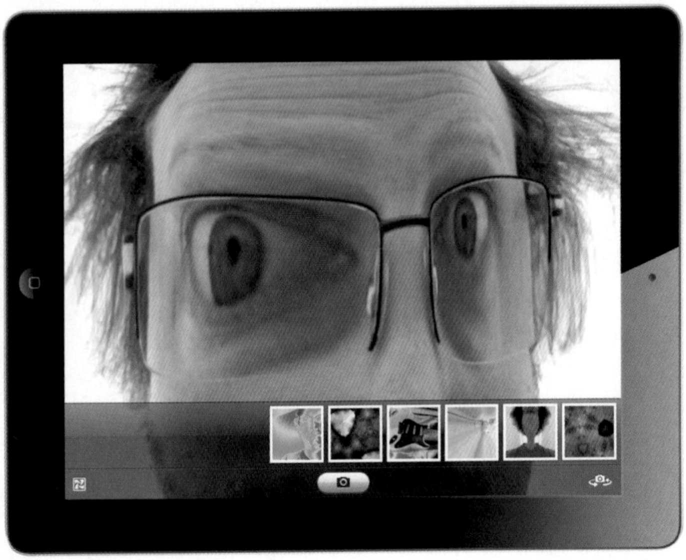

Task: Using Photo Booth's effects

Difficulty: Beginner

Time needed: 5 minutes

Photo Booth is a fun app to use, though under the hood it actually employs some pretty complex mathematics to generate the effects that are its trademark. Unfortunately it's not possible yet to record video in Photo Booth. The effects are centred around a grid and in the middle you'll see a 'normal' image. Above this are the thermal camera view, which translates light into different colours, X-ray which inverts the image into black and white, and a mirror that copies one side of the image to the other. To either side you'll find a kaleidoscope view that splits the image into different fractals and a light tunnel that creates a sort of zooming effect. Underneath are squeeze, twirl and stretch, which all distort the image in different ways. Where an effect has a 'focus' point, you can drag the screen with your finger to move it. Photo Booth is a fun way to create a profile picture for a social networking site, or just take zany snapshots while you're out and about.

Step-by-step | Photo Booth Get creative with Photo Booth

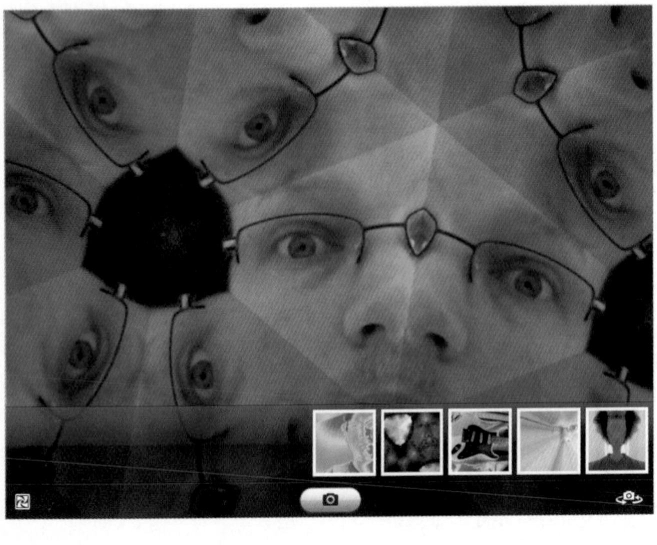

1: Try the kaleidoscope

Select the Kaleidoscope effect using the forward-facing camera and drag your finger on the screen to select the centre of the effect and so change how the rest of the effect behaves.

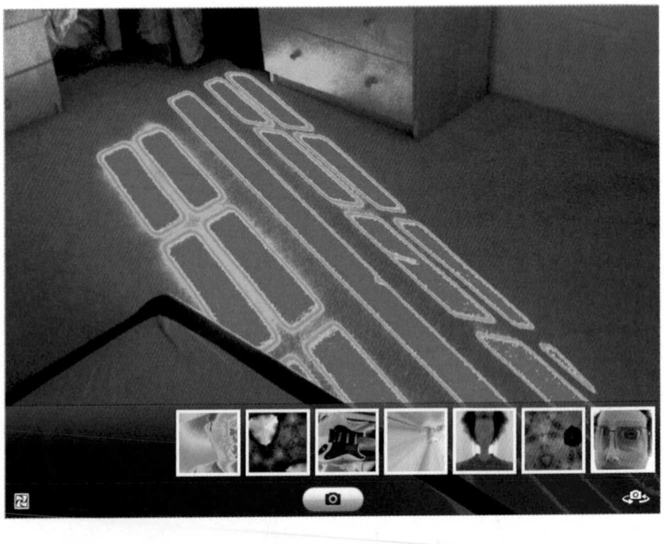

2: Try something strange

Here, some shadows are being cast through a glass door and by switching Photo Booth to thermal camera mode, we are able to capture a really striking effect with the rear-facing camera.

Photo Booth's effects

Choose from the different effects to get the kind of look that suits you…

X-ray
This effect puts everything into a negative view, changing light and dark around to give a moody look to your pictures. It's especially good when there's lots of natural light in the shot to begin with

Thermal camera
This isn't really a thermograph of course – they are extremely specialised pieces of equipment – but it uses the temperature and intensity of the light in the shot and converts these to colour-based information

The normal view
In case all the weirdness has got to you, there's always a 'normal' view in the centre to remind you what you're actually looking at

Effects with a focus
The distortion effects like stretch, tunnel and twirl have a central point that you can drag with your finger to change the way the effect is applied. Move the centre of the twirl effect, for example, and pinch to make it bigger or smaller

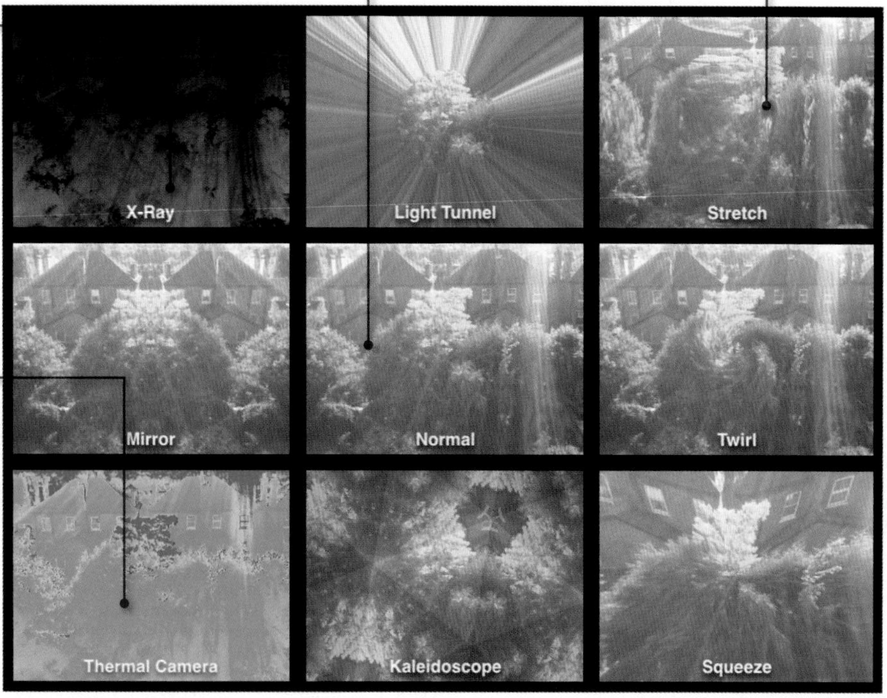

Knowledge base

Taking images further
Photo Booth is fun for taking odd snapshots, but you might also want to download a more advanced image editing app to your iPad to edit the images afterwards, maybe cropping them or further mangling them. There are many around, and one of the best free ones is Adobe Photoshop Express. This has good functionality and you can choose to make in-app purchases to have more advanced features if you feel you would like to at a later point.

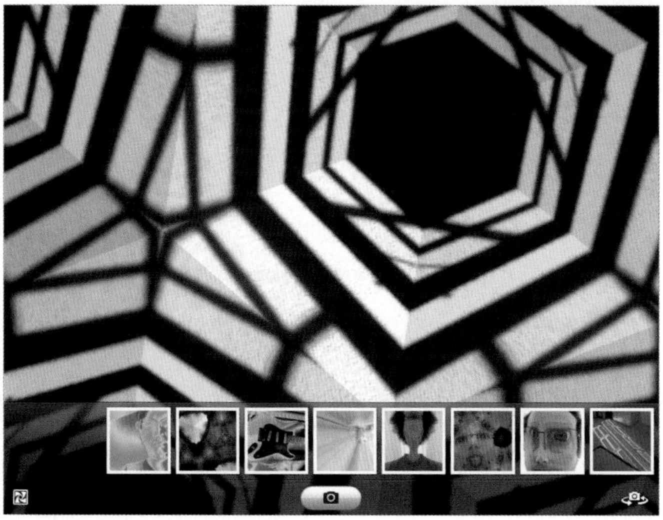

3: Change the view
Switching to the kaleidoscope effect with the camera pointing at the same scene, we can create a completely different kind of feel. Again you can drag and move the centre of the effect with your finger.

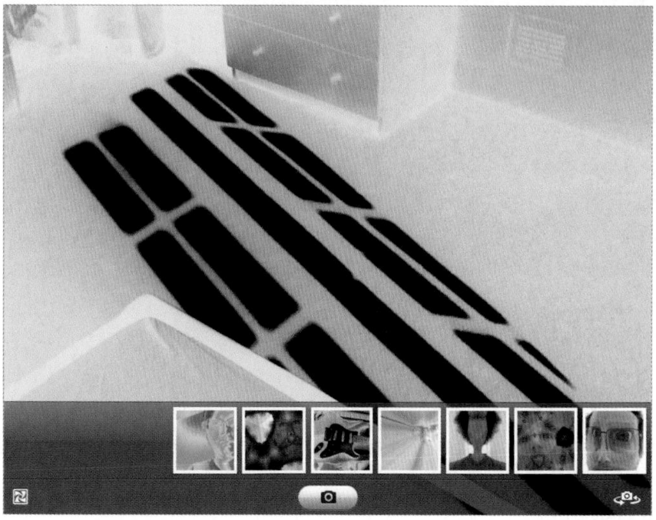

4: Back to front
Finally, try switching the same scene into X-ray effect mode and you will see the light and dark parts of the scene reversed. It's pretty odd but great fun to play with. Use it to take unusual snapshots.

Tutorial: Correct images with Photogene

Photogene is a photo correction tool that helps you crop images, rotate them, adjust colours, apply effects, use filters, and further manipulate photos to improve their quality

Task: Fix photographic images with Photogene

Difficulty: Beginner

Time needed: 45 minutes

Not every photograph looks perfect after you press the shutter button. With Photogene, you can correct an image by adjusting the colours and tweaking the exposure. You can also crop images to select just the best portion and add a border that looks like a picture frame. Thankfully, all of these tools are readily accessible on the iPad and provide a great deal of professional-level control. The effects and filters in Photogene are quite amazing. There are options to give images a cool Twenties retro look with lens shading, a black and white image, and a vivid colour treatment. Filters enhance an image with a pencil look or a posterised flat-colour look.

Not only is Photogene a good editor, but it also helps you adjust the pixel resolution of images. For example, you can downgrade a high-res photo to just 320 pixels in width to make it easier to email. The app also lets you post images to Twitter and Facebook, or send the final photograph via email.

Step-by-step | Photogene Fix your photo mistakes

1: Obtain an image

Either take a photo with the iPad 2's camera, or for the iPad 1 you can email photos to yourself and then save them to the Photo album, or download them from the web. When you start Photogene, select Photo Albums to find saved images.

2: Make simple adjustments

Before applying any filters and effects, you can crop an image by selecting only the portion you want. Press the Scissors icon (lower-left) and select the portion you want, then press Crop. Use the Rotate icon (second from left) to rotate the image.

Adjust and fix images on the iPad

Use the Photogene app to improve your images

Upload
Icons for returning to the gallery, uploading to Facebook and Twitter, changing resolution, and going through a tutorial to help you get more out of the program

Undo options
You can undo previous photo effects and corrections, or redo the last correction. The third icon (upper-left) allows you to return to the original image and start over

Size and rotation
Photogene lets you adjust the cropping of an image to select the portion you want. You can also rotate an image left or right, and flip horizontally or vertically

Effects and filters
Using the Effects button, you can apply effects such as Bleach (which removes harsh colours) or Reflect (which adds a reflection to the image). Filters also add pizzazz

Knowledge base

Add a frame
Adding a frame to a picture (icon in the lower-right) will add a frilly design or repeating pattern to the outer edge of your image. This frame is added to the outside and increases the pixel size of the image. When you save the image, the frame is also added so that, if you post the image to Facebook or Twitter, your friends will see the frame as part of the image (it is not just added to Photogene).

3: Apply effects and filters

The main purpose of Photogene is to adjust the colours of an image and apply effects and filters. Use the Effects icon (third from left) and the Filters icon (fourth from left). To adjust colours, press the colour icon on the bottom row.

4: Upload your image

You can also adjust the colour level (the icon looks like a bar graph) and add frames and borders. When you're done, press the globe icon (upper-right) to upload your photo to Twitter or Facebook. You can also copy it to the clipboard or email the image.

Tutorial: Turn your iPad into a photo frame

Not only is the iPad an incredible touch screen computer, but when it's not in use you can use it as a digital photo frame. Here's how…

Task: Set up a photo frame

Difficulty: Beginner

Time needed: 5 minutes

It's this kind of functionality and thought that makes Apple the great company that it is. We can imagine the meeting where the people are discussing the iPad and someone chimes in that it should be able to be used as a photo frame, and someone just says, 'Okay, we'll do that' – and then they make it happen and make it awesome. When you're not using it – which will be hardly ever, unless you're asleep – the iPad can become a very cool photo frame. It takes a few steps to set up, but once it's done you simply tap a button on the lock screen and the photos will start playing. In typical Apple fashion, you can assign transitions and pick which photos you want the iPad to display. If you have a particular album that you'd like to add to the iPad, you'll need to sync it to the device using iTunes.

Step-by-step | Settings Set up a photo frame

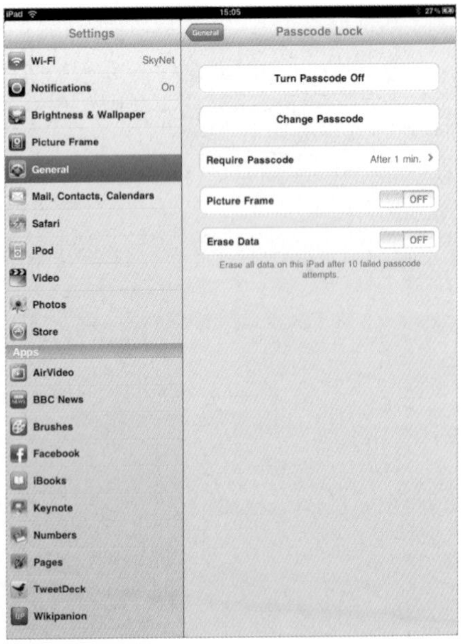

1: Passcode

Tap the settings icon on the home screen and then tap on 'General' and then 'Passcode'. If your passcode is already set up you'll have to enter it to edit the settings in this section.

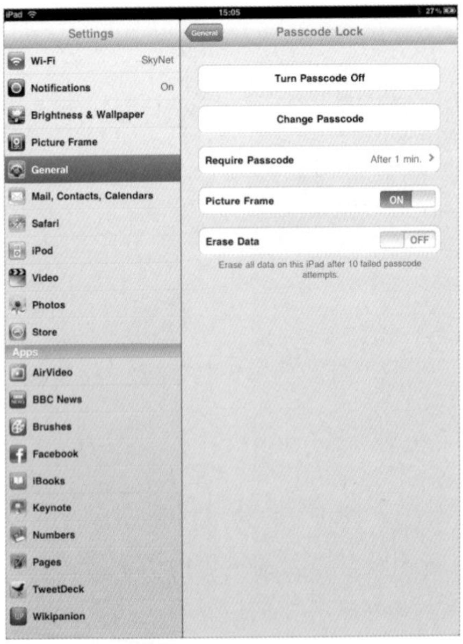

2: Picture frame

Tap the 'Picture Frame' button so you can clearly see that it is on. In order to make changes to the behaviour of this functionality, tap on the 'Picture Frame' menu above 'General' in the left-hand pane.

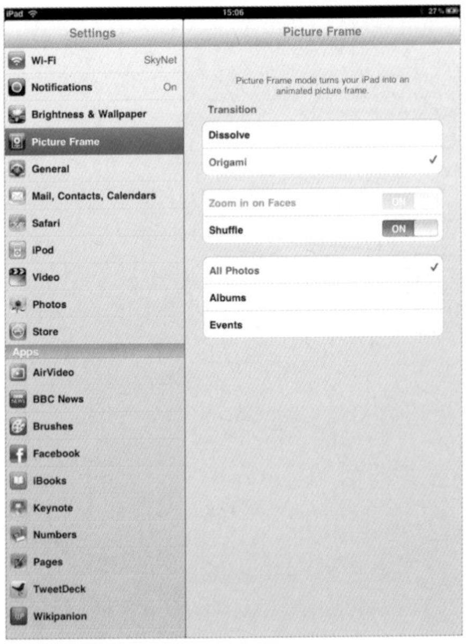

3: Lots of options

Here you can change the transitions, tell the iPad to zoom in on faces that it detects in the images, shuffle the pictures, and change which pictures are used in the photo frame.

Customising your photo frame

The iPad offers almost as many settings as a dedicated frame

Zoom in

The 'Zoom in on faces' option is especially useful if you have photo albums based on specific friends or family members

Great resolution

The fantastic high-res screen on the iPad makes your pictures look sumptuous and slideshows are simply mesmerising

Transition

There are only two transition types in the picture frame settings but both are really cool and very Apple-esque, so your snaps will look their best

Previews

In the events you choose from, you can see a preview of the pictures that are in them. This should make decisions much easier

Knowledge base

Not automatic

It's probably been done to save battery life, but there is no automatic setting to make the photo frame activate. You have to push the button on the lock screen each and every time you want it.

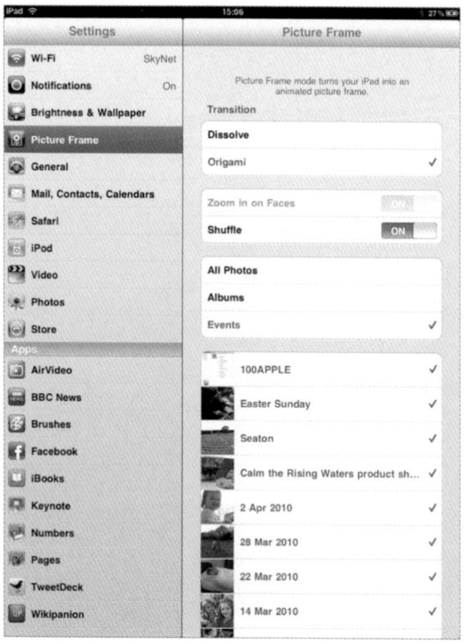

4: Lots of ticks

Tap on the 'Events' section to see all the events that you have added to the iPad. From here, you can tick the ones you want the iPad to display when in photo frame mode.

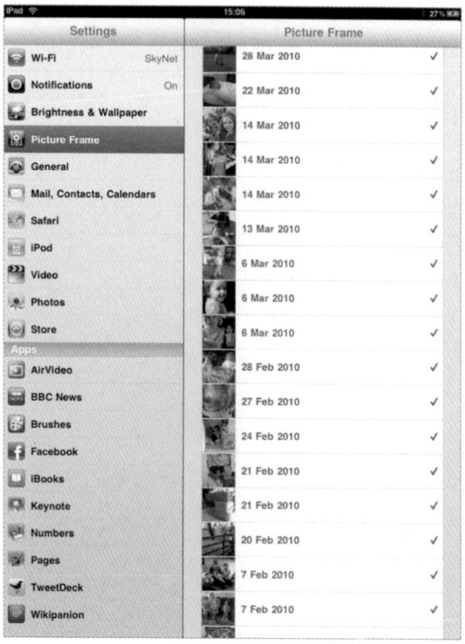

5: Flick it

No matter how many events you have catalogued in picture form on the iPad, you can easily flick up and down through them without ever leaving the main settings screen.

6: From the lock

Now, once the screen is locked, you'll have the option to tap the photo frame button next to the lock slider. Once tapped your photos will begin to display until you tell it to stop.

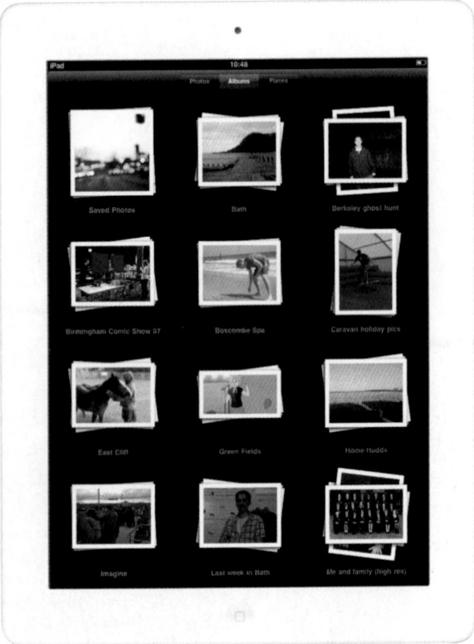

Tutorial: Create a photo slideshow on the iPad

Show your best pictures off with a cool slideshow, complete with transitions and your own music

Task: Creating a slideshow from your photos

Difficulty: Beginner

Time needed: 15 minutes

Apple has taken a lot of time and care over the Photos app on the iPad. We know this because it's a completely different app to the one that appears on the iPhone, even though they both share the same operating system. One of the things that sets this new Photos app apart is its ability to show picture slideshows, with far more control than the iPhone equivalent. A large part of this is, of course, down to the larger screen with greater resolution, but another part is the way the interface is so easy to use. Once you've learned how to create a slideshow, we're confident that you'll be so impressed that you'll be making them all the time. The real shame is that, unlike the desktop version in iPhoto, you can't save the results and share them with others. For now, though, just enjoy the brilliance of these slideshows.

Step-by-step | iPad Setting up a slideshow

1: Load it, tap it

Load the Photos app and then navigate to an album or a picture that you like. Then tap the 'Slideshow' button at the top of the interface to begin.

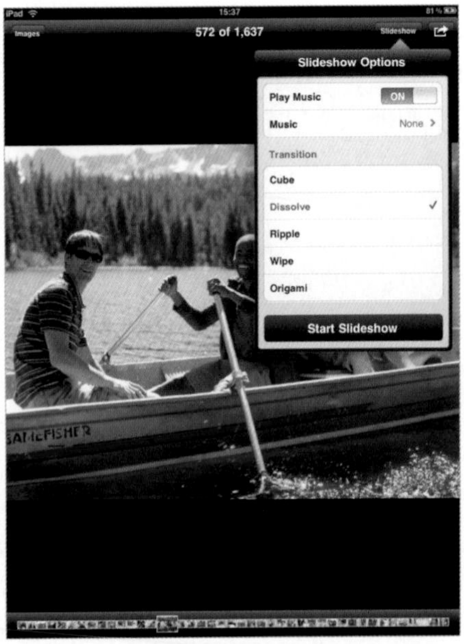

2: Options

The options window will appear and you can begin to customise your slideshow. Tap on one of the five transition you wish to use between photos.

3: Tune it

You can add music to the slideshow by tapping the music button. This will bring up access to all of your songs that have been synced from iTunes.

The iPad slideshow interface

Be amazed at how simply you can create a beautiful slideshow

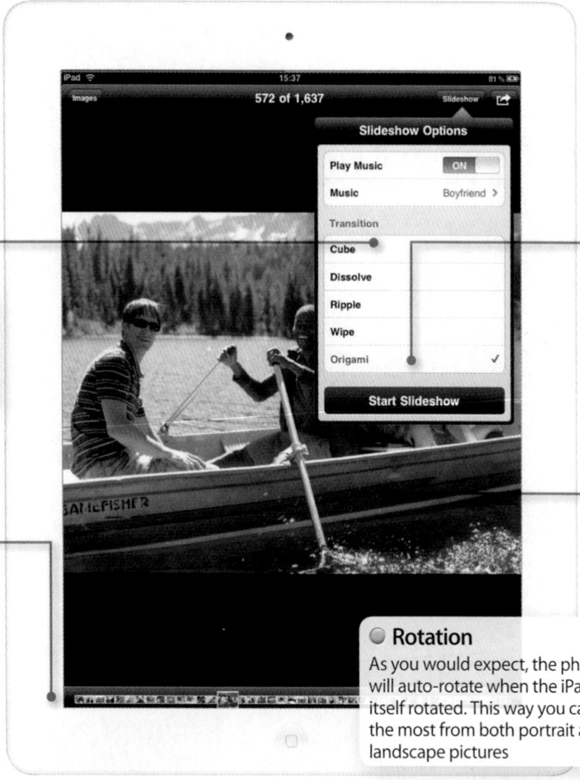

Pop-ups
Having windows within windows makes navigation on the iPad a complete joy. You pretty much always stay on the same page

Transitions
Origami is a new Apple transition type and it basically looks as though photos are folding out from under each other. Very cool

Scrubber
The Photos app has a cool and very easy to use scrubber at the bottom of the interface so you can navigate through a large number of pictures easily

Rotation
As you would expect, the photos will auto-rotate when the iPad is itself rotated. This way you can get the most from both portrait and landscape pictures

Knowledge base

Sounds
The integration of music into the slideshow adds a whole new dimension to watching your pictures. Your music can really set the mood. It is possible to create a playlist from the iPod app on the iPad, so you can create something specific on the fly.

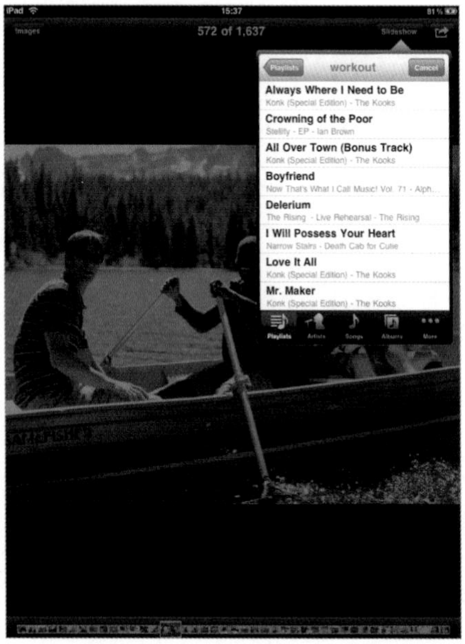

4: Playlist it
If you are organised you will already created a playlist for the slideshow and can use this now. Tap on whatever you wish to use to select it.

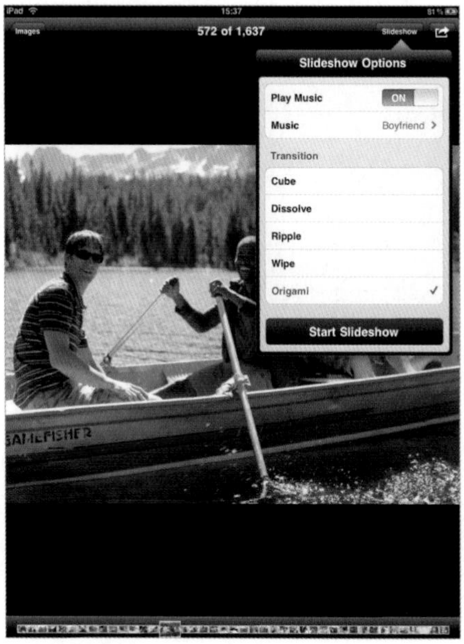

5: Ready, steady
Once you have everything in place, tap on Start Slideshow at the bottom of the Slideshow Options window. Your slideshow will begin immediately.

6: Watch in awe
You can now watch your favourite pictures from your most recent holiday or event, while listening to your favourite tunes while you do it.

Tutorial: Sketch creative ideas on your iPad

Master sketching on your iPad using the Adobe Ideas app and you will never want to put pencil to paper again

Task: Use the Adobe Ideas app and learn to sketch on your iPad

Difficulty: Intermediate

Time needed: 20 minutes

Designed for creative professionals, Adobe Ideas is an artistic application that allows you to sketch out ideas and graphics using your fingertips or stylus. You can doodle on photographs or sketch out drawings using a fantastic choice of pencil colours and blending opacity levels. The built-in line-smoothing technology also gives you professional graphic results.

There is plenty of room to expand with your creativity and canvas size, zooming out will allow you to sketch on a larger scale and you can also download the premium feature, layers.

All final artworks can be saved as JPEGs to your iPad album or exported via email as a PDF attachment. It is compatible with other Adobe software programmes so you can continue editing them on your desktop too.

The app's intuitive design makes it great for any on-the-go sketches and as it's easy to use, Adobe Ideas can be enjoyed by users at all artistic levels.

Step-by-step | Adobe Ideas Using Adobe Ideas to sketch creatively on your iPad

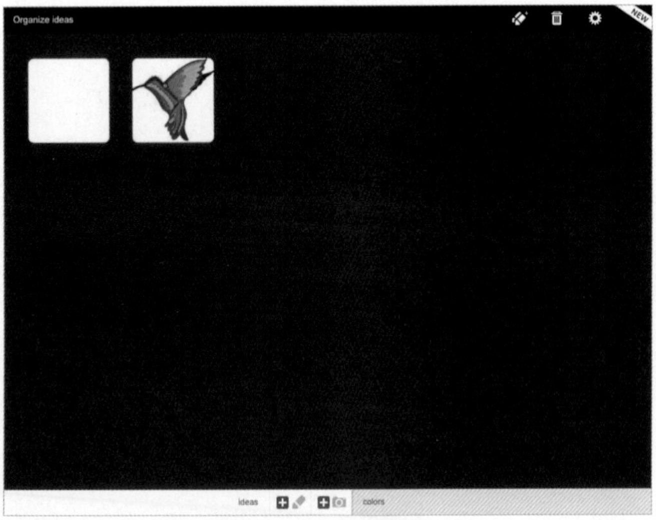

1: Sketching screen

Begin by opening the app. Your current idea sketches will appear on the organiser screen as thumbnails. To start a new sketch select the add sketch icon at the bottom of the screen (it looks like a pencil with a plus sign next to it). Use the tool bar on the left to select the pencil tool.

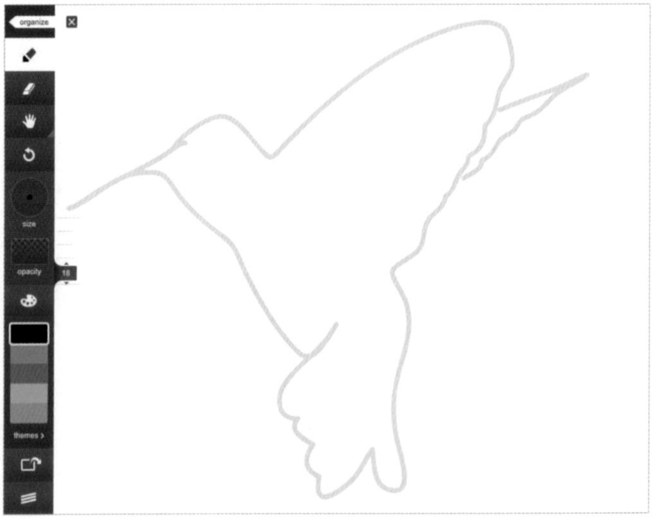

2: Outline your sketch

Change the brush size to suit your sketch and select a colour from the colour palette. For the initial outline we are using black and lowering the opacity to make a lighter brush outline that can be built upon and altered as the sketch progresses.

Sketching Screen

Understand your sketching screen options

Sketching Tools
You can select the pencil icon to sketch on the screen. Adjust the size and opacity of the brush by moving the selectable sliders; this can also be adjusted in the same way when correcting mistakes using the eraser tool

Colour Palette
The colour palette allows you to select a specific colour to paint with. You can also select the theme icon to work with an already set colour range or theme

Layer Icon
If you have downloaded the premium Layers feature you can build up, access and adjust your layers via the Layers icon

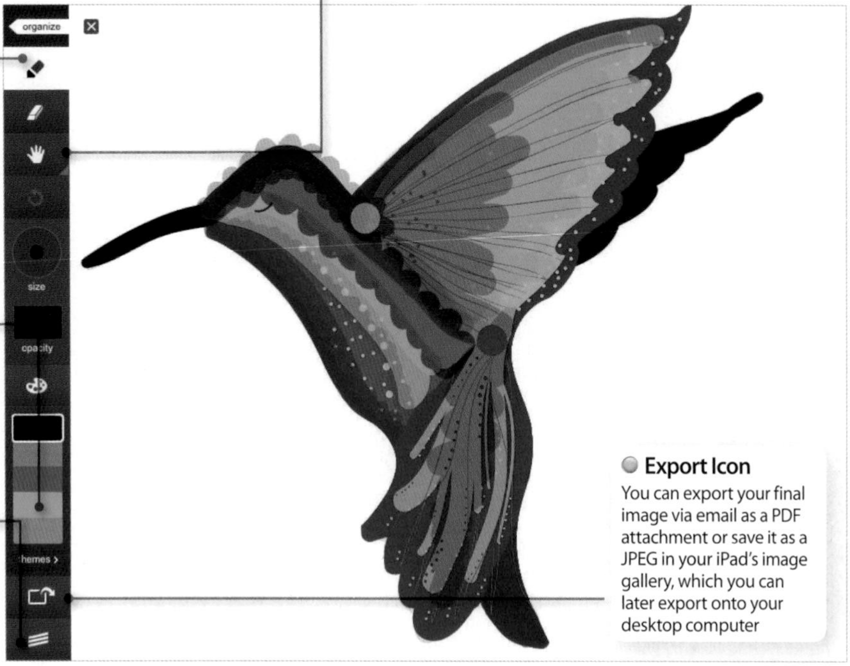

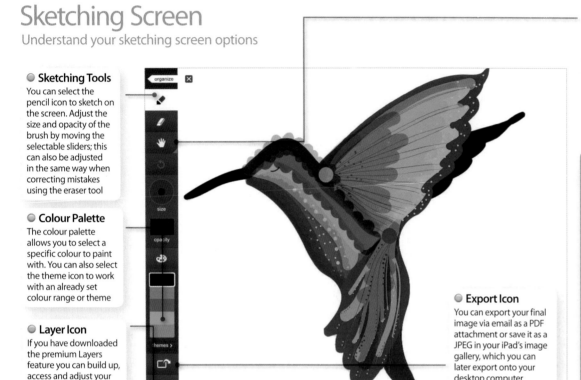

Hand Tool
Select the hand tool to zoom in, out and rotate your image. You can extend your canvas size up to nine screens by zooming out completely

Export Icon
You can export your final image via email as a PDF attachment or save it as a JPEG in your iPad's image gallery, which you can later export onto your desktop computer

Knowledge base

Premium feature – Layers

You can download layers to enhance the Adobe Ideas app. Layers will allow you build up gradually on your sketch and will give you more control over alterations and image changes. You can work on each layer individually, building up a drawing, adjusting their opacity or deleting any unwanted layers. The layers feature also allows you to use up to ten sketch layers including a photo layer in one drawing.

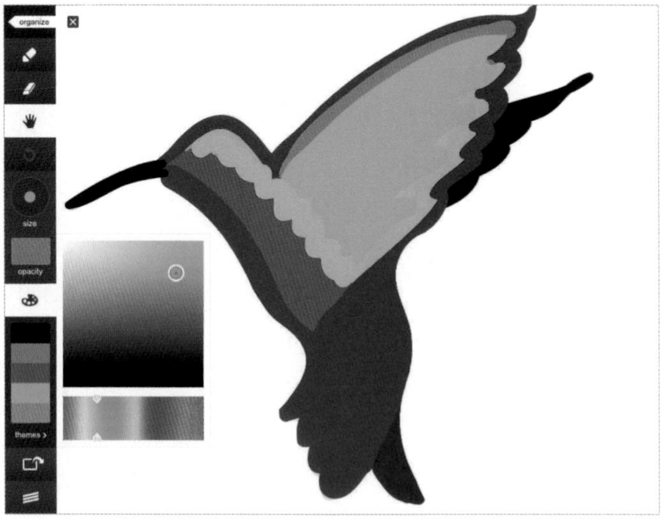

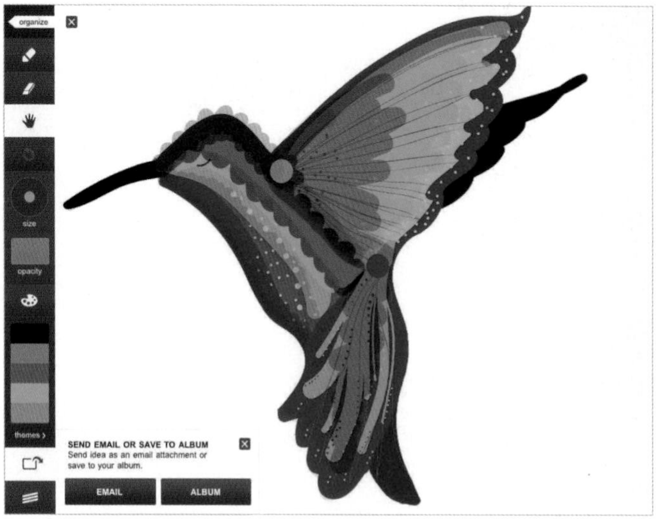

3: Selecting Colour

Use the colour palette icon to select a different colour or tone. Alternatively load a colour theme you have already prepared and select a colour sample to work with. Zoom into your sketch for more detailed work using the hand tool.

4: Save and Send

You can correct mistakes using the eraser or undo tool that can go back as far as 50 actions, including redos. Once you are satisfied, select the export icon (second from the bottom on the toolbar) and choose to save the image as a JPEG to your album or email it as a PDF file.

Tutorial: Get to know the Facebook app

If you have a Facebook account and don't want to bother using Safari to access it, there's an app that makes it much more compact. Here's how to use it

Task: Start using the Facebook app

Difficulty: Beginner

Time needed: 5 minutes

There are two benefits and one real downside to using the official Facebook app as opposed to simply accessing the site using Safari. First, the disadvantage is that the app is currently designed for the iPod/iPhone so it appears in the middle of the iPad screen. Tap on 2X to double it up to iPad size. The advantages are that it is far better organised and easier to use than the actual website and also, the app uses notifications to let you know immediately about responses to your actions, posts on your wall or requests from friends. Once the Facebook app is downloaded and installed on your iPad, you simply need to enter your email address and Facebook password to get going. So now let's go see some of the functions that make accessing your account on the move as much fun as the main site.

Step-by-step | Facebook Get friendly with this iPad app

1: Getting started

When the Facebook app is first run you will need to enter your email address and Facebook password to access your account. You'll notice that the first display which shows the News feed only fills the middle of the iPad screen. Tap on 2x to maximise the app.

2: Live news feeds

On the initial News feed page, there are five options. If you tap on Live Feed you can select from a range of notifications that you want displaying on this page instead. These include ones from Pages, Status updates, Photos, Links, Video, Notes and Groups.

Quick access to your profile

Here's all the features that revolve around your personal profile

Add a picture
Tap on the camera icon to upload a picture from your Photo Library and post it to your wall. After selecting the image you can then add a caption to it

See all your photos
Check out all the images in all the folders that you have uploaded. Tap on the Photos panel to show the folders. Tap on a folder to see the pictures

Your personal details
If you tap on the Info panel at the bottom of the screen, your mobile phone, personal description, birthday, email address, interests and favourite things are all listed

Enter your status
Type your status into this bar and it will appear on your profile. Your previous status updates, wall postings and comments from friends appear below

Knowledge base

Notifications from Facebook
The Facebook app supports push notifications. This means that when someone sends you a message, posts on your wall, asks to be a friend, tags you in a photo, posts an event or you get a friend confirmation, the Facebook server will send news of that to the app. If you aren't getting these then push notifications are turned off. Tap on the Settings app and then on the Facebook app under Apps. Tap on Push Notifications. This gives a list of everything you can be notified for. They can all be toggled on or off.

3: Post your status

The three options on the bar below the Facebook heading allow photos to be uploaded, your Status to be posted and to check in using Location services to show where you are. Tap on Status and enter what you are doing. Tap on Share when finished.

4: The main hub

Tap on the block of squares in the top left. This is the central hub of the Facebook app allowing access to all the website features including your Profile, Friends list, News feed, Messages, Places, Groups, Events, Chat and Notes. Tap Photos to see all the images you have uploaded.

Tutorial: Tweet from your iPad with the Twitter app

Love Twitter? Love your iPad? The free Twitter app gives you access to everything you want to do on Twitter with just a tap or two on your iPad

Task: Set up and use the Twitter app on your iPad

Difficulty: Beginner

Time needed: 10 minutes

If you've been using the web-based Twitter site on your iPad, you're missing out. First of all, the app is free. Also, it has almost all the features of the website and boasts great usability too. The Twitter app lets you manage followers, view and respond to mentions and direct messages, and you can even access multiple accounts. It lets you create new custom searches, save them, and delete them. You can also control all facets of your profile, from your image, to your URL and your biography. The interface is easy to use, with one-click access to mentions and messages. Ontop of all that, push notifications make it even more convenient.

This tutorial takes you through the major features of the iPad Twitter app. Before you begin, visit the App Store and install the app. The quickest way to find it is to search for Twitter, then Download and install the Twitter app.

Step-by-step | Twitter Use the iPad Twitter app

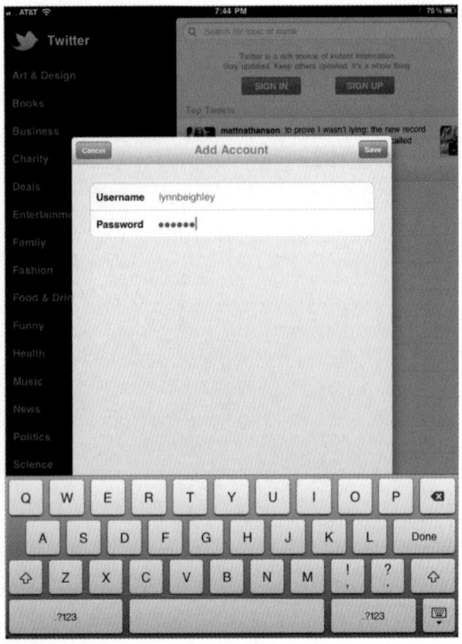

1: Set up an account

Install and start the Twitter app. Tap the Sign In button and enter a Username and Password. Tap Save. You will see your public Twitter feed displayed.

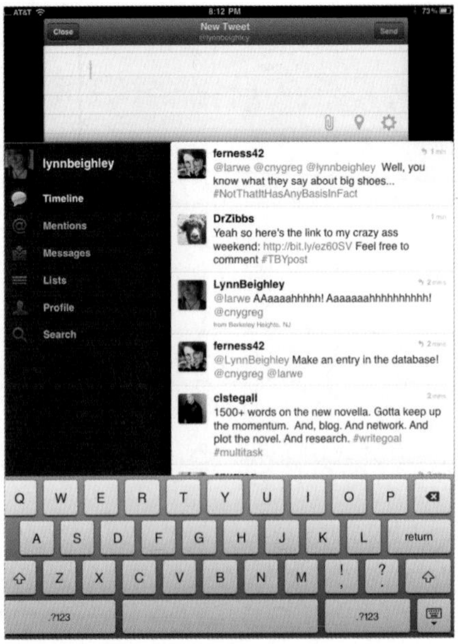

2: Send a tweet

Tap on the edit box, bottom left then type a tweet. When you're done, tap the Send button on the upper right. Your tweet will appear in your timeline.

3: Mentions and messages

Tap the Messages button to check Direct messages. To reply, tap the text box on the bottom of the screen, type your message and hit return.

Profile options

The Profile link opens your personal profile page. We look at the key parts…

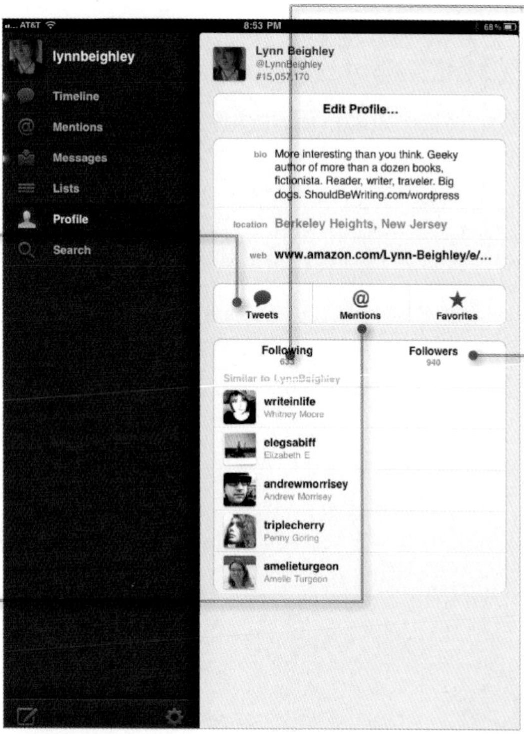

Tweets

Tap the Tweets button to see your tweets. If the Twitter app has a weakness, it's that it doesn't let you delete what you've tweeted. Hopefully the next iteration will build this in

Mentions

Tap the Mentions button, the @ sign, to see tweets people have made with your tweet handle in it. You can respond by tapping on the tweet and tapping the arrow above the tweet

Following

Tap the Following button to see a list of everyone you currently follow. If you want to unfollow, tap the person's name and then tap the Unfollow button

Followers

Tap the Followers button to see a list of everyone who currently follows you. You can follow back. If you want to block or report spam, tap the Settings icon on the upper right

Knowledge base

Search link

The Search button displays any saved searches, trending searches, and the search box. To create a new saved search, type your search in the search box, tap Search, and tap the Save Search button on the bottom right. Next time you tap the Search button, you will see your saved search. Remove the search by tapping the Remove Saved Search button with your search selected.

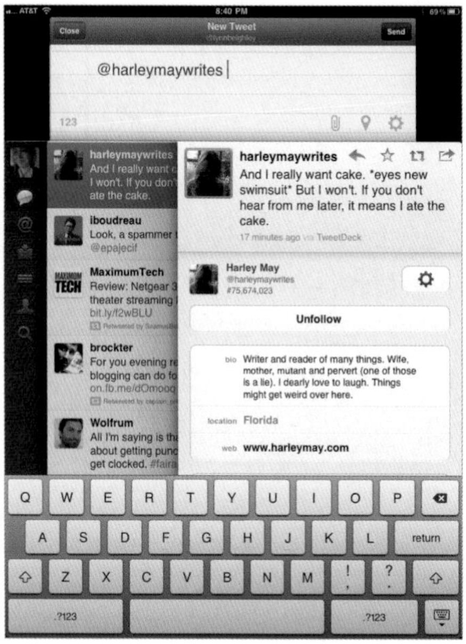

4: Respond to tweets

To respond to a specific person, tap their tweet and tap the left arrow. Tapping on an @name also lets you retweet, favorite, follow, and view their profile.

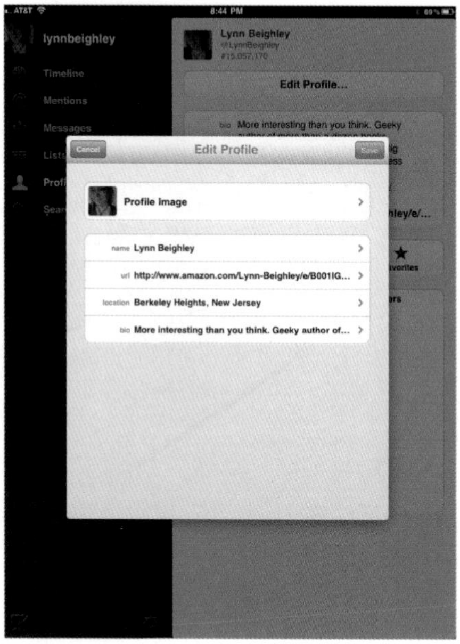

5: Manage your profile

Control your profile by tapping the Profile link on the left. Tap Edit Profile. From this screen, you can manage your image, name, URL, location and bio.

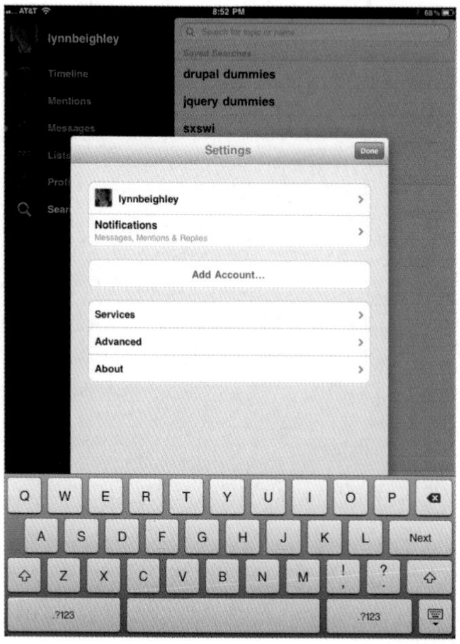

6: Add an account

If you have multiple accounts, you can add them. Tap the Gear icon on the bottom in the centre of the bar to open Settings, then tap Add Account.

Tutorial: Create a blog in the WordPress app

Setting up a personal blog is commonplace nowadays, but to make sure the content is timely and keeps your visitors coming back for more you need to update it frequently

Task: Start blogging whenever and wherever you like in minutes

Difficulty: Beginner

Time needed: 15 minutes

Blogging is fast becoming the de facto way to communicate with friends and complete strangers, and there are many services available to get you started. WordPress is one of the most popular options and is free whether you set up a blog on **wordpress.com** or host it on your own server. Whether you want to set up a family blog or something that you want the whole world to see, your words can be published in a matter of minutes, but the key to success is keeping the content updated frequently and that is not always practical.

You need not worry though, because the WordPress iPad app is the perfect companion for your new blog and makes editing and creating new posts child's play when on the move. It doesn't include all of the desktop features, but is more than powerful enough to create and edit posts and images when you do not have access to your desktop computer. Here we will show you how to set up a new blog and how to create your content on the iPad in a matter of minutes.

Step-by-step | WordPress for iPad **Mobile blogging in minutes**

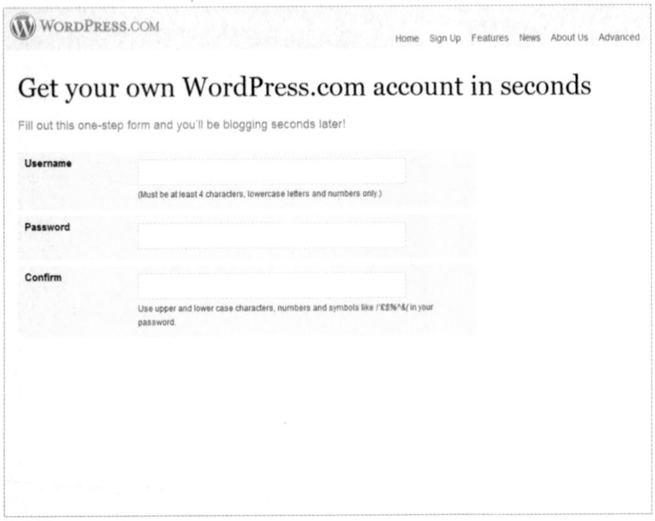

1: Create your blog

Go to **www.wordpress.com** and click the 'Sign up now' button. You will now be taken to a page where you have to input some information such as username and email address. Once you click submit you then need to confirm your email and you are ready to go.

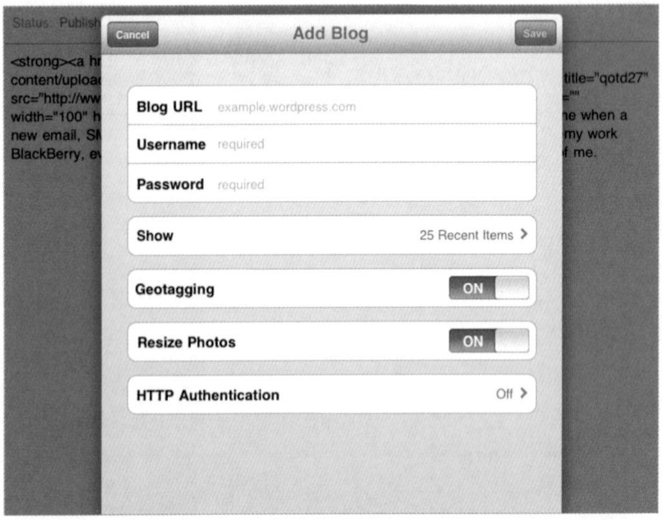

2: Make the blog mobile

Once you have set up your design etc, it is now time to set it up on your iPad. Install the free WordPress app, available from the App Store, and launch it. Press the '+' sign and enter your URL, username and password. You should now be all set to start blogging from your iPad.

King of the blogs

Create a great-looking blog while one the move

Add images
Adding images is easy and all you need to do is click the image icon and then choose a photo or graphic. It is a good idea to have some stock images loaded onto your iPad if you are likely to use them often

Settings
The Settings panel is always available and only one click away. This is especially handy because you can use different settings depending on the type of content you are publishing

Check your posts
A list of all posts, no matter what status they are in, is always available as well to allow for full management of your content on the go. You can also preview posts from this page

Post status
You can save posts as local drafts, published, private, draft or pending review for maximum flexibility. This lets you complete entries only when you have the time

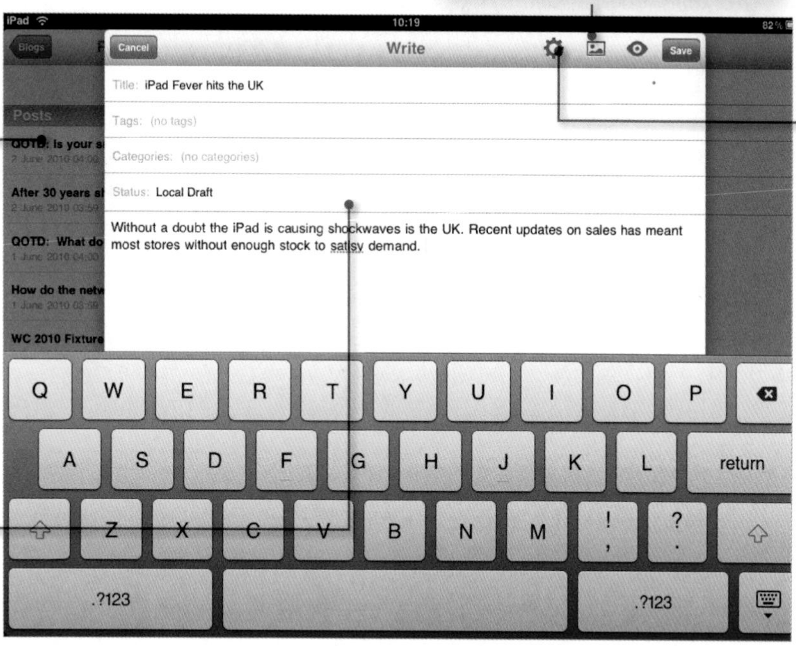

Knowledge base

HTML

HTML is the primary language behind most websites and some knowledge will help you to get the most out of the WordPress app. You only need to know a few snippets for most formatting and it will greatly enhance the appearance of your blog posts. As you get more experienced, the posts will look as though they were made on a desktop.

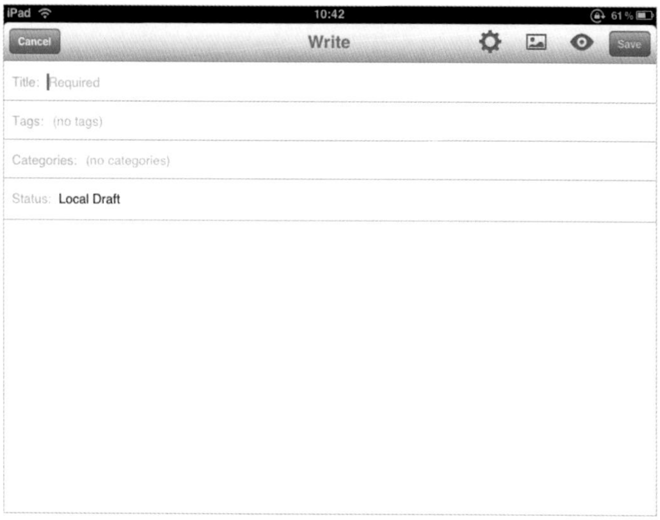

3: Write your first post

At the bottom you will see a 'Posts' icon. Click it and then click the 'create' icon top-right. At this point you need to insert a title, tags, categories and the main text for the entry. You can save the post as a local draft if you need to finish it later.

4: Add some style

Included is the ability to insert photos or links to other sites, but the default text formatting is plain. You can use basic HTML to add bold and italics so do some experimenting to see which works best for you. No matter what method you use, the whole process is simple and effective.

The iPad Productivity Guide

Get organised and manage multiple tasks with the iPad

The iPad is an astounding entertainment and lifestyle device, but it is also a fantastic tool to help you through a variety of task-based jobs. Whether you need to create a spreadsheet, send an attachment in an email or even perform a presentation, the iPad can solve all of these needs and more. The iPad Productivity Guide starts by showing you how to organise your Home screen into a filing system, as well as how to navigate around apps quickly, before taking you through the key apps for work. We'll show you how to print from your iPad, and even how to make it into a portable hard drive too. With these in-depth tutorials you'll soon be using the iPad to make your life more productive while on the move.

086 Manage your email account and learn how to use mailboxes and more.

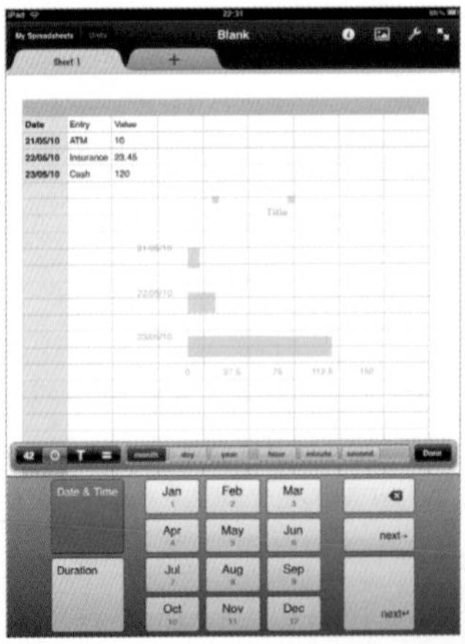

096 Use Numbers to create a variety of spreadsheets for every need.

Getting Started
Tap to Get Started with Keynote.
Scroll through the slides. Touch the images and text. And experience the most powerful presentation app ever designed for a mobile device.

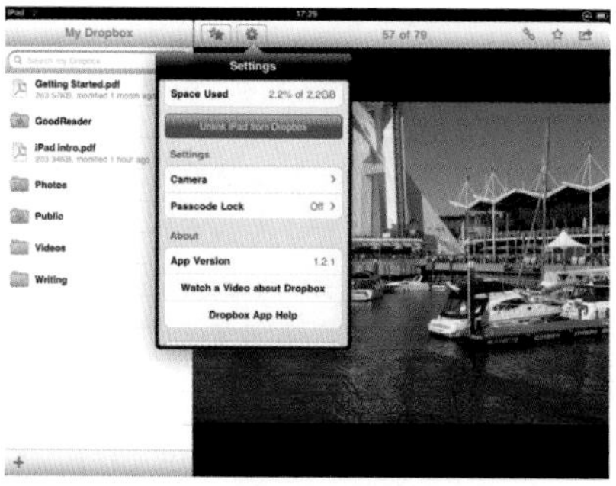
My Dropbox
Settings
Space Used
Camera
Passcode Lock
App Version
Watch a Video about Dropbox
Dropbox App Help
Getting Started.pdf
GoodReader
iPad intro.pdf
Photos
Public
Videos
Writing

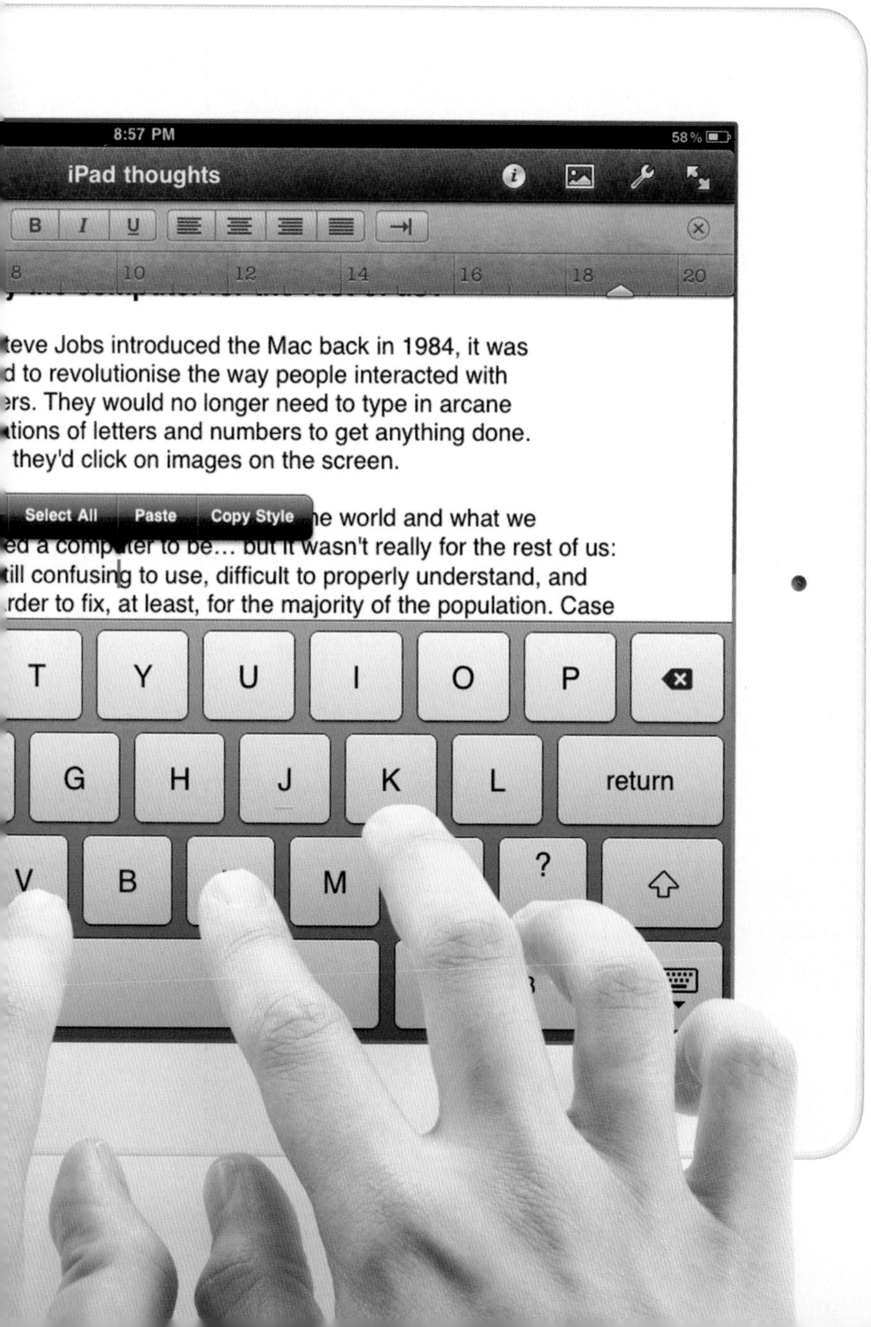
8:57 PM
58 %
iPad thoughts
Select All
Paste
Copy Style
return

Tutorial: Get to grips with iOS 4 folders

By organising all your apps into folders, they will be easier to find and access when you need them

Task: Organise your apps into folders

Difficulty: Beginner

Time needed: 5 minutes

With so many apps to choose from, it doesn't take long to build up a library of them that can get overwhelming to browse through, as many people have downloaded 50, 100 or even more. To find the apps you need on your iPad, you sometimes need to swipe through half a dozen screens looking for them. It's slow and tedious, especially if you can't remember which screen an app is on.

Fortunately, there is a solution, and you can organise apps into folders if you have iOS 4. This means that you can have a folder containing news apps, another with social networking, one for your favourite games and so on. You can reduce a dozen screens of apps into two or three, and organising apps this way enables you to find them faster and access them more easily.

A folder can contain up to 20 icons and a screen can contain 20 folders, so you can therefore have 400 apps on one screen! That's amazing, and it's so useful to organise apps this way. Once you've tried using folders, you will wonder how you managed without them.

Step-by-step | iOS 4 Organise your apps

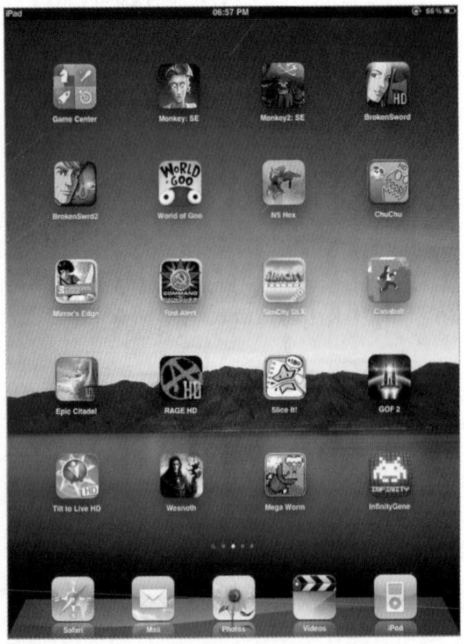

1: Select your apps

It's easier to create folders if the apps you want to use are on the same screen. Here we have several games that we want to keep in a Games folder.

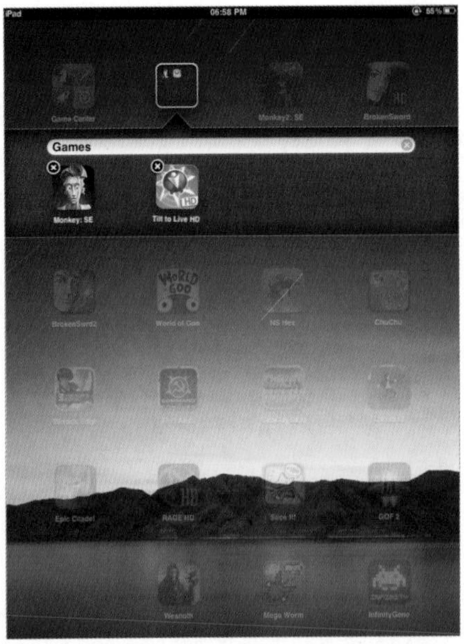

2: Create the folder

Tap and hold an app until they jiggle, then drag one and drop it on another. A folder is created containing the two apps, and a name is assigned.

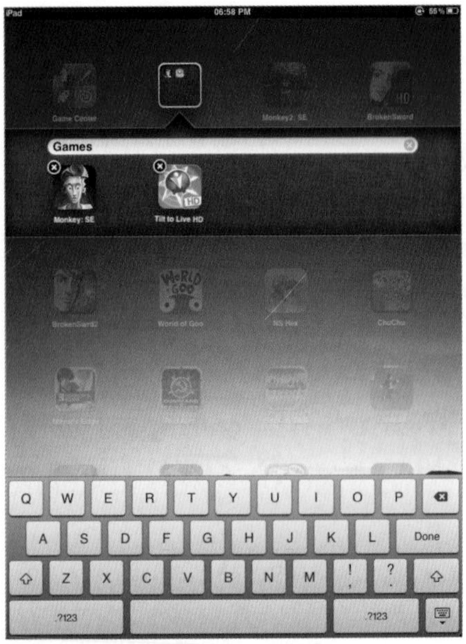

3: Edit the name

The default name is based on the category and it may or may not be suitable. Tap in the text box to bring up the keyboard and then edit the name.

Organise your utility apps

Customise your Utilities folder

The Utilities folder
Many of the default apps that you use occasionally can be hidden away in their own folder

Sort the apps
Tap and hold an app until they start to bounce about and then drag them around to rearrange the order. They scoot around to make space

Add your apps
You can add your own apps if you have utilities that you want to be able to access from the Home screen. Drag them and drop them on the folder

iOS 4 system vs user apps
Tap and hold an app in the Utilities folder and you'll discover that you can't delete iOS 4 system apps like the App Store or Calendar. You can only delete your own apps

Knowledge base

Folders in iTunes
You don't have to create, edit and organise folders on the iPad – you can do it using iTunes too. It works in the same way. Connect your iPad, select it in the left panel and then click the Apps tab. Folders are created in the same way by dropping one icon on top of another.

4: Add more apps
Tap Done to enter the name, then tap anywhere outside of the folder to return to the normal view. Now you can drag the other apps into the folder.

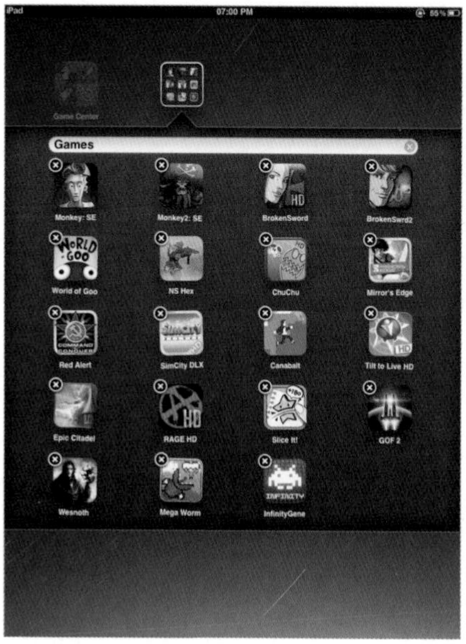

5: Rearrange the apps
Tap the folder to open it and you'll see all your apps. They may not be in the best order, so drag them around to rearrange them to suit you best.

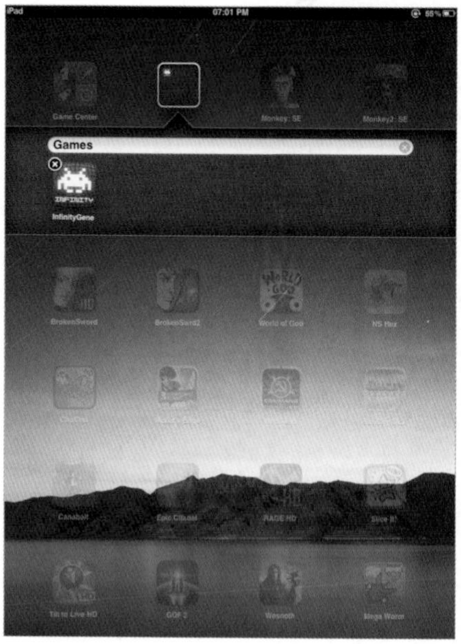

6: Delete a folder
It is not obvious how you delete folders, but it's easy. Tap and hold an app until they jiggle, then drag them out. Moving the last one deletes the folder.

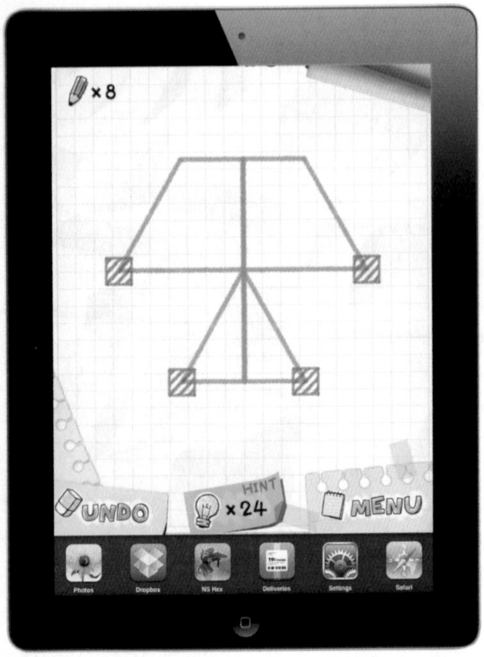

Tutorial: Move around apps quickly with the multitasking feature

Switching between apps has never been easier thanks to iOS 4's multitasking

Task: Easily switch between apps

Difficulty: Beginner

Time needed: 10 minutes

Multitasking was one of the most requested features by early iPad adopters, but it wasn't until iOS 4 that it became a reality. Previously when you pressed the Home button, an app would quit and that was the end of it, but now it is simply put in the background and you can bring it to the fore again and continue where you left off. You can be playing a game, for example, then switch to Mail to check for an important message, then carry on playing the game.

Some functions continue to run in apps when they are put into the background. For example, music continues to play from internet radio apps and your position continues to be logged by apps that use GPS. Not all apps continue running and some are just suspended, waiting for you to switch back so they can resume, but with this feature you can easily navigate back to them nonetheless.

Step-by-step | iOS 4 Task-switching tips

1: Start some apps

When you've just switched on, the memory and apps are cleared when you switch off. So start an app, press Home, start another and so on.

2: See the apps

Double-tap Home to see recently run apps. They're saved in the background and you can switch by tapping one and then switch back the same way.

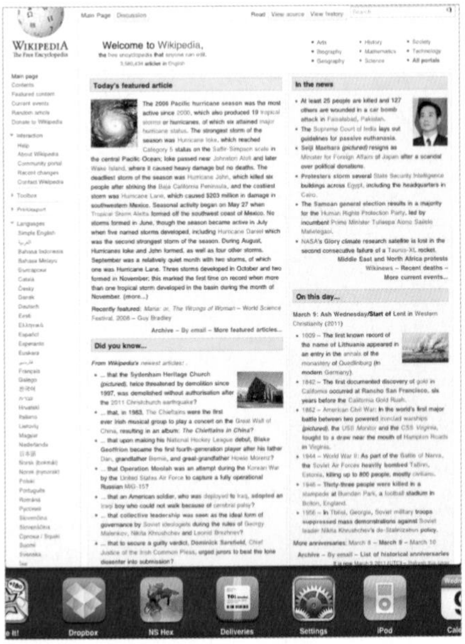

3: Swipe for more

Only six apps are displayed in the tray, but there may be more that you have recently been using. If so, swipe left to see them.

Mastering multitasking

How to switch between apps and close them down

Multitasking anywhere
Tapping the Home button displays the home screen or the screen you were last viewing, but your multi-tasking apps are still running in the background

Recent apps tray
The six most recently accessed apps are shown in the tray at the bottom of the screen. Swipe left and right to see the rest of the apps and access them

Knowledge base
Multitasking
Multitasking involves running more than one app at once, and an app will continue to function even though it is not on the screen. This is only partly true with iOS 4 and with most apps you really only get fast-task switching. A game doesn't continue to run when it's not on-screen for example; however, music will continue playing in the background.

Close an app
The only way to really quit an app is to double-tap the Home button and then tap and hold an icon until the red close button appears. Tap it to close an app

Home button
The Home button no longer quits apps, but puts them in the background. Double-tap it to open the multitasking tray and see all of the apps that are still running

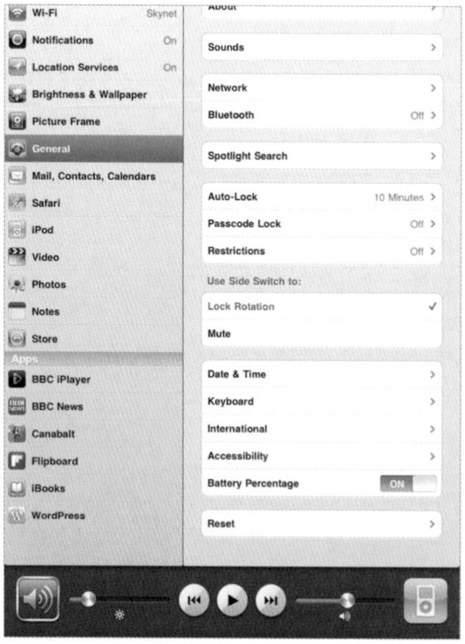

4: Use the iPod controls
If you swipe right as far as you can go, you'll see the iPod buttons, as well as brightness, volume and orientation controls. This can be useful.

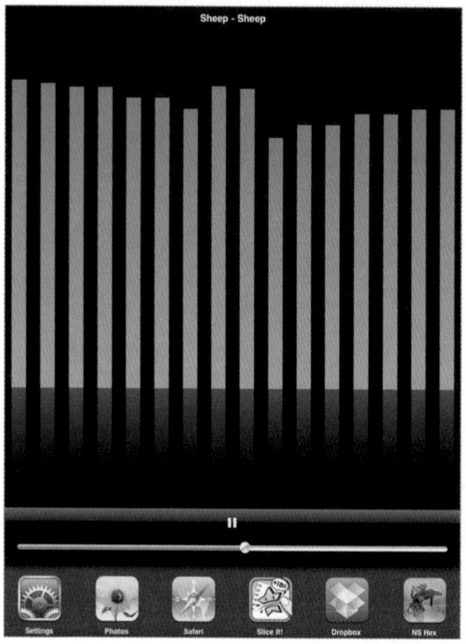

5: Non-stop apps
Some apps, like this one to play streaming internet radio, continue to play even when they are placed in the background and you're running another app.

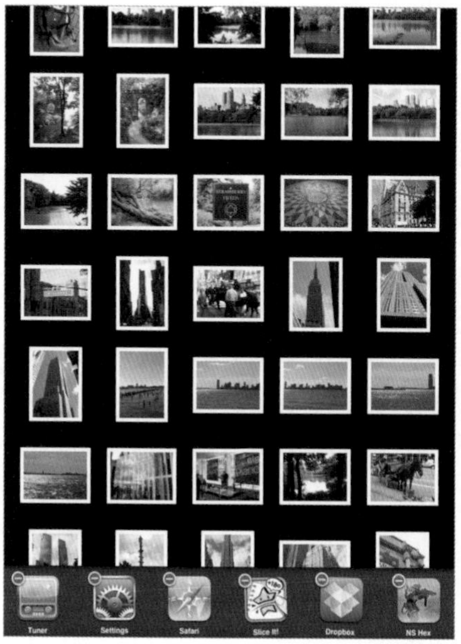

6: Really quit an app
Some apps freeze when you switch, but others carry on. To quit an app, tap and hold any of them until they jiggle, then tap the red corner button.

Tutorial: Managing emails

The Mail app on the iPad sets a new standard on how emails are managed from touch-enabled tablet devices. In this tutorial we show you how to manage your mail

Task: Organising emails
Difficulty: Beginner
Time needed: 15 minutes

Email is part of everybody's day-to-day life. Most of us start our day with it. In the old days, checking for emails would mean starting your fully fledged computer. With the introduction of the iPhone, this habit changed drastically. Most of us were using the device to check emails. Even though the iPhone has a decent Mail application, the small screen and lack of full-size keyboard was a problem. iPad's Mail app takes what is good about it on the iPhone and presents it with large screen and full-size keyboard. This provides the best email experience between the mobile devices.

Mail app supports most of the current generation technology such as automatic service discovery, Exchange Support, POP/IMAP support and built-in support for MobileMe, Gmail, Yahoo Mail and AOL. Mail app on the iPad also plays well with other related apps on the iPad, such as the Calendar.

In this tutorial we will look into doing a few of the more important tasks using the Mail app. It's all very easy – let us show you how…

Step-by-step | Mail Organising emails

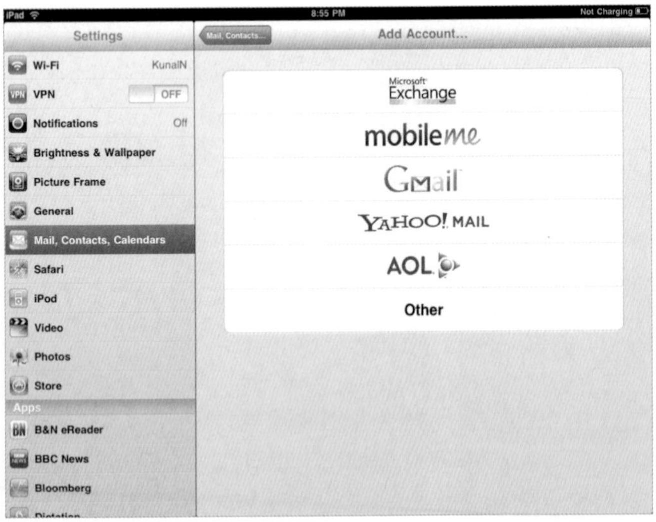

1: Adding an email account

Open Settings and select 'Mail, Contacts, Calendars'. You will now be presented with account types that you can use. Tapping on any one of the supported services will open the pop-up window asking for account details. Fill in the required information to set up your email account.

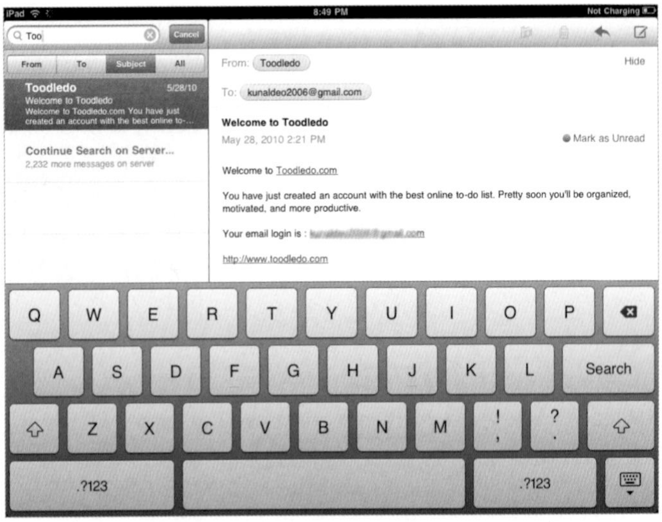

2: Searching for emails

Search for emails by typing onto the Search Box and selecting the From, To or Subject fields. Do a full text search by tapping All. By default this will only do a search on the emails that have been downloaded on the iPad. To do a full search you can tap on 'Continue Search on Server…'

You've got mail!

Working your way around the Mail app

Search box
This allows you to search your emails to find a specific one

Move message
This enables you to move a message to a folder (or mailbox)

Refresh mailbox
This checks the mail server for new messages and downloads them if available

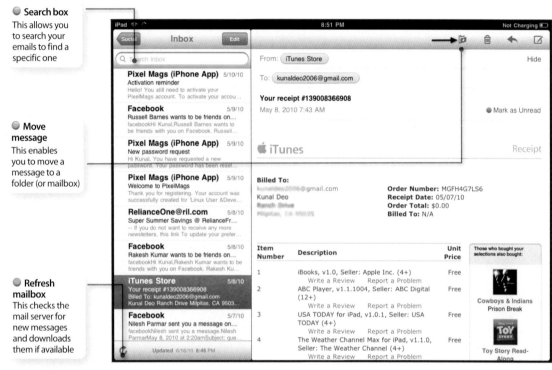

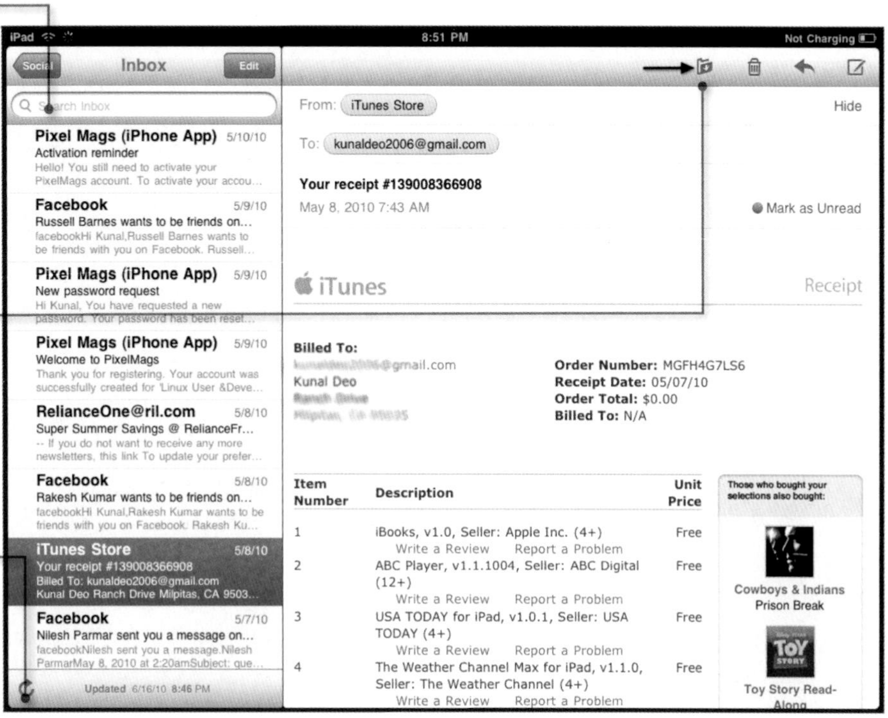

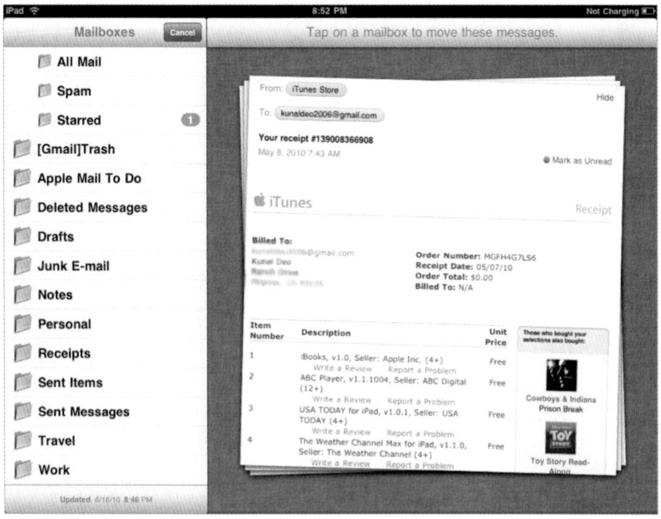

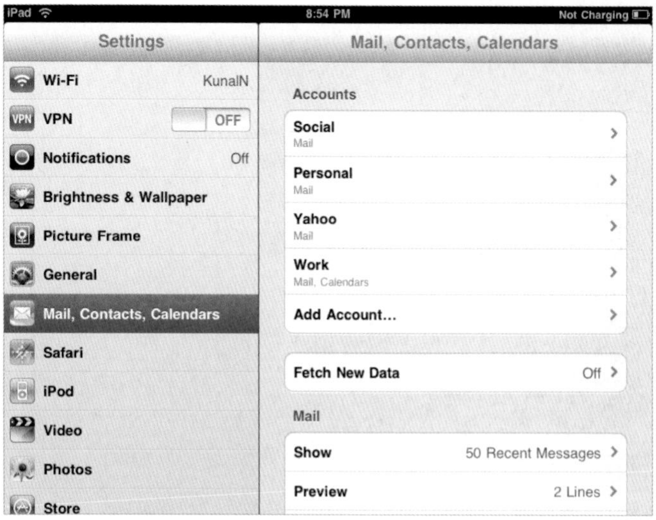

3: Moving messages between folders (mailboxes)

Tap Edit, then select all the messages that you want to move by tapping on the circles to the left of the message, then tap Move. Tapping Move will give you a list of folders available; tap on a folder to move the selected messages.

4: Sending a contact

You can configure a wide range of settings which control how Mail works. To access the settings for Mail, tap Settings (from the home screen), then 'Mail, Contacts, Calendars'. You can change the Account Settings, Mail, Default Account, Signature and more.

Knowledge base

Email Protocols

iPad's Mail app supports all major email protocols. These are:

1. Exchange ActiveSync: Exchange ActiveSync is a data synchronisation protocol that provides push synchronisation of emails, tasks, contacts between ActiveSync enabled devices and servers such as the iPhone.
2. IMAP (Internet Message Access Protocol): IMAP is a protocol for retrieving emails and working with mailboxes on a mail server using an email client. Email clients using IMAP generally leave messages on the server until the user explicitly deletes them. This and other characteristics of IMAP operation allow multiple clients to manage the same mailbox.
3. POP (Post Office Protocol): POP is similar to IMAP but does not provide support for using multiple clients using the same mailbox.

Tutorial: Using email attachments in Mail

The iPad is better suited for work than an iPhone. We'll show you how the iPad deals with email attachments

Task: Receive and amend email attachments from your iPad

Difficulty: Beginner

Time needed: 20 minutes

Whether you use a PC or a Mac, it's hard to imagine a day when you don't have to deal with email attachments. It therefore stands to reason that you're going to be faced with similar tasks while on your iPad. So, how exactly does the iPad handle attachments? That question will actually greatly depend on what's attached to your email message in the first place.

This tutorial will show you how you can work with your iPad to handle common files like photos, iWork or Microsoft Office documents and PDFs. They each behave in slightly different ways but the principle is actually very similar and it'll take you next to no time to find your way around the iPad interface.

But receiving attachments is only half the story. It's obvious that you'll also need to send them out too, which is why we'll cover that part as well. So pick up your iPad and let's see how all of this works.

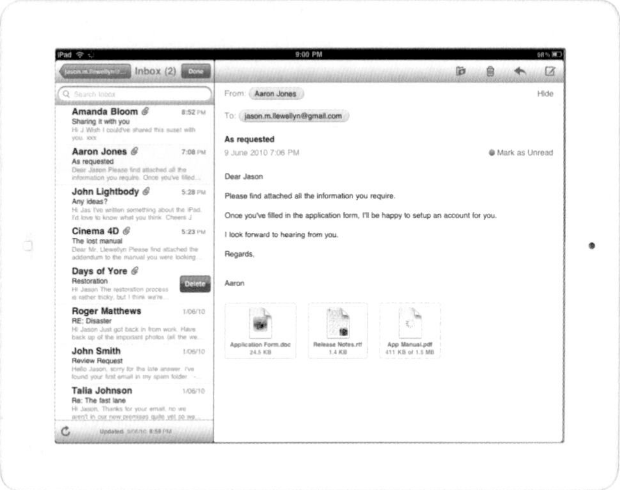

Email analysis

We break down the iPad's email and let you know all of the key functions and associated icons

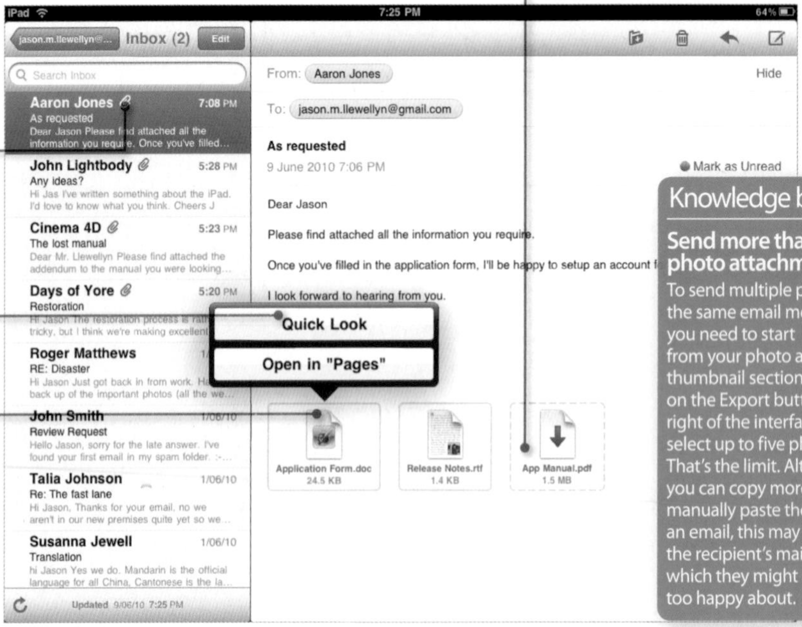

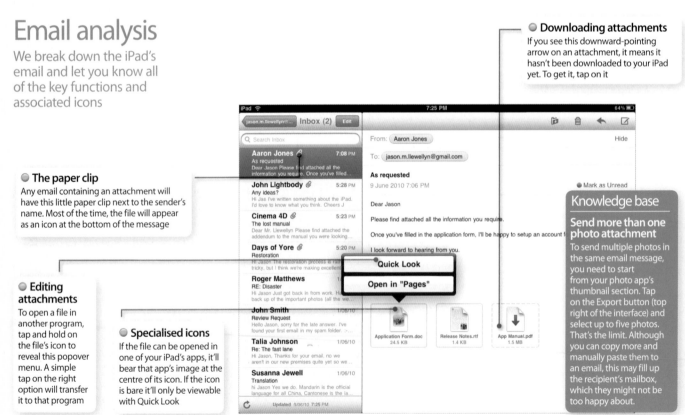

Downloading attachments

If you see this downward-pointing arrow on an attachment, it means it hasn't been downloaded to your iPad yet. To get it, tap on it

The paper clip

Any email containing an attachment will have this little paper clip next to the sender's name. Most of the time, the file will appear as an icon at the bottom of the message

Editing attachments

To open a file in another program, tap and hold on the file's icon to reveal this popover menu. A simple tap on the right option will transfer it to that program

Specialised icons

If the file can be opened in one of your iPad's apps, it'll bear that app's image at the centre of its icon. If the icon is bare it'll only be viewable with Quick Look

Knowledge base

Send more than one photo attachment

To send multiple photos in the same email message, you need to start from your photo app's thumbnail section. Tap on the Export button (top right of the interface) and select up to five photos. That's the limit. Although you can copy more and manually paste them to an email, this may fill up the recipient's mailbox, which they might not be too happy about.

Step-by-step | Mail Send and receive email attachments

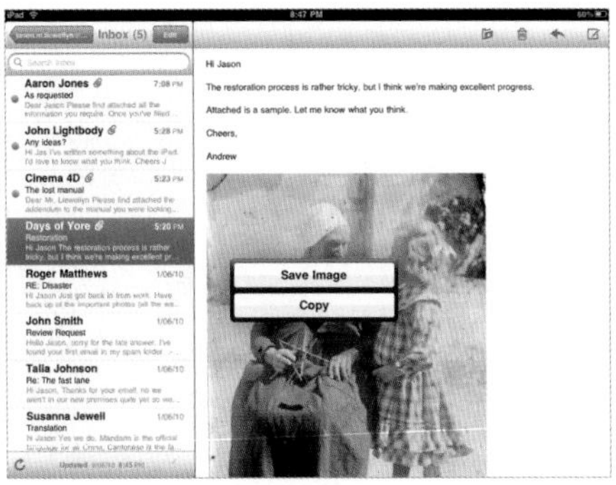

1: Into the photo app
When you're sent an image, adding it to your photo library is easy: tap and hold on it to reveal a popover menu. Select 'Save Image'.

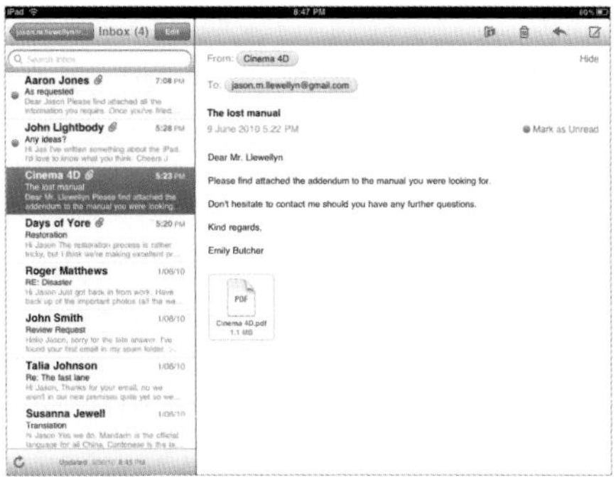

2: RTF and PDF files
If you're dealing with RTF files or PDFs, tapping on its icon will open it in Quick Look, where you can view and copy text, but you can't edit anything.

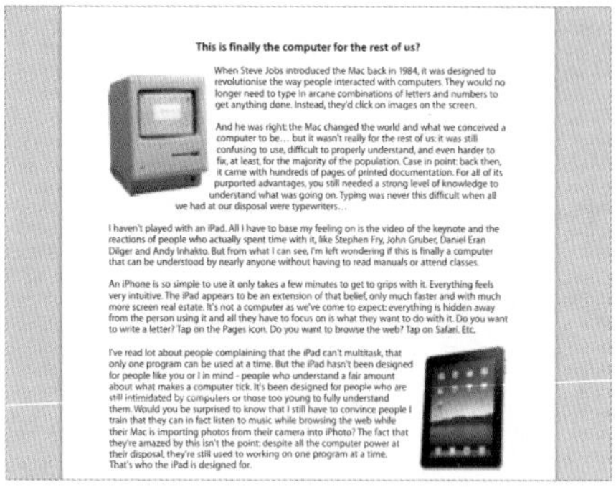

3: iWork and Office documents
With other documents like Word or Pages, tapping on it will lead to the same Quick Look section, but if you need to edit it, there's another way.

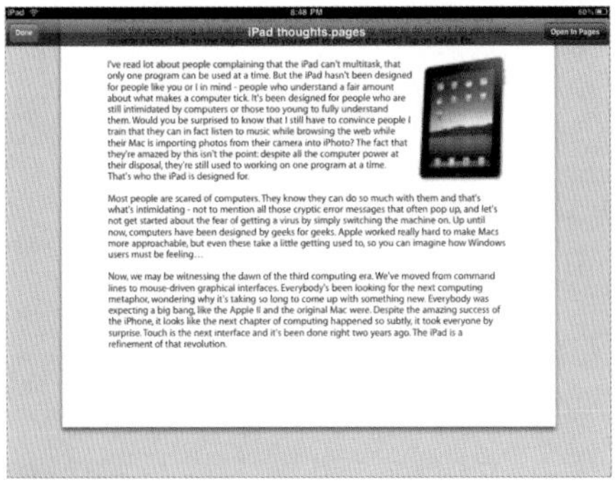

4: Getting out of Quick Look
To get out of Quick Look tap on the screen. You can choose 'Done' to get back to Mail or 'Open in Pages' if you own the Pages application. Do the former.

5: Open in an editing app
To get straight to Pages without going into Quick Look, tap and hold on the file's icon. This reveals a popover menu. Select Open in "Pages".

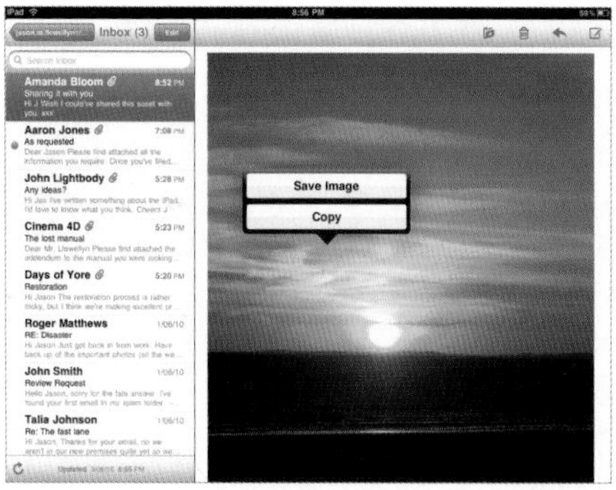

6: Copying a photo
Going back to a photo attachment, if you want to use it in iWork but not add it to your library, tap and hold on it, and select Copy from the popover menu.

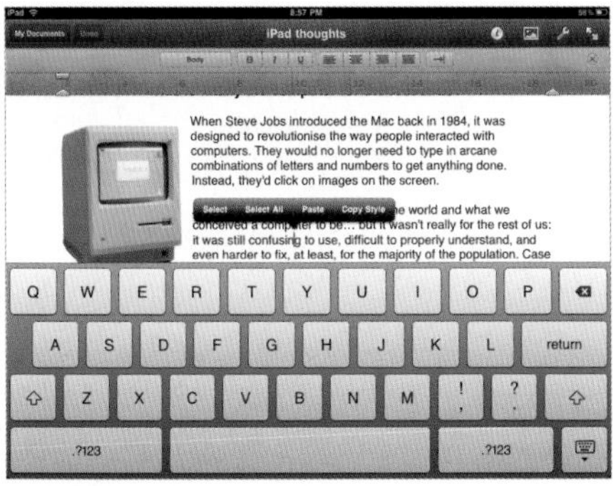

7: Pasting elsewhere
To open a document in Pages for instance (either an existing one or from an attachment), tap and hold to reveal a menu and select Paste to add that photo.

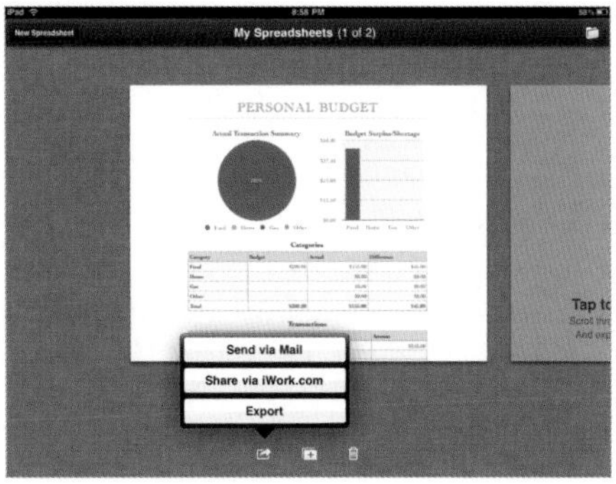

8: Attaching a file
To attach a file from one of your iWork apps, select a document from the Gallery, tap on the first button in the toolbar (lower left) and choose 'Send via Mail'.

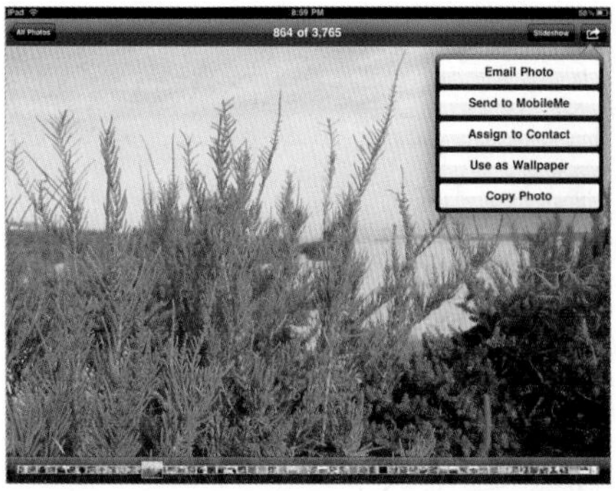

9: Attaching a photo
To send a photo, select it and tap on the same button, just as you did in the previous step. Only this time, it's located top right of the interface.

Tutorial: Syncing Notes with your Mac

The iPad's Notes app is a great way to keep track of ideas. And by syncing them over MobileMe you can access them anywhere

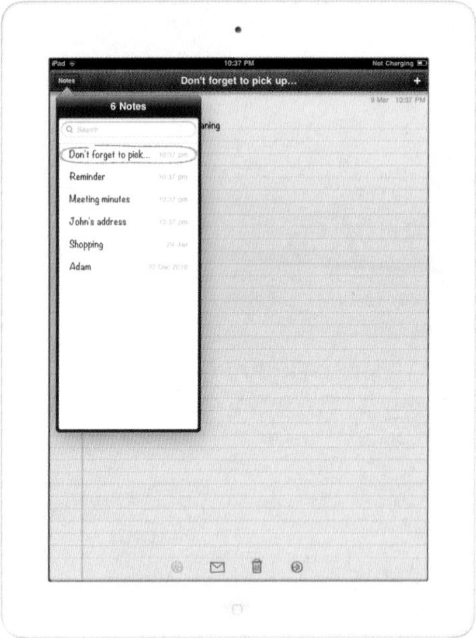

Task: Syncing your iPad with MobileMe

Difficulty: Beginner

Time needed: 10 minutes

Whether you're jotting down a shopping list, notes for a business proposal or a favourite quote, the iPad's Notes app is a great way to capture fleeting ideas. But until relatively recently, Notes was hamstrung with a critical flaw: there was no way to get notes made on your iPad back to your Mac. Thankfully things have improved markedly in recent iOS updates.

First, file syncing through iTunes was added, and now MobileMe subscribers – or anyone using an IMAP-based email account – can synchronise their notes without physically connecting their iPad to their computer. But MobileMe users have the advantage that synchronisation is two-way: notes you make on your iPad can appear automatically in Mac OS X's Mail application, while any jottings you create on the Mac can be synced over to your iPad.

But getting synchronisation arranged for the first time can be tricky. This tutorial shows you how to set things up to ensure that you're never without your best ideas.

Finding your way around Notes

The need-to-know functions

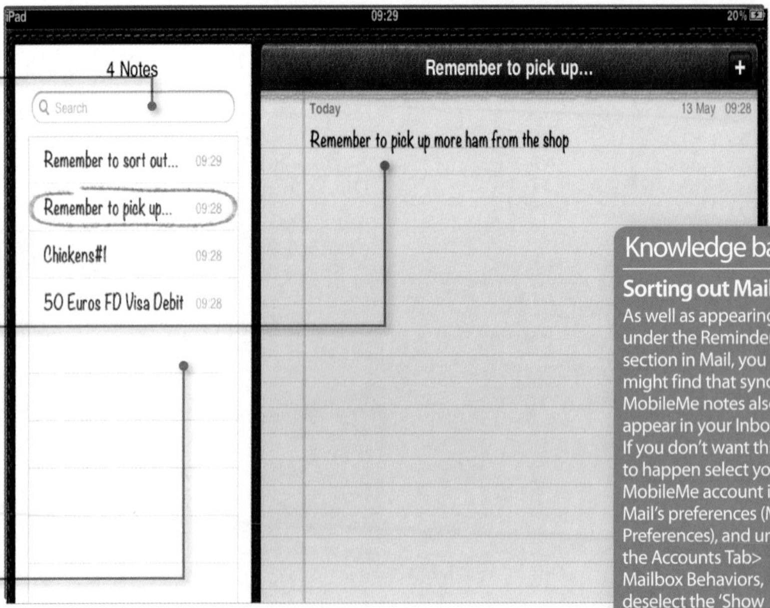

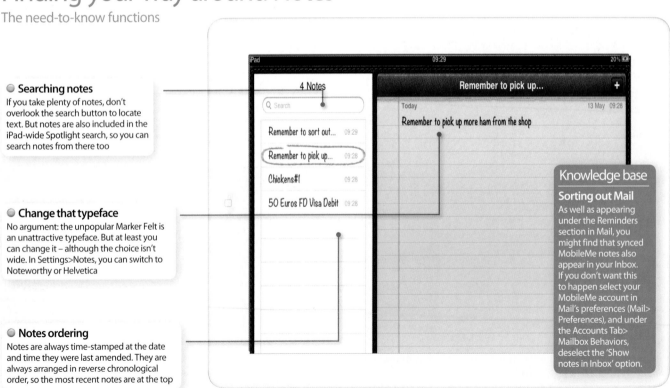

Searching notes
If you take plenty of notes, don't overlook the search button to locate text. But notes are also included in the iPad-wide Spotlight search, so you can search notes from there too

Change that typeface
No argument: the unpopular Marker Felt is an unattractive typeface. But at least you can change it – although the choice isn't wide. In Settings>Notes, you can switch to Noteworthy or Helvetica

Notes ordering
Notes are always time-stamped at the date and time they were last amended. They are always arranged in reverse chronological order, so the most recent notes are at the top

Knowledge base

Sorting out Mail

As well as appearing under the Reminders section in Mail, you might find that synced MobileMe notes also appear in your Inbox. If you don't want this to happen select your MobileMe account in Mail's preferences (Mail> Preferences), and under the Accounts Tab> Mailbox Behaviors, deselect the 'Show notes in Inbox' option.

Step-by-step | Notes Syncing Notes with your Mac

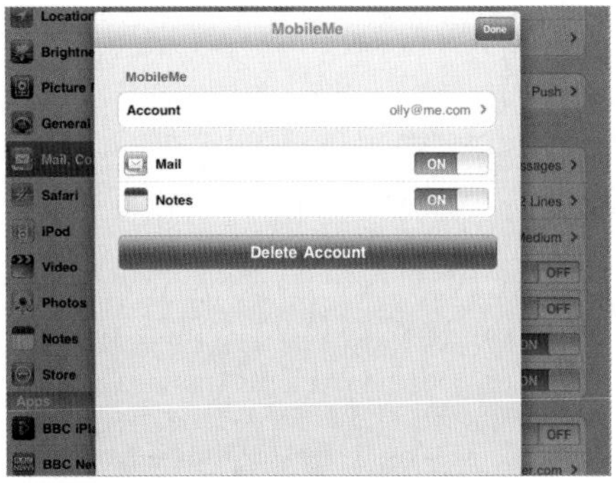

1: Add Notes syncing

To set up wireless syncing with MobileMe, go to Settings>Mail, Contacts, Calendars, tap the account to sync to and set the Notes slider to ON.

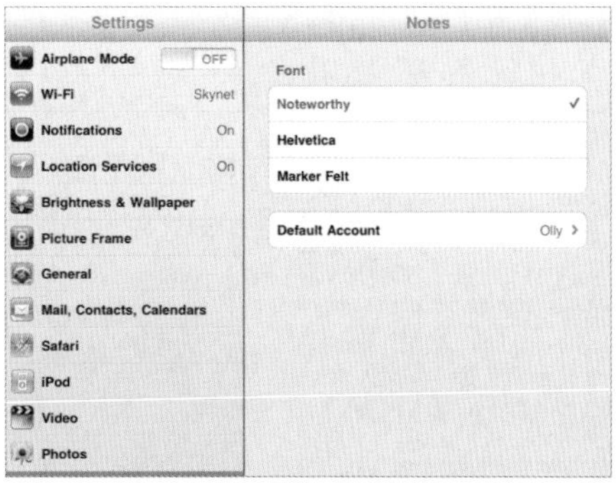

2: Set up your default account

To make sure all your notes default to your MobileMe account, open Settings>Notes. Tap Default Account and select MobileMe.

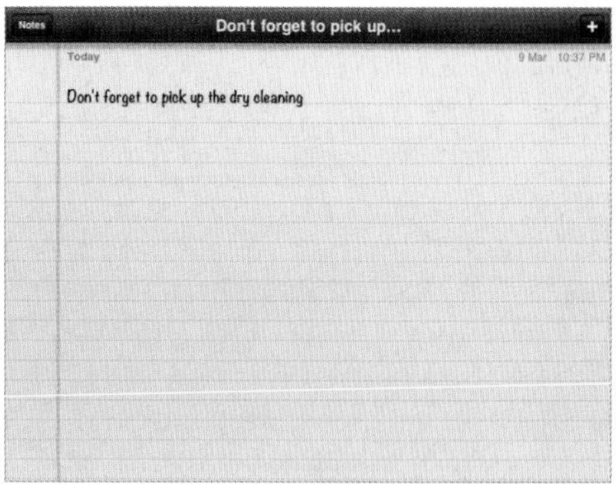

3: Syncing begins

You can now add entries to Notes and be confident that your content will instantaneously sync with your Mac whenever you tap the Done button.

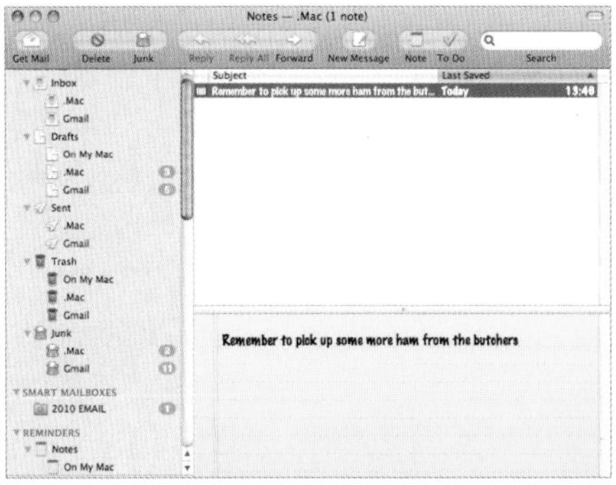

4: Synchronising with Mail

Back on the Mac, notes will be synced to Mail. Notes appear in the left-hand pane in a Notes folder under Reminders. You can create notes here too.

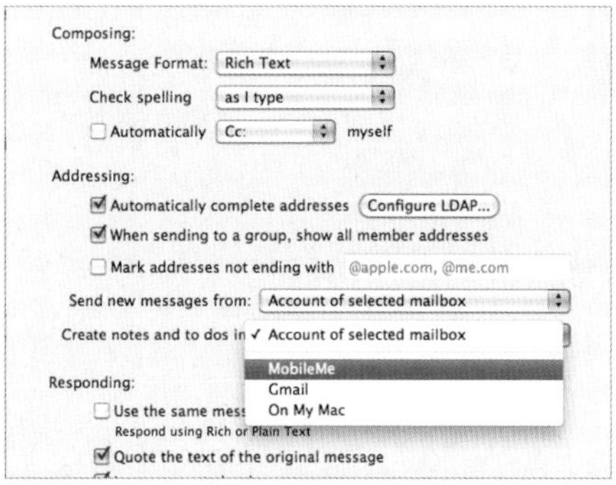

5: Two-way syncing

To sync notes back to your iPad, go to Mail> Preferences. Under the Composing tab, make sure 'Create notes and to dos in:' has MobileMe selected.

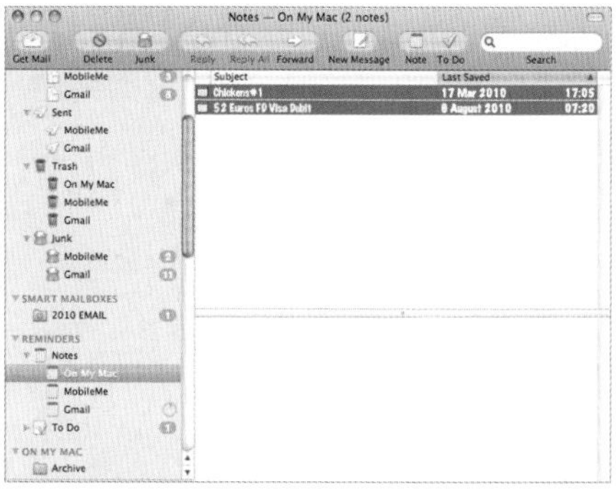

6: Moving notes

But what about notes you've already created in Mail? Under Reminders, click the disclosure triangle next to Notes. Choose the On My Mac folder.

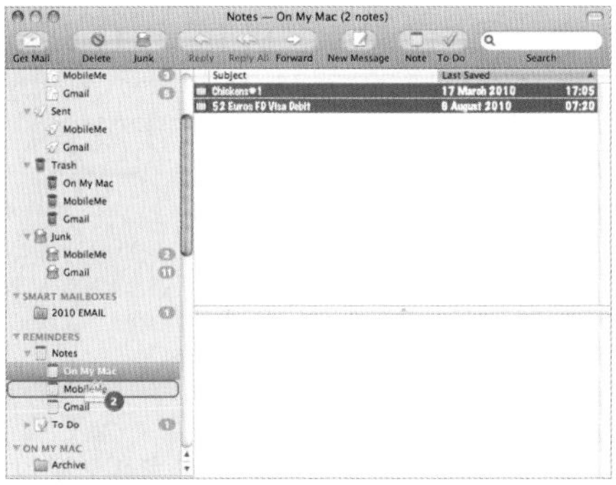

7: Add to MobileMe

Select the notes that appear in the Mail browser window and drag them to the MobileMe Notes folder. These will now be synced to your iPad.

8: Sync through iTunes

If you'd rather sync your notes through iTunes, first reverse the syncing you set up in step 1 in Settings>Mail, Contacts, Calendars.

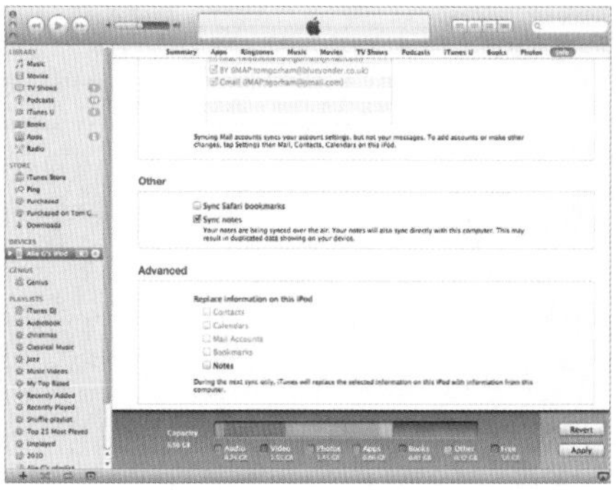

9: Manual syncing

In iTunes, select your iPad, click the Info tab and choose Sync notes under Other. Notes now appear under the Reminders section in Mail or Outlook.

Tutorial: Getting to know Pages

Apple's Pages takes the mobile word processing experience to a whole new level

Task: Learn to create with Pages in a matter of minutes

Difficulty: Beginner

Time needed: 20 minutes

Pages is not like most word processors – it combines the most used features in an interface that includes very few icons. Getting to know the app is not difficult, but it helps to understand where the main functions reside to get you started, and doing so will open up the power within. Despite the sparse interface it is packed with formatting options and clever tricks that make previously tiresome manoeuvres a thing of the past. For example, you can move an embedded image around an article and the words will automatically reposition themselves around it, and the included templates are customisable, which enables you to get creating in no time at all.

Not all specific needs are catered for, such as word count, but Apple has done a good job of defining the most used functions that people need and being able to share your creations without touching a desktop is another advantage. In this guide we will be showing you how to get started with Pages. As we stated earlier, this is not a standard word processor, but it may well become the one you use more than any other.

Step-by-step | Pages Create stunning documents on the move

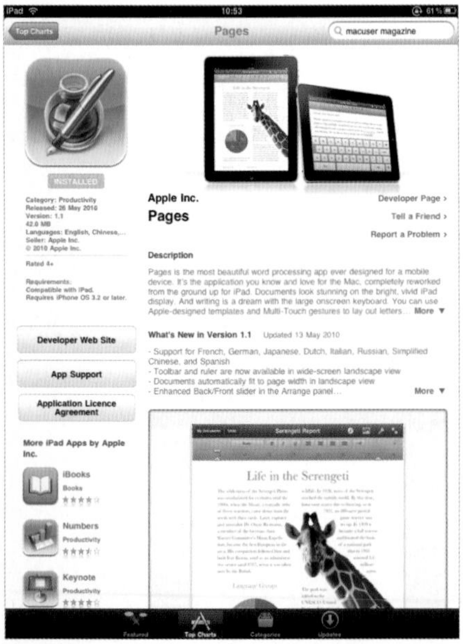

1: Grab the app

Search for 'Pages' in iTunes and purchase and install as normal. £5.99 may seem expensive for an iTunes app, but it is in fact very good value for a word processor with so many features.

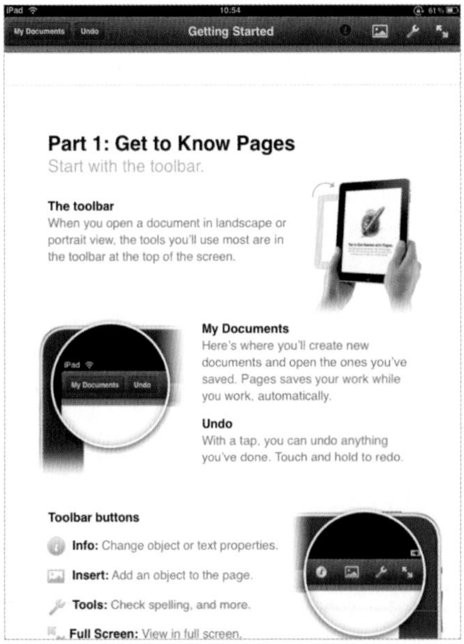

2: Have a look around

Pages is so obviously visual in the way it is designed that you could just have a wander around the icons and start typing, but the best place to start is the pre-loaded user manual.

3: Create your first document

In the first screen tap the '+' icon at the bottom and then tap New document. This will bring up a screen offering a selection of templates. You can choose anything from a blank page to a party invite.

Making the most of Pages

Learn all the tricks of the Pages trade…

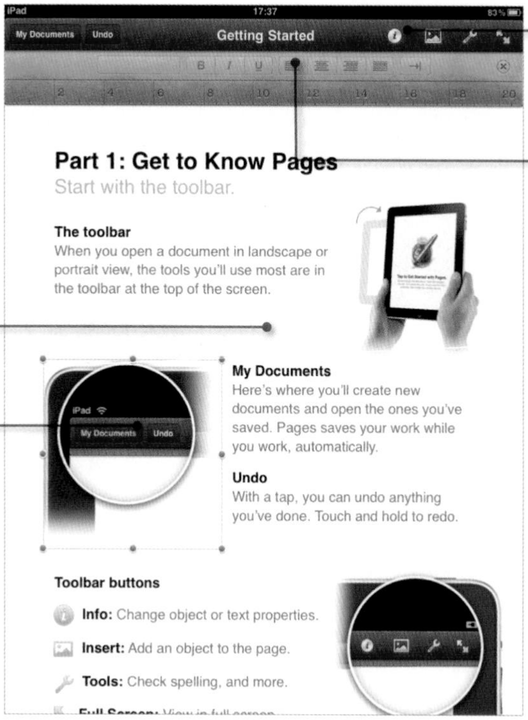
My Documents
Undo
Getting Started
Part 1: Get to Know Pages
Start with the toolbar.
The toolbar
When you open a document in landscape or portrait view, the tools you'll use most are in the toolbar at the top of the screen.
My Documents
Here's where you'll create new documents and open the ones you've saved. Pages saves your work while you work, automatically.
Undo
With a tap, you can undo anything you've done. Touch and hold to redo.
Toolbar buttons
Info: Change object or text properties.
Insert: Add an object to the page.
Tools: Check spelling, and more.

Document handling

Your completed documents are never far away. A tap of the 'My Documents' icon will bring up a page showing all of your saved work. Each document is saved automatically after every change

Easy image manipulation

Once inserted, images can be resized, moved and even twisted to the position you need. The words will automatically move to the right position

Extra formatting

Simply tap the 'i' icon to access extra formatting features such as bullet points, subtitles and headings. The options automatically change if you have an image highlighted

All the standards

All of the standard formatting options such as bold, italics and underline are easily accessible from the top bar. Highlight a word and click an icon for the desired effect

Knowledge base

Work with templates

Templates can make the process of creating eye-catching documents incredibly easy and Pages includes a variety of styles. Once you create a new document using a template you can change the images and all of the background text to your needs. You can also create your own templates for future use.

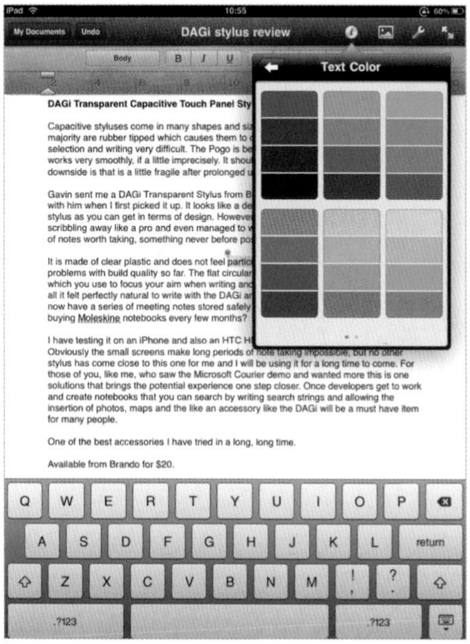

4: Test the options

Type a few words and then check the formatting options at the top. Select words by tapping and holding, at which point you can use the icons to format the text. Clicking 'i' gives further options.

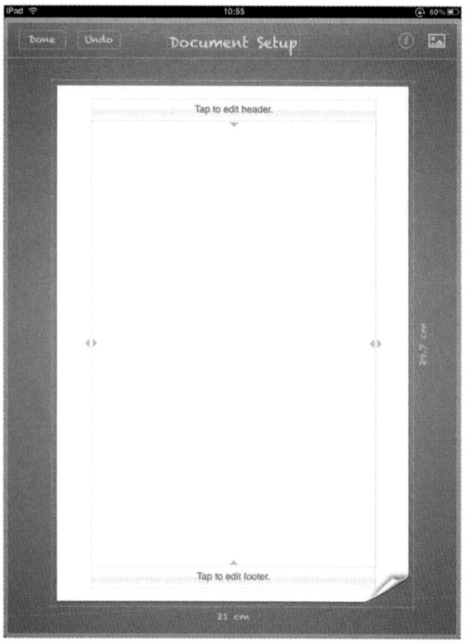

5: Delve deeper

Other options include a document setup wizard, defined by the top-right spanner icon and a quick tap of the picture icon lets you insert an image into your document.

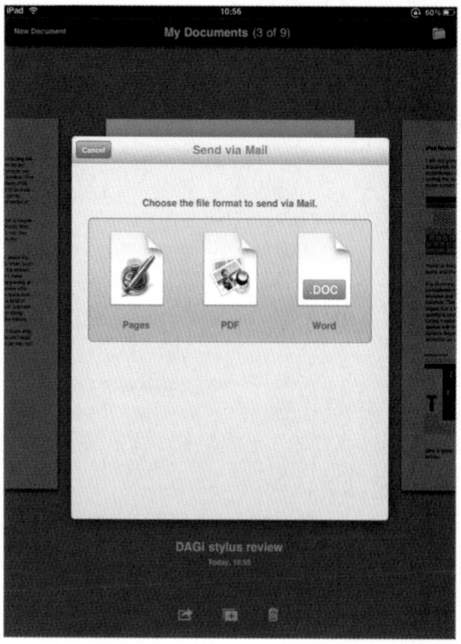

6: Share your work

You never need to save your work because Pages does it automatically whenever a change is made, but you can export it to PDF, Pages or Word format and send by email with the tap of one icon.

Tutorial: Perform professional presentations using the Keynote app

Keynote for iPad brings the Apple ethos of keeping things simple to the world of presentations

Task: Create quality presentations without the need of a desktop

Difficulty: Beginner

Time needed: 15 minutes

Creating presentations in PowerPoint has caused as much scratching of heads over the years as almost any other software solution. Despite this it has been widely used in the corporate world and to this day dominates the presentation software market. Keynote for iPad brings with it the advantage of being mobile, but it is also incredibly easy to use.

Because the iPad is finger driven, Apple has had to do away with the preciseness this type of software normally requires and has managed to make the entire process finger friendly and much quicker than the competition. It will still take some time to get used to, though, because the commands are different and at times it feels almost too easy. In this guide we will show you how to create your first presentation and how to make the most of the features and the fact that you can create wherever you are without the need for wires.

Using Keynote

Make your presentations look professional without needing to touch your desktop PC or Mac

Check your slides
All of your slides are available in the left-hand column and are previewed in great detail. You can also drag and drop them to change the order in which they will appear

Use the icons
These four simple icons hold within them a wealth of tweaks and tricks that will help you build a presentation in no time at all

Knowledge base

Animations

You can include a large variety of animations in your Keynote presentations which can also be previewed on the iPad itself. The trick is to only use them when necessary because overuse of animations will detract from the core message of any presentation. To animate an object, click the diamond-shaped icon and then choose the style that you require.

Shapes, text and more
The media available is almost unlimited and everything from simple text to photos and charts are available to you. You can then manipulate them once inserted into a slide

New slides
Adding a new slide requires a single tap on the '+' icon. Almost every function in Keynote only requires a tap or two and is highly intuitive to use

Step-by-step | Keynote Build a Keynote presentation

1: Get Keynote

Keynote is available on the iTunes App Store for £5.99 and is part of the iWork for iPad solution. All you need to do is purchase it and install it on your iPad as normal.

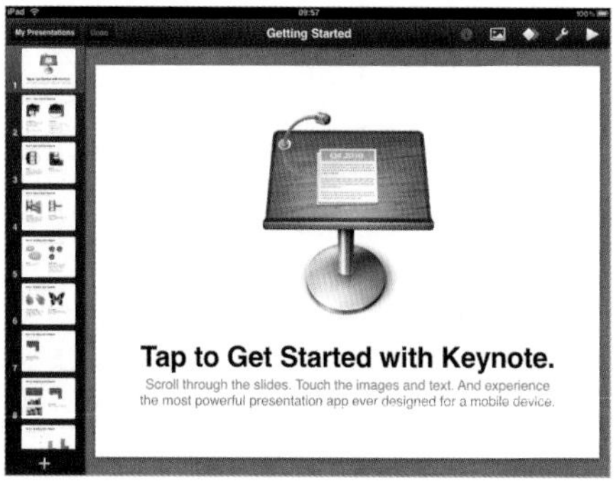

2: Read the manual

As you would expect from Apple, a manual is included in the app which is designed to get you up and running quickly.

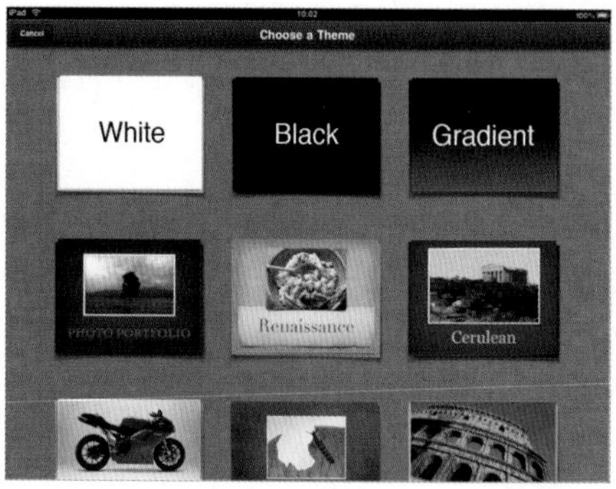

3: Create your first presentation

Click the '+' icon at the bottom and then select New Presentation. You can choose from 12 themes, but for the purposes of this guide select the White one.

4: Build your first slide

On the first slide, double-tap the photo and tap the small icon that pops up. You can replace the photo with an image of your choice from the photo library.

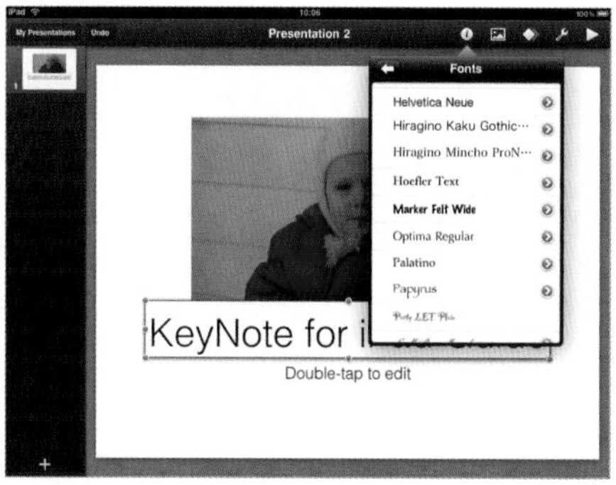

5: Use your words

Double-tap the text and add your own words. When done, tap on the words and tap the 'i' icon. This will bring up a selection of styles and colours for the text.

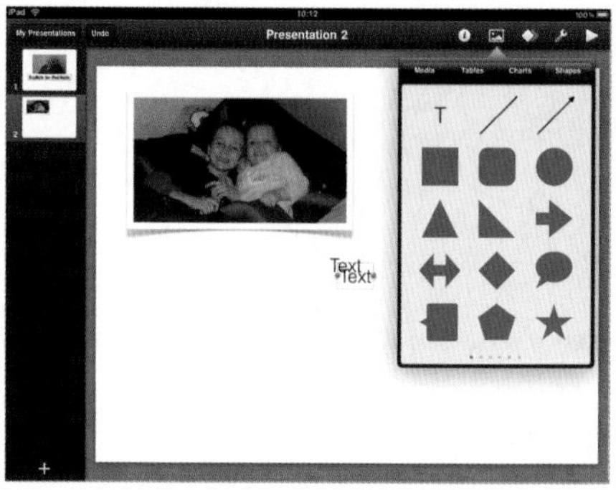

6: The important second slide

Tap the '+' icon on the bottom-left to create a second slide. Tap the picture icon at the top and then choose the 'Charts' tab. Tap the 'T' to insert a new text box.

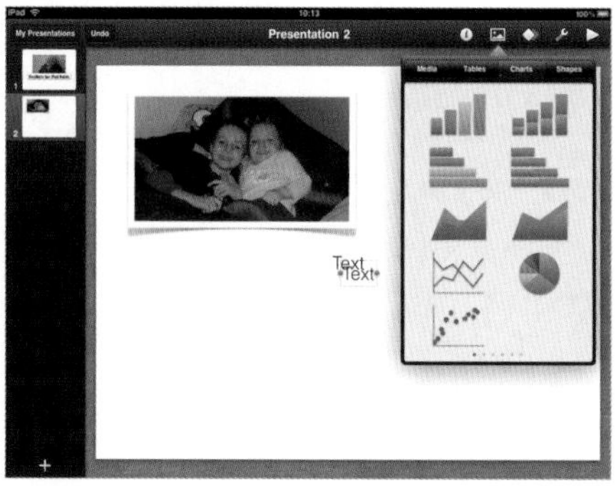

7: Add media

You will have noticed from the previous step that you can insert photos, tables, charts and many different shapes through the one command.

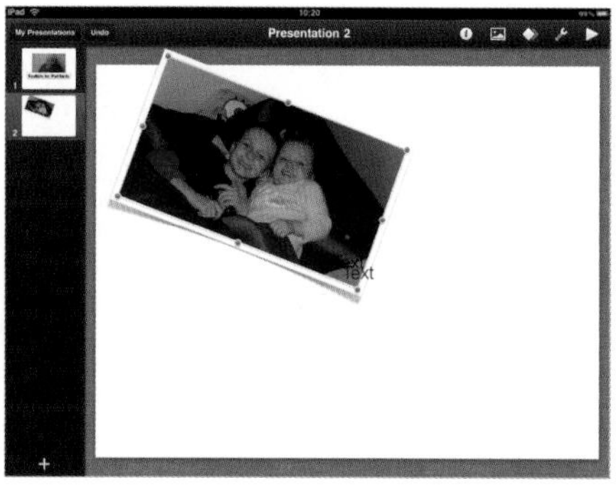

8: Time for tweaks

You can manipulate your media easily within Keynote. Tap a photo and then hold two fingers on it – you can now spin it round to any angle you like.

9: Share your work

Once you've finished you can share your work by tapping the left icon in the main document view. This will let you send it via email or to iWork.com.

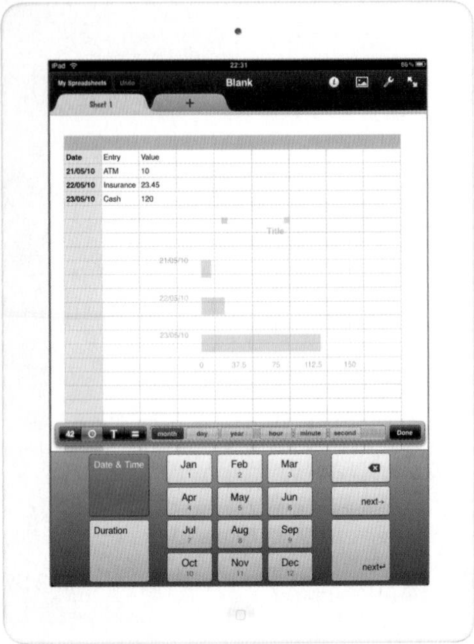

Tutorial: Use Numbers to create spreadsheets

With Numbers you can easily make some serious or silly spreadsheets to suit all tastes

Task: Learn to use Numbers for all of your spreadsheet needs

Difficulty: Beginner

Time needed: 20 minutes

Spreadsheets are a part of most people's lives these days and have taken on multiple roles in business and at home. Most spreadsheet programs tend to focus on the business side because this is where they are mainly used, but spreadsheets have a myriad of other uses that aren't often explored.

Numbers puts multiple uses front and centre with special templates built in and also brings a new way of working to the mobile user. However, the interface and function locations may feel alien to those that have used Excel for a long time and so a short introduction will help you to get to grips with the app quickly. There are a lot of functions built in to Numbers and some of these are not obvious, so take a look at these simple steps to start number-crunching straight away.

Step-by-step | Numbers Explore the power of Numbers

1: Grab the app

Numbers is on the App Store for £5.99, and although this may seem steep, it is excellent value for what you get. Once you have installed it you are ready to start.

2: Check out the manual

Apple has included a manual in Numbers. Because of the amount of features on offer, spare a few minutes to read it to speed things up later on.

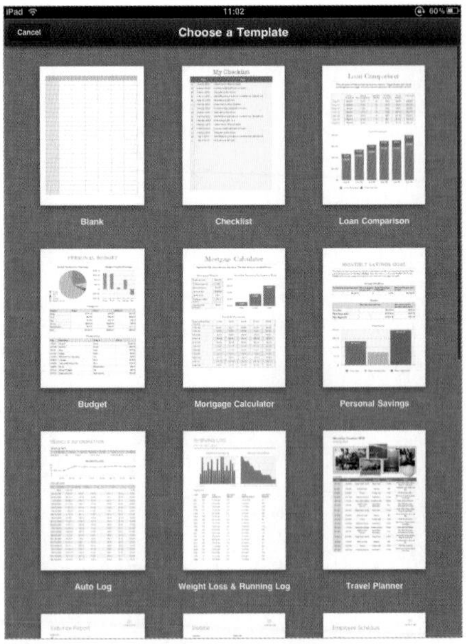

3: Your first spreadsheet

Tap the '+' icon at the bottom and click the New Spreadsheet option. You will be offered a choice of templates, from a blank sheet to a mortgage calculator.

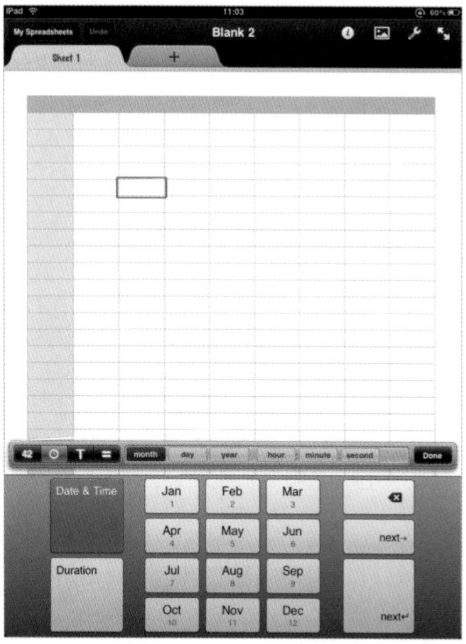

4: Adding data

Choose the blank one and double-tap an empty cell on the sheet. This brings up a dialog with four icons for numbers, date/time, text and formulas.

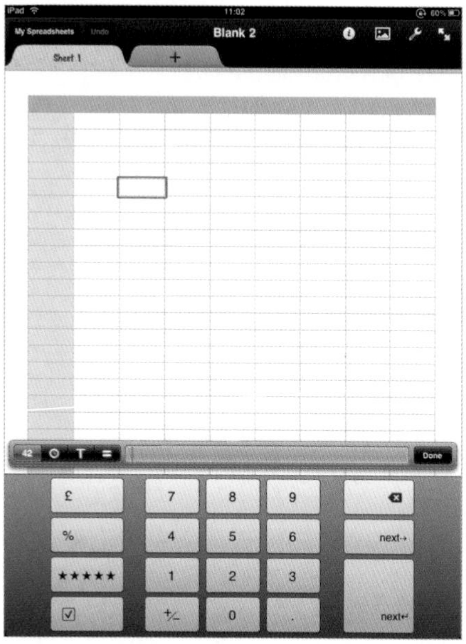

5: Handy shortcuts

Tapping any of the icons will bring up a dialog with shortcuts pertinent to the data you want to input. For example, the number icon brings up a number pad.

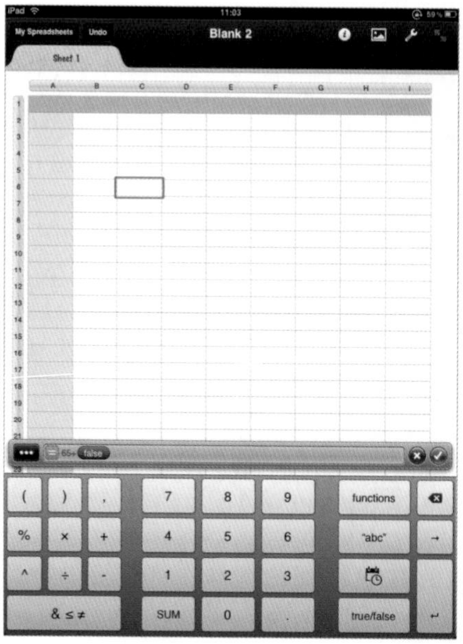

6: Use the data

If you tap the '=' icon you can choose from a wide range of simple functions that will pop up such as 'SUM' and true/false.

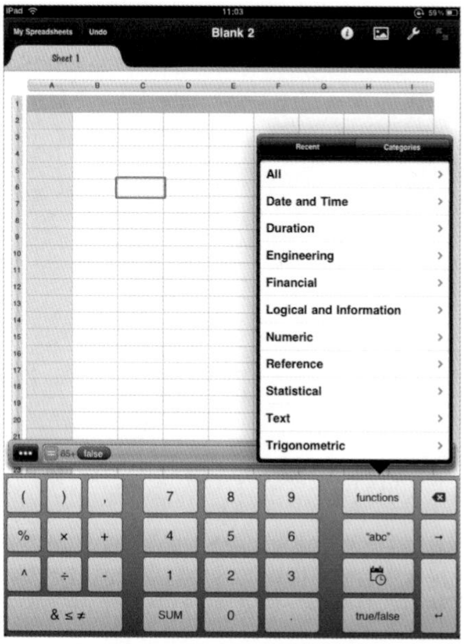

7: Advanced functions

The functions button is a window to some serious capability and includes categories of functions such as Trigonometric, Engineering and Statistical.

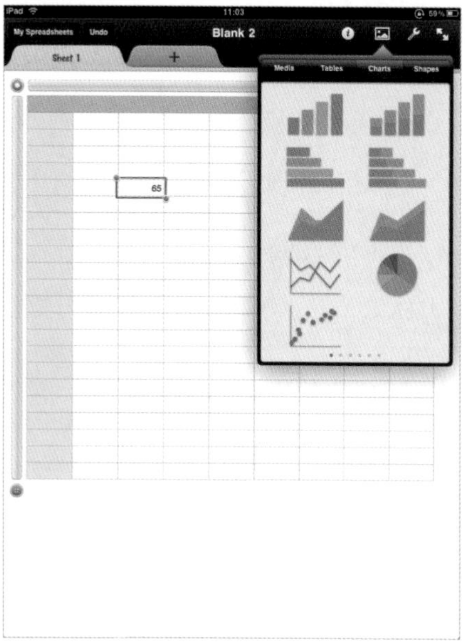

8: Add some media

Once you have your basic data built you can tap the picture icon in the top-right and insert photos, tables and shapes that will help to make the data more visual.

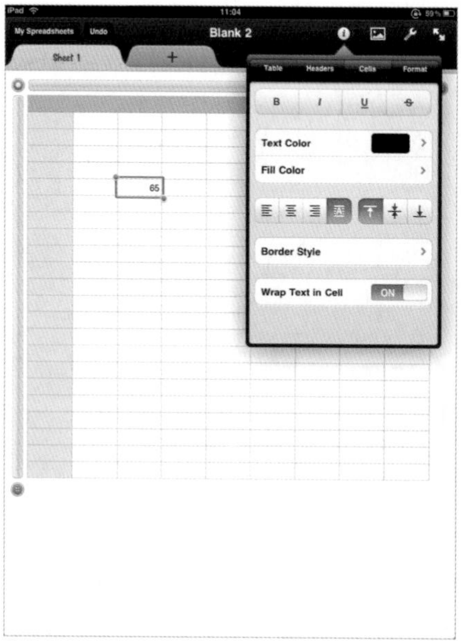

9: Practise your touch

Numbers is touch only and this will present problems at first, but with practise it feels natural. The interface looks simple, but it hides a huge range of options.

Productivity

Tutorial: Transfer files using Dropbox

Do you often transfer files between your Mac, iPhone and iPad? Learn how life can be so much easier with Dropbox. You'll never need a USB stick again…

Task: Use Dropbox to transfer files between your Mac and iPad

Difficulty: Intermediate

Time needed: 15 minutes

With cloud computing on the increase, life is getting easier and more convenient for all computer users. Take Dropbox for example, until recently the only way to transfer files between two computers was to either email them or copy them onto a USB stick. A tiresome chore if you regularly work using several machines. Thankfully, Dropbox makes this task so much easier. By installing the app on your Mac, PC, iPhone or iPad, any files you drop onto it will be accessible – instantly – on all the other devices. No longer will you need to carry a USB stick in your pocket or search through the drawers for one, everything you need will be on one of your favourite devices.

Best of all, a 2GB account is free! Follow us as we explain how to set up and use Dropbox to copy files between your Mac and iPad. It's so easy and convenient you'll wonder how you ever managed without it…

Using Dropbox on the iPad

Never will you need a USB stick again

Passcode Lock

Prevent others from accessing your Dropbox account by setting a Passcode Lock – it works exactly the same as the passcode built into the iPhone OS. Just remember the code you use!

Space Used

Dropbox includes 2GB of free online storage (you can purchase more from the website). To see how much space you've used, tap the Settings button

Camera settings

Select the quality of photos uploaded from your iPad by pressing the Camera button – a slider enables you to tweak the image quality. Note that higher settings will take longer to upload, and take up more space

Navigation

Use the menu on the left to browse your files and folders. When viewing a file, you can pinch-to-zoom, scroll and click-and-hold to navigate and share files

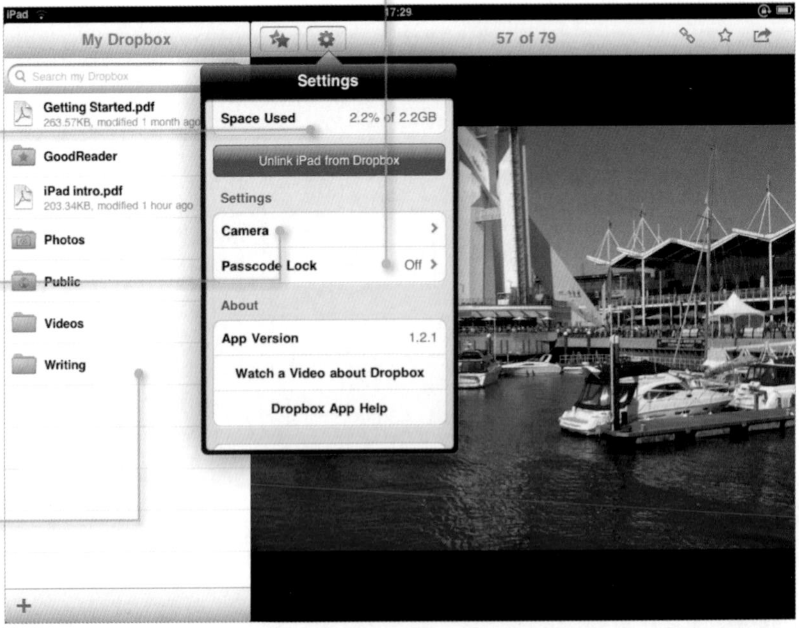

Step-by-step | Dropbox Transfer files through the cloud

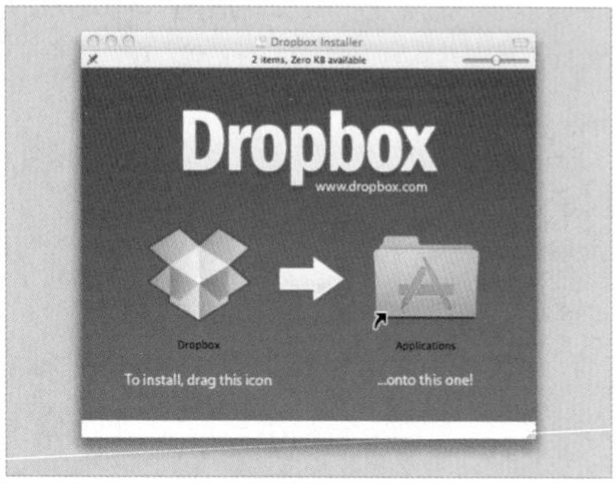

1: Download and sign up

The first step is to install Dropbox on every device that you wish to share files between. It's free from the App Store and **www.dropbox.com**.

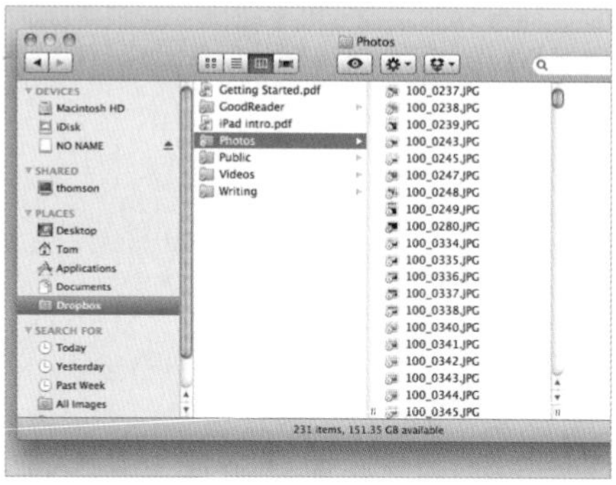

2: Start on the Mac

Once installed on your Mac you'll see a Dropbox folder under the Places tab on every Finder window. Drag any files you wish to transfer into this folder.

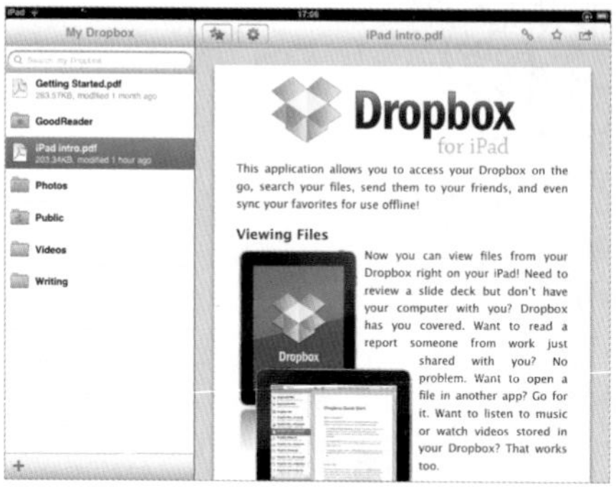

3: In the cloud

These files are automatically copied to the Dropbox server in the cloud, and you can now access them from your iPad. Load up Dropbox and sign in.

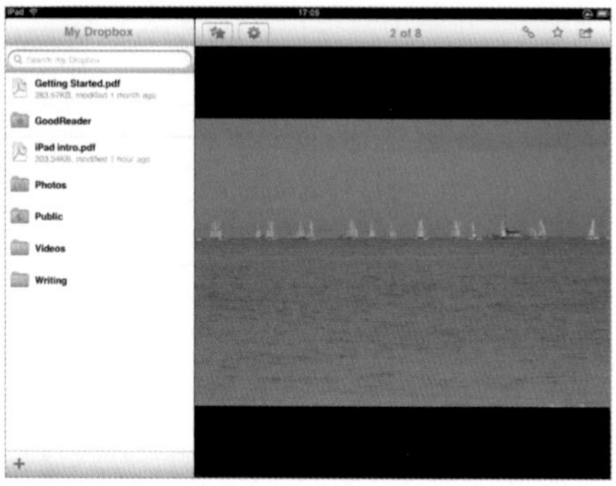

4: Browsing files

Turn your iPad on its side to go into landscape mode, you'll see a menu down the left-hand side – here's where you can browse through folders.

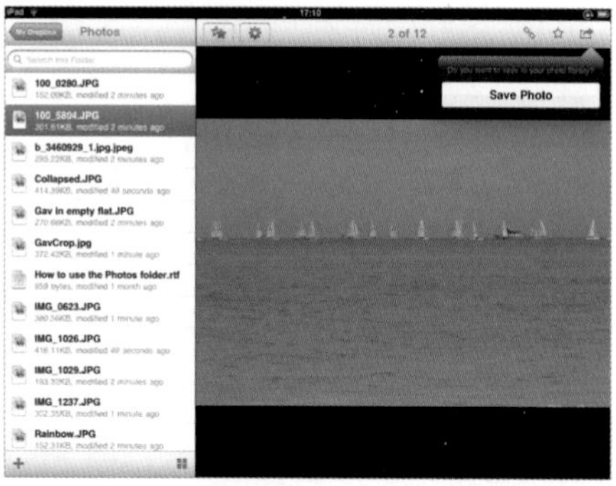

5: Saving photos

As you can see, we've copied some photos to our Dropbox Photos folder. To save a photo to your iPad, press the share button in the top-right corner.

6: Delete files

You can delete files and folders by swiping a finger across them. These files will be deleted from your Dropbox account – not just your iPad.

7: Share files

You can share files with friends by emailing them a weblink of the file in your account. Tap the chain link in the top-right corner, and enter an email address.

8: Upload photos

To upload files from your iPad to your account, tap the + button in the bottom-left corner. You can upload photos from your Photo Album.

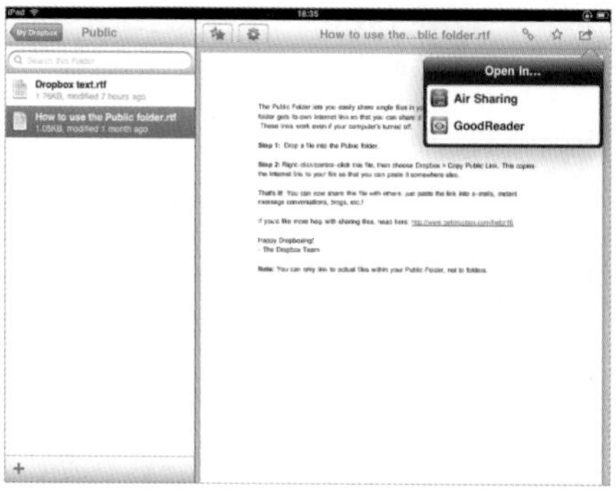

9: Another app

To open a file in the relevant app (for example a .pages file in Pages), tap the share button in the top-right corner and select the app.

Tutorial: Use AirPrint to print files

Yes, believe it or not, you can actually print from your iPad – but there are some tricks you should know about. Here are our secrets to iPad printing…

Task: Print from your iPad
Difficulty: Beginner
Time needed: 5 minutes

When critics sought to find flaws in the iPad on its release, one weakness they focused on was its inability to print. At the time, for a permanent record of anything on your iPad's screen you had to email a copy to your Mac or PC and print it from there. But the arrival of iOS 4.2 ended those complaints by bringing printing to the iPad's set of features.

AirPrint works with most popular iPad applications, such as Pages, Safari and Photos. It works over a local Wi-Fi network, so to use it you need to be on the same network as the printer you plan to use. The catch is that the iPad only prints to AirPrint-compatible printers, currently restricted to a limited range (a full list can be found at **http://bit.ly/euwjbk**). But the good news is that some third-party utilities enable you to print to any printer on your network (see Knowledge Base). For now, however, we help you get to grips with AirPrint and get you printing from your iPad with ease.

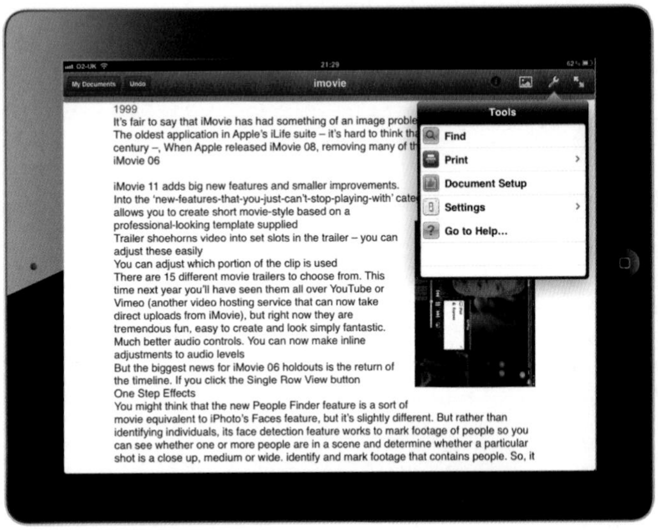

Step-by-step | AirPrint How to print a webpage

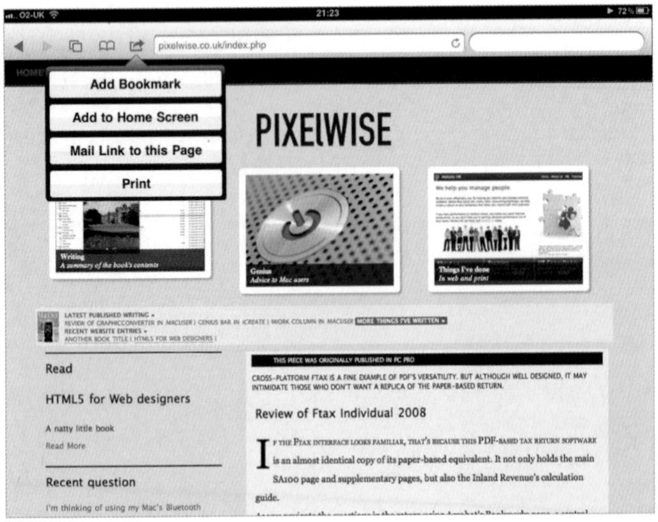

1: Choose the page to print

Many iPad apps now support printing, and most use the same technique. To print a page in Safari, for example, navigate to the page you want to print, click the arrow icon at the top of the screen, and select the Print option from the drop-down menu.

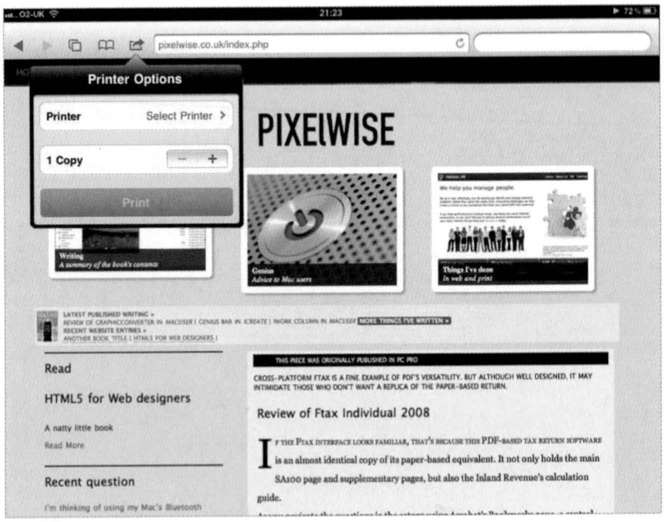

2: Choose the printer

Your iPad doesn't automatically know which printer you want to print to. The first time you print from an application, you will be prompted to select a printer. You will have to tap Select Printer to make your choice from the available printers.

Printing on the iPad

Most iPad apps follow the same approach when printing

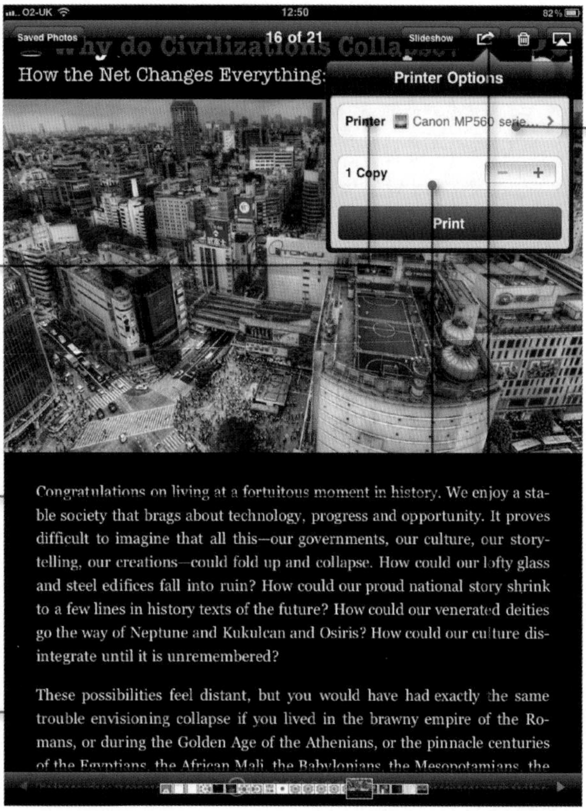

Options
Currently Apple restricts the type of printer you can print to, but here we're using the Printopia utility to print to a non-AirPrint-compatible Canon printer

Number of copies
Quickly choose the number of copies you would like to print by tapping the '+' or '-' buttons. Depending on the options that your printer supports, you may see additional choices here

Find the Print icon
In most apps that support printing, the printing option is found under the same 'arrow in box' icon

Switching printers
The iPad remembers your chosen printer, but if you want to change printer, just tap the printer in the list and you will be taken to another drop-down menu showing all of the available options

Knowledge base

Print to any printer
So what do you do if you don't have a AirPrint-ready printer? One way around this limitation is to use Printopia (**www.ecamm.com/mac/printopia**), a Mac utility that when installed lets your iPad print to any printer attached to your Mac, even it isn't AirPrint compatible. It also adds a 'virtual printer' that lets you send PDFs or JPEGs directly from your iPad to your Mac.

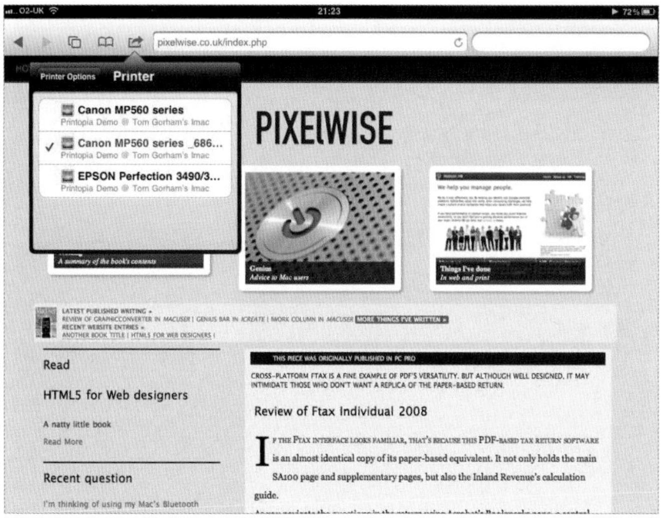

3: The printer list

As long as you're on the same Wi-Fi network as your printers, you should see every AirPrint-enabled device in this list. Choose the device that you would like to print the webpage to, so you can select any further printing options.

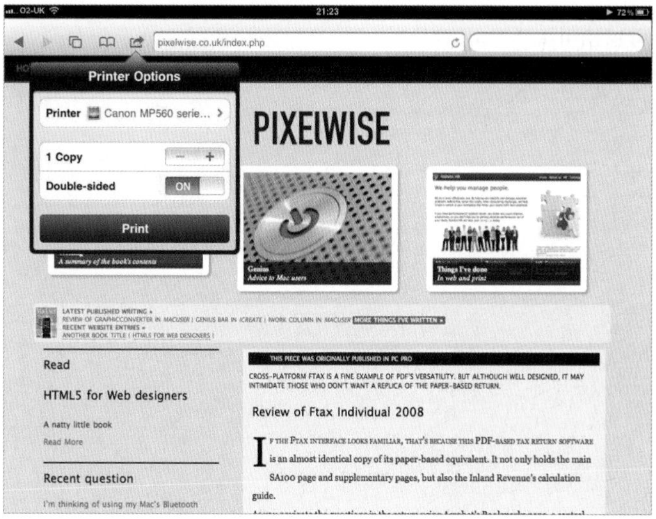

4: Choosing options

Depending on the printer you have selected, you may get other printing options. For example, if your printer supports double-sided printing, this may appear as an option. When you're happy with the options you have chosen, tap the Print button and the page will be printed.

Tutorial: Make a wireless hard drive out of your iPad with Air Sharing HD

This simple app turns your iPad into a storage device…

Task: Discover how to share files between a Mac and iPad

Difficulty: Intermediate

Time needed: 10 minutes

The iPad would make a fantastic portable hard drive, especially the 64GB model – that is if users could access the hard disk space from their Mac. Thankfully there's a solution at hand, with a clever app titled Air Sharing HD.

It enables you to wirelessly mount your iPad as an accessible drive on your Mac, giving you the ability to store files on the free memory, view and download email attachments, print documents and share files with other users. Priced £5.99, the app provides an easy and efficient way to store your important documents. All it requires to work is a Mac and a Wi-Fi connection.

In this tutorial we'll explain how to install the program on the iPad and share files. Any iPhone or iPod touch users are in luck, as there's a version of Air Sharing available for these devices, and the following tuition will work for all three devices.

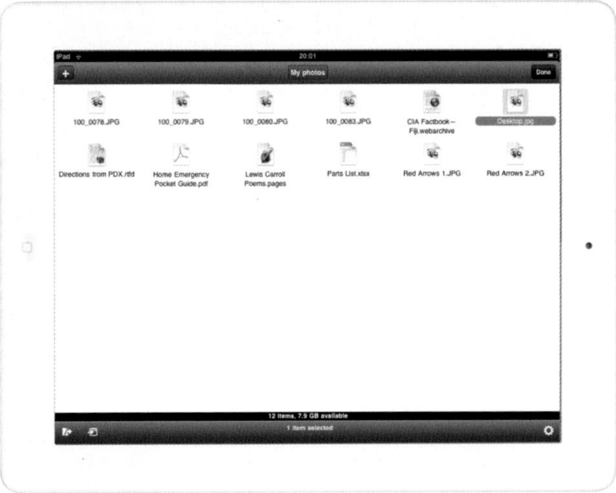

Go hands free

Air Sharing HD has some great features. Here we give you some further pointers for using this clever app that turns the iPad into a portable hard drive dream

Navigation

When opened, Air Sharing HD will show you the root folder. Tap on any folder to view the files within. To navigate back to the root folder, press the button in the top-left hand corner

Settings

In the bottom-right corner of the screen is the settings button. Tap it to turn sharing on and off, set an app passcode lock, tell the app to sleep after a certain time of period, set up a slideshow and edit the file browser

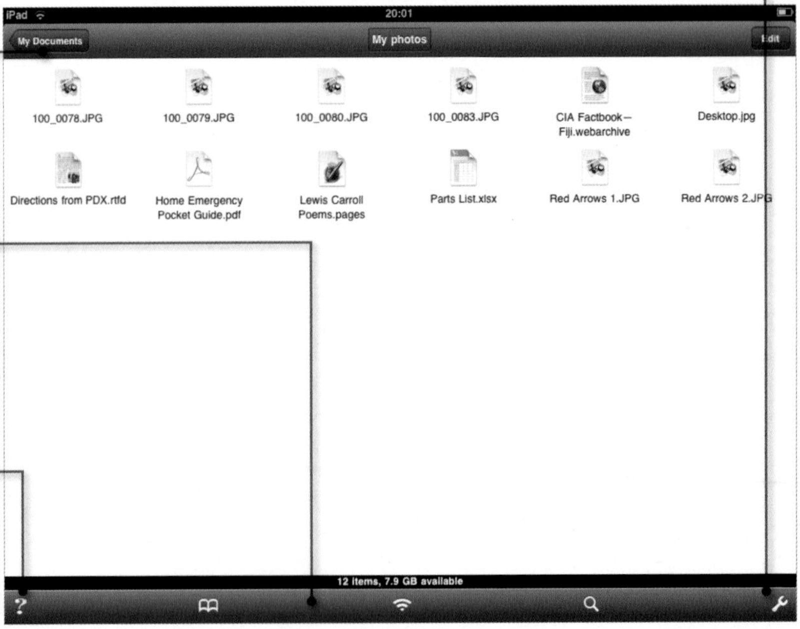

Three more icons

You'll see three buttons at the centre of the screen at the bottom. Search enables you to look for files, bookmarks will show your favourite files and the Wi-Fi icon gives you the option to select which network to connect to

Help Topics

Press the question mark at the bottom of the screen to access Help. From here you can discover how to setup Air Sharing HD on Windows and Linux, access remote servers and add a new server

Knowledge base

Edit button

Press the edit button at the top of the screen to access some desktop-class features. Once selected, simply tap on any number of files to edit them. Options include the ability to rename files, copy, move to another folder, compress as a zip, duplicate and delete – features not typically found on the iPad. You can also print and email any relevant files.

Step-by-step | Air Sharing HD Installing, sharing and editing

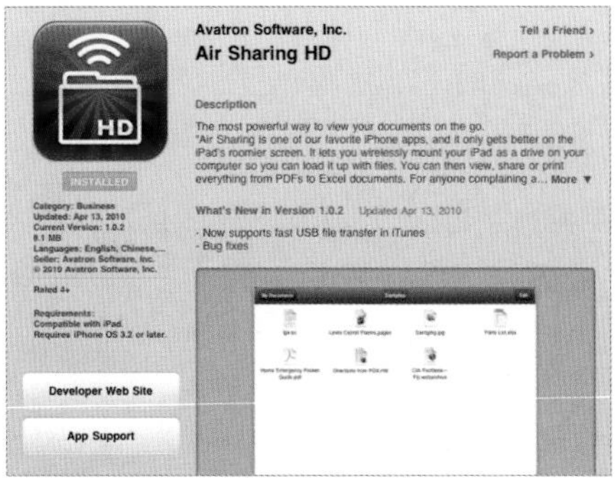

1: Install and share

Download Air Sharing HD from the App Store. Once installed, open it on your iPad, tap the settings button in the bottom-right corner, and ensure Sharing is on.

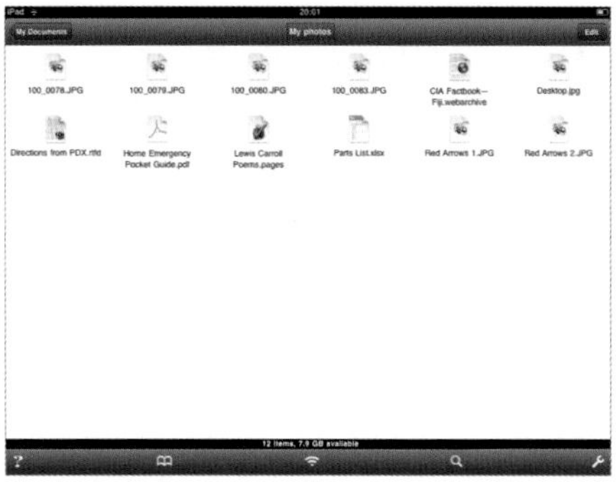

2: Find the IP

To connect to your iPad from a Mac you'll need to find the IP address of the iPad. Open the program and tap the spanner icon in the bottom corner of the screen.

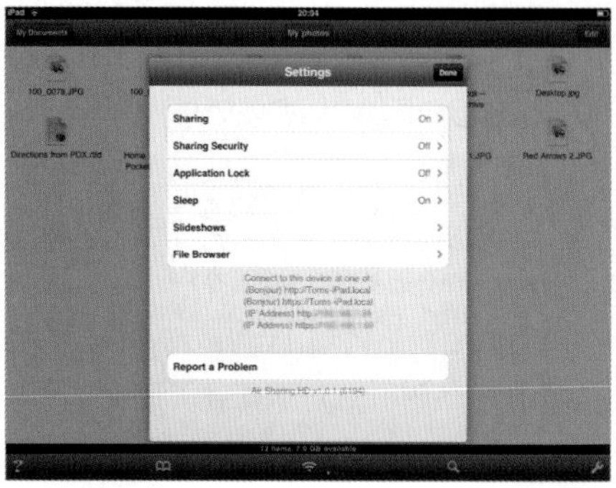

3: IP address

Towards the bottom of the pop-up window are a set of connection listings. Your iPad's IP address will be at the bottom, for example http://162.XXX.0.0.

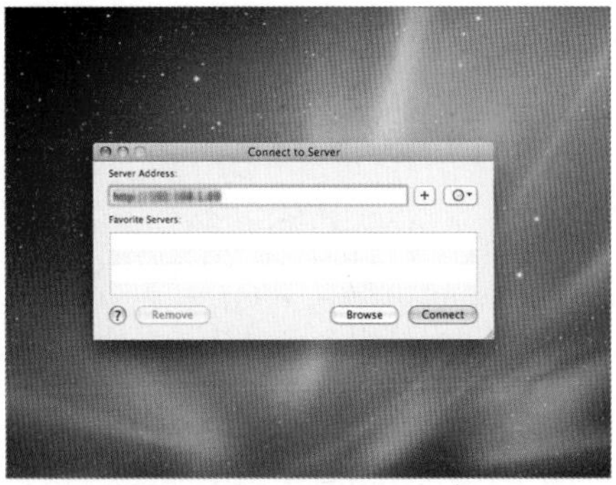

4: Connect to your Mac

Make sure your Mac is on and connected to the same Wi-Fi connection as the iPad, and press Command-K to bring up the Connect to Server window.

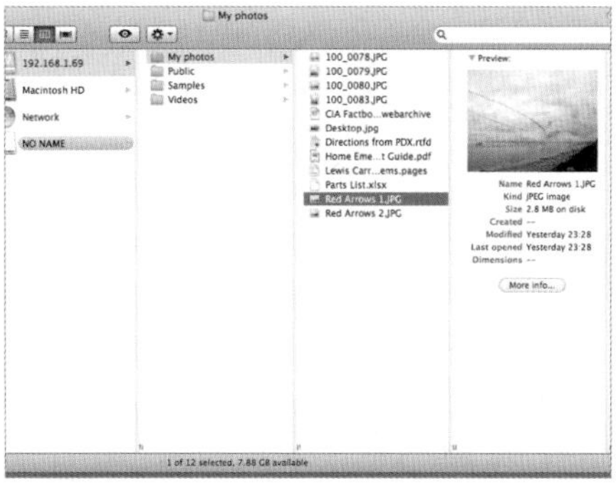

5: Time to connect

Enter the IP address for your iPad, for example http://162.XXX.0.0. Press Connect, and the Finder will open a window displaying the contents of your iPad.

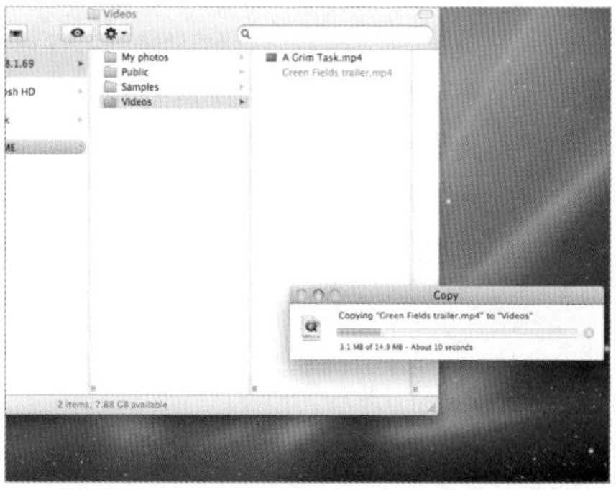

6: Copy files across

You can now drag-and-drop folders and files onto your iPad. Create folders if you wish to organise them. On the iPad, you'll see copied files in Air Sharing HD.

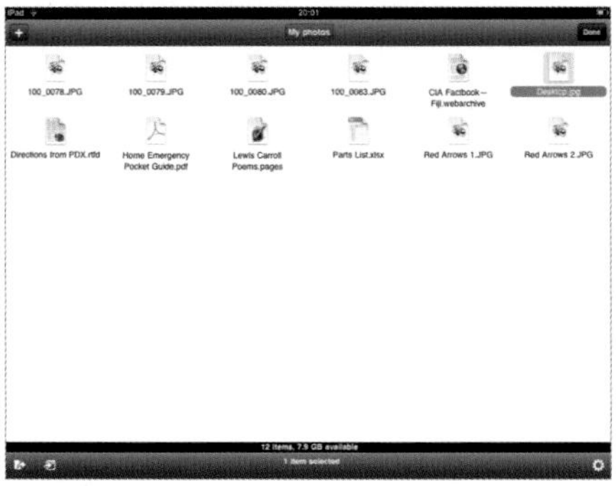

7: Edit on your iPad

You can edit files on the iPad in a number of ways. Tap the Edit button in the top-right of the screen, select a file, and press the cog wheel at the bottom.

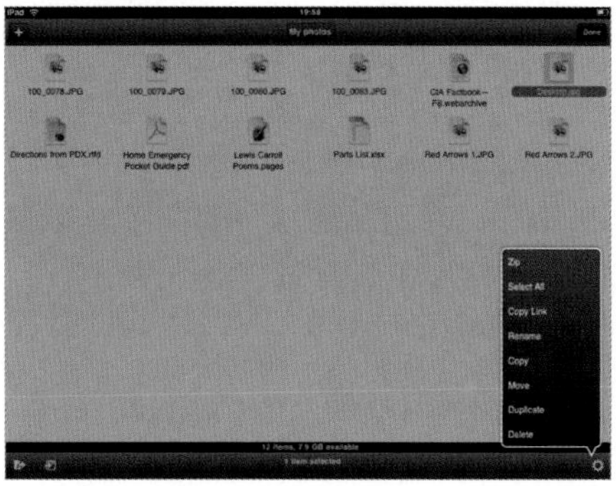

8: Delete, zip and rename

You'll discover it's possible to rename files, zip them, copy, move, duplicate and delete. To select more than one file to edit, simply tap as many as you need.

9: Print and email

You can also print images, email them and save to Photos. To do this press this file icon in the lower corner of the screen. To print you'll need a wireless printer.

Tutorial: Control a computer with your iPad

The iDisplay app is indispensable because it allows you to view and control your computer screen, run slideshows, use a database, and even play Flash movies (sort of)

Task: View and control your desktop

Difficulty: Advanced

Time needed: One hour

The Apple iPad is a very powerful device, but it is not exactly a full computer. It does not run full commercial-quality software apps, such as a photo application developed for the desktop; it has no features for browsing network drives and copying files; and it does not play Flash movies. Yet, with iDisplay, it can perform all of these tasks – as long as you are willing to spend some time setting it up.

Essentially, the iPad is like a window into your computer (the app supports Mac OS X and Windows XP). You load a small program on your computer, available at **shapeservices.com**, then install the app. With the app running on your iPad, you can then enable iDisplay to share your desktop over Wi-Fi. Once you do, you can control the mouse on your iPad, start applications, edit a photo in Photoshop, and even play a movie. Note that for all of these tasks, iDisplay will run slowly. Flash movies will play but, depending on the speed of your Wi-Fi network, they will run slowly.

Step-by-step | iDisplay View your screen

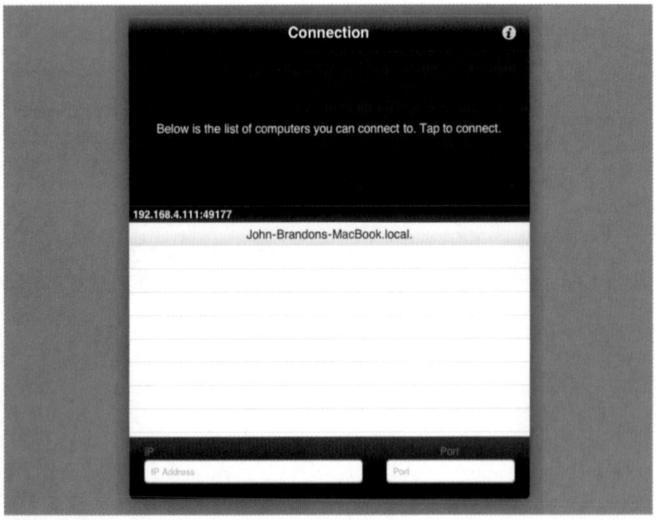

1: Load the apps

Load the iDisplay app (**www.shapeservices.com**) on your computer and start it, then load the iDisplay app on your iPad. You may need to adjust some screen size settings as prompted. On the iPad, select your desktop from the Connection box.

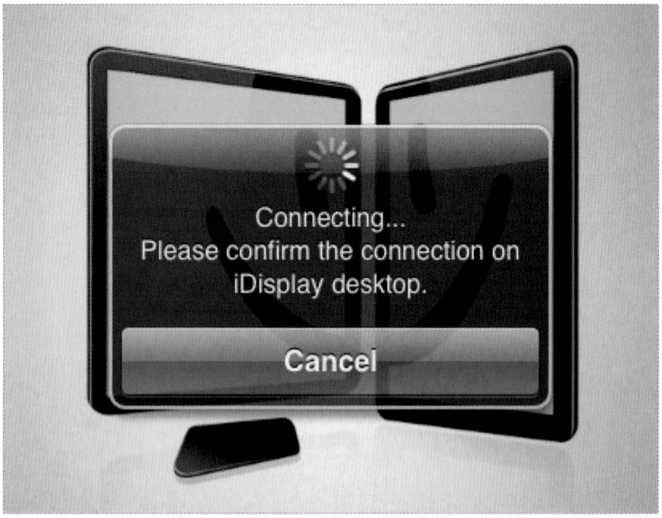

2: Confirm the app

Now switch back to your desktop. You will see a prompt to confirm the iDisplay app appear on screen, so click the Confirm button. Now go back to the iPad and you will see your desktop on its screen, ready for you to control remotely.

Use iDisplay on your iPad

Control your computer with your iPad's screen

Screen share
You can see that iDisplay is running on your computer. At any time, you can close down this app to shutdown iDisplay on your computer

Start apps
You can start any app – even those from Adobe and Microsoft – and control them using your iPad. Screen refresh times for these apps depends on the speed of your Wi-Fi network

Status updates
You can even set how iDisplay works on your Mac while accessing it from your iPad. Go to the yellow iDisplay icon and set options for screen size and screen location

Servers
Another great use of iDisplay is using it to copy files from your local drive to a server. Just open the drives you want and select the files, then click and hold down and drag to the new location

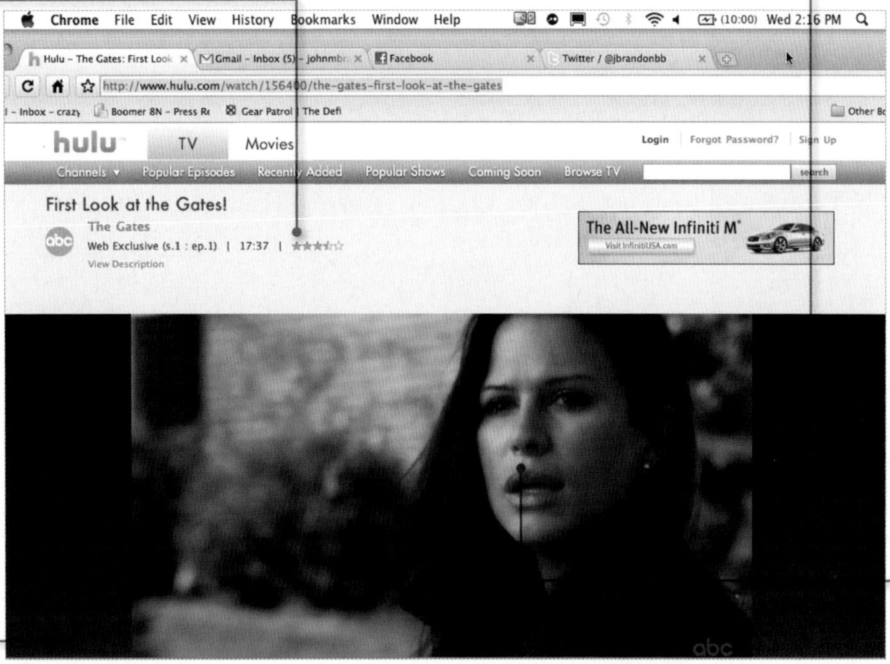

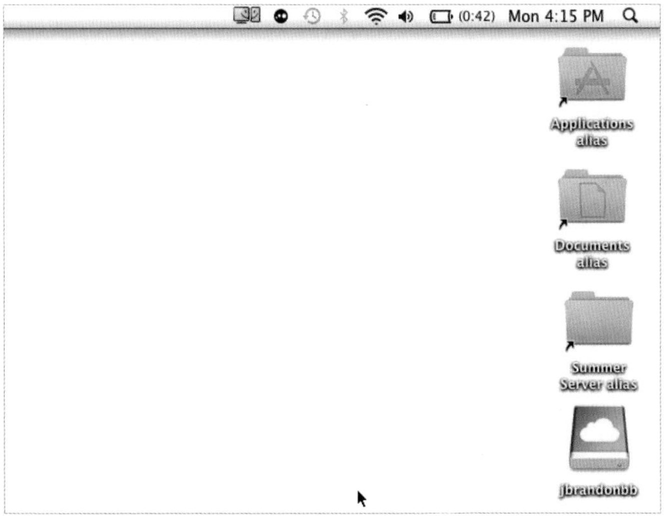

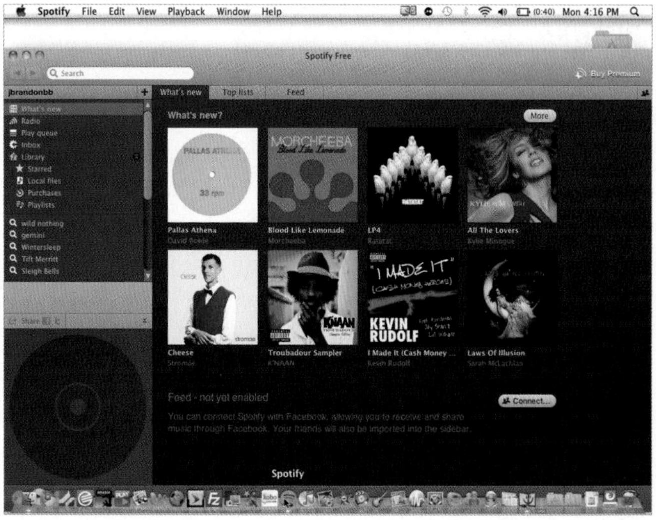

3: Control apps

To use your computer on the iPad, you will have to press and hold on the mouse icon, then drag it over to where you want to go. Double-tap on the iPad's screen to make a selection on your computer, whether it be opening a file or accessing media.

4: Connect users

Once an app is running (Spotify, for example) you can go to your computer and keep using it by taking control of the mouse, even as iDisplay is still running on your iPad. Any changes that you make will appear on the iPad as well.

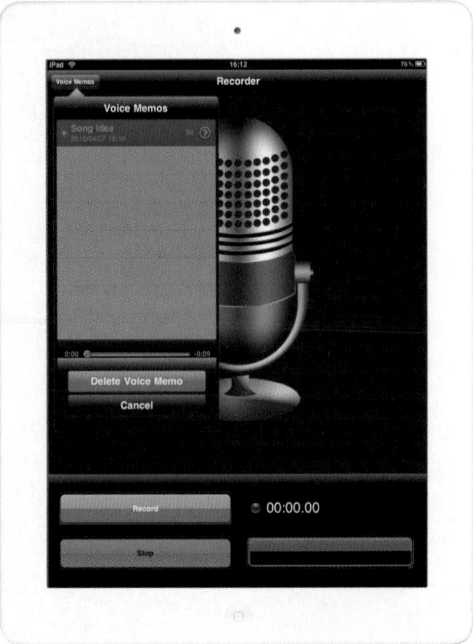

Tutorial: Take down voice notes on your iPad

There's no native Voice Memos app on the iPad, so use this great free option instead…

Task: Record a voice memo on your iPad

Difficulty: Beginner

Time needed: 10 minutes

While we're absolutely sure that the App Store will throw out any number of novel uses for a 10-inch touch screen, we were a little surprised that Apple didn't include the voice recording app from the iPhone 3GS on this device. We could pontificate over the reasons, but its all academic as there is an incredibly Apple-esque app out there which is free to download. This app is beautifully made, it looks great on the screen and it works incredibly well. The free version limits a couple of features, like emailing the memo, but for the purpose of recording thoughts and the like it's more than adequate. The menu system is as simple and Apple-like as you would want, and within a few minutes of discovery you can know everything there is to know. It's extra functionality like this that elevates Apple devices beyond the combination of great hardware and in-house software. It's a very useful app that, once you get used to using it, will become a go-to app when you don't have time to type or just want to hear how something sounds.

Step-by-step | Voice Memos Record and tag a voice memo

1: Load it, record it

Load the Voice Memos for iPad app and hit the red Record button to begin recording. The iPad mic is at the bottom of the device below the home button.

2: Level check

The green bars indicate when the microphone detects audio. Make sure the level doesn't run into the red, otherwise the sound will distort.

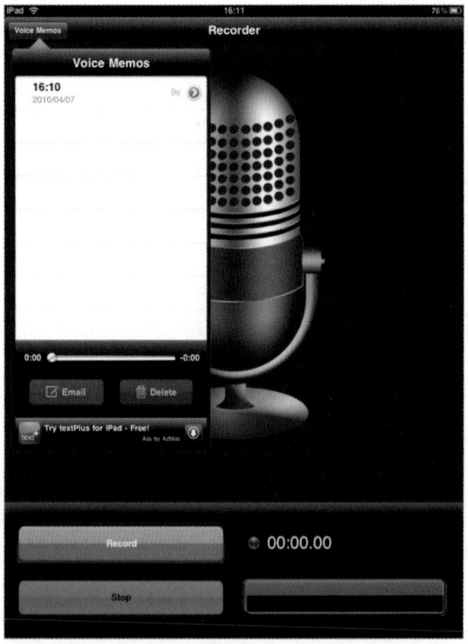

3: Finished and view

When you've finished recording you can view the stored memos by tapping the Voice Memos button. Memos are organised by date.

Record voice memos on the iPad

Download the free Voice Memos app and get recording

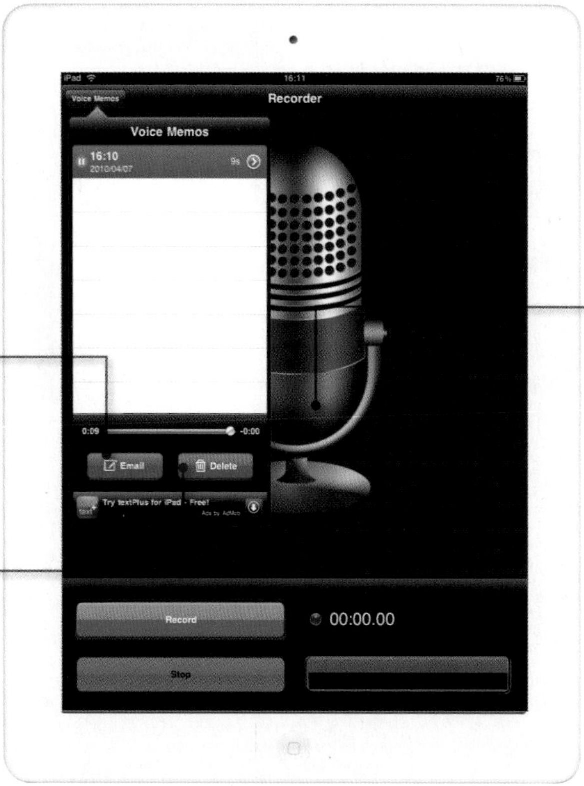

Email

You can send memos out to people via email, but only if you have bought the full version of the app. If you don't plan to send any memos you don't need the full version

Delete

Once you've finished with a memo and wish to discard it just hit the Delete key. It's best to do this regularly as you don't want to waste space on the iPad

Ad support

The reason such an excellent app like this can be on the App Store for free is because it is ad supported. Advertisers pay to have their ads running along the bottom of the open windows

Interface

The whole interface is about as Apple-like as you could want. We're surprised the Voice Memos app didn't make it over to the iPad from the iPhone 3GS

Knowledge base

Sound

The microphone on the iPad isn't of amazing quality, but it is certainly good enough for basic use. The speakers on the iPad are of much better quality, and resemble those of a MacBook more than the iPhone.

4: Playback

Tap on the blue arrow to play the memo. You can see the progress as it plays. You can also see how long is left and how much has been played.

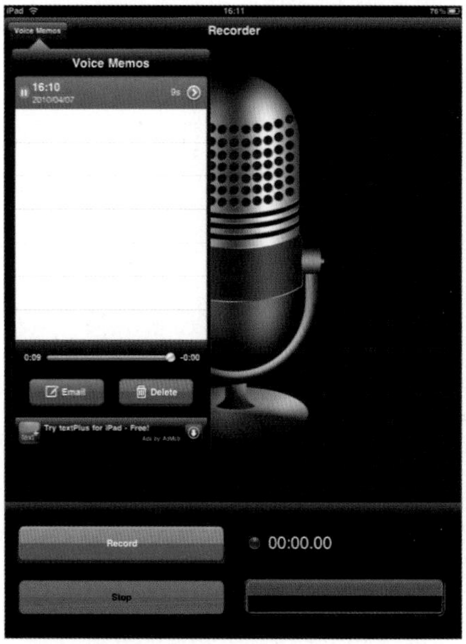

5: Add a tag

You can add a tag to each memo so you know what each one is. Tap the blue arrow in the top-right of the pop-out window to see the next screen.

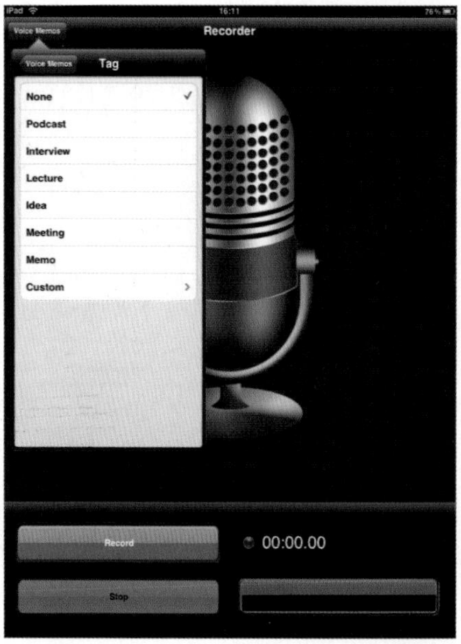

6: Tick it

On this screen, tick the tag you want to label the memo with (Podcast, Interview, Lecture, etc). If you want you can also create a customised tag.

The iPad Entertainment Guide

Turn your iPad into the ultimate multimedia device

This book proves that the iPad is many different things, all at once, but one thing it excels in is its ability to act as a portable media machine. From allowing you to read an infinite number of books in this movable library, to listening to music and watching movies wherever you are, the iPad does it all. The iPad Entertainment Guide takes you step by step through intuitive playlists, as well as sharing media. From streaming videos to playing multiplayer games online, through editing music and movies using GarageBand and iMovie, we have your entertainment needs covered right here with these in-depth guides.

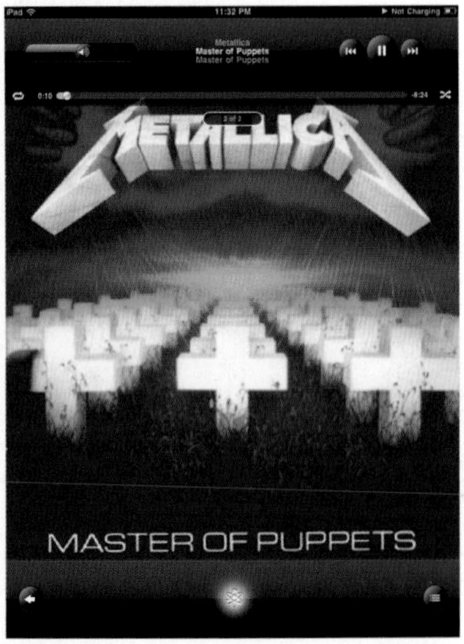

114 Master the iPod's more advanced controls and increase its potential.

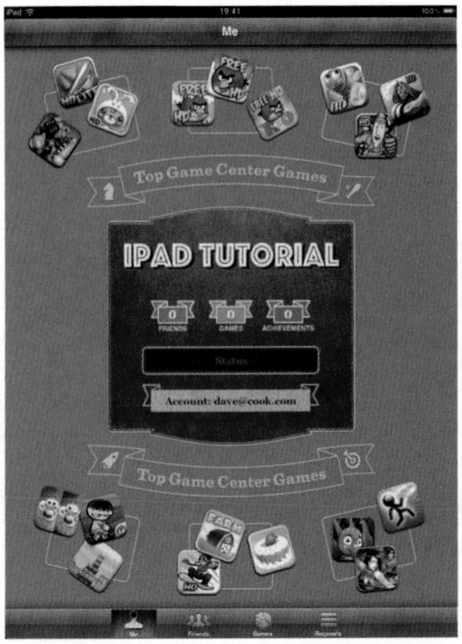

126 Create a Games Center account and play multiplayer online games and more.

124 Use your iPad to stream music and videos to other devices in your house.

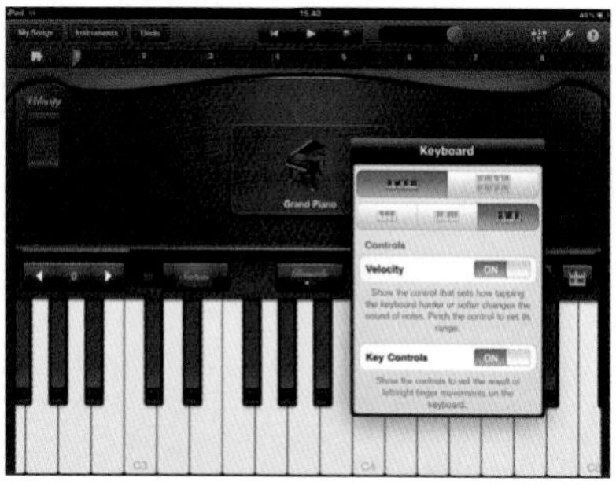

134 Learn how to make the best of the piano in GarageBand to create fantastic sounds.

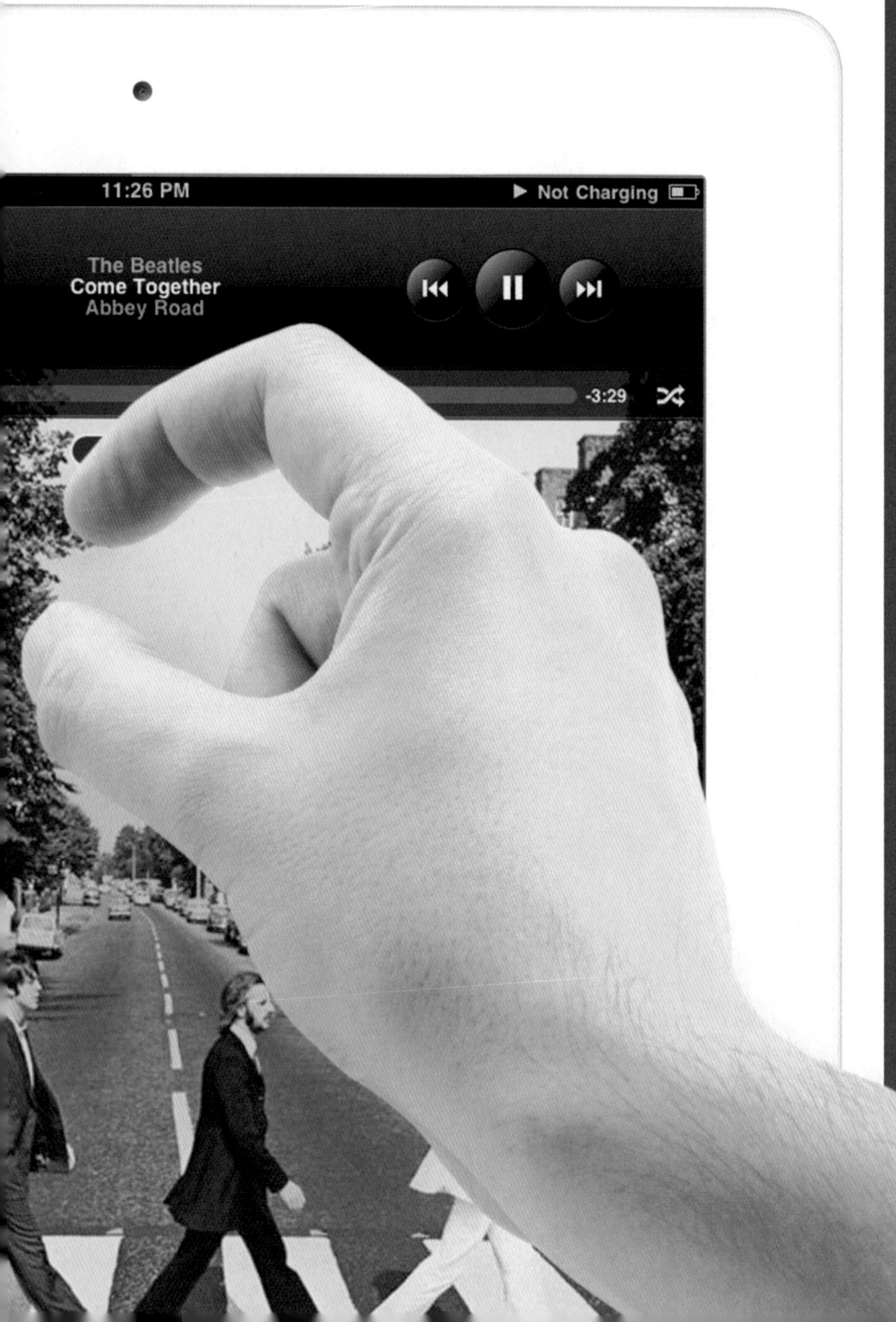

Tutorial: Bookmark and highlight in iBooks

Learn how to easily find your favourite quotes, sections and pages in digital books

Task: Add a bookmark in iBooks

Difficulty: Beginner

Time needed: 5 minutes

iBooks is a really fantastic eReader that allows you to carry a whole bookcase around with you while on the move. You can even customise the fonts, brightness and other settings to suit your needs and create a reading experience like no other. But if you have a wealth of books on your iPad, it could become hard to find your way around; thankfully, not only are your iBooks organised into a library that's easy to navigate, but you can also bookmark text so that you can easily find the bit you are looking for among the piles and piles residing on your digital bookshelf.

The ability to highlight text is also a welcome feature. You can even select what colour you want to highlight the text in, which helps when you want to colour code certain bits to signify certain things. This is particularly useful for text book research. In this step-by-step tutorial we will show you how to easily use bookmarks and highlights with iBooks.

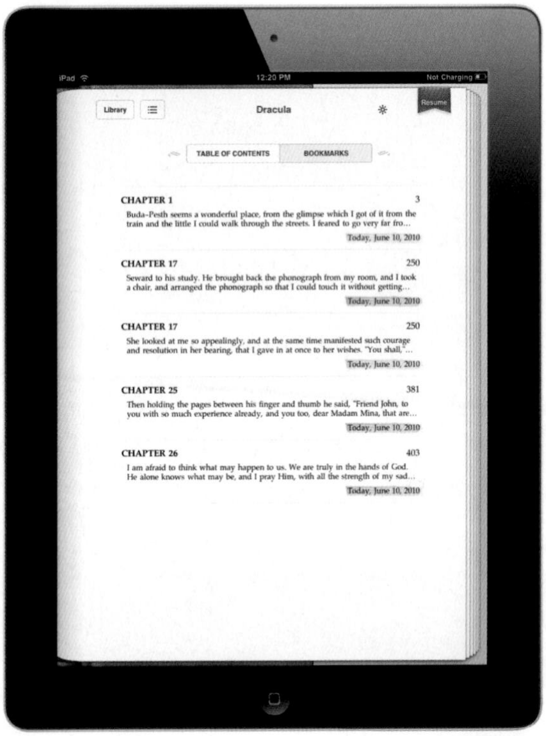

Step-by-step | iBooks Using Bookmarks in iBooks

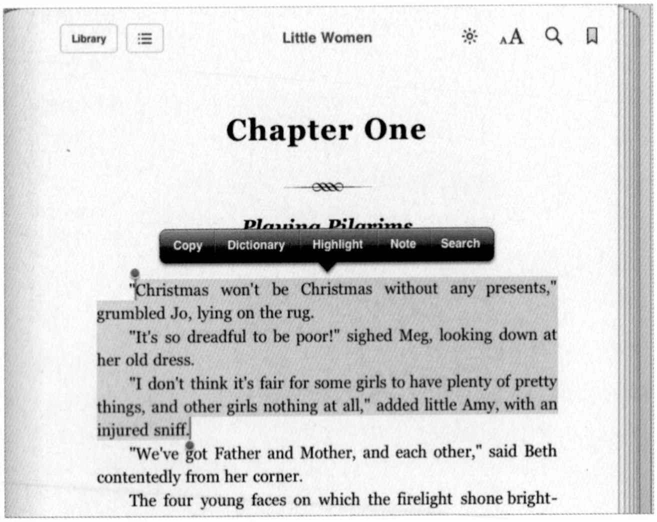

1: Select text to bookmark

Double tap anywhere (or press on a word) on the book to open the Options bar. Move the blue circles to select a region of text that you want to bookmark or highlight. It is similar to the cut-copy-paste mechanism available everywhere in the iOS.

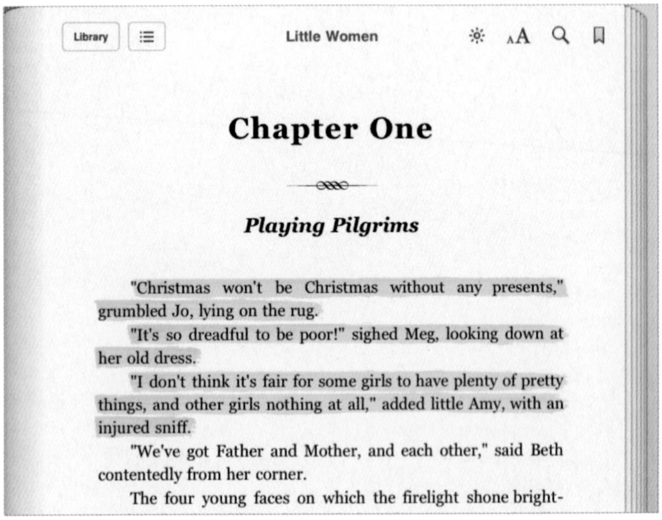

2: Highlight text

When you select text in this way, it will bring up a menu that allows you to copy, search and more. One of the options is Highlight, and all you need to do is select this and you'll be able to clearly find specific bits of text without having to read the whole thing again.

iBooks interface

Having a look inside iBooks

TOC and Bookmarks
Tap on this button to access the Bookmarks and Table of Contents of the current book

Adjust font size
Tapping on this icon in the top right-hand corner allows you to adjust the font size

Search book
Tapping this magnifying glass image allows you to do a full text search on the current book

Bookmark
Tapping this icon allows you to instantly bookmark text

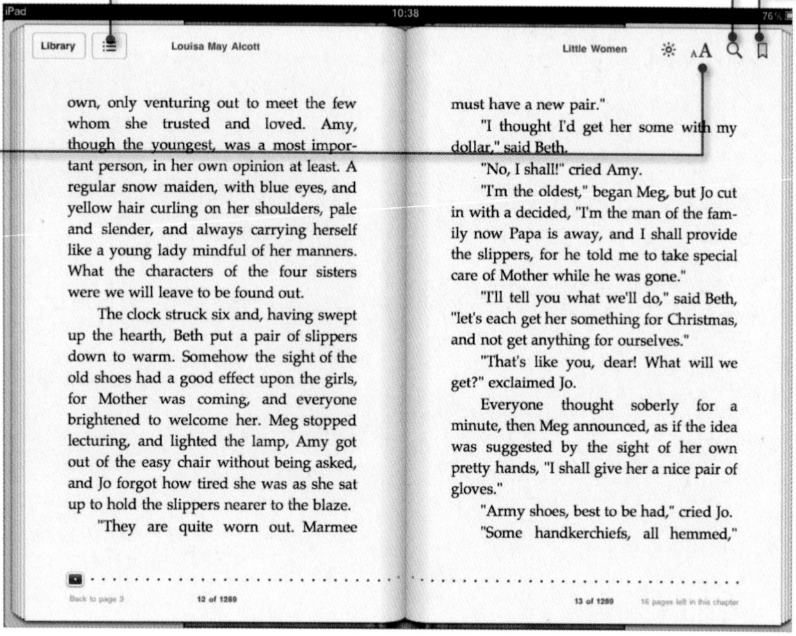

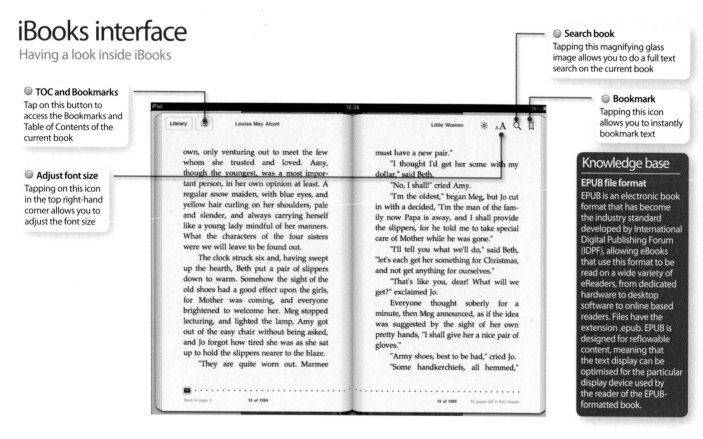

Knowledge base

EPUB file format

EPUB is an electronic book format that has become the industry standard developed by International Digital Publishing Forum (IDPF), allowing eBooks that use this format to be read on a wide variety of eReaders, from dedicated hardware to desktop software to online based readers. Files have the extension .epub. EPUB is designed for reflowable content, meaning that the text display can be optimised for the particular display device used by the reader of the EPUB-formatted book.

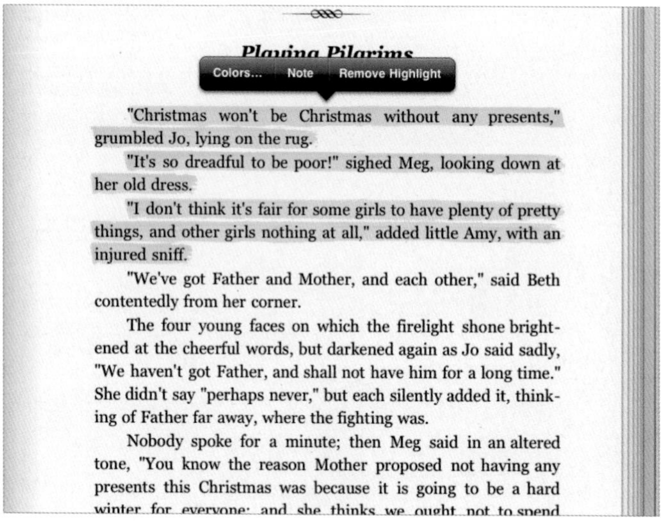

3: Change colour of highlighted text

You can change the colour of highlighted text to organise it better. You can choose from five colours, namely yellow, green, blue, pink and purple. To change the colour, tap on the highlighted text, tap the Colors… option and then select a different colour.

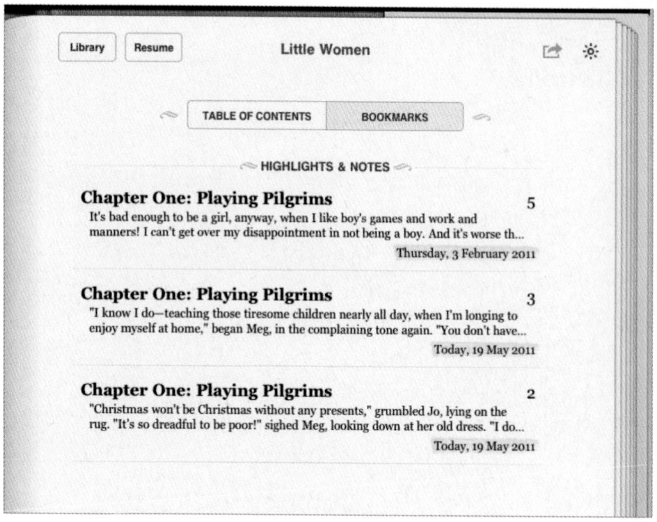

4: Bookmark the selected text/region

Once the text has been highlighted, tap on the bookmark icon found in the top-right of the screen. Selecting the list icon next to the Library button will then take you to the bookmark menu. Tapping on the bookmark you want will take you to the relevant page.

Tutorial: Use Kindle to read eBooks

Build up a library of books on your iPad's Kindle app, so you can read your favourite authors on the go

Task: Read eBooks on your iPad using the Kindle app
Difficulty: Beginner
Time needed: 10 minutes

Before iPads where invented, we had to lug our holiday reading around on slabs of processed dead tree. Printed books (especially chunky hard backs with massive page counts) took up valuable space in our suitcase, and ate into our precious baggage weight allowance to boot.

In these digital days, the Kindle app provides a much more convenient way of storing our holiday (or day to day) reading. As well as enabling us to read electronic books (or eBooks) on the iPad's screen, we can use Kindle to shop for them as well. This saves us the hassle of popping out to the high street bookshop (or having to anxiously wait for the postman to deliver books in time for our holiday's departure date).

Kindle was initially a handheld tablet invented by retail giant Amazon to enable book lovers to read digital copies of books. However, iPad owners can download the free Kindle app and turn their iPad into a Kindle reader with ease (saving them the expense of buying a dedicated digital book reader).

Step-by-step | Kindle Learn how to get eBooks onto your iPad

1: Open Kindle

Download the Kindle app for free from the App Store and install it on your iPad. Tapping on the Kindle icon takes you to the Home screen. This is where your books will be stored. To find some reading material, click on the 'Shop in Kindle Store' button at the top right.

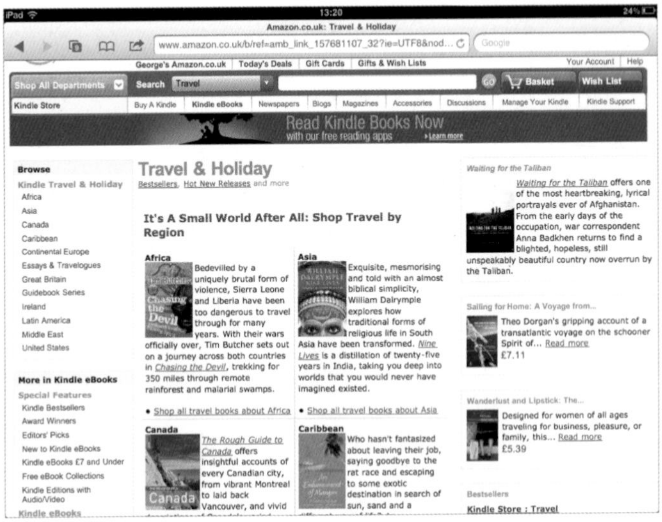

2: Go shopping

The Kindle eBook store is part of the Amazon website, so there are plenty of books to choose from. Peruse one of the featured new books on the Kindle Store's homepage, or browse through your favourite categories by clicking on a link like Travel & Holiday.

Interact with a Kindle eBook

Discover the extra bells and whistles you get from an eBook

Explore bookmarks
Click here to jump to specific notes or bookmarks that you've created. This saves you the hassle of trying to remember where important information is stored in your eBook

Notes and highlight
To help you find a particular bit of text at a later date, hold your finger down on it and drag to make a selection. You can then type in a note or select a highlight colour

Interactive links
As with webpages, links to content in other parts of the eBook are underlined, so you can jump to different chapters or sections of the book in a click. This interactivity gives eBooks a real edge over their paper predecessors

Customise pages
Lost your glasses? No problem! Use this section to create your own big print edition in a click, or you can inverse the text so that you're reading white letters on a black background

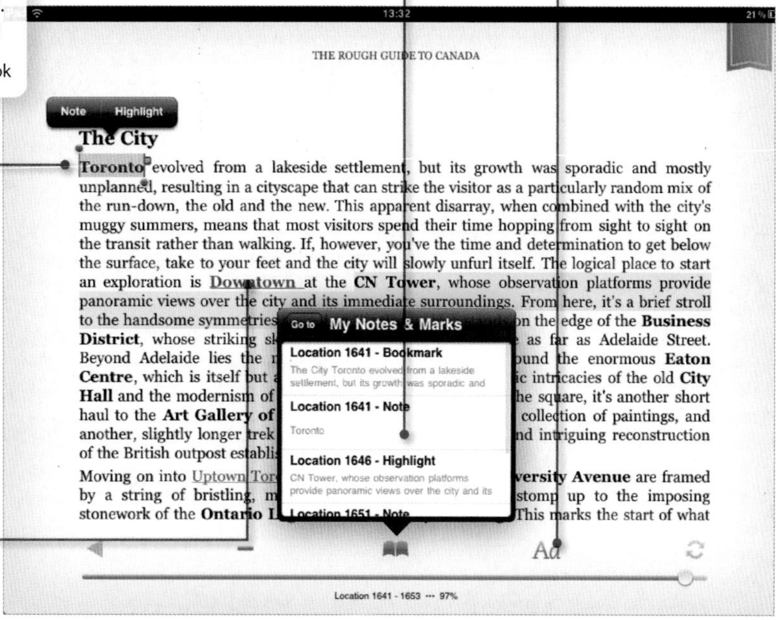

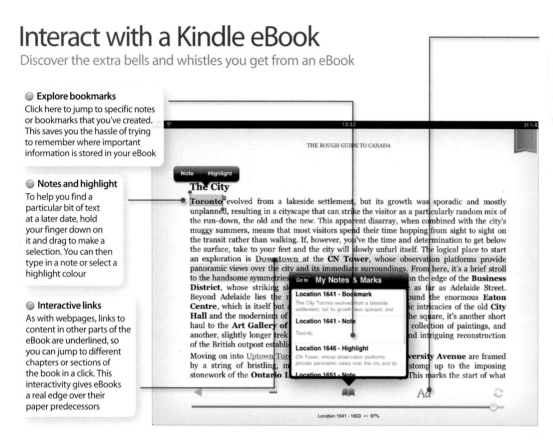

Knowledge base

Fabulous freebies
As well as downloading sample chapters from many new eBooks, you can download entire books for free using the Kindle eBook reader. This is a great way to catch up with the classics of literature. Simply click on the link to the online Kindle store to launch it in Safari, then scroll down to the Free eBook Editions link in the Special Features section. You can then browse through thousands of books in Kindle's Popular Classics range and enjoy adventure tales featuring Conan Doyle's Sherlock Holmes, or chill your spine with the classic work of HP Lovecraft.

3: Download your book

Tap on a thumbnail to discover more about a book, and read customer reviews to help you make an informed choice. If you fancy buying the book tap the 'Buy now with 1-click' button. Alternatively, download a free sample chapter. Make sure you set the 'Deliver to the iPad' option.

4: Start reading

To read a downloaded book, tap on its cover in your Kindle Home screen. Turn pages by tapping the screen (or swiping left or right). You can tap the top-right corner to bookmark a page (instead of creasing down the corner in traditional printed book).

Tutorial: Utilise the iPod app's advanced controls

Once your music starts, how do you alter what you hear? Your iPad has a few hidden controls to help you

Task: Control the iPod app on your iPad

Difficulty: Beginner

Time needed: 10 minutes

So how do you control your music without the click wheel of a traditional iPod? All the controls are obviously touch-based and the interface is designed to only show you what you need at a specific time so that you don't get overwhelmed with a plethora unnecessary options.

Your iPad's standard media playback controls are very straightforward: once a song starts playing you can pause and resume playback, alter the volume or skip to the previous or next song in the list thanks to the buttons at the top of the screen. But there are more controls hidden in the background that allow you to do more than just listen. These allow you to scrub through your track, play the current song over and over again, and even help you create a Genius playlist based on the track you're currently listening to. This tutorial will show you how all of these controls work.

Step-by-step | iPod Learn how to use the advanced controls

1: Looping

Launch the iPod app and select a song. Tap the artwork to reveal controls, then tap on the leftmost button at the top to start looping songs.

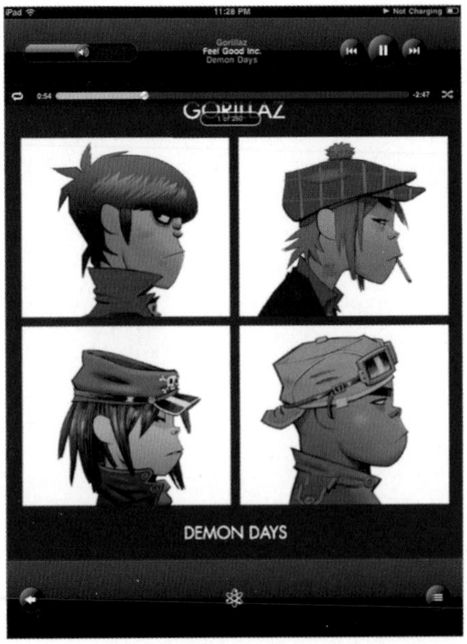

2: Randomness

If you'd rather not know what the next song is going to be, tap the symbol on the opposite side. Doing so will shuffle your songs from this point on.

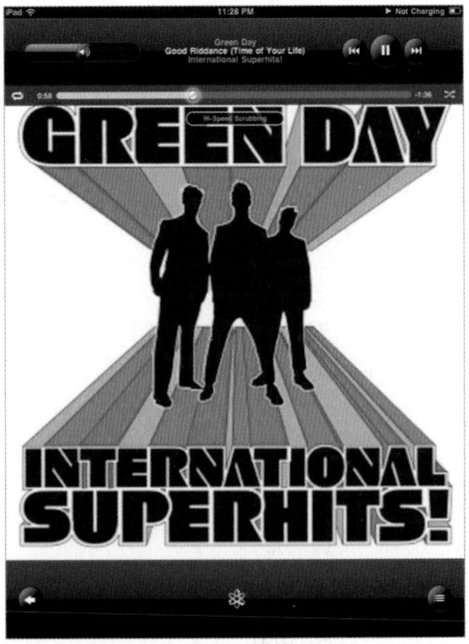

3: Scrubbing

The line at the top, between these buttons, represents the track's duration. Drag the circle that travels along it to skip through the song.

Making more of the music

The iPod app controls dissected for you

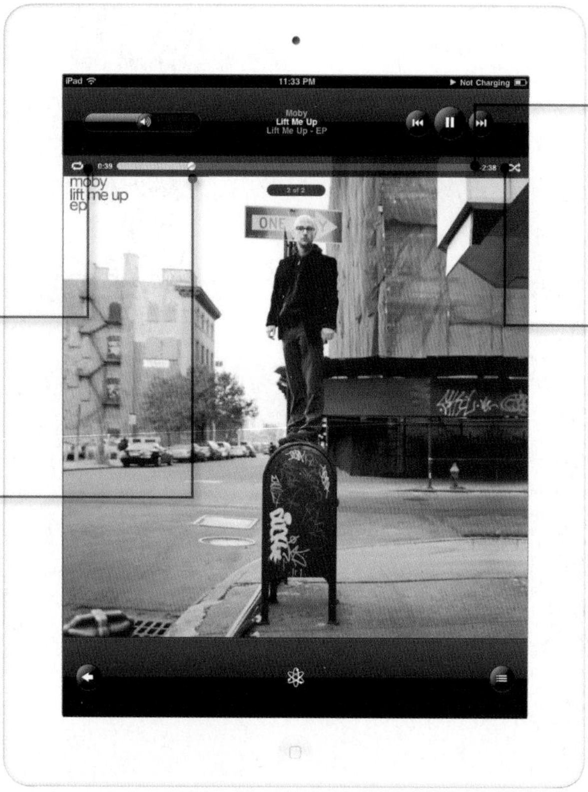

Play it again

If you like the song you're hearing so much you'd like to listen to it again, tap this button twice to loop playback for that song only

Music is circular

This little circle represents the playhead and shows you where you are within your song, using the bar it travels on as the overall duration of your track

Time gentlemen, please

These numbers tell you how much time has elapsed since the song started playing (on the left), and how much time remains (on the right)

Tap to cancel

Once a button is selected, it turns blue to indicate that the option is now active. To turn it off again, tap on it once more

Knowledge base

Precise scrubbing

Scrubbing left or right to move to a different section of your track can feel very imprecise. However, there's a very exact way to control your experience: tap on the circle that represents your current location along the track then move your finger down. The further down you go the more precise you'll scrub as you move left or right.

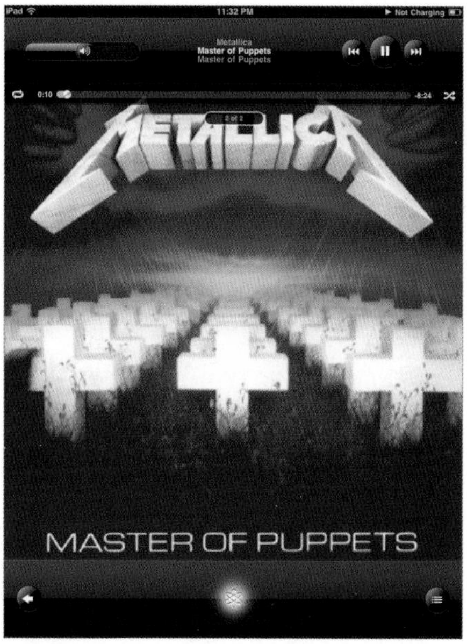

4: Genius

Should you want your iPad to provide you with tracks that go well with the current song, tap the middle button at the bottom to initiate Genius.

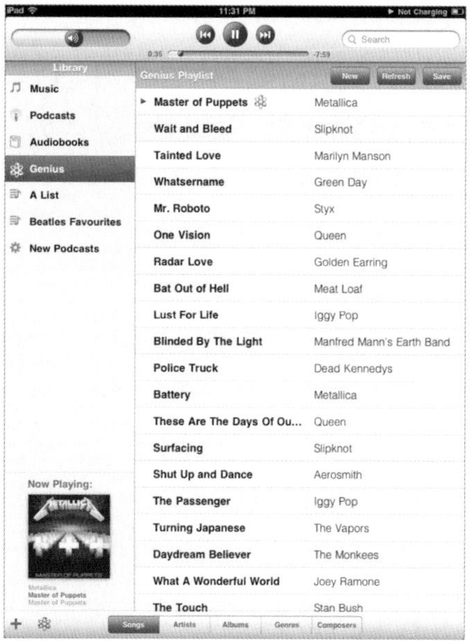

5: Playlist

A new playlist is automatically created for you with a selection of songs from your library. If you're not happy with the results, tap on the Refresh button.

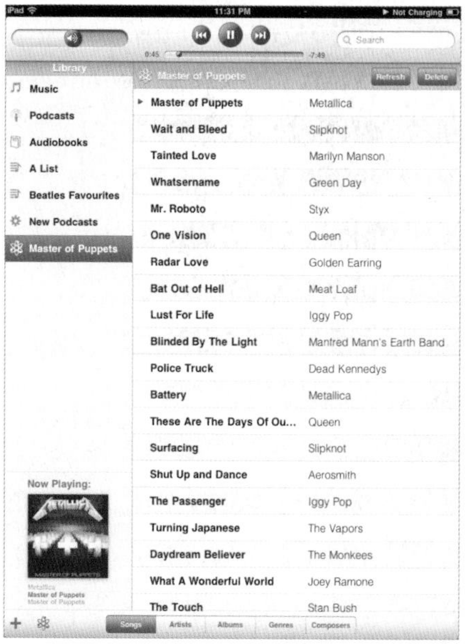

6: Saved

Tap on Save, to turn the selection into a playlist that you can access at any time. It will bear the name of the original song used to create it.

Tutorial: Create Genius playlists on the iPad

Making your own special playlist is great but by letting the iPad do all the hard work you can get some really cool musical mixes

Task: Make and save Genius playlists quickly and easily

Difficulty: Beginner

Time needed: 2 minutes

Keeping track of all the music on your iPad can be a bit of a pain. It's surprising how much music you can fit onto even just the 16GB version. With all that music it makes sense to keep track of it all and to create playlists.

Of course, listening to whole albums is fine, but then we all have our favourite tracks and like to hear them more often than others. Creating playlists manually is a great way of doing this, but it's time consuming and if you don't keep them updated they soon get tiresome.

You could just stick your whole music collection on random, but even this throws up issues like those hidden tracks or fillers that ruin a smooth transition, or the odd song you're bored of hearing. The best solution may well be Genius mixes.

Apple has created a tool that lets you select a track and automatically create a playlist of music that complements each other. It's a great way of keeping the music going around a certain theme and in the main it's incredibly reliable.

Step-by-step | iPod Make Genius mixes on the iPad

1: Open iPod

Fire up your iPad and then launch the iPod applications. Tap on Music at the top-left of the Library column. Scroll down until you find a song that would make a good foundation for your playlist; this will be the basis of your list so make sure you pick something good!

2: Make a Genius mix

When you have found a track that most suits your current mood, tap on it to start it playing. When you're ready, tap on the Genius symbol that you can find tucked away at the bottom-left of the screen, next to the + symbol.

Playlists on the iPad

Create your own Genius playlist

Library
All of your playlists are shown here and each Genius mix is named after the first track you use to make the playlist. To start your playlist tap on it and then on the top track

Delete a playlist
If you get bored with a playlist or have too many to comfortably use your library then you can delete it very easily. Tap on the playlist and then tap on Delete to get rid of the Genius mix

Knowledge base

Genius mixes
Contrary to what you might think, Genius mixes aren't just randomly thrown together and Apple is working behind the scenes to make the music fit. iTunes assesses your music collection and from an extensive database puts together the tracks that go best

Genius mix
The Genius mix icon can be used at any time to make a new playlist, even from existing Genius playlists. Simply tap it to create a playlist based on the currently playing track

Views
To view your music collection in any of five different views simply tap on one of the five options. Making Genius mixes is simpler if you view your music as Songs, however

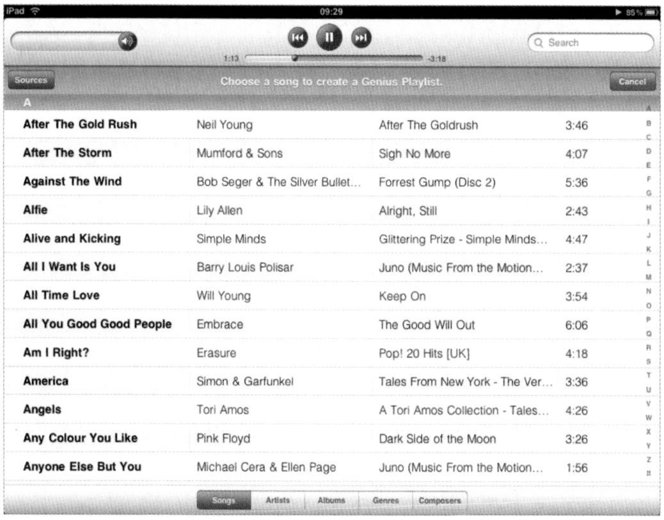

3: Asses your mix

You'll see that a new playlist called Genius has been added to your library and that songs have already been populated to it. If you don't like the tracks simply tap on Refresh, or if you'd prefer to choose a different starting point tap New.

4: Save your playlist

Once you are happy with the tracks that are on your playlist all you have to do is click on Save. The playlist that was called Genius is now renamed to the starting track of your Genius mix. By default a Genius mix contains 25 tracks.

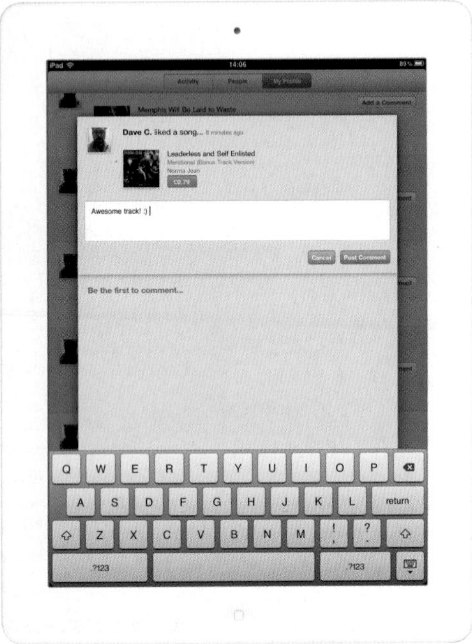

Tutorial: Set up a Ping account in iTunes

Open up the social aspects of iTunes with Ping, Apple's expansive music network. Follow artists, compare music tastes and more

Task: Create a Ping account and start using its features

Difficulty: Intermediate

Time needed: 10 minutes

Ping is designed to give iTunes a personal touch by opening it up to social networking. It's a simple service to set up initially and once your account is created, it can be used to recommend your favourite tracks to the masses. But on the other hand, it allows for friend recommendations as well, helping you find new artists and tracks attuned to your favourite genres.

In iTunes you can hover over a track on your playlist and use the 'Ping' drop-down to 'like' a song. The more songs you like, the better the automated recommendation service becomes at flagging up songs that may be of interest to you. Better yet, songs that have been recommended to you can be bought straight from the alert via iTunes.

You can even go beyond iTunes by syncing your Twitter feed, which automatically posts recommendations to your feed for all to see. Although this does give rise to a large amount of Ping spam on your feed, so beware of how often you do this.

Ping in a nutshell

How to get the most out of Ping

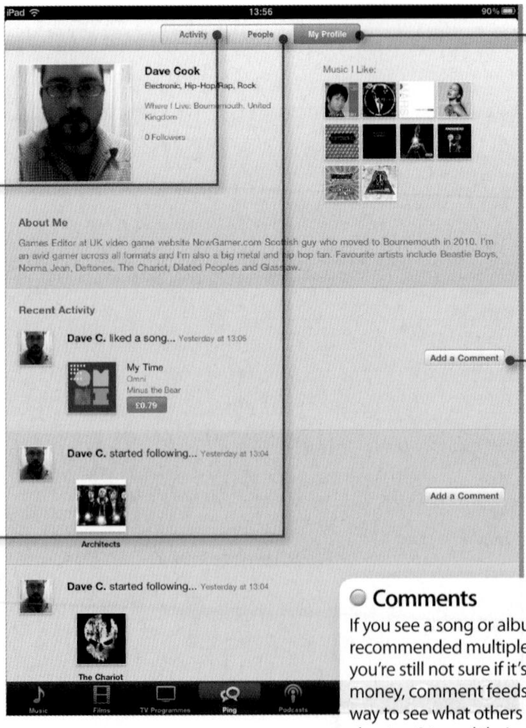

Activity tab

The Activity tab shows all of your friends' recommendations and actions. This is updated every time something new happens. It also lets you buy songs that friends recommend straight from the feed

People tab

The People tab shows you all of your friends' activity in one stream, or all of the activity from bands you follow. It's comparable to Twitter's streaming list format, and like the Activity tab it is updated every time something new happens

My Profile

This tab displays all of your recent activity including your recommendations, your bio, who you are following and more. It even lets you buy recommended tracks straight from the feed

Comments

If you see a song or album recommended multiple times but you're still not sure if it's worth the money, comment feeds are a good way to see what others are saying about artists and their music

Knowledge base

Music Networks

While it is a neat concept, Ping does have a few competitors out there already. Both Last.fm and Spotify house integrated social networking options that are easy to use and help foster a sense of community. All three are fundamentally sound, but each of them has unique features that warrant checking them all out. You're literally spoiled for choice.

Step-by-step | Ping Create your Ping account

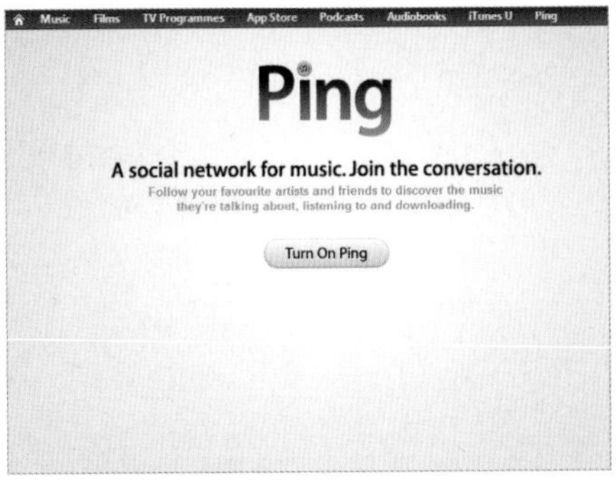

1: Turn on Ping

On your home computer or laptop, sign into iTunes and click 'Ping' on the left menu. The following menu within the iTunes Store will ask you to turn on Ping. Click the button to get started with the registration process.

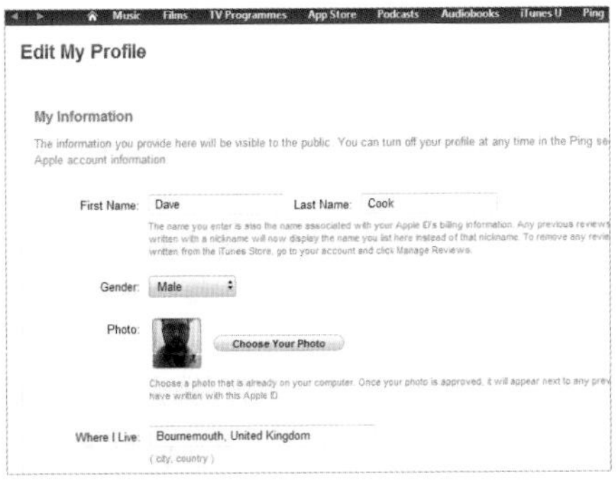

2: Register your account

A few pages of registration fields will follow, together with the option to upload your profile picture. Simply fill out the required fields and enter your biography to give your Ping profile more of a personal touch.

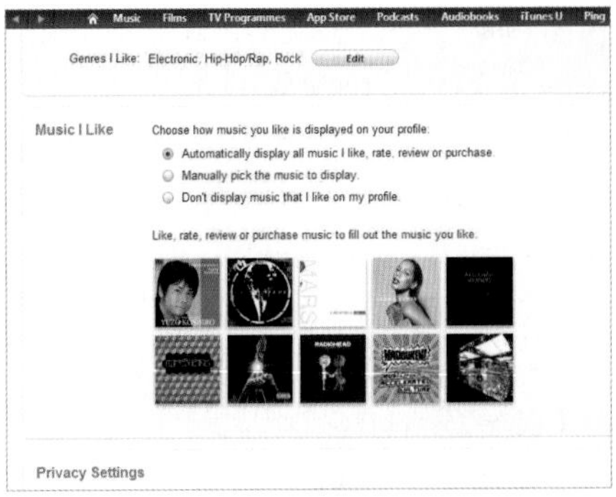

3: Set your tastes

You can select up to three favourite music genres when you are setting up your account. This may seem a bit trivial, but it actually helps Ping send you artist recommendations based on the music that you like.

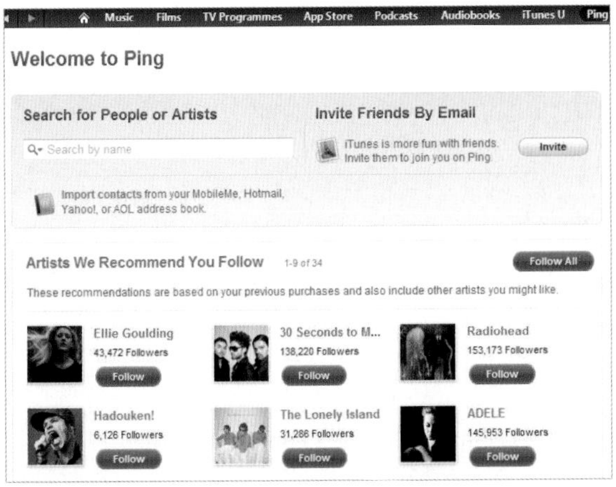

4: Make it social

Ping lets you sync to your email contacts and Twitter feed so you can recommend tracks, compare tastes and more. Simply trawl your contacts automatically or add people manually to get rolling.

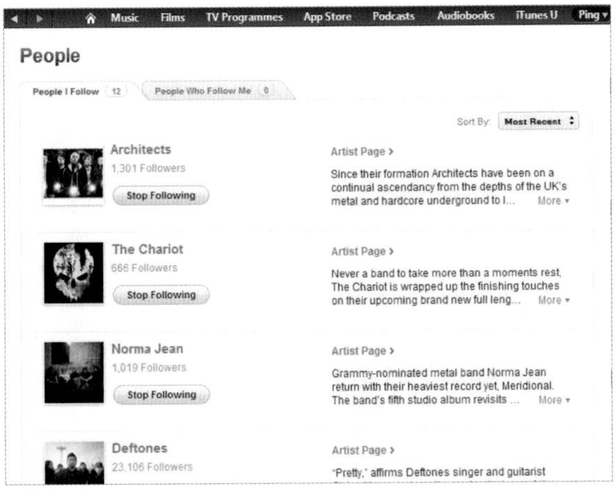

5: Follow some artists

Networking with other users aside, you can also follow bands to keep abreast of their new releases, latest news, tour dates and much more. Hit the 'People' tab to keep an eye on artists you follow, or use the search bar to find new artists.

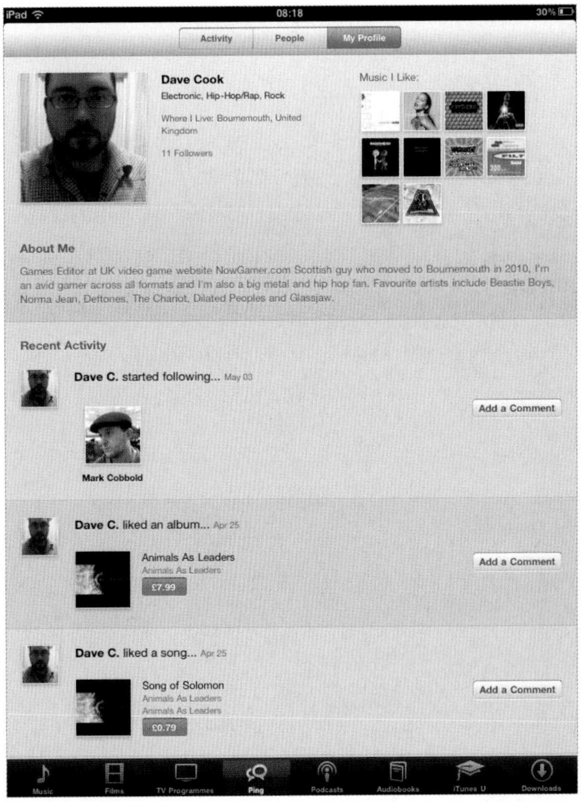

6: Ping on iPad

You're all set! Now go on to your iPad, fire up iTunes and hit the Ping tab to start using the same account on the move. All of the features are the same, so there is no trimming back on the iPad version whatsoever.

Tutorial: Watch videos using Home Sharing

With the most recent version of iTunes and iOS, you can now view movies and TV shows on your iPad that you have purchased in iTunes on your PC or Mac

Task: Watch a video on your iPad currently on your PC or Mac in iTunes

Difficulty: Beginner

Time needed: 3 minutes

Have you ever wanted to use your iPad to view a movie you have on iTunes on your computer? With the recent iOS 4.3 update, your iPad has the ability to use the iTunes Home Sharing feature, which allows you to connect your iPad to your PC or Mac iTunes software. You can then view movies and TV shows that you have downloaded to your computer's iTunes on any iPads in your local network.

Your iPad can wirelessly connect to your computer's iTunes program, allowing you to browse videos currently downloaded to your computer. You don't need to download these movies or TV shows to your iPad. Instead, when you view a video, your computer streams the movie to your iPad. Keep in mind that you can share your purchased movies and TV shows, but you cannot share movie rentals.

This tutorial takes you through turning on Home Sharing and connecting to your computer's iTunes with your iPad.

Step-by-step | Home Sharing Share movies with your iPad

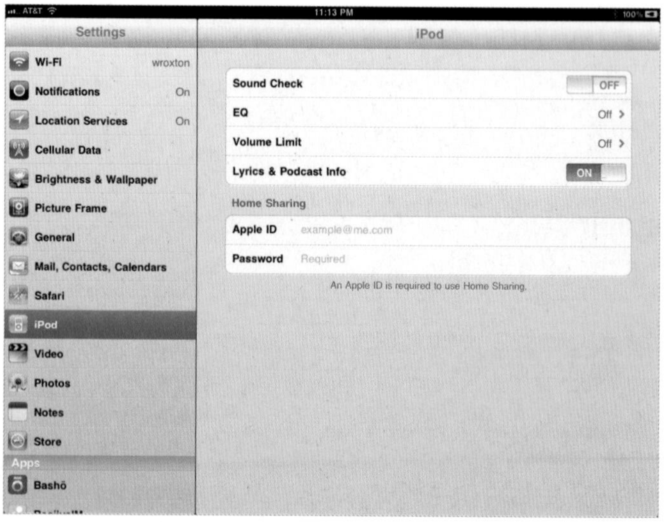

1: Activate Home Sharing

On the PC or Mac with the videos you wish to share, start the iTunes application. Choose Advanced>Turn on Home Sharing. Enter your Apple ID and Password and click Create Home Share. Leave iTunes running.

2: Change iPad Settings

Open Settings on your iPad. Tap the iPod icon on the left. Under Home Sharing, enter the same Apple ID and password that you entered in iTunes in the last step. This allows your iPad to connect with your iTunes.

Shared iTunes Library

Navigating a shared library in the Videos app

Shared button
Tap the Shared button to get back to the main Shared screen. The Shared screen displays all the iTunes video libraries your iPad can currently access

Movies
The Movies button on the shared library screen displays all movies that have been purchased and downloaded to iTunes on your PC or Mac. Rental movies cannot be shared and will not be visible

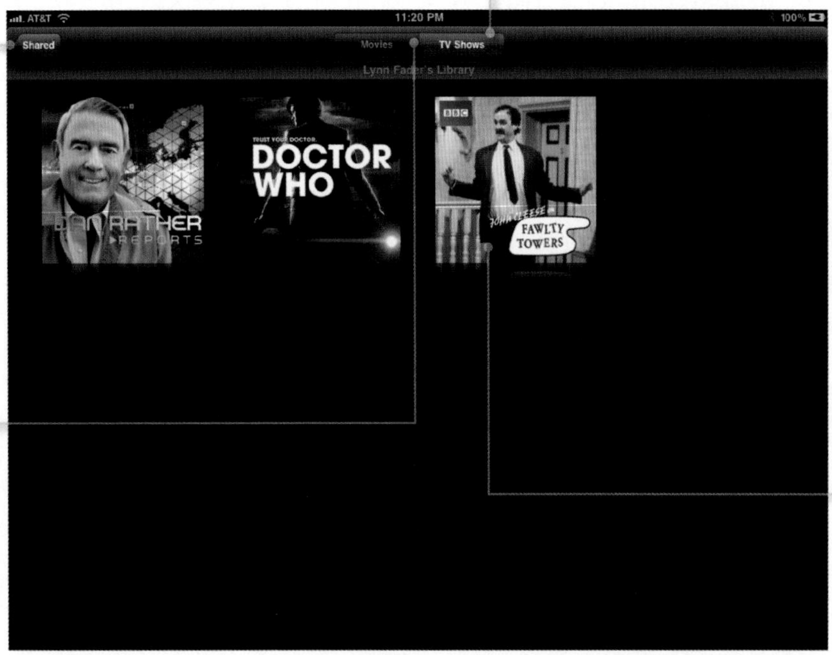

TV Shows
Tap TV Shows to view thumbnails for series. If there are multiple episodes for the same show in your library, they will all appear in a list under a single thumbnail

Knowledge base

iTunes authorisation
Apple keeps track of how many computers are allowed to play or share a given purchased video. When you purchase iTunes videos, you can share the purchased videos from a maximum of five authorised computers. You may have to authorise your iTunes when you turn on Home Sharing for the first time, which will count towards your five authorisations.

Thumbnail poster
Movies and TV shows appear as thumbnail posters. To begin streaming the video from your computer's iTunes, tap the thumbnail. This will display a detail screen

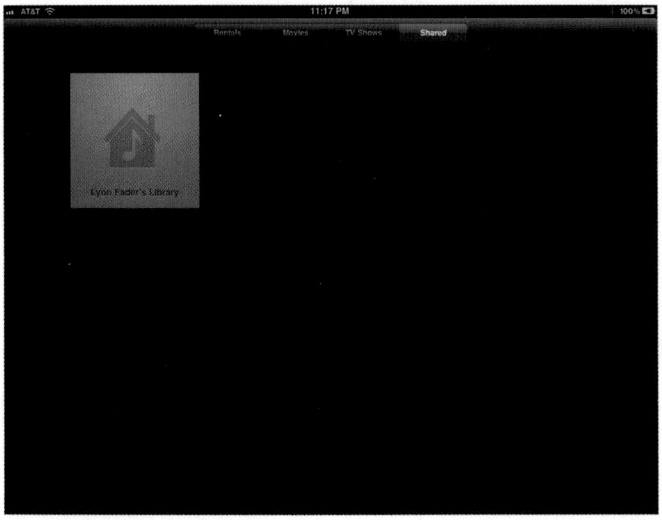

3: Open videos

Close the iPad's Settings and tap on the Videos app. You should see the Shared button on the top right of the screen. When you tap this, you see an icon for your computer's shared iTunes video library.

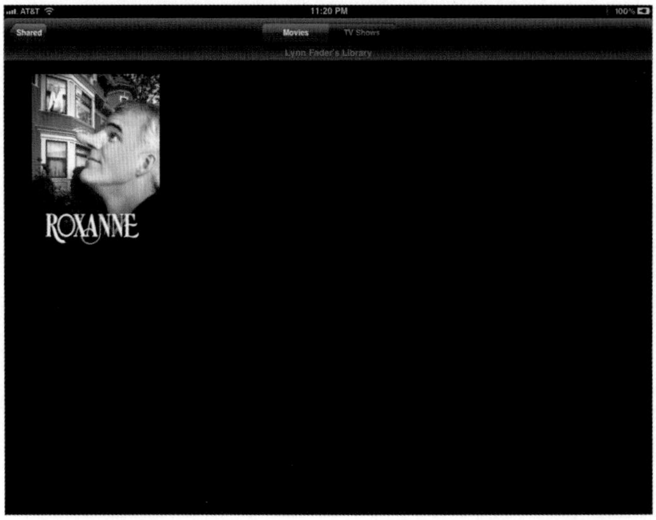

4: Play a video

Tap the iTunes library to view available videos. If you have both movies and TV shows in your iTunes library, you will see two buttons at the top allowing you to switch between them. Tap the video you wish to view.

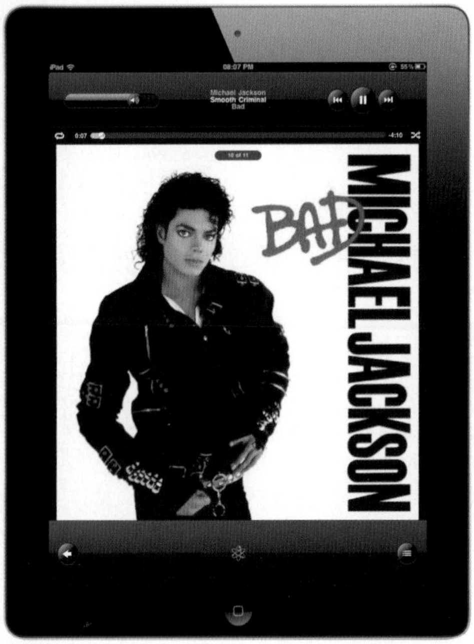

Tutorial: Use Apple's Remote to control iTunes

Through the magic of Wi-Fi, this free app from Apple allows you to control iTunes and Apple TV from your iPad without leaving the sofa

Task: Turn your iPad into a remote control

Difficulty: Beginner

Time needed: 10 minutes

Remote transforms your iPad into a wireless remote control for iTunes and Apple TV, enabling you to choose songs and playlists as if you were sat at your computer. It's especially useful if you have a remote set of speakers set up via AirTunes. As long as your iPad is on the same Wi-Fi network as your computer, you can use Remote to control what's playing on your iTunes library on the Mac upstairs in the bedroom, for example, while you listen to speakers connected to an AirPort Express in the living room. The app works equally well with the Apple TV, too, enabling you to search for movies or TV episodes via the pop-up keyboard, pause, fast-forward and rewind.

Search for 'Remote' in the App Store and download and install the app as normal. Here we'll illustrate how to set the app up to control your Mac's iTunes library.

Step-by-step | Remote Take control of iTunes

1: Scan the network

Launch the Remote app and select the Add an iTunes Library option. This will search for iTunes libraries on the local network.

2: Home Sharing

Alternatively, Home Sharing will find other devices using the feature, so if your computers are networked already you can save a bit of effort.

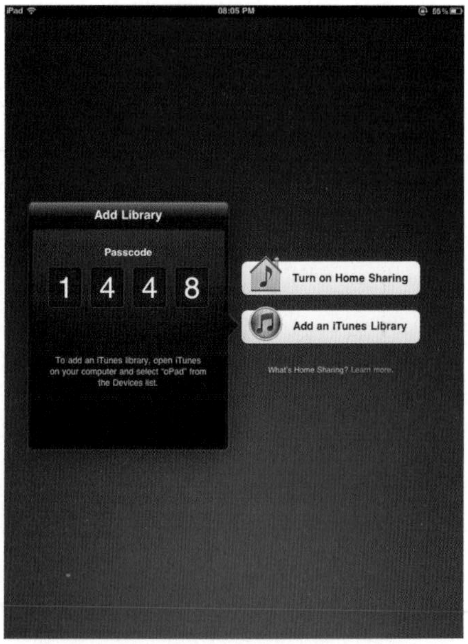

3: Get passcode

If you're adding a library manually, a four-digit passcode is displayed on your iPad's screen. This will be used to link it to the computer.

Navigate iTunes

Take control of the music you listen to

Genius

The app allows you to access the Genius Mixes portion of iTunes, so you can automatically construct playlists made up of similar types of tune

Artistic endeavour

Tap the Artists tab to search for tracks by an alphabetical list of artists

Playlist paradise

All of your iTunes playlists are accessible from within the app, and you can even make new ones by tapping the + button

Now Playing

Tapping the Now Playing button will make the current album art full screen and give you the same controls as the iPod app

Knowledge base

Home Sharing

Home Sharing is a method of syncing purchases from the iTunes Store between multiple computers in your household (see page 120). The machines all have to be on the same Wi-Fi network for it to work, and you can set it to sync automatically or just to transfer files manually between computers. Remote will automatically find the iTunes libraries and Apple TVs that have Home Sharing turned on.

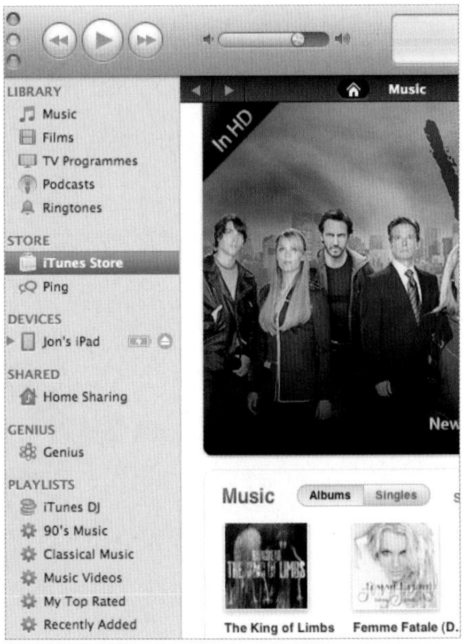

4: Choose device

On the computer you want to control, open iTunes and select 'iPad' from the devices list on the library panel on the left-hand side.

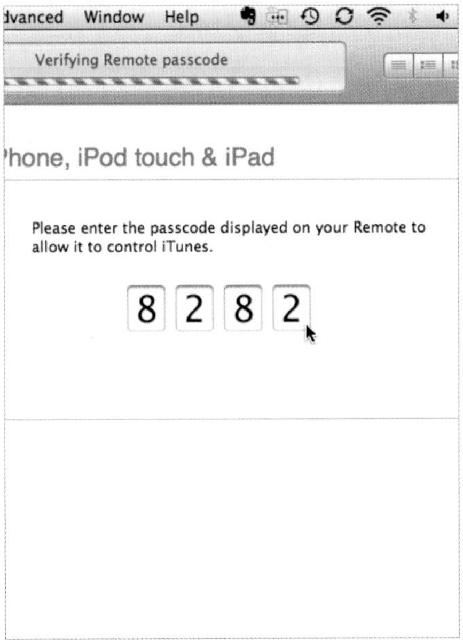

5: Enter passcode

Enter the passcode displayed on your iPad's screen into the boxes on your computer's screen to sync up both devices.

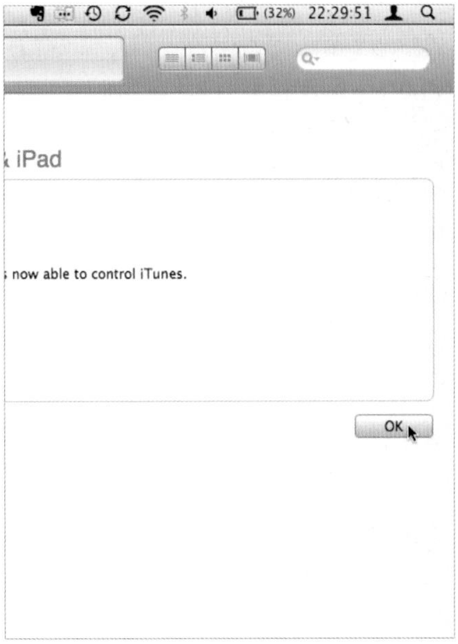

6: Take control

Click OK once the code has been verified. You now have full control of iTunes from your iPad, anywhere within Wi-Fi range.

Tutorial: Stream audio and video

You can turn your iPad into your home media hub by streaming audio and video to other devices in your house. Here's how…

Task: Stream media to your iPad

Difficulty: Intermediate

Time needed: 15 minutes

While it's really great to be able to carry your favourite films, photos and music with you on your iPad, let's be honest: the joy is a personal one, as the iPad's speakers and screen are hardly built for sharing with a wider audience. Or at least it would be without the iPad's killer feature: AirPlay. It allows you to stream your iPad's music, video and images wirelessly across a local network.

The only extra you need to use AirPlay is a compatible device to stream your iPad's content to. This could be an Apple TV, AirPlay-enabled stereo speakers – of which there are several available on the market – or an AirPort Express wireless base station, which comes with a socket that enables it to connect your iPad to a home stereo system. A button tap is all it takes to free your audio and video and watch films on the big screen, or listen to your music collection on your best speakers. No wires required. We take you through how to get connected and streaming.

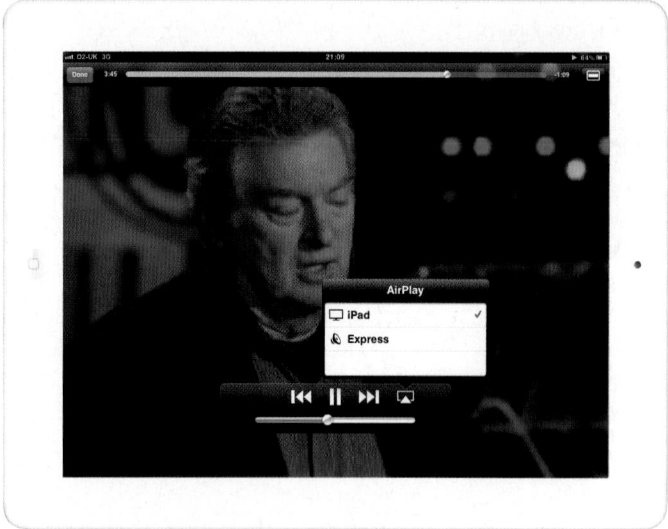

Step-by-step | AirPlay Set up your AirPlay connection

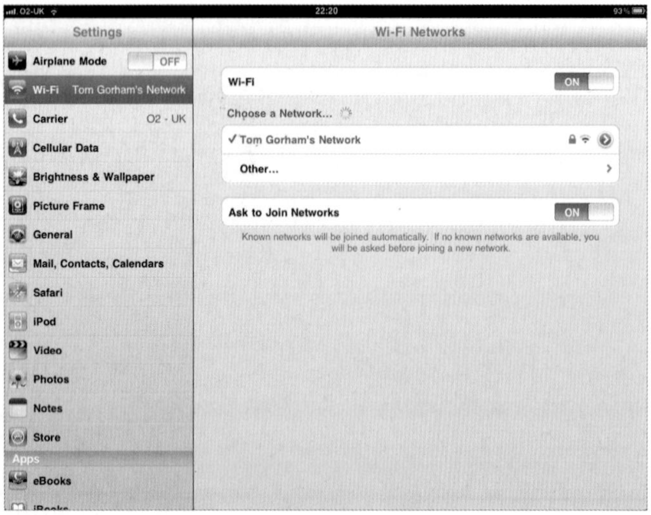

1: Check wireless settings

AirPlay works over a local Wi-Fi network, so check that your iPad and the device you're streaming to are on the same network. You can set this up on the iPad by tapping Settings and choosing the Wi-Fi option. If your network is secured, you will need to enter its password.

2: Open the media

When your devices are properly connected, start playing the media on the iPad that you want to stream to another device. When you play a movie or a song on your iPad tap the AirPlay icon (a hollow rectangle with a solid triangle) that appears on the media controller.

AirPlay on the iPad in action

AirPlay is an impressive technology, but it's pretty simple to use

Audio or video?
The speaker icon here indicates that only audio will be streamed to the external device. If you see a TV icon instead, video will also be streamed over AirPlay

AirPlay's icon
The AirPlay icon itself is just a simple box with an arrow. The same icon appears on all iOS devices, and in iTunes on the Mac and PC too

More than video
It isn't just the media itself that can be sent over AirPlay. Song titles, artists, album names and artwork can all appear on AirPlay-enabled speakers that have graphical displays

Knowledge base

AirPlay everywhere

AirPlay is a clever wireless technology, the usefulness of which isn't restricted to the iPad. In fact, any iOS device with iOS 4.2 or later installed on it can use AirPlay – and so can the iTunes application on Mac OSX. AirPlay features are also present in Apple's free Remote iPad and iPhone app, which allows you to control an iTunes library from an iOS device. But not all video can be streamed using AirPlay. At the time of writing, video streaming from the iPad is limited to media streamed from Apple's own apps – other apps can only stream audio.

3: Choose your output

When you tap the AirPlay icon, a pop-up menu will appear, offering a choice of AirPlay-enabled devices. The currently selected output has a tick next to it, and it should be your iPad. Tap the name of the device you want to stream to.

4: Streaming in action

Unfortunately, you're not able to watch the same video in two places at once. Once you have selected another output device from the list, the video or audio is sent there within a couple of seconds. The iPad's screen will go blank!

Tutorial: Set up a Games Center account

We show you how to enter into a world of fun games, fierce competition and social gaming with Game Center

Task: Create a user account and get started with Game Center

Difficulty: Intermediate

Time needed: 10 minutes

Like Open Feint before it, Apple's Game Center is a multi-purpose gaming service that gives users a platform to befriend other gamers, engage in multiplayer, compete for online leaderboard supremacy and earn unlockable achievements. It comes preloaded on devices with iOS 4 and above installed, and it significantly enhances your iPad as a gaming platform.

Once you follow the initial set-up instructions, there is a wealth of options available to you. From the top menu you can clearly see your friend, game and achievement counters, while the bottom tab bar lets you access Game Center's menus. 'Games' is the most in-depth, displaying all of your Game Center-enabled games, as well as your global ranking on the online leaderboards. Within each game's menu, you can also see how many achievements you have unlocked, get details on locked achievements and recommend the app to a friend. It's a solid service that brings together the best games available on one dedicated platform.

Step-by-step | Game Center Set up your new account

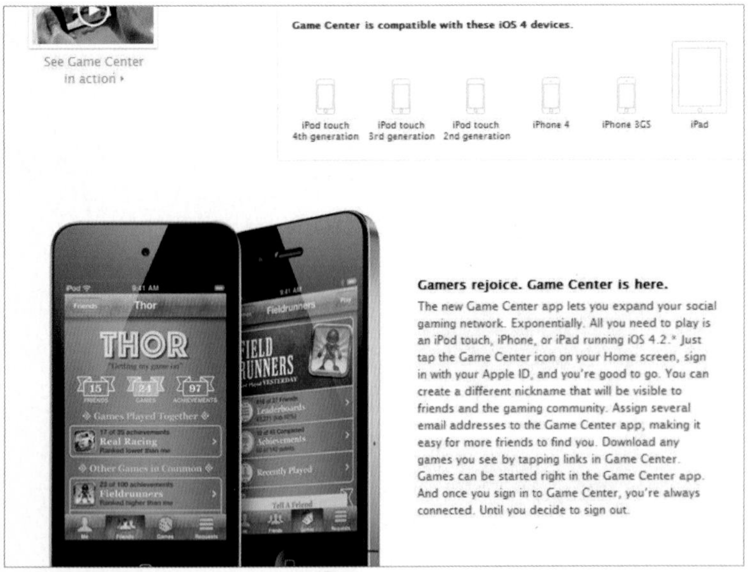
See Game Center in action ›
Game Center is compatible with these iOS 4 devices.
iPod touch 4th generation
iPod touch 3rd generation
iPod touch 2nd generation
iPhone 4
iPhone 3GS
iPad
Gamers rejoice. Game Center is here.
The new Game Center app lets you expand your social gaming network. Exponentially. All you need to play is an iPod touch, iPhone, or iPad running iOS 4.2.* Just tap the Game Center icon on your Home screen, sign in with your Apple ID, and you're good to go. You can create a different nickname that will be visible to friends and the gaming community. Assign several email addresses to the Game Center app, making it easy for more friends to find you. Download any games you see by tapping links in Game Center. Games can be started right in the Game Center app. And once you sign in to Game Center, you're always connected. Until you decide to sign out.

1: Get updated

Game Center runs on iPads running iOS 4 and above. It's unlikely your device will be running anything less, but it always pays to ensure your iPad is running the latest firmware available. Hook it up to iTunes and download any new updates before proceeding.

2: Open an account

Once in Game Center, tap the 'Create New Account' option. The app will ask you to input your location and date of birth, as well as accepting the terms and conditions. This is straightforward, but the next step requires a bit of thought.

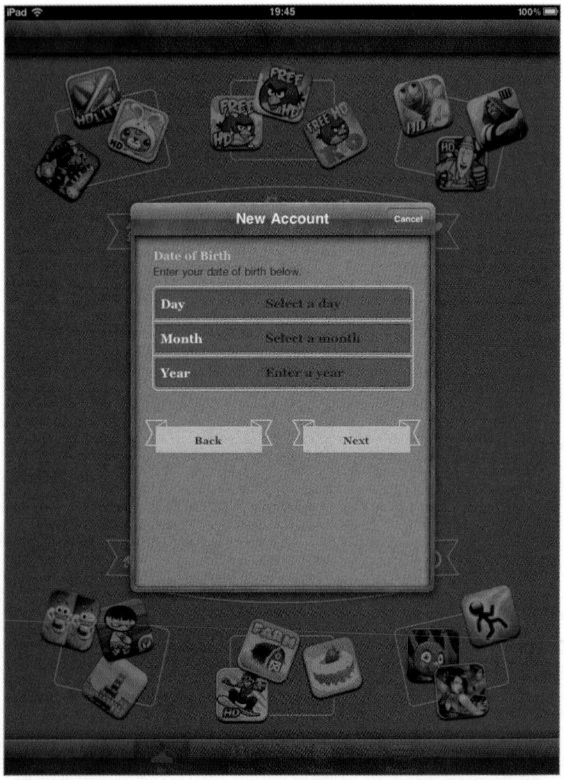

Welcome to Game Center

Enter a world of fun and friends

Top Game Center games
Promoted or top-selling apps will refresh along the top and bottom of Game Center's top menu. You can tap app icons to be taken to their respective iTunes pages to buy them

The Games tab
Tapping 'Games' will bring up an overview of all your Games Center-enabled apps. Here, you can view achievements, online leaderboard rank, and recommend the app to friends

Your Friends list
Tapping 'Friends' will bring up a list of your connected friends, together with their achievements and recent games. In order for them to appear here, you must accept their friend request

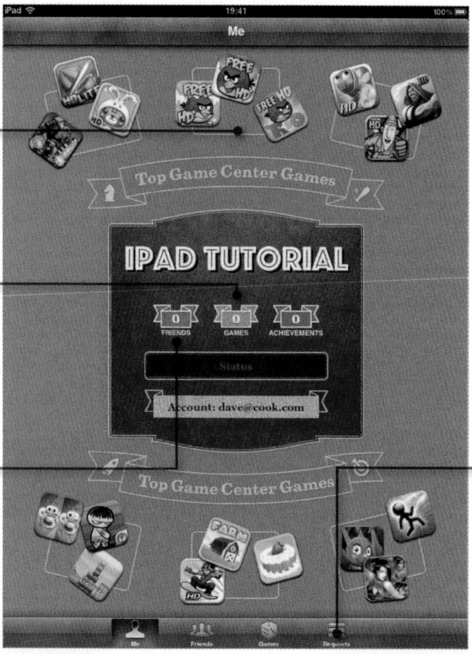

Requests list
The 'Requests' tab houses your pending friends requests. You can also send out requests if you know the email address tethered to a person's Apple ID. Once a request is accepted, the person is instantly added to your list

Knowledge base

Rival Platforms
Just like the console gaming world, iTunes plays host to two competing game platforms – Open Feint and Game Center – both vying for a place as the best gaming format the iOS has to offer. Both services have a wealth of superb features, such as Game Center's social features and Open Feint's free game deals. Both are well worth trying.

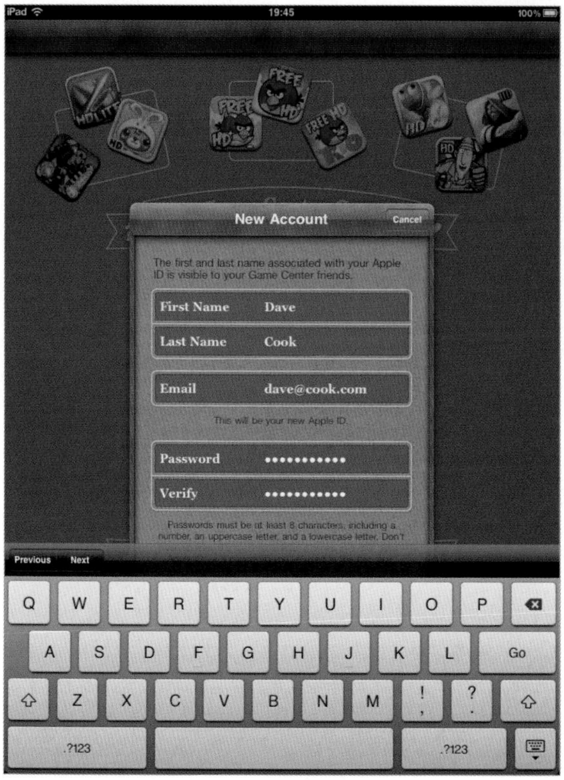

3: Register with iTunes

On the next page, you will be asked to input more data. Entering the email address associated with your existing Apple ID will automatically add your Game Center-enabled apps to the library. Otherwise, enter an unassociated email address to start from scratch.

4: Start playing today

Once your details have been entered, the app will return to the top menu. In the 'Games' tab you can get your account started properly by tapping 'Find Game Center Games'. This will take you straight to iTunes so you can start building your library.

Tutorial: Utilise settings in GarageBand to record a track

Recording in GarageBand is even easier when you understand the tools and settings available to help capture a perfect take

Task: Make recording easier by utilising the many settings in GarageBand

Difficulty: Intermediate

Time needed: 10 minutes

GarageBand lets you record both MIDI and audio, and each serves a different purpose. MIDI is a form of musical information that's widely used in music technology, and involves telling software which notes to play back, in what order, how hard and so on. MIDI in GarageBand is recorded by creating a software instrument and then tapping the relevant parts of the screen to enter notes at specific points. Interestingly you can also connect certain models of USB MIDI keyboard via the camera connection kit and play notes in using this.

Your performances might not be perfect, and that's where quantization comes in. Quantization is when the software pulls the notes into the correct timing using a grid that you specify. When it comes to recording sound, GarageBand can use your iPad's built-in mic or a specialised audio attachment like IK Multimedia's iRig, which has a special guitar or mic input. We show you how to make use of the settings while recording.

Step-by-step | GarageBand Exploring GarageBand's settings

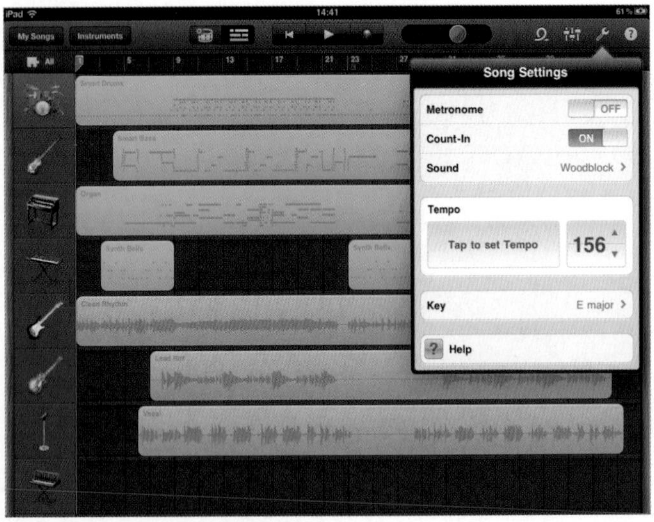

1: Open the Settings

Click on the spanner icon to open the Settings window. Turn the metronome on if you want to have a click track during recording, which is great for programming beats in the correct time. Also activate the count in to give you a run-up before recording.

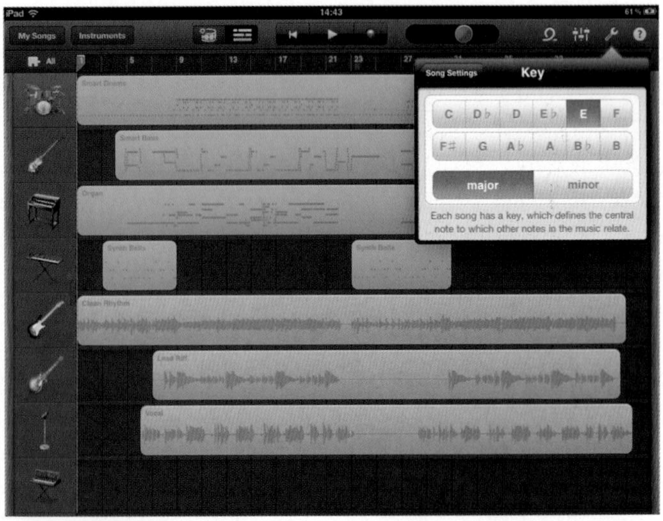

2: Set the tempo

In the Tempo section you can choose the speed of the track by using the numerical field or by tapping the Tap box to set your own speed. Use the Key section to set the root key of the song – just tap on the key you require.

Recording audio in GarageBand

Using the Audio Recorder you can set up and record sound from a mic, guitar or any other source…

Noise Gate
Use the Noise Gate function to cut off any sound that falls below a certain threshold. This is useful for making sure that when you pause between singing lines of a song, for example, room noise is not accidentally recorded

Audio recorder presets
You can choose presets for the Audio Recorder module, such as small or large room, telephone line or even loudhailer. These provide quick and easy ways to affect the sound of the track to suit your needs

Settings menus
Use the global and per-track settings boxes to change the fundamental characteristics of the song – its tempo, key and the effects applied to tracks, as well as using a click track and quantizing

Knowledge base

Audio interfacing
The iPad can record through its built-in mic but to record proper guitar, bass or vocals you will need a proper interface, such as IK Multimedia's iRig or the upcoming Alesis StudioDock. These provide professional level audio interfacing and microphone connectivity.

Use effects
Certain audio recording presets have effect controls. Here for example you can change the amount of compression and distortion applied to the channel

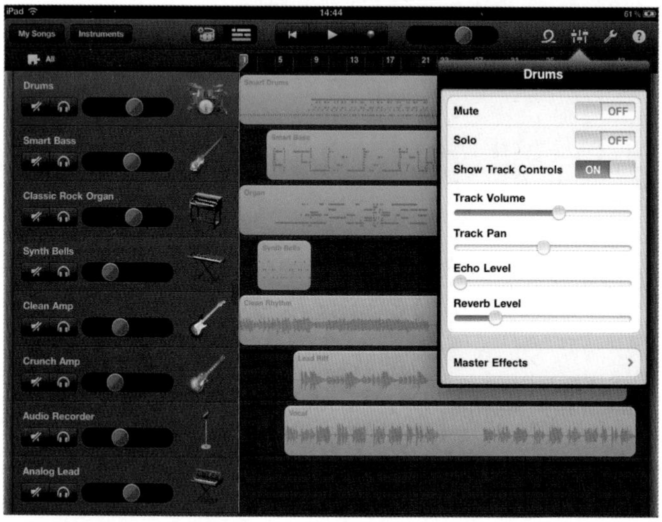

3: Set up a track
Select a track in a project and then click on the mixer icon at the top-right corner of the screen. For each track you can set it to Mute or Solo, show or hide its track controls and also set its volume and pan plus any echo and reverb that is being applied.

4: Set up audio recording
Select an Audio Recorder module and you will see some preset recording setups available. Click on the Plug icon at the top left to call up the Noise Gate, and turn this on and set a threshold level to cancel out all noise below that level such as hiss.

Tutorial: Edit your GarageBand projects

Making music in GarageBand on your iPad is great fun, but you need to know how to edit to get the most out of it

Task: Master editing of your GarageBand projects
Difficulty: Intermediate
Time needed: 10 minutes

Transitioning GarageBand from the Mac to the very different form of the iPad was no mean feat, and Apple has done a remarkable job. In truth, although the applications share a name they are quite different to use, thanks to the touch interface of the iPad being so different to the mouse and keyboard. You can record MIDI either by tapping the screen or by attaching a keyboard though the camera connection kit and record virtual instruments. Unfortunately as things stand it's not possible to edit the notes in MIDI clips after recording, except overdubbing drum parts. You can also record audio tracks, and these clips like MIDI can be split and moved around the timeline, copied, pasted and cut to create your arrangements. As you might expect, the majority of the editing on the iPad version is done by pressing and holding on clips and choosing an edit function. For more advanced editing, you can send the project back to your Mac to be opened in GarageBand or Logic.

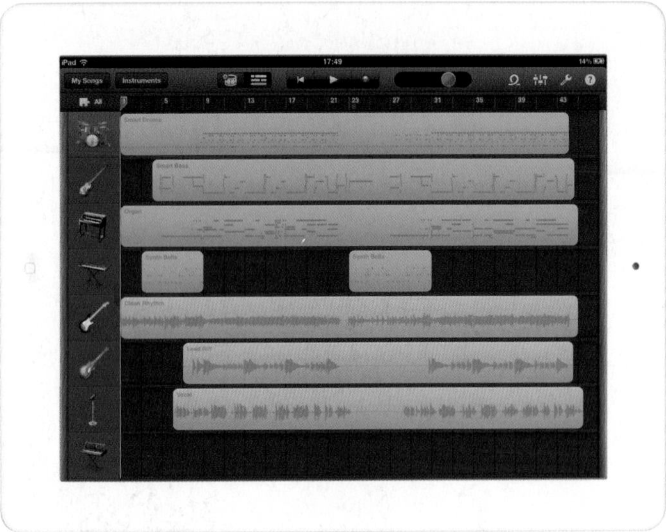

Step-by-step | GarageBand Master editing in GarageBand

1: Edit a MIDI clip

To start editing a track, tap once on a recorded MIDI clip. From the resulting contextual menu you can choose to cut, copy or delete it, or to trim or split the clip. If it's not already looped you also get the option to Loop it.

2: Extend a loop

Once you have specified that a clip should be looped, you will see a circle icon appear on its right-hand edge. This can then be dragged to the right to extend the loop for as long as you like to create the exact sound you want.

GarageBand's timeline

GarageBand packs a lot of functionality into a surprisingly compact space…

Song Sections

Sequencing in GarageBand is done by building up sections of a song, each with a set number of bars. These can be managed using the Song Sections window. You can duplicate sections and modify them to create variations

MIDI clips

MIDI that you record into GarageBand is used to trigger virtual instruments, and the clips and loops arranged in the timeline. Unfortunately you can only overdub notes at present, not manually edit them one by one, which would be useful

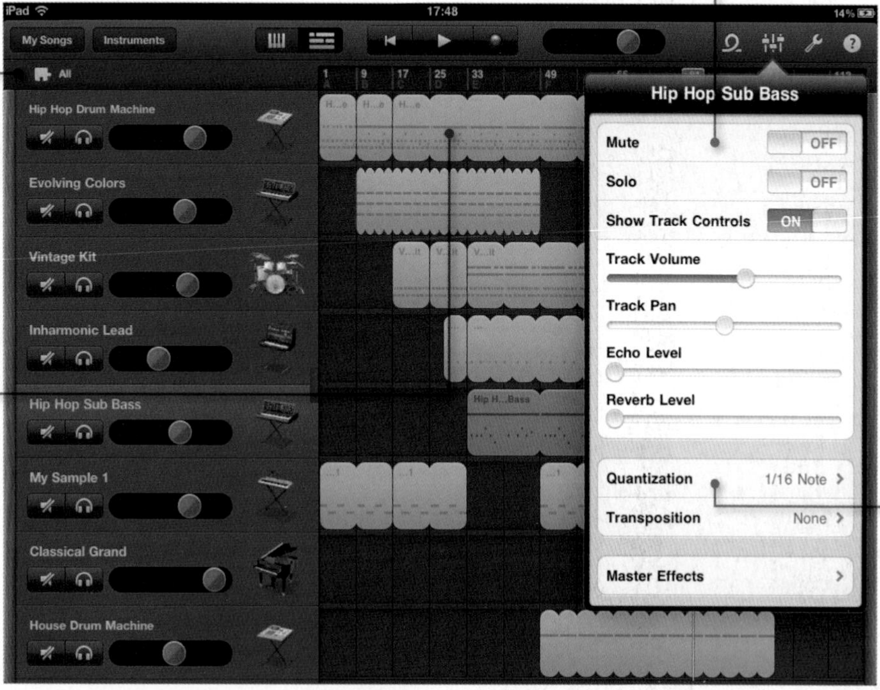

Settings

Each track has a settings section, and you can control its volume, as well as its echo and reverb levels, to give sounds more space in the mix

Knowledge base

Connect a keyboard

Although you can tap the screen to program MIDI instruments, it's also possible to connect any class compliant MIDI keyboard – requiring no special drivers – over USB via the camera connection kit. This means you can play using a keyboard, which is a much more natural and expressive experience than using the screen.

Quantization

When you record MIDI, it's hard to get the perfect timing straight off. By using quantization you are able to have the note snapped to the correct timing values

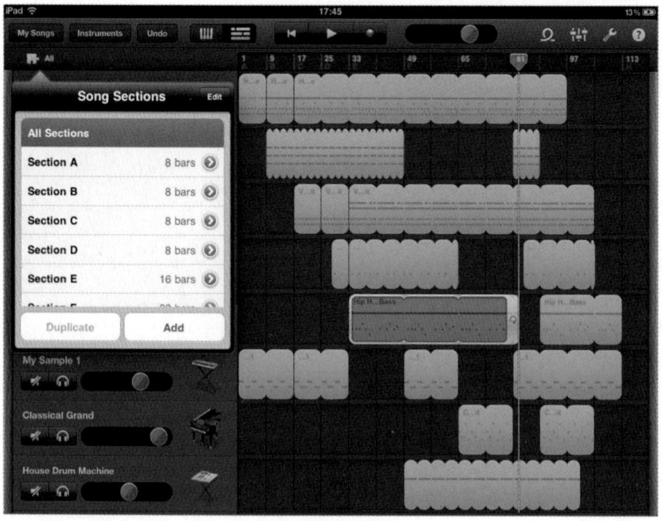

3: Modify song sections

Press the Song Sections button at the top left of the interface and you will then see all available sections. Click to add a new one or duplicate an existing one, and tap the Bars arrow to specify a new length up to 32 bars.

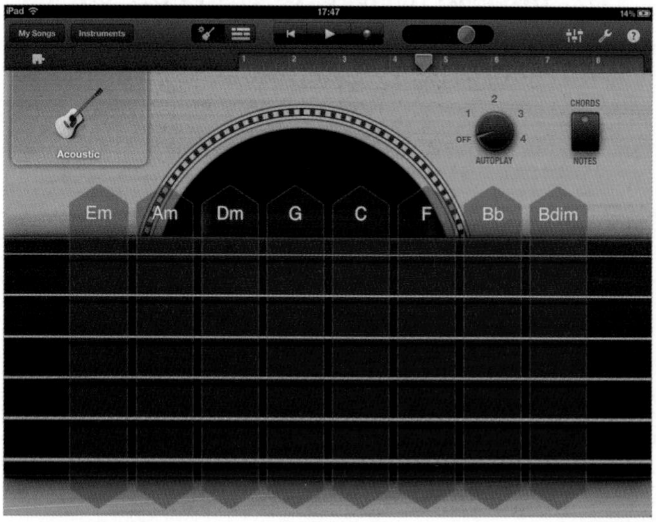

4: Edit an instrument

For any instrument or Smart track that your project may include, double tap on the track itself to return to the instrument's edit window. Then you can make any changes you may require to its sound or overdub a new MIDI part.

Tutorial: Use the GarageBand guitar

Even if you're not a guitarist, GarageBand's guitar can help you make great music thanks to some nifty tools and tricks. We show you how to get the most out of it

Task: Master the GarageBand guitar
Difficulty: Intermediate
Time needed: 15 minutes

One of GarageBand's best features is the quality and flexibility of its excellent built-in instruments. While keyboards and drums are fairly easy to do on a touch screen, guitars are more tricky. Which makes it all the more amazing that GarageBand's guitar is so remarkably easy to use.

For a start you get a choice of guitars, and there are a couple of ways to play it. In Notes view, you see the fretboard and the strings, and pressing a string will play a note. Drag and hold to bend the note and the guitar reacts just like a real guitar. Naturally you can play several notes at once using multiple fingers, or switch to Chords mode. This lets you play whole chords just by pressing the relevant area. An autoplay function creates a range of different strummed styles, making instant music. Back in Notes view you can alter the scale of the guitar so that it's not just standard tuning. Using scales extends the functionality of the guitars and makes this an even more playable instrument.

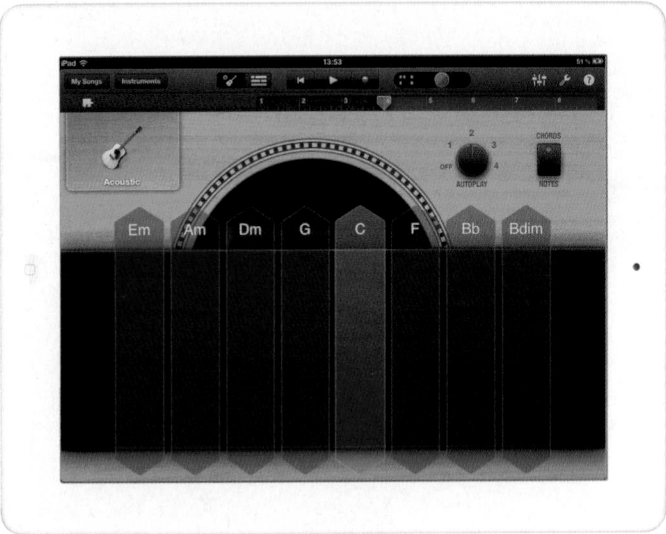

Step-by-step | GarageBand Master the GarageBand guitar

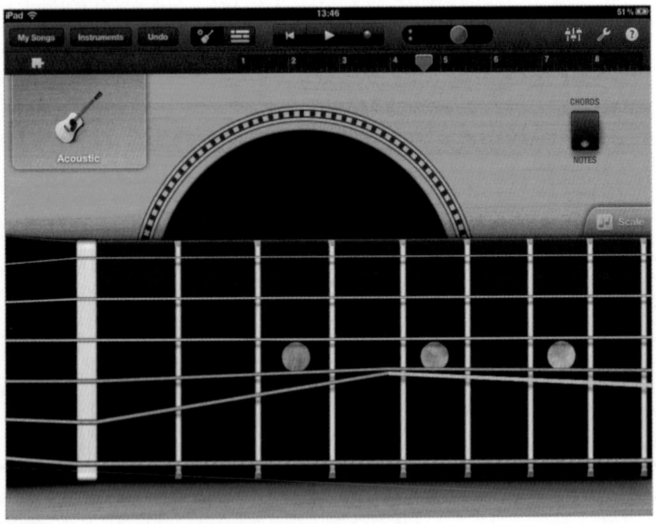

1: Choose a guitar

Load a guitar and choose a model from the top left of the screen. In Notes view, press and hold a string on the fretboard to play a note. Drag your finger up or down to bend the note.

2: Change the scale

Click on the Scale button to choose a new scale. Select Major Blues for example, and the strings are adjusted so that they play different notes. Try different scale types to see how they sound.

Guitars in GarageBand

There's more to GarageBand's guitar than meets the eye

Instruments
Click on the Instruments button to be taken back to the main instruments list to reassign the track to use another kind of instrument

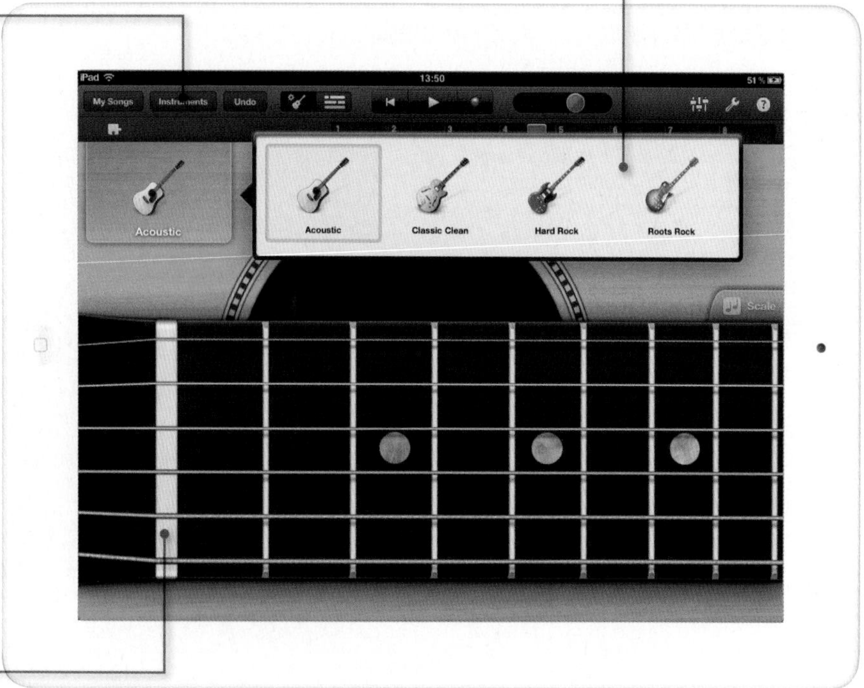

Fretboard
Tap on the fretboard to play strings. Drag your finger to bend notes, and use more than one finger to play multiple notes at once

Guitar chooser
Tap here to choose from the guitars. The acoustic sounds clean and bright, and the three electric guitars have effects added that you can tweak

Knowledge base

Recording chords
With Chord Autoplay mode activated, you can hit Record and create a sequence of chords, pressing to change them as the song progresses. Back in Song view, you will see the chords recorded onto a MIDI track as notes. These can be looped, moved, split or deleted as you see fit to help you structure your song.

Scales
Use different scales to change the tuning and setup of the guitar. This is handy for playing different kinds of music like blues or oriental styles

3: Play chords

Switch to Chords mode and you will see the fretboard display change to group the chords together for ease of playing. Run your finger up or down a chord to play it as if with a plectrum.

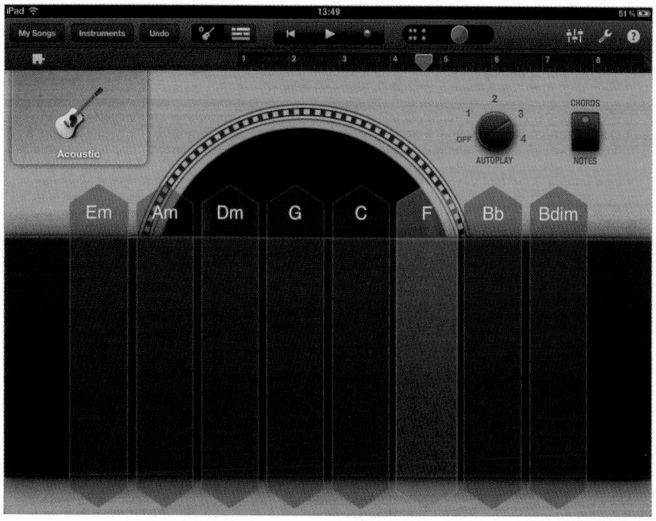

4: Use autoplay

Select one of the four Autoplay modes and hit a chord. GarageBand will play back a preset strummed or picked pattern. Click on another chord name to change the chord playback, and repeat this to create a song.

Tutorial: Master the GarageBand piano

Create music from the grand piano on your iPad. Here's how to use the manual set of pianos and synths in GarageBand to provide the ideal tinkling ivory soundtrack

Task: How to set up and use the piano

Difficulty: Intermediate

Time needed: 15 minutes

Unlike most GarageBand instruments, the Piano requires some playing ability in order to create anything other than a discordant cacophony of keyboard-based sounds. There is one method of creating something that has an automatic process, which is the Arpeggiator, but it's not that great so if you can't play the keys, you're better off using the Smart Piano instead. The other issue is that even if you can play, instead of the 86 keys on a decent keyboard there are only a maximum of 31 using the very thin keys, doubling up to 62 if using top and bottom racks. The thin keys are hard to hit unless you have small fingers, but the medium size keys have 27 while the broad keys have just 19 keys per rack. You need to try them out to see which ones your fingers can play. It's vital that you know what part the instrument is going to play in the song from the start. This determines how you set up the sections for recording. For short interludes or highlights, use 8-bar sections, for piano-driven songs use 32-bar ones.

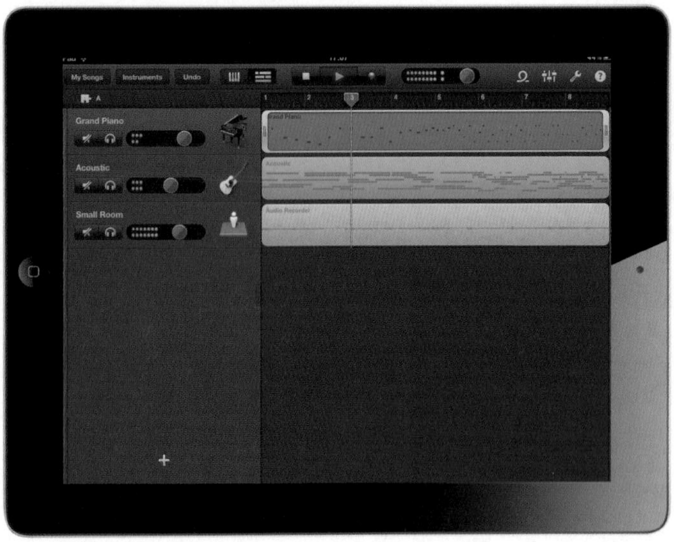

Step-by-step | GarageBand Creating a piano-based track

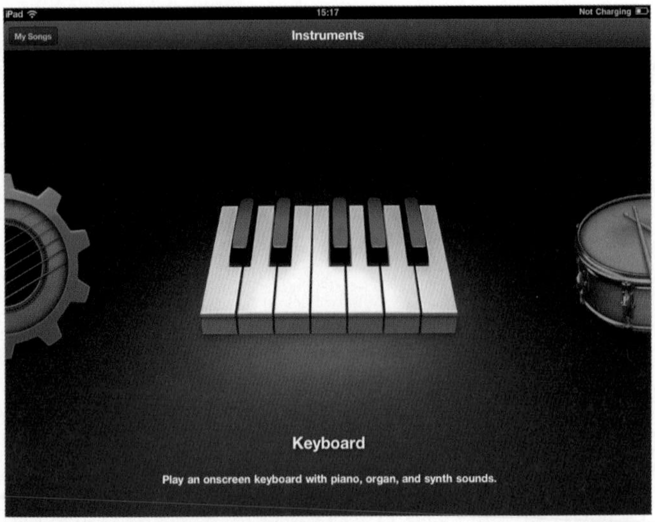

01: Lay the groundwork

Tap on New Song and select Piano as the instrument group to use. Select the Grand Piano as the specific instrument from the group. To set the length of the first piano section tap on the Song Section icon and ensure it is set to 8 bars.

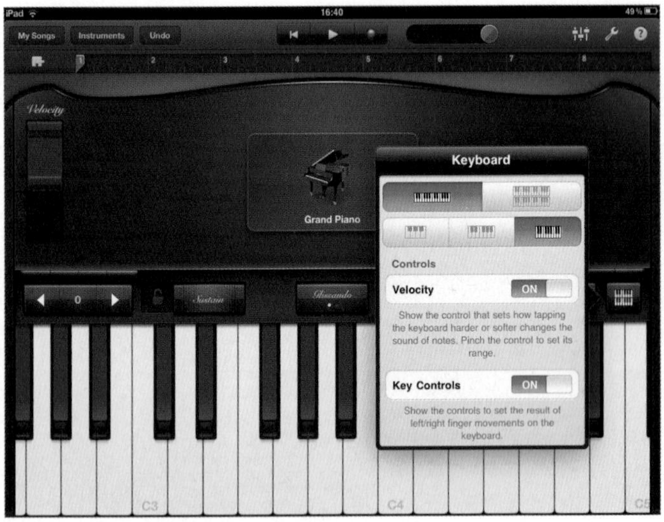

02: Change settings

To get the very best out of the Grand Piano, tap and hold the bottom of the Velocity marker and move upwards. Now shove the Sustain slide in the centre of the screen to the right so that it is on then tap on the Keyboard icon on the right.

Around the Piano panel

The options and extra features explored

Bash them hard
With the Velocity slider extended it takes quite a whack to get full volume. The range sets the minimum and maximum volumes for key presses. Increase the minimum for louder results

Automated playing
The one method of getting an automated result out of the Piano is to use the Arpeggiator to play chord notes. Move the Sustain bar to the right to lock the sequence and then play the keys to transpose it

How many keys
The keyboard can be set up with three different widths of keys and either a double rack of them for a maximum 62 keys or with a keyboard that scrolls left and right as you play it

Record the track
You can have an intro and a metronome ticking to help time the playing. The red record button starts recording onto the Section selected. The bar along the top shows how long the section is

Knowledge base

More keyboards
In the Piano section there are just two actual pianos but lots of synths. The keys work differently and a new feature is added to the Glissando button. It has a Pitch option, which means that the note is extended when held and the pitch modified by a set of four controls on the right. These contain mix, cutoff, volume attack and volume release dials. Also, the sound of the key as it sustains can be modified with pitch and modulation wheels that work like on a real synth.

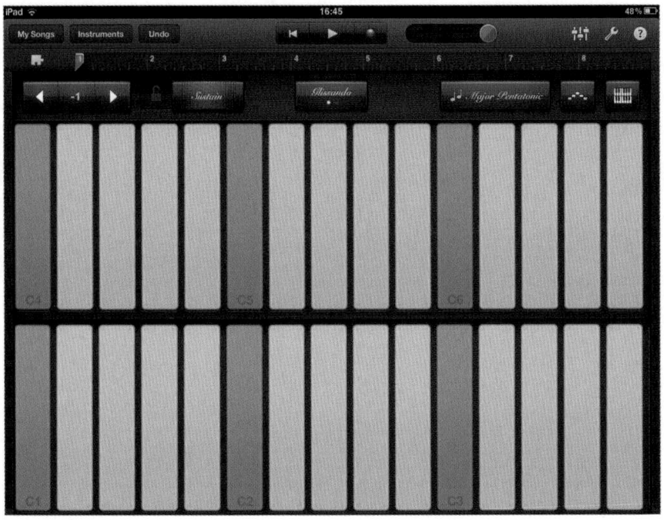

03: Dual keyboards

Select the mid-sized keyboards and a top and bottom rack. Tap on the Scale button and select Major Pentatonic for a scale of complimentary notes. Move the Glissando slider to the right so it says Scroll and set up the keys so they don't overlap. Then turn it back to Glissando.

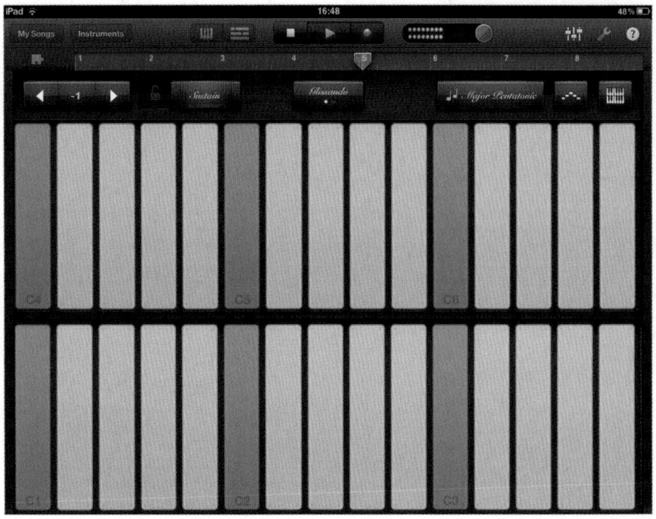

04: Play that song

Tap on the red Record button and play your opening 8-bar track introduction to the piece. When finished, tap on Song Section then on Add and create a 32-bar section for the main body of the song. Play and record that then repeat for additional sections.

Tutorial: Banging the drum in GarageBand

Don't rely on the Smart Drums, go manual and create sets of patterns and effects for your GarageBand tunes. Here's how to create at 16-beat track drum section

Task: Creating a drum track using GarageBand
Difficulty: Intermediate
Time needed: 20 minutes

There are two sets of drums that can be used in GarageBand. The Smart Drums and the regular Drums. The Smart set just consist of placing drum symbols on a grid to create the overall pattern. The standard Drums come with three standard kits and three drum machines. The drum kits involve more manual playing with your fingers, but can still use some automation to provide the main track over which additional drum sounds can be placed.

The first thing to do is to plan out your drum sequences in terms of Song Sections so that you have drum sections for the intro, main song, chorus and ending. How varied these are is completely up to you but they are split into Sections with user-defined bars. The default option is 8 bars, which lasts around 18 seconds. You can just copy these, but it's a little easier if your main sections are 16 bars long and that's what we are recording here in the step-by-step found below.

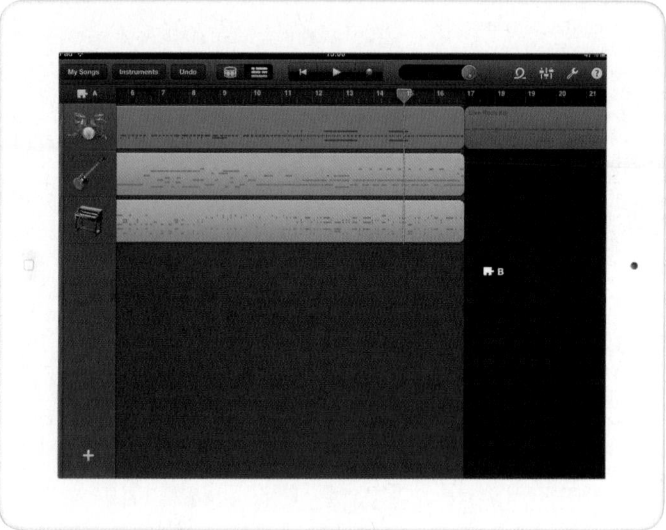

Step-by-step | GarageBand Making a drum track

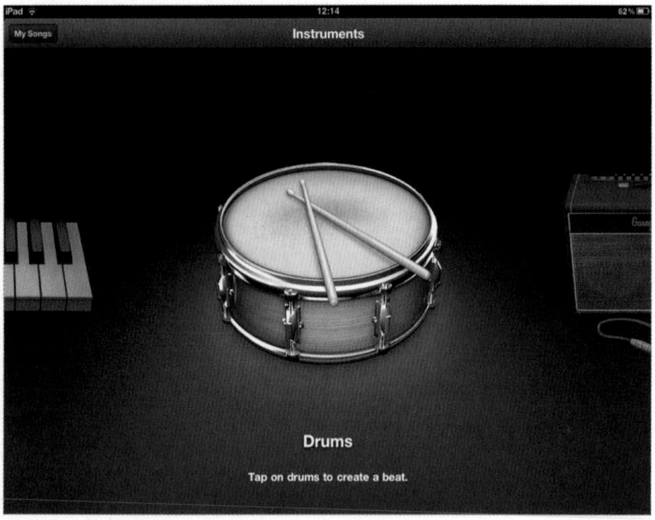

1: Set up the track

Load up GarageBand and then tap on My Songs to exit out of any current songs that are already loaded. Then you just need to tap on the plus sign to create a new song and select Drums as the first instrument to use.

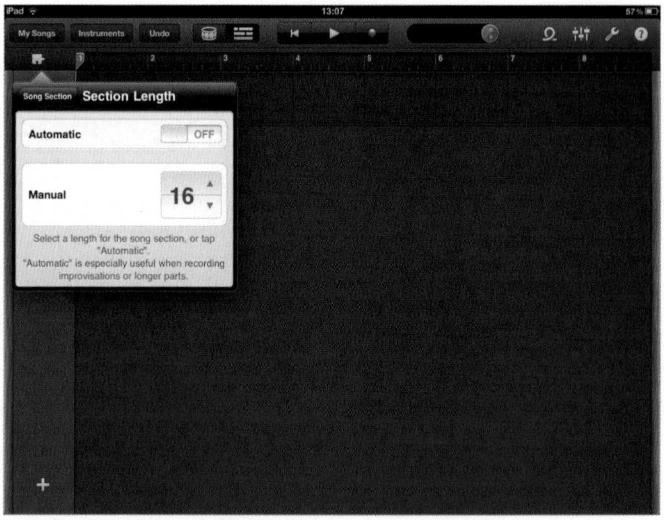

2: Main drum track

Go to the Track view then tap on the Section Length icon in the left corner. Tap on Section A and change this to 16 for a longer track. Then, tap on the red record button and place two fingers on the Snare Drum, one above the other.

Around the kit

There are more options than you might think for a set of drums that you just tap

Instrument and song

The Drum icon shows that you are currently using this equipment to play and record with. Tap on the track selection icon next to it to switch over to the songtrack editing mode

Recording options

Here are the Mixer options including setting the volume, master effects, amount of reverb from the kit and also the echo level to make it sound more cavernous. You can turn off the multi-effect drum recording mode as well

Set the length

The Song Section icon allows each section to be duplicated and the length to be set to a specific number of bars like 8, 16 and 32 or to be left on Automatic for a free-form recording session. Tap on Add for the next Section

Hit the beat

The drums are impact sensitive so the harder you tap them, the louder the noise they make. Some drums and symbols also make more than one type of noise depending on where you tap them

Knowledge base

Automated drums

As well as the drum kit here, there's also the Smart Drum. To use this you place the drum elements on a grid that sets how loud and how complex the tune is. This is useful for a generic piece of drum sound in the middle of tracks but you'll want to mess it up with some individual sounds for the intro, chorus and finish. Although we used the Snare drum in the step-by-step, you could set up the Low Tom for the main drumbeat using the manual drum kits.

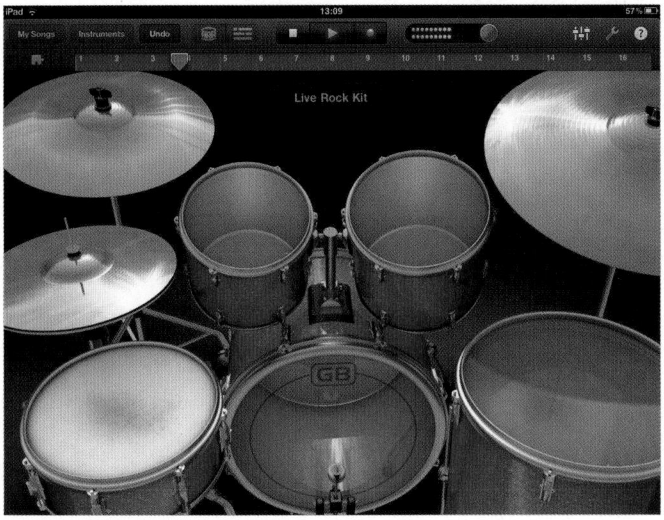

3: Start drumming

Move your fingers apart vertically to increase the volume, then twist them sideways to increase the drum speed. Record your main Snare sound all the way through to the end of the 16-bar track then tap on the stop button.

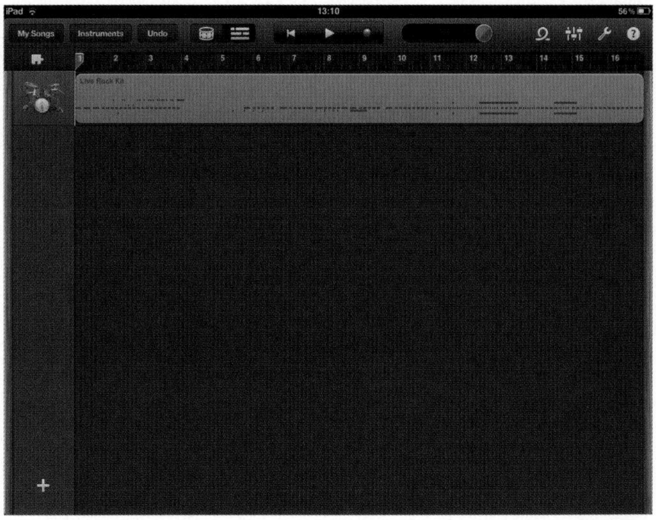

4: Add the rest

Move the counter back to the start of the track. Tap on Record again and as the existing drum track plays, add Bass drum effects throughout the track. Repeat the process for cymbals and hi-hat. This is the opening drum track that can be duplicated.

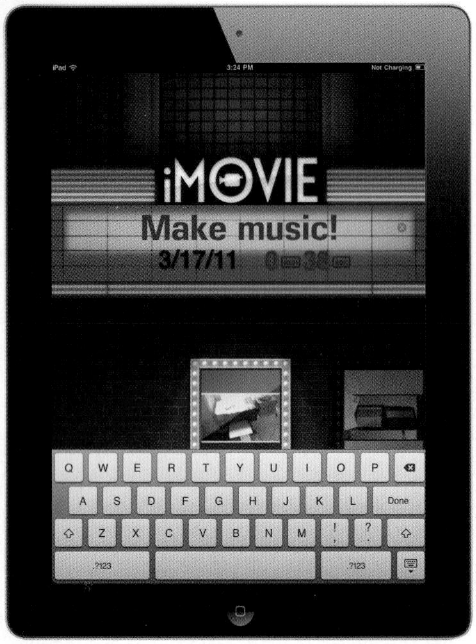

Tutorial: Create a movie on the iPad 2 with iMovie

Creating and exporting a film with iMovie on the iPad is easy, if you know a few important tips and tricks…

Task: Create and export a movie on the iPad

Difficulty: Beginner

Time needed: 10 minutes

The iMovie app is basic enough to appeal to anyone, but could be used by a serious filmmaker who just wants to create a basic film from footage that you shoot on the device itself. The basic idea is that, like the Mac version, you shoot some video clips and then add them into one continuous movie. You can insert transition effects such as a spotlight fill, and include titles that introduce the film or specific sections. And, you can add multiple audio tracks and trims clips down to size. When you are done, you can export the final creation to a plethora of video services, including YouTube and Vimeo, and even export directly to Facebook.

The app works fast on the iPad 2, allowing you to create movies with ease. We take you through how to create and share your films using this fantastic app.

Step-by-step | iMovie Create a film in iMovie for iPad

1: Add clips

When you open iMovie and start a project, you will see a bin of video clips. Select the ones you want and click the arrow to add them.

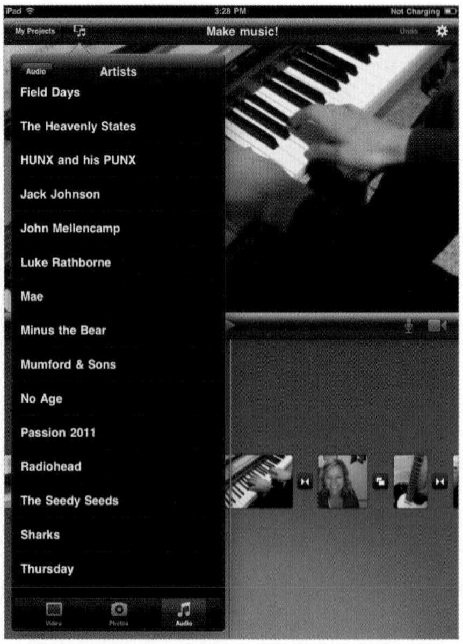

2: Add audio

You can also add audio clips – just select the Audio tab on the bottom of the screen. Add the ones you want to coincide with your video footage.

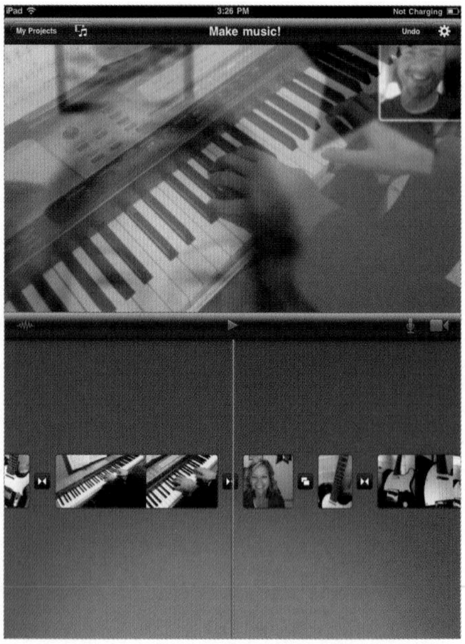

3: Scrub

Piece together your clips and swipe with two fingers to zoom in. Double-tap to add text titles. Press the VCR-like play button to see the results.

Movie projects

The main iMovie home screen shows you all available projects you can edit

Name the project
At the main screen of iMovie, you can name your project. Tap the current name and type what you want to use for the movie title. This will be used for sharing the movie as well

Knowledge base

Adding videos
Adding movies to iMovie is more trouble than you might think. For some reason, when you copy movies over from your computer using iTunes, these video files do not show up in the video bin. The app prefers a very specific size and format. However, one workaround is that you can email QuickTime movie files to yourself, then download them to the Photos app.

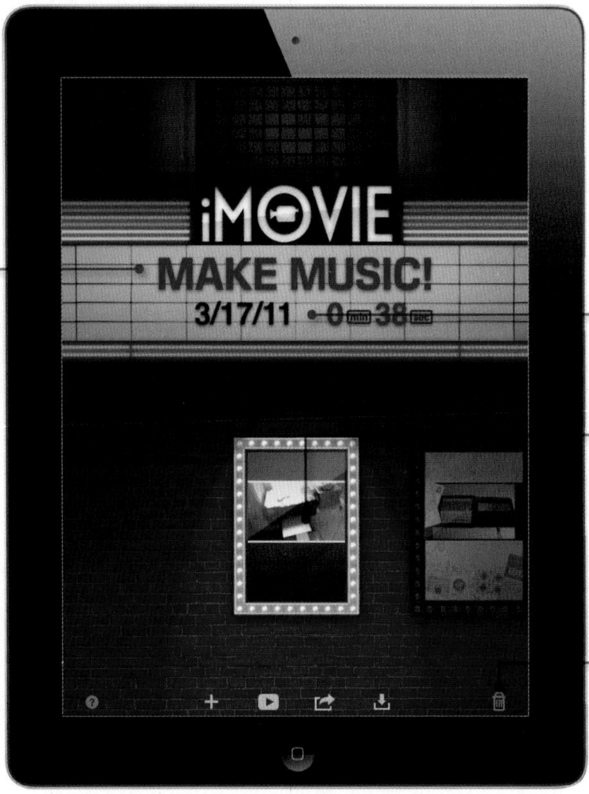

Date and time
You can quickly check the date and time for the currently selected movie project. If you see a time that does not look right, you can select that project and perform editing tasks

Choose project
Swipe to the right to see any additional projects and note their date and time. For the current project, you can share the movie to video services such as Vimeo

Delete
At the main screen for iMovie, you can also select a project and delete the film to save space on your iPad 2. The app will confirm that you really want to delete your work

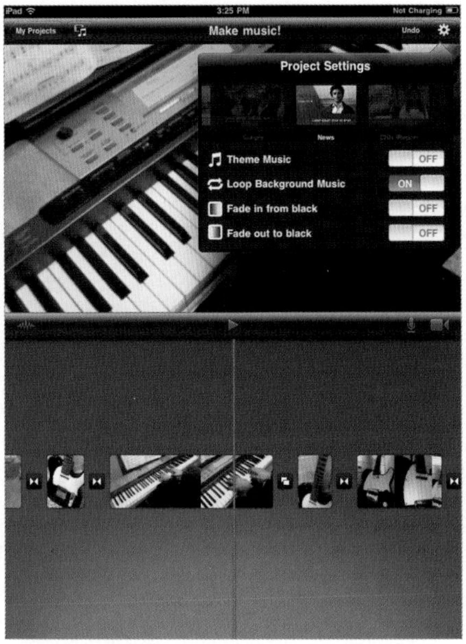

4: Settings
You can change the theme used for transitions. Select Settings and choose a new theme. You can also enable or disable the background track.

5: Share
Once you have created the movie, press the My Projects button to return to the main menu. Press the Share button that looks like an arrow.

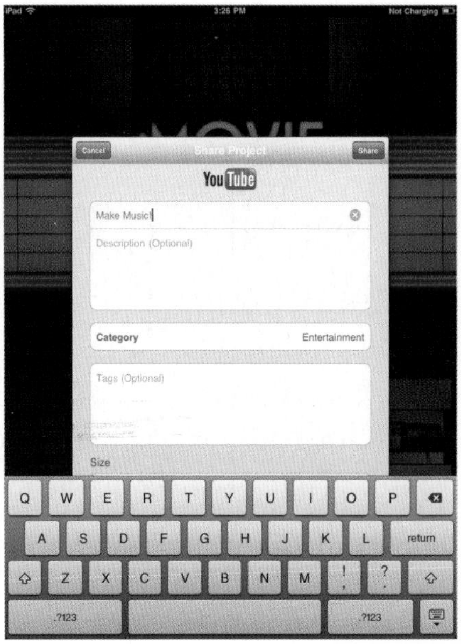

6: Upload
Select the service you want to use. For YouTube, you will need to enter your account info, name the movie, and provide a description. Press Share.

Tutorial: Master precision editing in iMovie

iMovie on the iPad 2 lets you edit the video you shoot with the on-board 720p video camera. You can also add music, transitions, photos and upload straight to the web

Task: Make your iMovie videos perfect with this precision editing guide

Difficulty: Intermediate

Time needed: 15 minutes

The iPad 2 is now able to shoot HD video, and this opens up a whole world of new possibilities for movie making. Apple has ported its iMovie software to the device, though it only runs on the latest hardware, so you'll need an iPad 2. Capturing video is easy enough, though you aren't able to easily import videos from an alternative camera or from your Mac thanks to the way that iMovie encodes the video it captures. It's possible to save captured video to your Camera Roll, and also to send projects to iMovie on your Mac for further editing, so you can use these options to move your media around. Editing is easy in the timeline thanks to the iPad's touch-screen interface. Clips can be dragged and dropped into projects, moved around and split, shortened and lengthened all with a few simple gestures. It's even possible to add stills with the Ken Burns effect to make your projects more interesting.

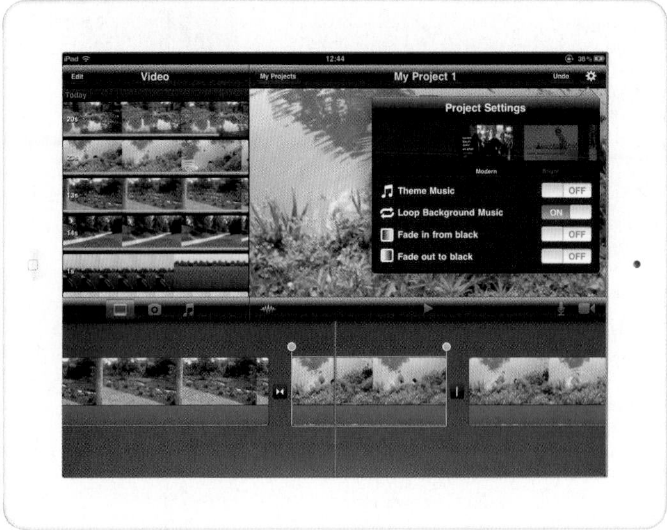

Step-by-step | iMovie Editing in iMovie

1: Move clips around

Clips can be dragged from the project bin into the timeline and once there, they can be picked up and rearranged by pressing and holding on them, then moving them to a new location. To remove a clip from the timeline you can simply drag it out and it will disappear.

2: Split clips

To split a clip, move the timeline so that the playhead is over the point at which you want to make the edit. Then tap once to select the clip and it is outlined in yellow. Swipe your finger down across the clip and it will be split in two.

iMovie's editing features

Fine tune your movies using these great tools…

Project bin
Here you'll see the clips that you have recorded on your iPad. Drag and drop ones you want in a project from the bin onto the timeline

Media chooser
Browse from your movie bin, your photo library and your music library to find material for your projects

Knowledge base

Back and forth

iMovie isn't very flexible when it comes to importing video from other sources – it's very fiddly to do. It's great at exporting though, and gives you options to compress and upload to a number of popular video sites as well as sending the movie to iTunes, or as a project to iMovie on your Mac.

Clip handles
Drag the handle at the right-hand edge of a clip to the left to shorten it, or back to the right to restore its original length

Playhead
Place the playhead at the point you'd like to cut. Select the clip by tapping and swipe your finger down to make the edit

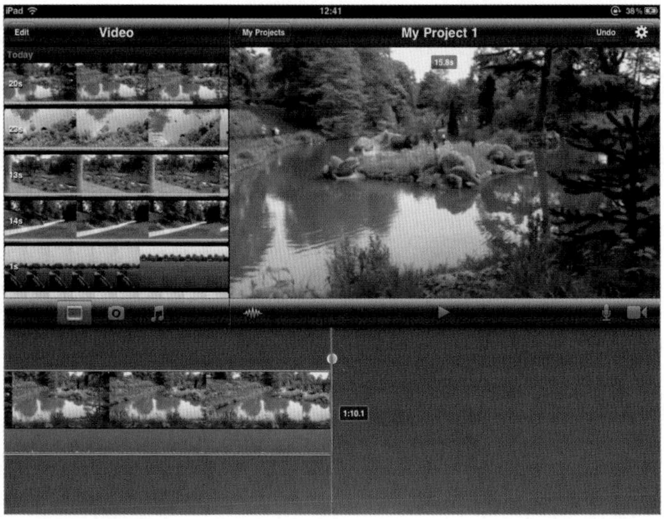

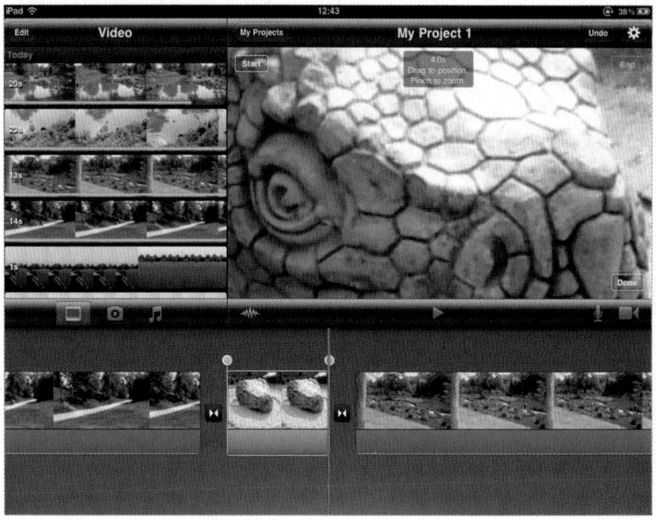

3: Change clip duration

To change the length of a clip, single tap to select it, and then scroll to the end. You can pick up the yellow handle at the end of the clip and drag it to the left to shorten it, or right to restore its original length. This only works with the right-hand slider, not the left.

4: Edit a picture

Drag a picture in from your image library and place it into the timeline. Use the handles to change its length if required. Drag and pinch on the image to set the zoom level at the start and end of the clip, then play back to preview it.

Tutorial: Use transitions in iMovie projects

Having transitions in your iMovie projects will make them look more professional, so it's a good idea to know how they work, and how to tweak them to suit your tastes…

Task: Master iMovie transitions to create professional videos

Difficulty: Intermediate

Time needed: 15 minutes

When you make movies, you will need to use some sort of transitions at some point. Basic cuts from one shot to another are fine, but transitions make things more interesting and help to create a more natural flow. As well as fades at the start and end of a project, you might want to use crossfades or dissolves between scenes, or some of the more complex transitions that iMovie has. Editing transitions is also possible, and rather easier on the iPad 2 version than on the smaller screens of the other devices. Being able to control the timing of transitions is great because it lets you opt either for quick changes for a more urgent feel, or more slow and leisurely ones for a more relaxed pace. By double-clicking on a transition you open its editor window and are able to slide the handles to change its duration, as well as selecting from preset durations and selecting a transition type. Explore transitions to achieve a more professional look to your film projects.

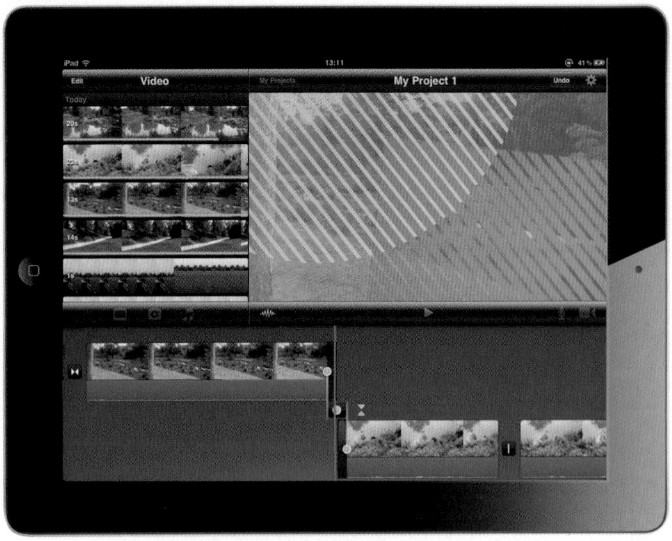

Step-by-step | iMovie Using transitions in iMovie

1: Set up start and end fades

Go to the settings menu at the top-right corner of the screen and tap on it to reveal the project settings window. Here you can switch on fades from and to black for the start and end of the project, as well as choosing some options for the music.

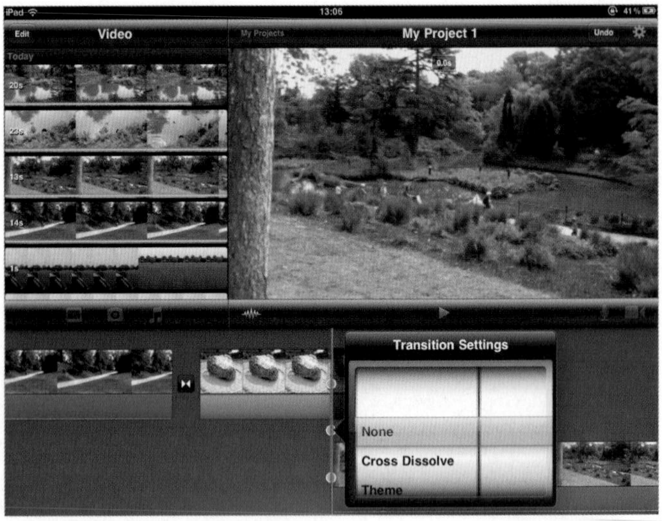

2: Select a transition

When you drop a clip into the timeline, iMovie automatically creates a transition. If you don't want one, you can double-click on it and choose 'None' from the list. Or you can just leave it as the default cross dissolve if that's what you want.

Transitions in iMovie

Master transitions for a better finished product

Transition Settings
Control the transition here, choosing a preset length and a transition type. You also have the option to choose 'None' if you want a straight cut to happen

Transition editor
Click on the dual arrows to expand the transition editor and view the way the clips overlap. Click on the yellow dot in the centre to open the Transition Settings window

Knowledge base

Power hungry

The iPad version of iMovie only works officially on the iPad 2, and this is partly because of its dual core processor but also because it has 512MB RAM as opposed to the original iPad's 256MB. The iPhone and iPod Touch models supported also have 512MB, making them compatible as well.

Project settings
Tap on the project settings section to switch fades from and to black on and off for the project and also to choose a theme. The theme determines which transitions are available

Timeline
Transitions are inserted automatically and also rendered in the background, so as soon as one is on the timeline you can preview it to see it played back, then edit it

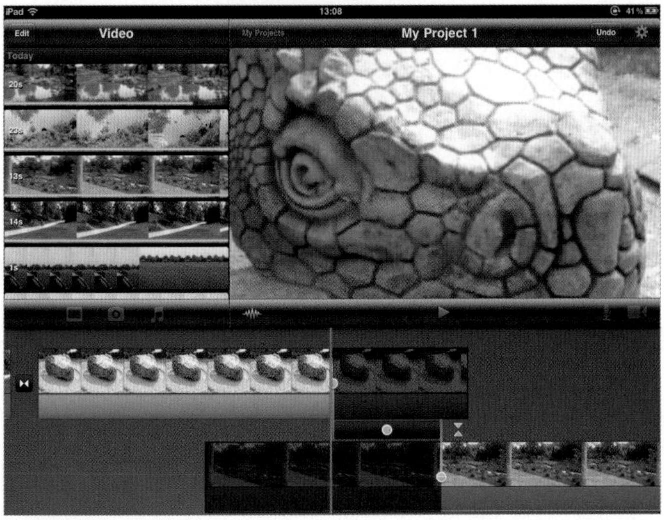

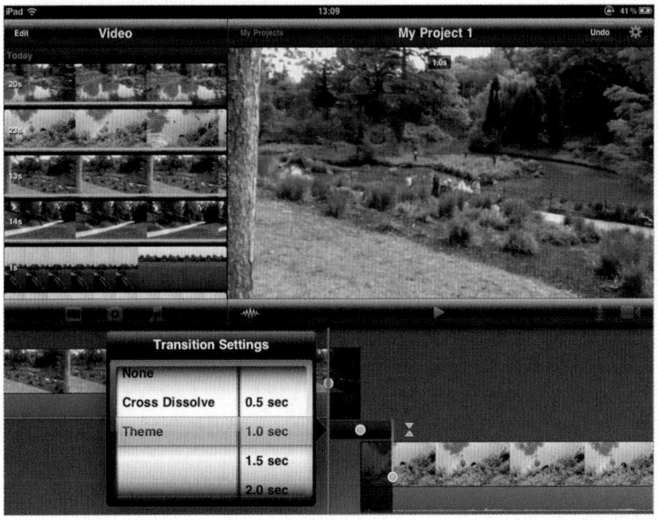

3: Edit the transition

You need to tap on the dual arrows by the transition to open up its editor view. You can then pinch to zoom in if you like, for far greater precision. Drag either clip to move it and so change the point at which the transition occurs.

4: Use theme transitions

Switch the transition type to 'Theme' and you will use whichever transition is contained within the project theme. Choose the theme from the project settings menu. Scroll through the transition in the timeline to see it take effect.

The iPad Essential Apps Guide

The apps you simply have to own

There are over 350,000 apps currently available on the App Store, and that number is increasing every day at a fast pace. There are a plethora of apps to make you fitter, apps to get you to sleep, apps to help you with your working life, apps to turn your photo into a zombie… and a whole load more. As more and more developers are releasing their products, it can be ridiculously hard to know which ones to pick. Within this swirling swamp of applications, The Essential Apps Guide is here to show you all the must-have apps that will really improve your iPad's functionality. Covering every section of the App Store, from Social Networking and Travel to Utilities and Games, this guide points you in the right direction. There is an app for anything you could possibly dream of, and these are the very best.

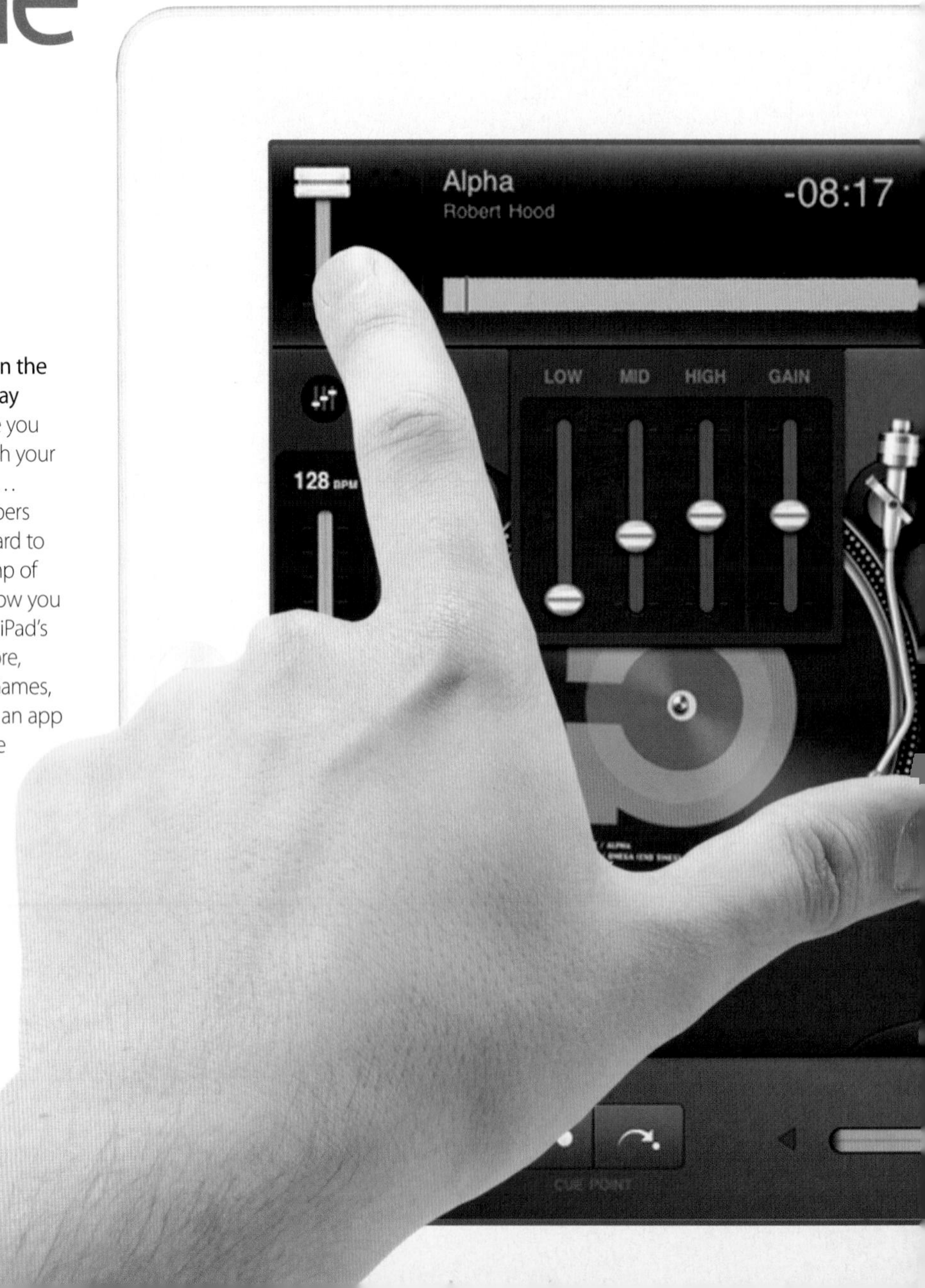

The iPad Book

APP REVIEWS

No SIM
10:40
28 %
Calendar
Contacts
Notes
Maps
App Store
iTunes
YouTube
Videos
Twitter
ebay
Spotify
Game Center
iBooks
Dropbox
GarageBand
Safari
Photos
Mail
Settings
iPod

Ultimate guide to iPad apps

Ensure your iPad is never out of your hands by packing it with apps that you'll return to time and time again

There are more than 300,000 apps in the App Store. Choosing which ones to select and download is no easy task, hence the need for publications such as this one. But there are some apps which nobody should do without – the apps which will help make your life easier and more pleasurable.

We've chosen 30 apps which we feel you must download. They have been split into three categories, Productivity, Entertainment and Lifestyle, so you can easily find the kind of app you need. Covering areas as diverse as apps that allow you to read comics to ones that let you create music on your iPad, these are the applications that will extend the functionality of your device much further, and allow you to get the most out of your purchase. A great many of them are free, too, so you don't have to worry about splashing too much cash. Have fun.

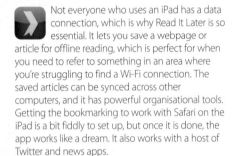

Entertainment

After a hard day, we all want to kick back and relax. How we do that depends on the mood we are in, but with so many apps out there catering for wildly different tastes, there will certainly be something for you.

Some people like to curl up with a good book or magazine, and there is certainly enough reading material for you to enjoy. Many publishers have put the printed word into a format you can enjoy digitally, saving trees in the process. And while you are devouring the text, you can slip on some music. Streaming is the order of the day, and there are apps to help you take advantage of that.

If you want to sit and chill in front of a good programme or catch up on the latest news, you can do that too. Faster connection speeds mean you can even enjoy live streams of big events or rolling coverage. And if you want to let off some steam or engage your brain, try a game. After all, there are thousands of them to enjoy.

Read It Later Pro

Price: £1.79/$2.99
Developer: Idea Shower

Not everyone who uses an iPad has a data connection, which is why Read It Later is so essential. It lets you save a webpage or article for offline reading, which is perfect for when you need to refer to something in an area where you're struggling to find a Wi-Fi connection. The saved articles can be synced across other computers, and it has powerful organisational tools. Getting the bookmarking to work with Safari on the iPad is a bit fiddly to set up, but once it is done, the app works like a dream. It also works with a host of Twitter and news apps.

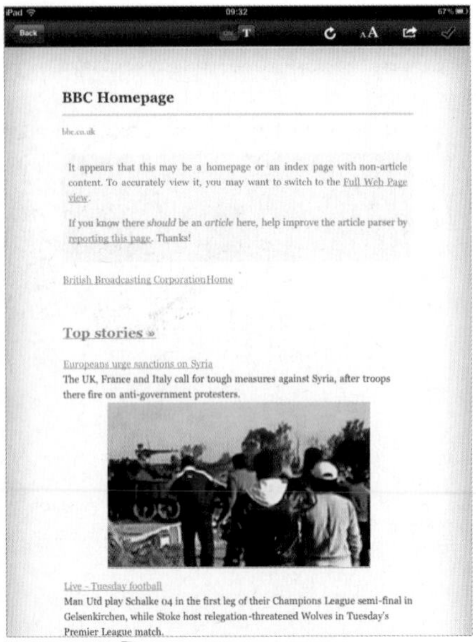

Getting Safari to work with Read It Later isn't straightforward, but it's worth doing.

Comics

Price: Free
Developer: comiXology

Comics has a brilliant way of presenting graphic novels, and the built-in reader is wonderful. There's a good selection of free comics to get you started, and you flick through their pages in the same way as you would navigate a selection of photos, giving it a fluid and natural feel. It's a class app with great features, including automatic bookmarking and the ability to see a full series. You can also buy print copies – the app lets you know where your nearest store is. It can be a little slow at times, but if you enjoy comics, then you must try this.

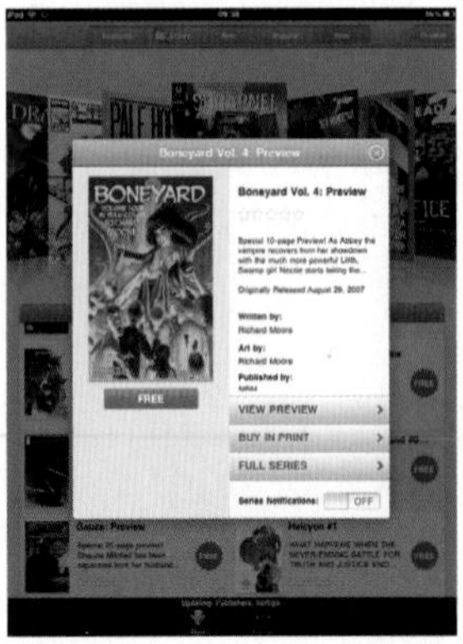

Buying a comic is simple, and you can see if there is a print copy available.

iBooks

Price: Free
Developer: Apple Inc

We're getting to the point where reading books on paper is starting to feel rather quaint. Apps such as iBooks and Kindle are now making major inroads. With iBooks, you can instantly access the iBooks Store and buy the latest tomes using your iTunes account. They download straight to the app, appearing on a set of virtual bookshelves. As a nice addition, you can view PDFs too. Using iBooks to read a novel is a joyful experience.

"Comics has a brilliant way of presenting graphic novels"

It's worth downloading a free book – there are plenty to choose from.

Last.fm

Price: Free
Developer: Last.fm

Last.fm is a free music-based social networking app that lets you create your own song lists, and allows you to discover new music. It is built for the iPhone, but works well on the iPad too. The emphasis is on the music rather than the social aspect, but it's still feature-laden. You can start a new station and search for fresh tunes by inserting your favourite artist, tag or user, and streaming is very fast. Songs play even when you quit the app.

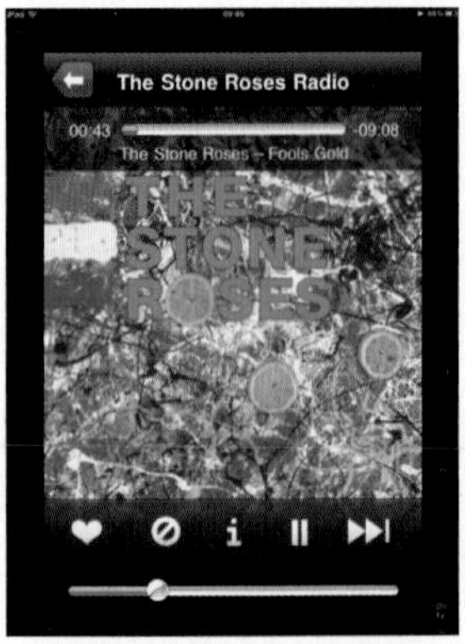

You need to be a subscriber to listen to the radio function.

Cut The Rope HD

Price: £1.19/£1.99
Developer: Chillingo Ltd

After the Angry Birds craze came Cut The Rope, another amazing game from Chillingo. The concept is so simple, and yet it makes effective use of the iPad screen. The idea is that you slice through ropes in order to collect stars and feed Om Nom with some delicious candy. There are dozens and dozens of puzzles to get through before you reach the end of this colourful, cute and addictive game.

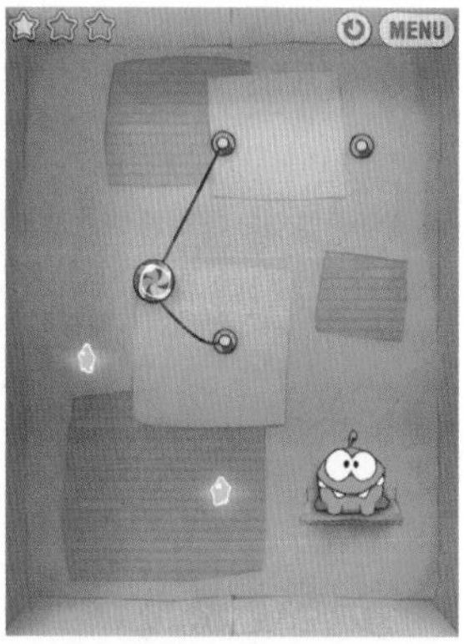

The game starts off easy enough, but soon becomes incredibly difficult.

Spotify

Price: Free
Developer: Spotify

Spotify lets you stream tunes to your iPad – via an iPhone app – as long as you are paying a monthly subscription. Songs play at a bit rate of around 160kps, and the app has the ability to save music to your iPhone, allowing you to listen to songs offline, perfect for when you're travelling by air or Tube.

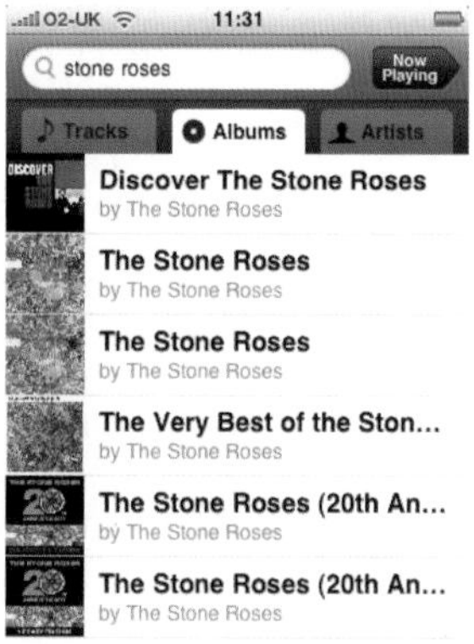

The search functions are great, letting you sift through millions of songs.

Sky News for iPad

Price: Free
Developer: BSkyB

The Sky News app lets you view live footage from the popular UK television news channel, as well as select dozens of individual stories, each accompanied by video. Streaming is fast, and the quality and breadth of news is astounding. Sky News for iPad is as slick as the coverage itself.

The strength of the Sky News app is in its extensive video coverage.

"Show Infinity Blade to anyone who doubts the iPad"

Infinity Blade

Price: £3.49/$5.99
Developer: Chair Entertainment Group

Infinity Blade is the app to show anyone who doubts the iPad as a gaming platform. The graphics will blow you away in this third-person action role-playing game, which has intuitive controls and loads of baddies to slay. The touchscreen is used to cast spells, attack, dodge and block through many battles. Wholly addictive.

The excellent control system is one of Infinity Blade's selling points, but it takes a while to master.

Pianist Pro

Price: £2.99/$4.99
Developer: Mark Terry

Pianist Pro puts a piano at your fingertips, complete with beats and a whole host of different sounds ranging from an organ to an acoustic guitar. It includes a full set of piano keys, but to see them all you have to slide the keyboard at the top of the screen. It includes recording abilities, and is great for a spot of practice.

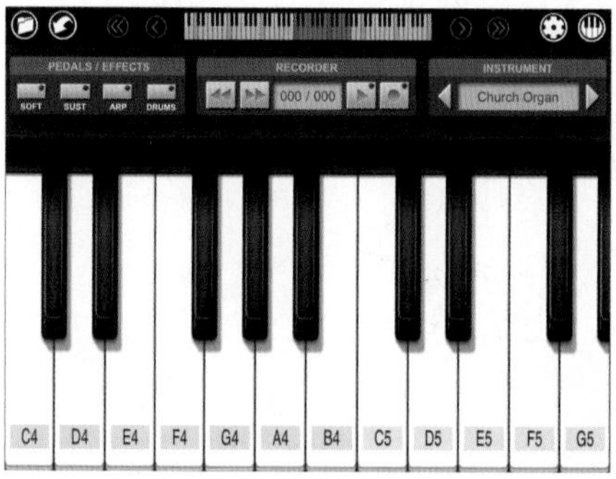

The keys are large and inviting with all the major features placed above them so they don't get in the way.

"djay effectively allows you to turn your iPad into a virtual DJ rig"

djay

Price: £11.99/$19.99
Developer: algoriddim GmbH

In some ways, the iPad is becoming the Atari ST of today. Its power and large screen means the device has bags of potential. With djay, however, the emphasis is on play, giving you the chance to have a good session on the decks, letting you blend songs into each other and beatmatch, with the iPad screen effectively becoming a virtual DJ rig. You get channel mixers, volume controls, pitch blend sliders and a whole lot more.

Get two records going, and record your very own slice of music.

Lifestyle

Since the dawn of the internet, our lives have changed immeasurably. Lifestyles are based as much online as they are off. Nowadays, we find ourselves glued to social networks during quiet evenings, or we find ourselves blogging the minutiae of our lives to anybody who cares to read, often in no more than 140 characters.

But we still need time to do everyday 'real activities' like cooking and take time out to chill with some music. And there are times when we become utterly lost, and need a bit of guidance, or just pointing towards the nearest bar. Lifestyle apps fit into your day-to-day lives, offering help and guidance, and even a spot of shopping.

In some ways, they are the middle ground between work and play – the things you just do because they are creative or essential. And here, we present ten of the most essential apps for you to download, making life that bit more laidback and enjoyable.

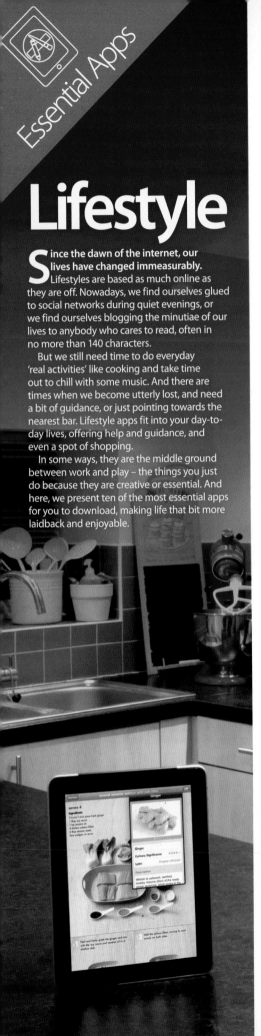

iMovie

Price: £2.99/$4.99
Developer: Apple Inc

To use iMovie, you must be in possession of an iPad 2. But with this loaded on to your device, you will be able to edit your HD film masterpieces, using its abilities to trim clips, manipulate the timeline and use a variety of themes, including neon and CNN iReport, all with accompanying soundtracks to boot.

Twitter

Price: Free
Developer: Twitter

Twitter's own iPad Tweeting client is top notch, making it simple to follow other users, post your own thoughts and search for topics or names. The front end is a breeze to navigate, and replying to messages and retweeting are just mere button pushes away. The app makes good use of the large iPad screen, and is split into two, with menu options to the left and other people's Tweets to the right. If you click on a Tweet that includes a reference to a webpage or image, that material is displayed so you don't have to tap through to Safari.

Twitter utilises the iPad screen very well, with an intuitive and neat interface.

Photo Cookbook

Price: £2.99/$4.99
Developer: projektagentur GmbH

Just flicking through the Photo Cookbook app is enough to make your mouth water. With 80 delicious-looking recipes – split into four categories – its unique selling points are the stunning hi-res photographs of dishes, which the app claims take less than 30 minutes to make. There are only a handful of steps to each recipe, so you're not drowned in a sea of instructions, and yet they are clearly explained, so we had few problems making them. Recipes can be emailed, and there is a baking app available too.

There are 20 recipes in each category giving you loads of choice.

Friendly for Facebook

Price: Free
Developer: Oecoway

Given the fact that Facebook still hasn't produced a dedicated iPad app, the market is currently effectively sewn up by Friendly for Facebook. It puts much of the functionality of Facebook on the tablet device, and makes a great job of presenting your profile, wall and messages. You can upload photos, write notes and update your status. The app also notifies you of your friends' birthdays, allowing you to switch between accounts and use a PIN code to secure your details.

Friendly for Facebook is probably the best iPad Facebook app out there.

Windowshop

Price: Free
Developer: AMZN Mobile LLC

Amazon has made a real name for itself as a global internet retailer. The Windowshop app by Amazon lets you search and buy from the UK store. Products are clearly displayed in columns, and clicking on each one brings up a pop-up window that allows you to purchase or find out more. Wish lists can be drawn up, and you can access you account details from within the app.

Amazon's app is a real window to the online store, with great search facilities.

"Skype is an app everyone should download now"

WebMD

Price: Free
Developer: WebMD Health

WebMD provides accurate health advice, and is neatly packaged, giving a solid overview of ailments, accompanied by symptoms and related articles. The Symptom Checker shows you a picture of the body, and by tapping on the area of concern you can call up a list of symptoms, and then narrow down the possible conditions.

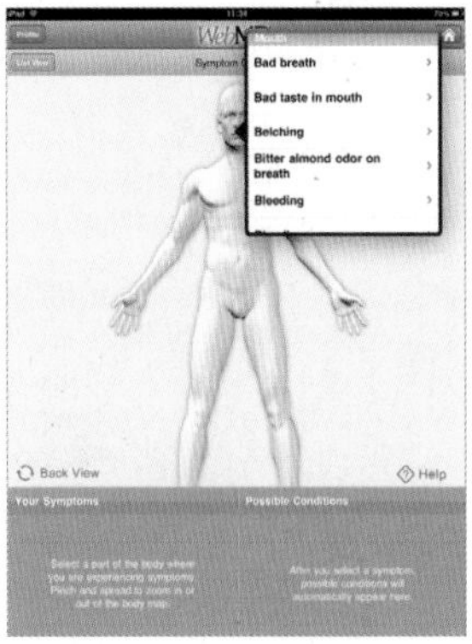

Using an image of the human body, you can narrow down your symptoms.

Around Me

Price: Free
Developer: Tweakersoft

Around Me is actually produced for the iPhone, but it taps into the iPad's location features. It still enables you to find anything, though, from banks and bars to hotels and parking. It's fast, and displays a phone number of the venue if one is available, as well as a Google map of its location. You can share the location on Facebook, Twitter, SMS or email.

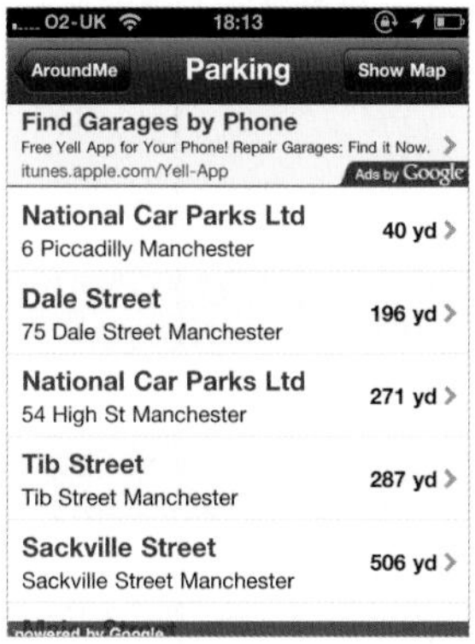

Around Me allows you to find a variety of different services.

eBay

Price: £3.49/$5.99
Developer: eBay Inc

Anyone who uses eBay will find the online auction giant's iPad app to be a pretty useful download. Feedback can be monitored and left, and you can send messages to buyers and sellers, search for items, keep a check on your eBay account, and see at a glance which items you're watching, buying or selling. The drop-down menus gives you everything you need, except for one thing. You can't sell items using the app, which to be honest is the only place it really falls short.

Large images of the latest deals are shown as soon as you load the app.

GarageBand

Price: £2.99/$4.99
Developer: Apple Inc

GarageBand is very different on the iPad to the Mac, where it has cultivated a professional reputation. On the iPad, it's much more accessible, letting you choose from a variety of instruments, and allowing you to play them. Its eight-track recorder means it does have further uses, however.

The guitar is one of many instruments built into GarageBand, and you can record as you play.

Skype

Price: Free **Developer:** Skype Software

With Skype, you instantly have a phone in your hand capable of making free calls to other Skype users, as long as you're in a place with Wi-Fi. This app is made for the iPhone, but it's brilliant for phoning people across the world at low cost. It also boasts two-way video calling, although you'll need an iPad 2. It's one app everyone should download given the sheer number of Skype users out there.

Productivity

Life isn't always fun. Sometimes you have to work or complete tasks, and that is where productivity apps come into their own, often making these times less intrusive and dull.

The best apps are those that save you stress and worry. It may be that you need to make some quick amendments to a word-processing document while you are on the move, or you may want to jot down an idea or thought, visually sketching it and making annotations. Or you may be looking to produce a good-looking presentation for the boss while sitting on the train, then save it to the cloud to work on when you get back to your desk.

There are apps to help you do all of these things and so much more, making you better organised and easing some of the most time-zapping tasks, ultimately giving you more free time.

Atomic Web Browser

Price: £0.59/$0.99
Developer: Richard Trautvetter

Safari has long been a poor relation among web browsers, but many believe it's the only one they can use on the iPad. Not so. Download Atomic. Not only is it lightning fast, but it also taps into some of the most popular online activities with Facebook and Twitter integration. Webpages fill the entire screen, and you can use tab browsing. The browser supports AirPrint, and downloaded files can be sent to Dropbox or opened in apps. URLs can be shared, and you can block ads and save webpages for offline viewing.

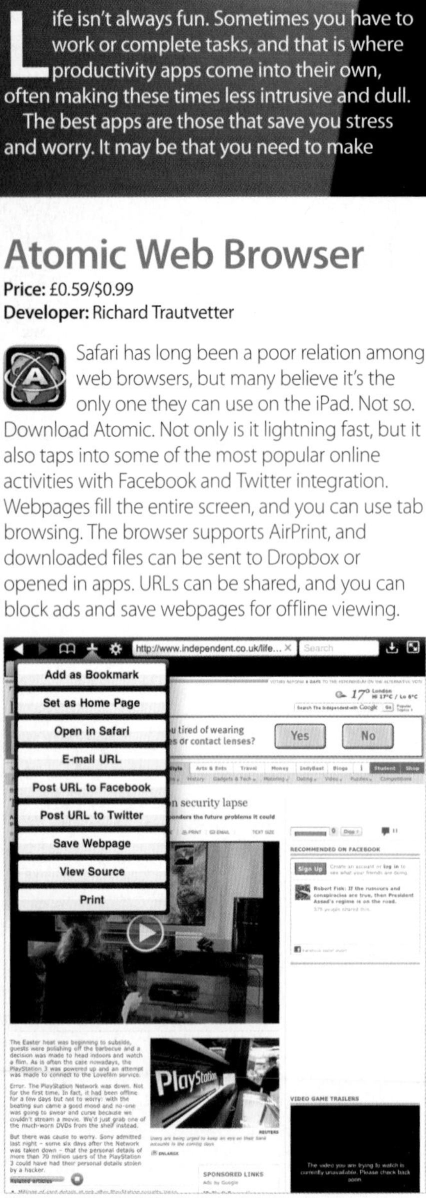

URLs can be posted to Facebook, Twitter or emailed, and pages can be saved or the source viewed.

GoDocs For iPad

Price: £2.99/$4.99
Developer: Nikita Lutsenko

As the iPad lets you sync email accounts from multiple service providers, it makes sense that Google Mail users can have access to Google Docs as well. Unfortunately, this isn't the case. Enter GoDocs, a handy app that gives you direct, secure access to your Google Docs at speed. From the top menu, you can browse your documents, open them, edit them, and save them on the cloud. It's an expansive toolset that gives you 100 per cent of the features you would expect from Google Docs online.

Documents can be tweaked at leisure, drawing in a range of editing options.

Calculator Pro

Price: £1.19/$1.99
Developer: MYW Productions

For some reason, Apple did not include a calculator with the iPad. Welcome, then, Calculator Pro, an excellent calc that also includes advanced functions. It's a good-looking app that works incredibly well – to get the scientific mode, you simply tilt the iPad. There are memory buttons, and if you tap in the wrong number, you simply swipe to delete the digits. There are skins available to customise, but you have to pay extra.

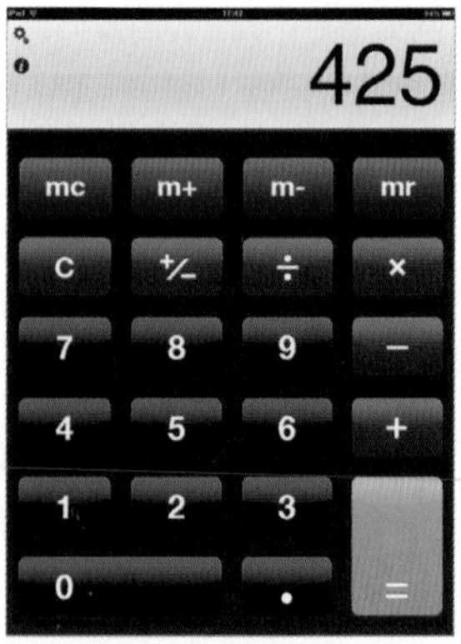

In portrait mode, the calculator looks like one huge desktop offering.

Dropbox

Price: Free
Developer: Dropbox, Inc

There are some apps we couldn't live without, and Dropbox is one of them, letting you store your files online. It's free, and as long as you don't use more than 2GB of storage, you won't have to pay a penny. The idea is you install Dropbox on your PC or Mac, and place files within the folder. They will then be accessible on your iPad, and vice versa. Dropbox supports all manner of files including PDFs.

"There are some apps we can't live without – Dropbox is one of them"

All your cloud files can be viewed – clicking one opens it up with Dropbox .

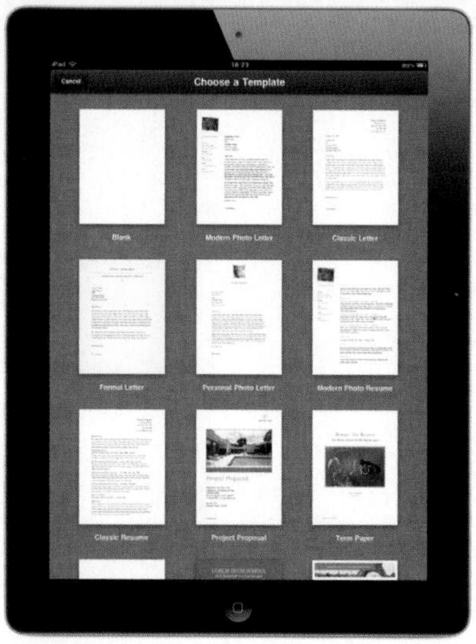

Pages

Price: £5.99/$9.99
Developer: Apple Inc

Considering the price, Pages is nothing less than amazing. You're getting a fully featured word processor that doubles up as a flexible desktop publishing package (indeed, attempts have been made – rather successfully – to lay out magazine pages using it). You are able to use a host of paragraph and character styles, align text and apply custom fonts. Images can be moved, re-sized and rotated. Documents can be emailed or shared via iTunes, and you can, of course, print too. All in all, it's a must-have app.

iTranslate – free translator

Price: £2.99/$4.99
Developer: Sonico GmbH

Although the translations are not always spot on, and take a little bit of deciphering, using iTranslate to make sense of a piece of foreign prose is still nifty. Copy and paste text into the main box, tell the app which languages you are using, and the translation is quickly made.

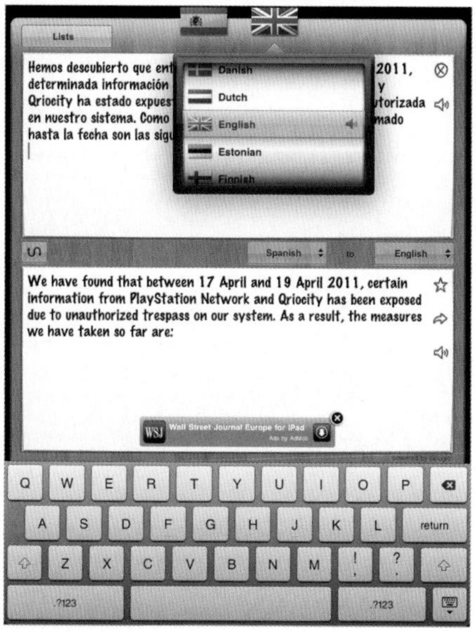

Documents To Go

Price: £5.99/$9.99
Developer: DataViz, Inc

Documents To Go is two things in one: an office suite which allows for editing, and a file repository. You can change documents, and save them to the cloud. The app works with Microsoft Office files (whether it be Word, PowerPoint or Excel), and also works perfectly with iWork files.

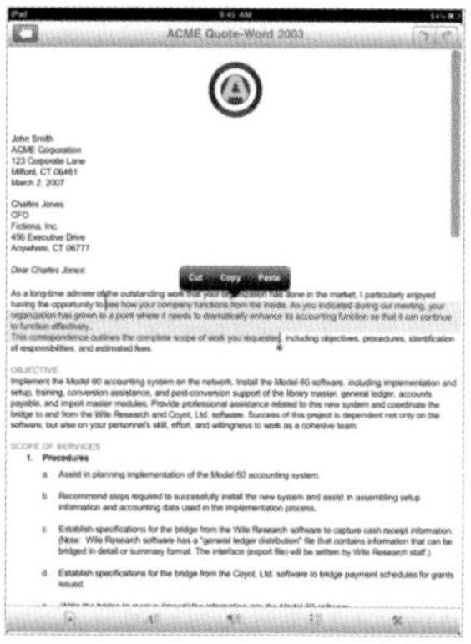

With Documents To Go, you get a full office suite for your iPhone.

iCurrency iPad – The Currency Exchange Rates Converter

Price: £0.59/$0.99
Developer: Sollico Software

There is no doubt that iCurrency is easy and intuitive to use. By typing in an amount, the conversion takes place instantly. It has more than 150 currencies, and a handy exchange rate chart.

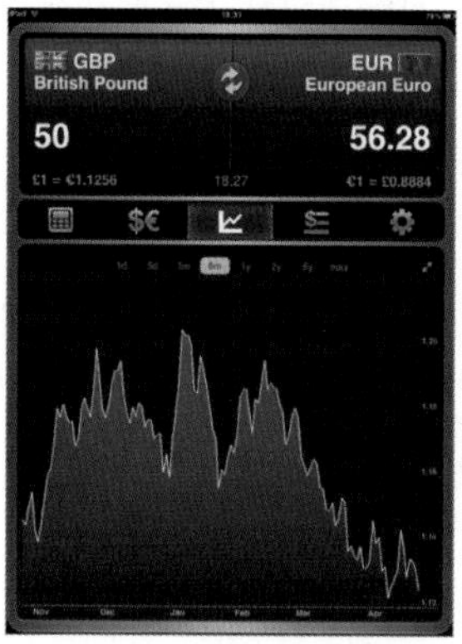

The currency rates are displayed at the top, and there's a wealth of options.

Dragon Dictation

Price: Free
Developer: Nuance Communications

This is one powerful app, and all the more remarkable for being free. By tapping record and speaking, an uncannily accurate transcription is produced that can be edited. The result can be emailed or sent and are saved for future reference.

Depending how long you're recording for, the results can show up in seconds.

"Documents To Go is both an office suite which allows for editing, and a file repository"

Awesome Note for iPad

Price: £2.99/$4.99
Developer: BRID

If, like us, you tend to find your sticky notes are flung across your desk, then Awesome Note for iPad is well worth the asking price. It lets you produce colour-coded notes that are placed within folders ranging from ideas, travel and shopping to work, study and to-do lists. Adding notes is easy; tap the + button, and you can view all notes at a glance, viewing them in a variety of ways, including date order. With Evernote and Google Docs syncing, it really is awesome.

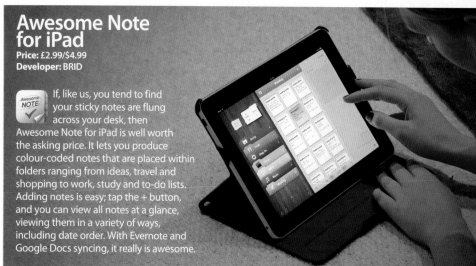

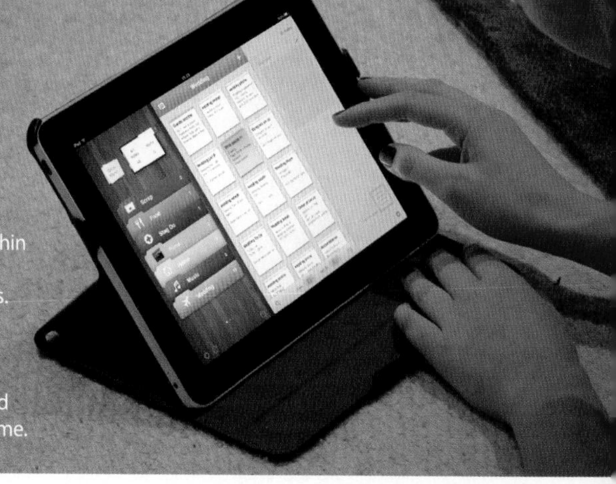

Price: Free Developer: Adobe

Adobe Photoshop Express

Professional photo editing on your iPad from an industry powerhouse

Adobe is one of the premiere photography software companies and now it has brought its industry standard Photoshop application to the iPad. This version doesn't even come close to the original in terms of features but what it does provide are some stripped down functions in an incredibly slick and easy to use application. If you own the original iPad, which doesn't have a camera, you will have to sync some pictures you've already taken. When it loads you have to select a picture to edit and from there you can do a number of cool things to enhance what your camera has already achieved.

The most basic functions are things like cropping and adding borders and on a more professional level you can adjust brightness, saturation and contrast. You can also add preset effects in a very simple way too. You can save your creations back to your picture library or upload them to Photoshop online (but this requires a membership). If we're totally honest there are far more advanced image editing apps on the store, though we doubt any are as polished as Adobe's offering. The app is so easy to use that you can fumble your way into expertly enhancing your pictures without trying too hard. If you have used the desktop Photoshop app, however, then this will fall far short of your initial expectations.

■ In the opening interface, there are some cool tips and tricks presented in typical flashy Adobe style.

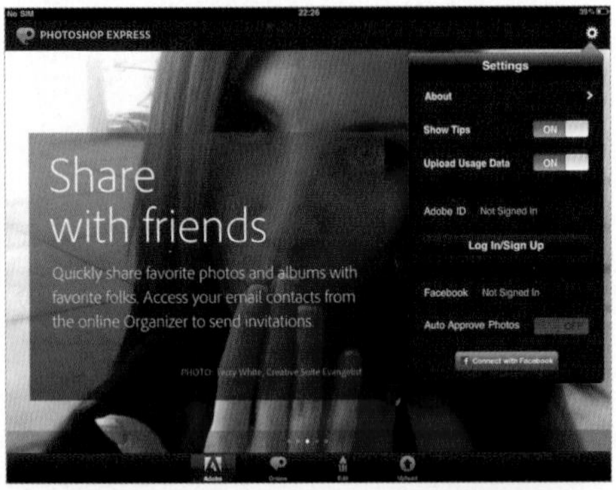

■ In the settings panel you can also connect with Facebook and upload pictures to your wall and add captions as you do it.

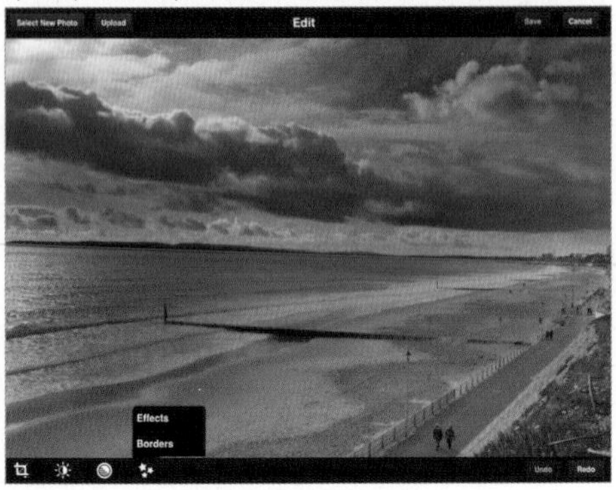

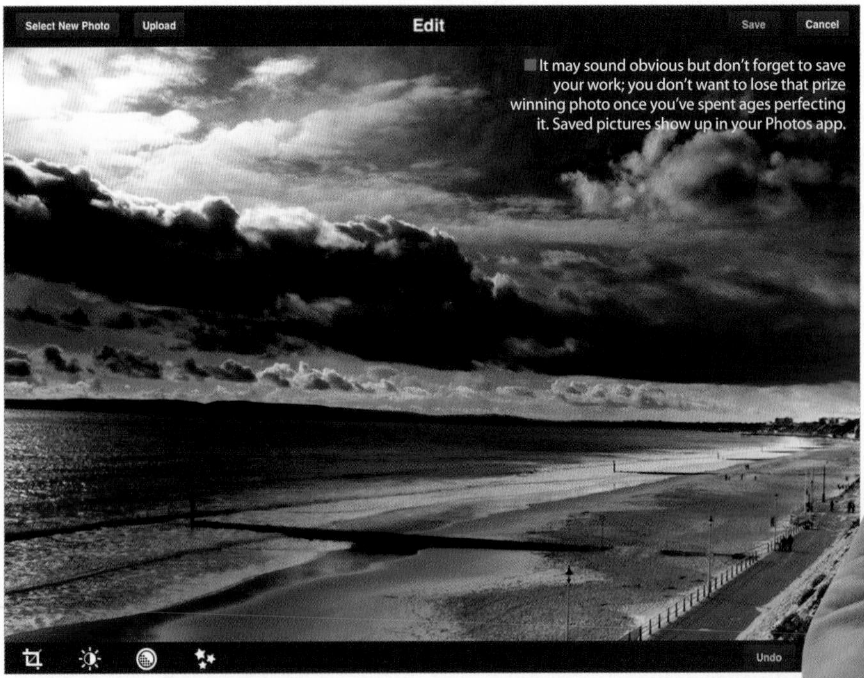

■ It may sound obvious but don't forget to save your work; you don't want to lose that prize winning photo once you've spent ages perfecting it. Saved pictures show up in your Photos app.

■ This final button in the tools section gives you access to the effects and borders – these are really for the finishing touches to your pictures.

Overall Rating ★★★★☆

Price: £1.19/$1.99 Developer: Global Delight Technologies

Photo Delight

Hand paint some colour into your pics with this cool app

Although there are a number of apps with similar functions available within the App Store, Photo Delight nevertheless manages to score highly thanks to its ease of use, smart tools and great options.

The reasons for this success are plenty. Firstly, its got some pretty smart styling, making the picture you load to edit look like it's on an easel. Down the side of the interface are the tools and options and the setup works in landscape and portrait. When you load a file from your library, you will find that it has been turned black and white, giving you the option of finger-painting the colour back into the picture.

On top of that simple system are a couple of other cool features. The first is the mask tool, which can be used to more easily view the area you are going to colourise. You also have the option of using different sized brushes, and you can choose between a soft or hard brush to reveal colour in a more subtle or obvious way. A great, easy to use app that's very rewarding.

■ The mask tool is a great way to see what you are painting in, adding your touch input in a red that's hard to miss. After that, use the colourise tab to flood the colour back into it.

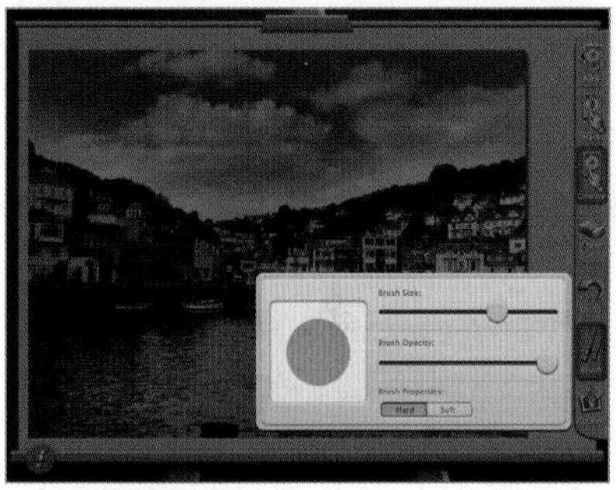

■ Altering the brush size allows you to get in close to areas that need fine detail. The bigger brush sizes also let you easily sweep through much bigger areas quickly.

■ In the options menu you can do all kinds of things with your picture. You can save the session, add the picture to your clipboard to take into another app, or share it with the world as it is. The pop-up menus make life a breeze.

■ Use your finger to 'paint' colour back into your photos. The results can be stunning and the touch input make this a highly enjoyable experience.

Overall Rating ★★★★★

Price: £1.19/$1.99 **Developer:** Red Software

Animation Creator HD

Create incredible animations on your iPad with just a flick of your fingers…

If you ever had any doubts about the potential of the software on the App Store then now is the time to cast them aside. We doubt even Steve Jobs himself could have envisioned a time where artists could create animations using their iPads. And yet when you load an app like Animation HD you almost feel as though the tablet computer was invented for this very purpose.

Once you have created a new project and tapped the toolbox button to show you the options you are ready to get cracking. You can select backgrounds, change painting/drawing tools and, of course, colours. Once you've started your animation you can use the plus button to add the next frame with onion skinning or you can copy the frame to add to it. For more ambitious users there is also the option to add layers like a Photoshop document. The colour palette is a little disappointing, it must be said, but you can use a sliding scale of colours to create more desirable tones if you so wish. The brush choices are cool, as is the ability to easily alter the brush size.

If you are artistic then you will undoubtedly get some enjoyment from this app. It's simple, easy to use and a great deal of fun, not to mention great value. Well worth a download.

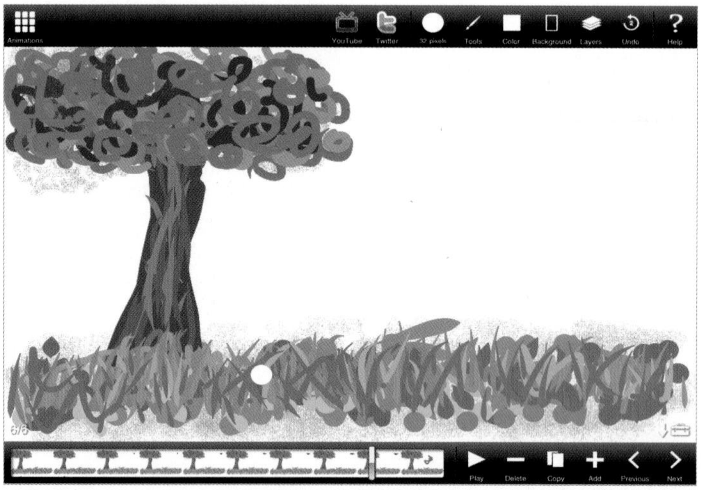

■ Add layers easily by using this drop-down menu. Just remember which layer you are editing.

■ You'll use the brush tool most as it feels the most natural to paint with using your finger. Tap the button to change tools.

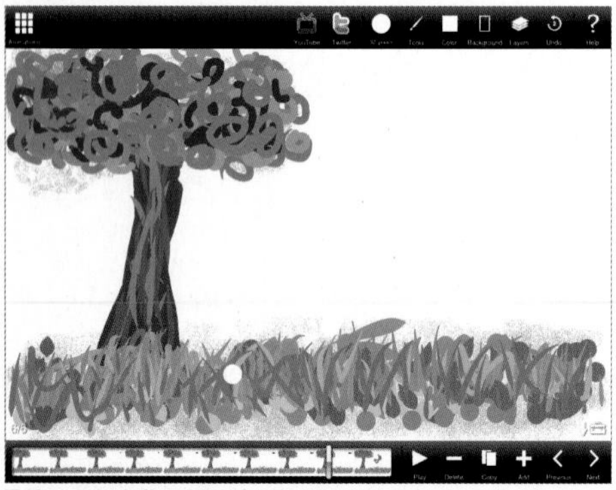

■ The controls for adding frames is simple, so you can rattle through animations if you're doing something straightforward.

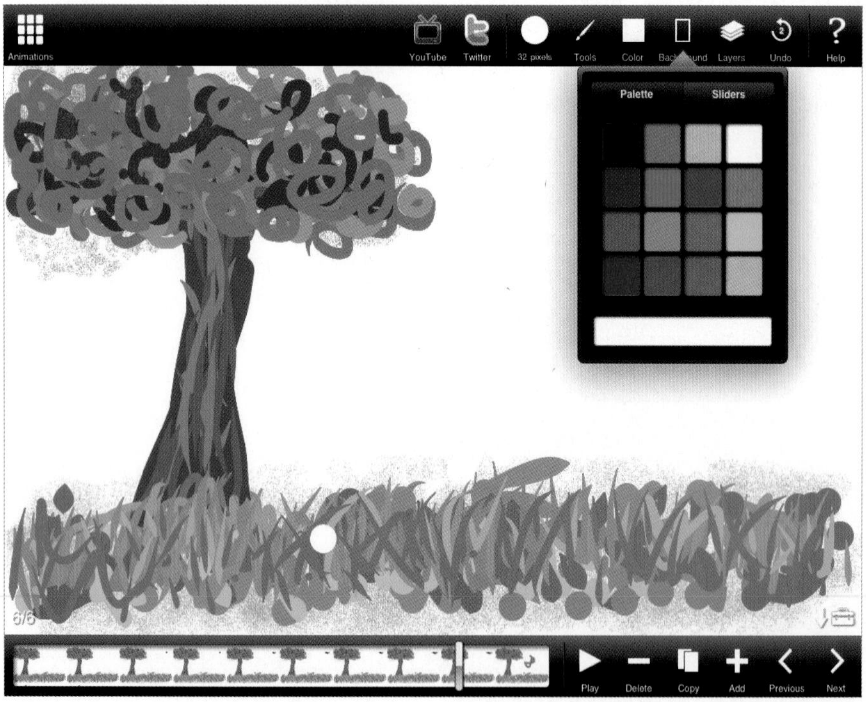

■ The colour palette is a bit poor but you can use a sliding scale to get more subtle variations, though this can be tricky if you are not used to doing it.

Overall Rating ★★★★★

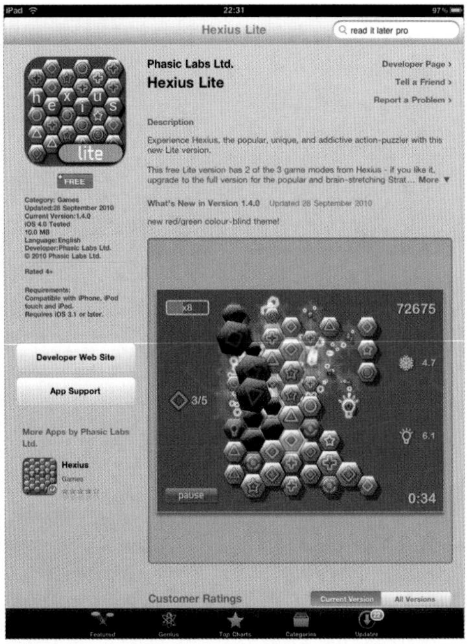

■ Once you've selected an app you're taken to the App Store.

Price: Free Developer: AppShopper

AppShopper

Ensure you never miss an app bargain again

AppShopper.com is a website for finding out about all the best app bargains, and now it has its own app. This works as you'd expect, giving you the latest updates of the best and cheapest apps. Major updates are given to you and it's possible to integrate your own apps into the store so you know when they're due an update.

The app itself is easy to navigate, being split into Filters as well as Sections. Filters enable you to do everything from searching for free apps, to browsing apps by category or just looking through your updates, while Sections is split into Popular, What's New, My Apps, Wish List and a general search feature.

The biggest downside is that it's skewed towards the US-based users, meaning that all the prices are currently only in dollars. It also doesn't tell you if an app is available in your region, or if it's in English. Despite these annoyances, however, AppShopper remains a highly useful little app for finding bargains.

Overall Rating ★★★★★

Cocktails HD

Tom Cruise will have nothing on you after you buy this app

Don't know your Bloody Bulls from your Bloody Marys? Thought a Manhattan was somewhere in New York? Then this is the app for you, as it will turn you into a cocktail expert quicker than you can say Tom Cruise.

Cocktails HD at its most basic is a guide to making cocktails. And yet, thanks to fantastic presentation, easy to learn steps and stunning images, it becomes a completely unmissable app that any cocktail connoisseur will not want to ever be without.

Cocktails are split into eight categories ranging from Shooters to Martinis and come with full instructions for making them, along with the required ingredients. If that's not enough there are also handy guides that explain everything from correctly shaking your chosen drinks to even how to correctly serve wine and beer.

While there's nothing here that's not easily available on the internet, it's all put together with so much care and attention and the drinks look so mouth-watering that you'll always want to keep it handy in order to try out your latest tipple. There's even a nice little feature where you can shake your iPad and the app will choose you a random cocktail.

If you've always been interested in mixing cocktails or have a big party coming up you'll find this app to be the perfect reference guide. Now excuse us, we've got some Harvey Wallbangers and Strawberry Daiquiris to make.

Price: £2.99/$4.99 Developer: Pocket Cocktails

■ The presentation throughout Cocktails HD is absolutely superb, with clutter-free menus and easy to follow advice.

Overall Rating ★★★★★

Price: £2.99/$5.99 **Developer:** Guinness World Records

Guinness World Records: At Your Fingertips

If you want to be a record breaker, this is what you need…

Spread across a handful of extreme categories (including Tallest, Craziest and Most Expensive), Guinness World Records: At Your Fingertips offers users an interesting insight into what it takes to become a legend amongst generations of drunks. This may occasionally require doing a little more than withstanding the pain of a needle or forgetting that falling causes death, but oh well.

Each category contains perhaps half a dozen or so separate entries chronicling various individuals' life work, making good use of the device's features through a range of interactive elements. These are often as simple as dots placed upon items of note that will bring up small portions of text thereon. Using the constant connectivity of Apple's devices, the Guinness World Record for typing the alphabet backwards could very well be yours by the middle of next year. Sure, that hardly matches the 100 metres for prestige, but it's a start.

Aside perhaps from three-dimensional diagrams to manipulate, offering that additional level of presentational pizzazz, it's difficult to claim value for money isn't present here.

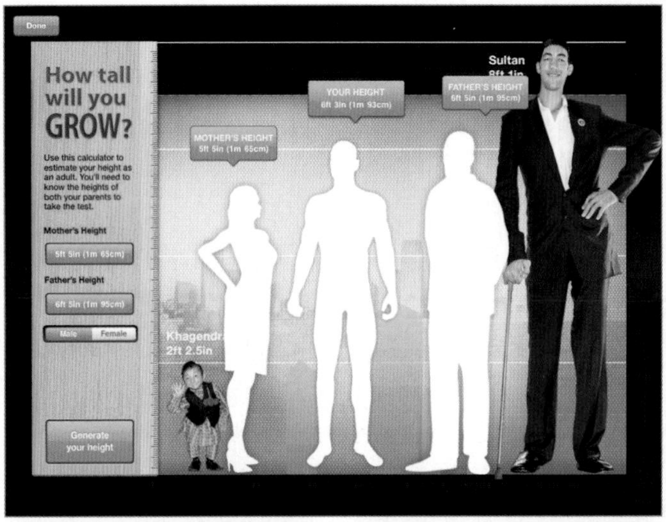

Here the interactive element involves children having their eventual height predicted.

Records are illustrated using annotated diagrams that can be prodded at will.

A library of striking imagery is on hand to demonstrate how extraordinary each feat is. Or person, of course. Here, the world's tallest living man is spoiling a game of basketball.

Video links are included within some write-ups, depicting better than words ever could the feat achieved, such as a scene depicting the prologue to Usain Bolt's 100m sprint title.

Overall Rating

★★★★☆

Price: Free **Developer:** BBC Worldwide LTD

Good Food Magazine (for iPad)

How to bring a print magazine to iPad and do it well

The BBC is renowned for its food programmes. Complementing the on-screen cookery masterclass is the brilliant *Good Food Magazine*. Within the pages, you'll find seasonal recipes, hints and tips from top cookery writers, fantastic features, dream kitchens, and all the latest gadgets.

Now, the BBC has brought the *Good Food Magazine* to the iPad. Here, each issue displays all its glorious photography and mouth-watering recipes on a platform that does it justice.

So, what's to like? Firstly, the layout: it starts off like a conventional magazine, but touch the bottom of the screen, and you can view each spread as a thumbnail. Tap on one, and it springs up to full screen. If you're not sure what you want to cook, the filter on the contents spread will allow you to narrow recipes down into certain categories.

There's more to each page, though. We like the tools spread here; tap the image you want to read about, and the text relating to it appears to the side. Each recipe front image has a flip button that reveals the ingredients and cooking instructions. Tap the little 'i' icon, and a box will appear telling your more about a certain ingredient, and even let you know the various health benefits. You can either view instructions as you would in a book, or tap the blue 'Cook' icon, and you'll be presented with the steps individually in a larger type face.

One of our favourite features has to be the shopping list option. If you find something you'd like to cook, click on the list icon, and all the ingredients (and amounts) are listed. If you already have some stock cubes in the cupboard for instance, it's possible to edit the list down, and the list will grow with each additional recipe you request. Take your iPad to the local supermarket, and tick off items as you put them in your trolley. If the shop doesn't have that special ingredient, simply click on the glossary, and find the food to discover what it is and what you can substitute it with.

The icing on the cake has to be the exclusive video clips that feature tips and from the Good Food team, which ensure you get great results every time.

■ The app is free, but you will need to buy the content.

■ The stunning photography is rendered beautifully on the iPad's HD screen. It'll certainly tempt you to cook it.

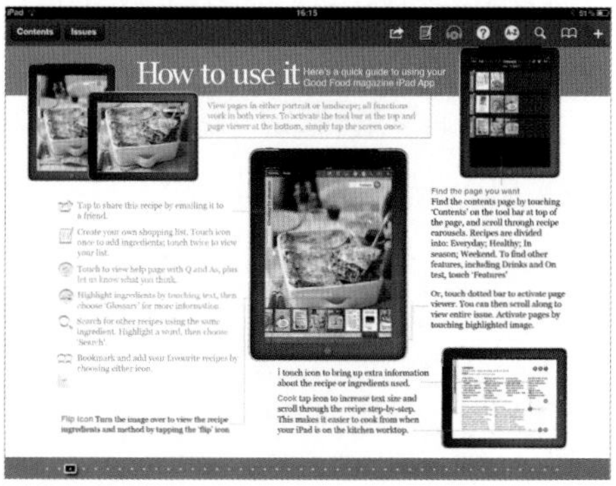

■ Handy tutorials will guide you on how to use the app.

Overall Rating ★★★★★

Price: Free **Developer:** Jonathan George

Boxcar

The news not when it happens, but as it happens…

Oddly, if you've no friends in this world whatsoever, Boxcar is certainly the app for you – though we sincerely doubt that was Jonathan George's intention in creating it.

More central to its existence is the plethora of social networking options available. Whether it's Twitter, Facebook, Foursquare, Google Buzz or any other portal, there's no shortage of places to keep up with current events of a serious or comedic nature. Trouble is, having so many sources can lead to confusion amid the bundles of data being thrown in the unsuspecting user's direction each day.

Boxcar addresses this situation by breaking down each of the above providers – along with email and RSS feeds – providing push notifications to your Apple device the very instant one person or outlet updates. Rather than having to scroll through perhaps hundreds of Twitter feeds, or the copious output of Facebook friends, it is now possible to cherry-pick the most valuable contacts across all fields, and be updated on them instantly.

What's more, with specific relevance to Twitter, if you're interested in all the members of a particular band, magazine team or perhaps newsroom, the app makes slotting all of their Tweets together into a whole just that little bit easier. Naturally, if the idea of receiving push notifications every time an acquaintance has breakfast seems like hell, you can restrict the app's functionality to certain times (though sadly not days of the week). This app does rely upon advertising support to survive (unless you're okay with the £4.99/$9.99 ad removal fee), but there's little denying Boxcar's streamlining functions are pretty useful in this multi-multimedia world.

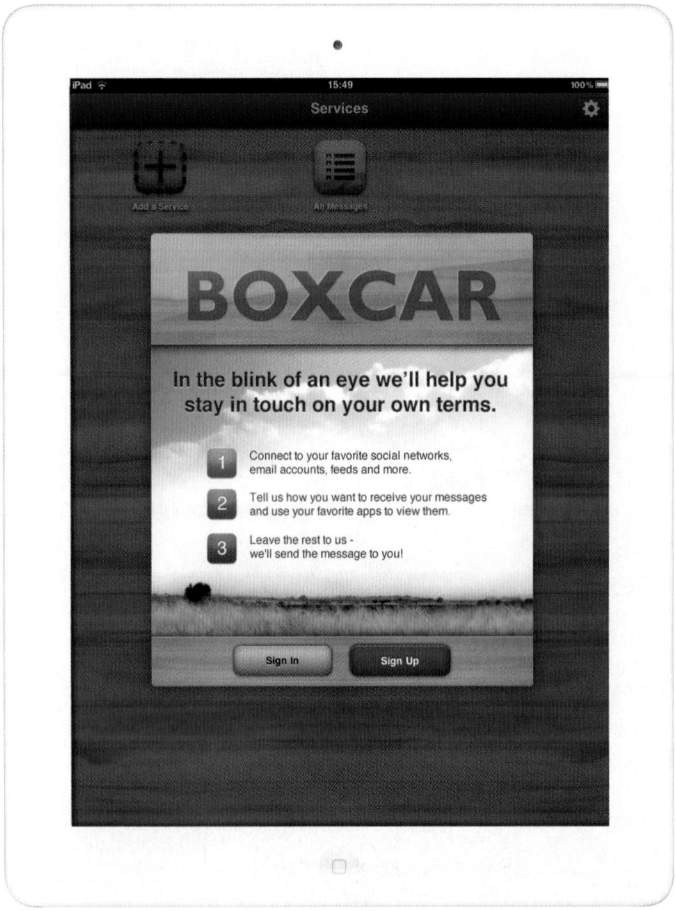

■ Popular social networking services can be added or removed from the app's repertoire with ease.

Overall Rating ★★★★★

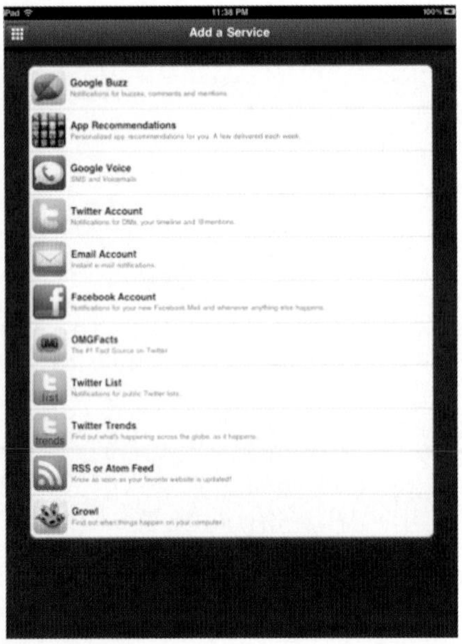

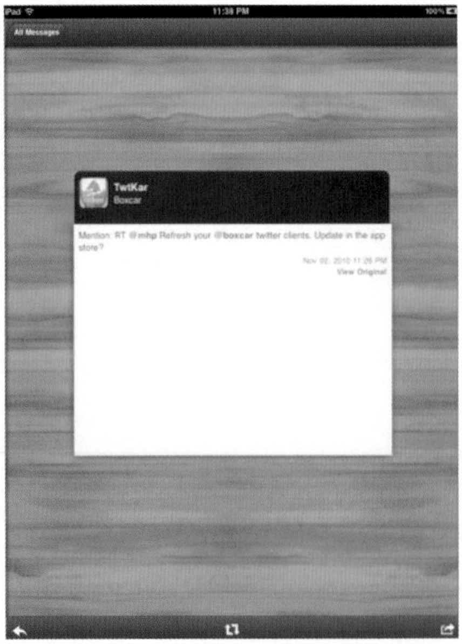

Price: Free **Developer:** AOL Inc

Engadget for iPad

The essential technology news app comes to iPad – and is better than ever

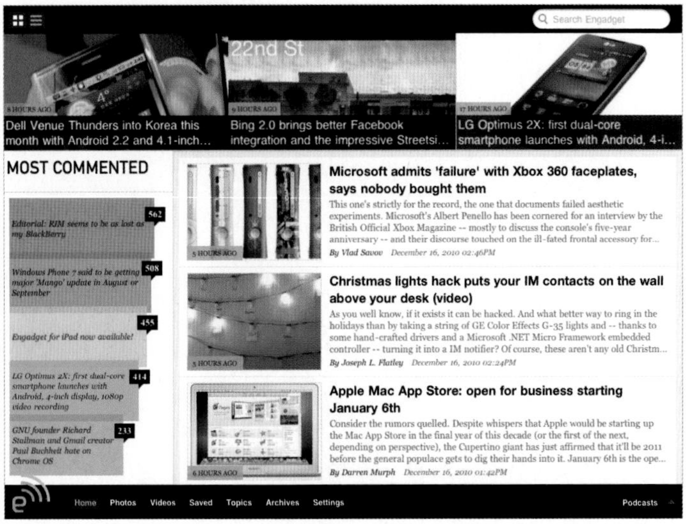

The Engadget app on the iPhone brought a wealth of technology news to your fingertips, and now the app has grown onto iPad and it's better than ever.

Upon loading the app you can tap into four channels: Engadget, iMobile, Engadget HD and alt.Engadget, and are served up a rich feast of regularly updated news stories, plus photo galleries and video feeds. The screen is efficiently presented with scrollable stories across a top bar, and news previews in the main window that you can tap on to be taken through to the full story and accompanying links. What's more, a handy side-tab allows you to post comments on any of the stories, and a side-column on the front page displays the most-commented stories.

The app is completed by launch pads along the bottom of the screen that take you to photo and video galleries, saved stories, hot topics and news archives. But the real icing on the cake is the 'Podcasts' tab that lets you listen to Engadget's latest audio feeds within the app itself.

Whether you have an enthusiastic interest in technology or simply want to gaze at how a great news app should be done, Engadget is a must-download app that is a joy to behold.

Overall Rating ★★★★★

Go Run Magazine

Thinking about running? Then this app will help you along every step of the way

Price: £0.59/$0.99 **Developer:** PixelMags

We all pledge, usually in an alcohol-induced haze on New Year's Eve, to rid our bodies of toxins and get fit for the forthcoming year. Granted, such resolutions are usually swiftly forgotten about, but if you are serious about improving your fitness then the Go Run Magazine app provides the perfect springboard for your ambitions.

This digital magazine is geared towards runners of all abilities, offering useful tips that can be read on the move and practical advice on training and nutrition. When you download the app you will get part one of 'The Beginner's Guide To Running', which is the first of many in-app books that will steadily help you enhance your running skills. In fact, the app pledges to help you train for your first 5K run from scratch in just 12 weeks!

The pages of this eBook are informative and eye-catching without constantly bombarding you with text. Everything is kept waffle-free in bite-sized segments, providing only the essential information you need to get going, which is generally friendly and encouraging.

The app is easy to navigate, thanks to the handy scroll bar at the foot of the page, and zooming in is done simply by tapping on the page. There are also tabs to search for keywords and share the content with a friend.

So whether you're an existing runner eager to take on board additional expert advice to better prepare you for your next big race, or just thinking about getting into a new exercise regime and need tips on conditioning your body and buying the right gear, then this is the app for you.

■ The scroll bar at the foot of the page allows for a simple and user-friendly navigational system.

■ The Go Run Magazine app is ideal for runners of all abilities and disciplines.

Overall Rating ★★★★★

Price: £6.99/$11.99 Developer: Ilya Plavunov

OMGuitar Advanced Synth Guitar

We finger the hottest musical instrument app

One of many synthesisers available in the App Store, OMGuitar is slightly different to the rest in that it is designed to retain the crucial human element that can fill music with feeling. The strings on the virtual guitar are sensitive to so many different types of interaction, not just tapping and strumming, but also note bending and muting. Importantly, the app can also distinguish the speed and rhythm with which you strum the strings, allowing you to attach your own personality onto the performance.

Actually playing the app as though it's an instrument inevitably feels a little tricky at first. It's obviously not played entirely like a real guitar, but neither is it a simple synthesiser that you can play by just pushing buttons. Instead, it's intended that the iPad be held in the lap so that one hand can freely strum, while the other grips either the top or bottom of the device in order to manipulate the chord buttons on the screen. It does take a little getting used to, but eventually becomes second nature and is smooth to play.

In terms of features, OMGuitar is very flexible. There are six different types of simulated guitars to choose from, half electric and the other half acoustic, while ten in-built effects, such as distortion or phaser, allow for further customisation. Naturally, the app allows you to record in .wav format and save directly to iTunes, while full MIDI support is promised for a future update. Other than that, the only way OMGuitar can possibly be improved. More guitar types, more effects and so on. All of which will come with time.

As it stands, OMGuitar is the best guitar synthesizer on the App Store. But who is it designed for? It's certainly a fun novelty if approached as a distracting digital toy, but the high price almost pushes the app out of the range of most dabblers. As a serious musical synthesizer program, the price is a bargain and we've heard from many musicians who agree and have regularly used the app for composing and even recording. And who are we to disagree?

Overall Rating ★★★★★

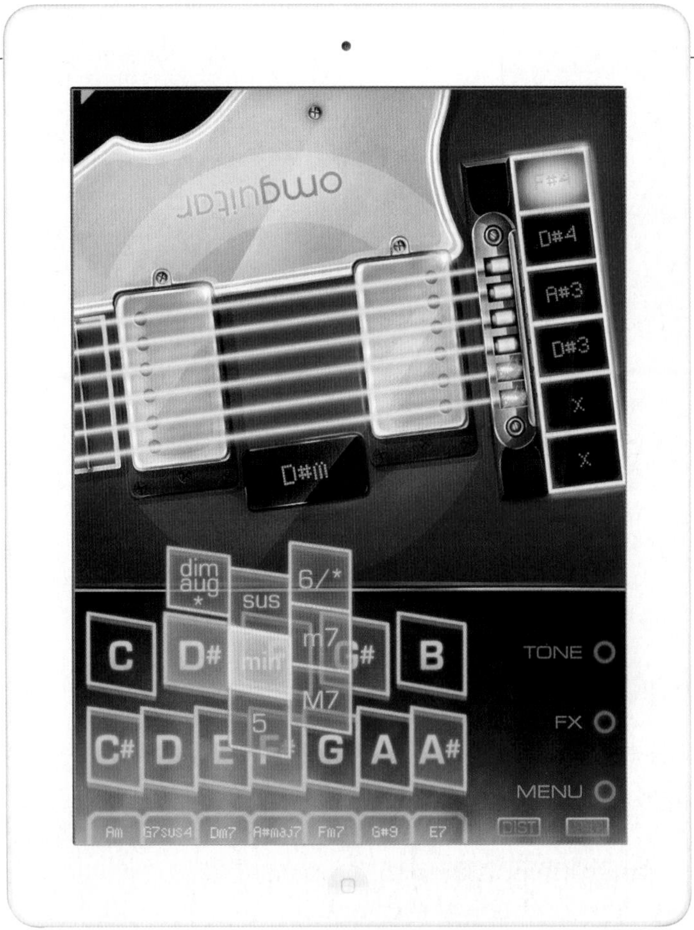

■ The way buttons bring up transparent menus, which overlap the others, is a nice space-saving touch.

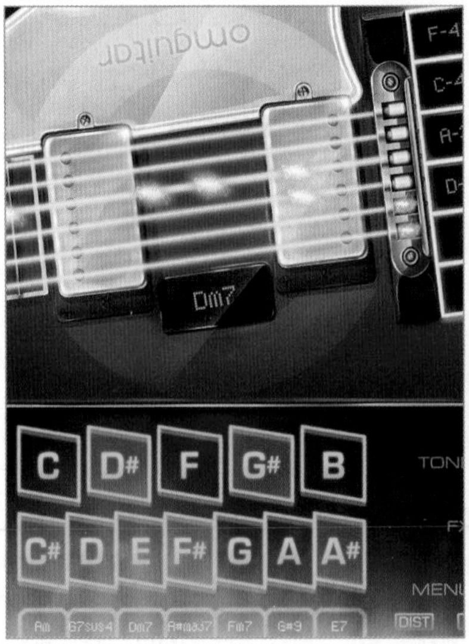

■ Little waves of noise ripple through the strings when you strum, just to offer some reassuring visual feedback.

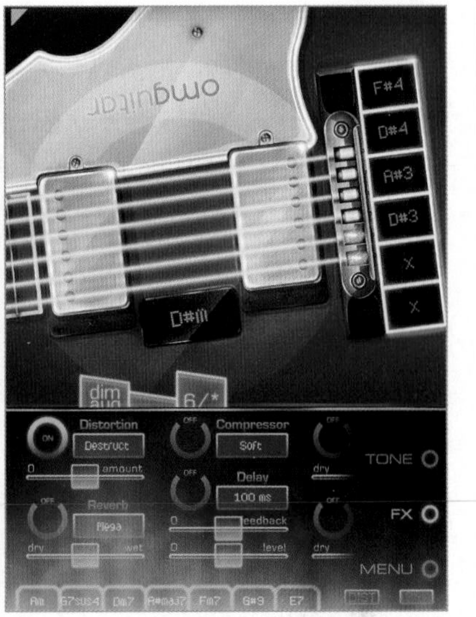

■ A wide range of effects are possible. You could lose hours fiddling around with them.

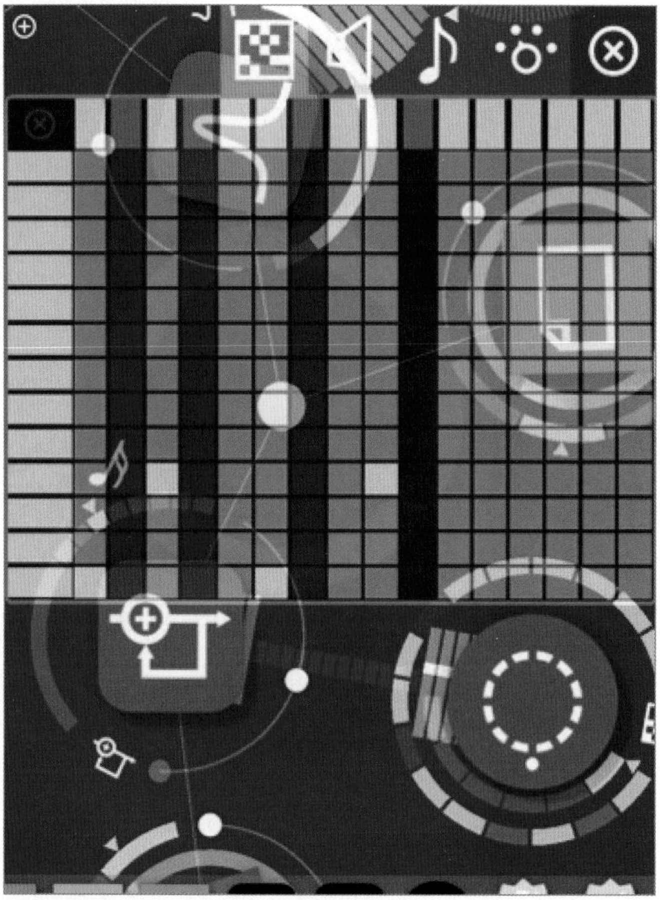

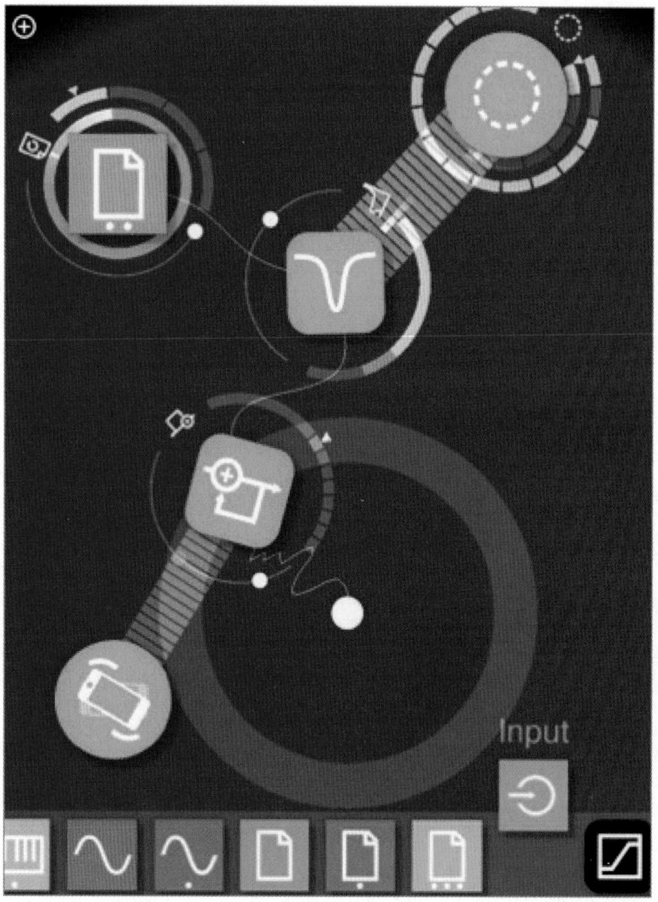

■ Get too many tangibles going on and Reactable Mobile struggles to keep up with it all. Most of the time it's just fine, though.

Price: £5.99/$9.99 **Developer:** Reactable Systems SL

Reactable mobile

Getting to grips with the coolest synthesiser on iPad

Best described as a futuristic synthesiser, the Reactable is a circular table, backlit with a deep blue light, to be used in a darkened room. The table itself is a touch-sensitive computer display that reacts to objects, called tangibles, that are placed on the screen, moved around and rotated. This creates different sorts of music depending on the type of tangibles that are placed on the table, their spatial relationship to one another and the way in which they are manipulated. It's a very cool, almost sci-fi idea, and one that has been used by a number of high-profile performers including Björk. Sadly, at a price of around £8,500, the Reactable is far out of the reach of your average bedroom DJ, which is where Reactable Mobile comes in…

At a mere £5.99, Reactable Mobile is much more affordable than its tabletop counterpart and does a pretty good impression of it too. Just like the original, it allows you to place various synthesiser functions onto the surface and play around with them to create your own music in real time. On the iPhone, it's a rather cramped affair, but on the larger iPad screen, laid down flat on a table or other surface, we felt like we were getting a fair approximation of the original technology, especially with the room to use both hands freely.

There's a mind boggling array of options at your fingertips – loop players, oscillators, wave shapers, sequencers and all number of other things we don't really understand but are sure will be most welcome with the musically inclined, especially as the software allows you to incorporate your own samples into the mix. As amateurs, we had a lot of fun simply experimenting with the 'tangibles' and were surprised by the music we were able to create, suggesting that those who know what they're doing will be able to produce exceptional results. Just about the only fault we encountered was that the software struggled to keep up when we overloaded it with too many tangibles at once but that may not be such big a deal. After all, how many bands do you see use more than a handful of instruments at once?

Overall Rating ★★★★★

Price: Free Developer: Amidio Inc

LoopJ™ Interactive DJ Station

Become a mixing marvel with this fantastic free app

LoopJ Interactive DJ Station is an interesting combination of a loop player and DJ device, but can be somewhat confusing for the uninitiated. Instead of being presented with dials or sliders, here you are given 20 pads that require different techniques to create effects. Press and hold to preview the sound, tap to queue it, double-tap for an immediate start or stop, drag up or down to control the volume of a loop, drag left for a HP filter, right for HP and so on. It's complicated, but natural once you get the hang of it.

The cool thing is that two tracks can play at the same time, and the decks are always properly synced via a timestretch algorithm based on the BPM value you set at the bottom of the screen. You can crossfade to change the balance between tracks, and there are effects that you can add by moving the circle to the appropriate position on a graph. The app currently only comes with Delay, Gate and Repeater options, so it will be nice to see further effects added in future updates.

You have five sample tracks to experiment with, but you can add your own ones for free. You can also record to WAV and M4A files through an in-app purchase.

This app is better suited for more experienced dance DJs and musicians, though, but there is a lot of fun and experimentation to be had for those less used to mixing, and as a free app it offers users a lot. Some excellent results can be achieved, and we just hope future updates will bring more options along the way.

Overall Rating ★★★★★

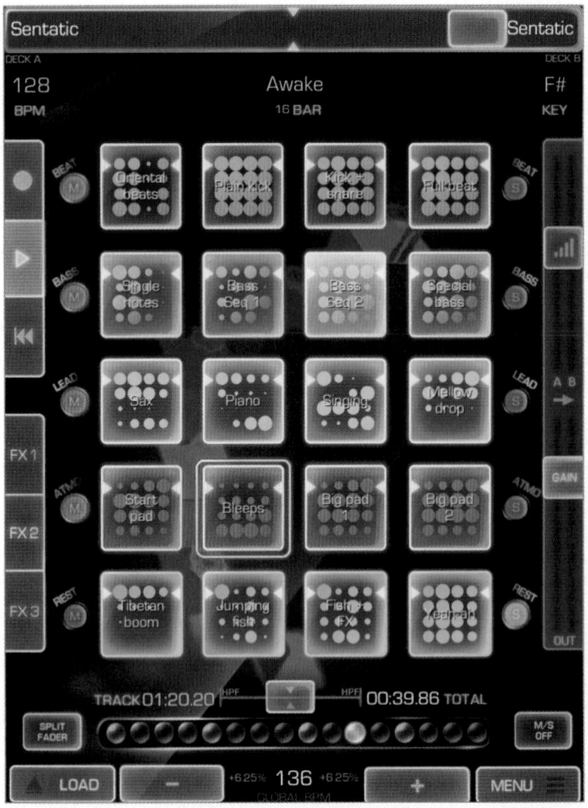

■ Double-tap on the square for it to immediately start playing.

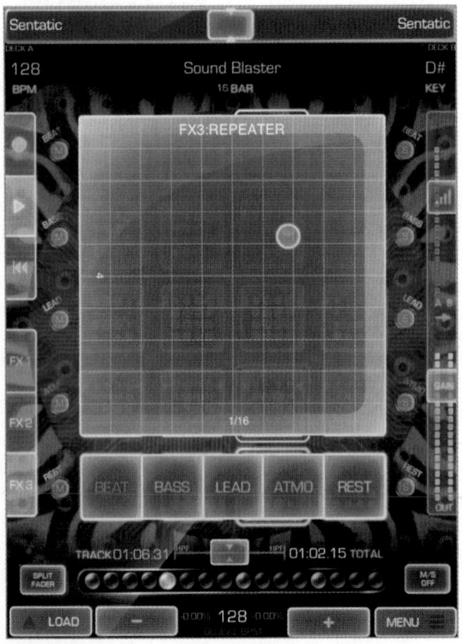

■ Move the Gain slider with your finger. This command is clearly much easier to work out than the others.

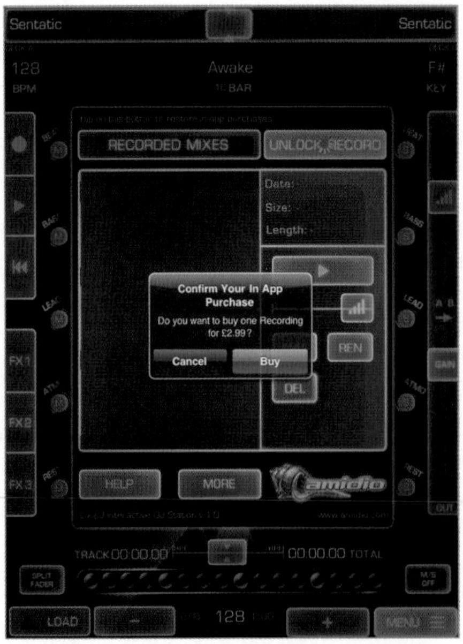

■ You have to pay for recording capabilities, but the price is reasonable considering the app is free.

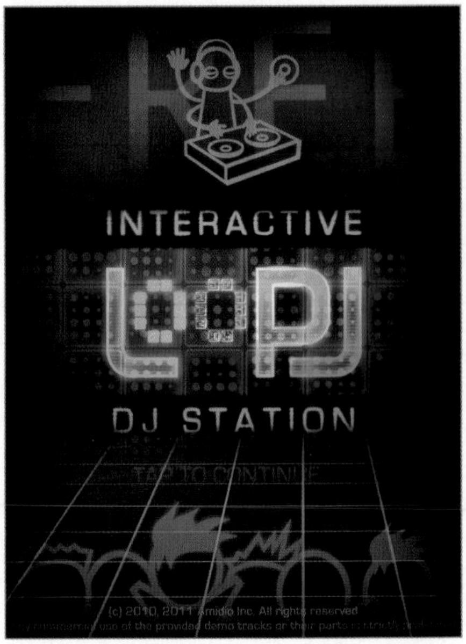

■ In among the features is a split fader, but this isn't active yet, but it will be a nice addition in a future update.

Price: £1.19/$1.99 **Developer:** PixelMags

SciFiNow

The world's leading science fiction magazine comes to the iPad

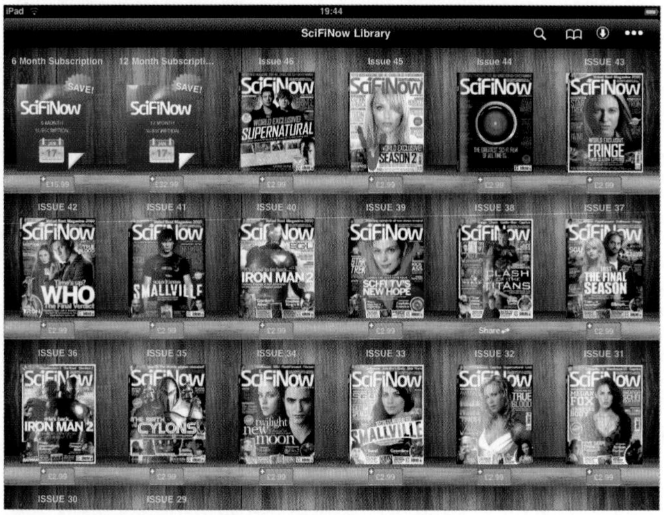

The debate as to whether the internet or a handheld magazine is better is never going to die. Both boast positive and negatives that the other would love to include/exclude and it's unlikely one will ever ride out on top. What will, however, is a mix of both. *SciFiNow* is a perfect example.

Giving you a free issue of the magazine when you purchase the app, it opens up the ability to buy every back copy released and gives you instant access to the monthly publication as soon as it goes on-sale. Reading *SciFiNow* on iPad is a treat. Flicking through the pages with your fingers or zooming into a particular article, which is heightened thanks to the iPad's slick resolution and speed, is effortless and makes the experience as good as having the actual print magazine. In some instances it's even easier as bookmarking a page or searching for a particular feature is as simple as a touch of a button. You can even share an issue with a friend who also has the app installed, making the app as close to its real-life counterpart as possible. Ideal for reading on the train or any long journey, the *SciFiNow* app is perfect to get your science fiction fix on the move if you fancy an alternative to having paper between your fingers, or just want to save shelf space.

Overall Rating ★★★★★

Tap TV

Watch classic movies and cartoons plus the best of YouTube on your iPad

Price: Free **Developer:** TapMedia

■ While you'll find some hi-res new cartoons on the Tap TV system, most content is old and grainy, but still well worth watching.

There are many different ways you can watch video on the iPad, but the truth is that videos are only as good as the source they come from. What Tap TV offers is the ability to 'tap' into an extensive archive of videos to watch via Wi-Fi at any time you see fit. As you might expect, the app is split into a diverse range of channels: movies, cartoons, documentaries, App TV, audiobooks, Magic TV, Best of YouTube and Silent Classics. Unfortunately, when it comes to movies or cartoons you're unlikely to find anything particularly new on Tap TV, but it's a great source of ancient classics that you can educate or just plain torture your kids with, or watch on your own for pure nostalgia value (and the inevitable swell of mild disappointment that accompanies returning to your childhood favourites).

We found some excellent old Warner Bros. cartoons lurking in the lists, and some great Charlie Chaplin movies that you probably won't have seen for years! There are new videos too, though, particularly on the documentaries and App TV channels.

The app is well laid out with easy-to-navigate menus, although we did find that the thumbnail videos took a little while to propagate through the system, giving the app a sluggish feel at times. Of course, this is down to internet speed more than anything, so the overall success of the app would be much improved if you have a super-fast Wi-Fi connection at home.

Overall Rating ★★★★★

Price: £2.39/$3.99 **Developer:** BBC Worldwide Ltd

Doctor Who: The Mazes Of Time

Comic-book fun comes alive in this action-packed adventure

The story behind *The Mazes Of Time* is simple. The Doctor and Amy Pond answer a distress call to save the members of a family who have been warped off to different time zones that range from an Incan world to a sprawling Dalek ship.

It's a fairly simplistic story, but it does allow for a nice range of locations, even if they're aren't rendered to any great degree. But while it's not much to look at, the all-important gameplay is of a far better standard, with the Doctor and Amy having to work together to clear each area. Initially, puzzles consist of straightforward switches that must be pressed, and doorways that must be opened, but they do require more head-scratching later on.

Amy and the Doctor are very different in the way they are used to solve puzzles. The light-footed Amy is able to easily move along cracked tiles and crawl under small areas, while the stronger Doctor has the ability to push large crates and clamber over high objects. You can also switch between the two characters at will, which further adds to the game's strategy.

The game won't take you more than five hours to complete, but it's a highly entertaining romp, thanks to its recognisable heroes and villains, solid presentation and the fact that it's just a lot of fun to play. Yes, it's squarely aimed at kids, and yes it's a little too easy for its own good, but there is much for fanatics to love here.

Overall Rating ★★★★★

■ The game isn't much to look at but the gameplay is fun.

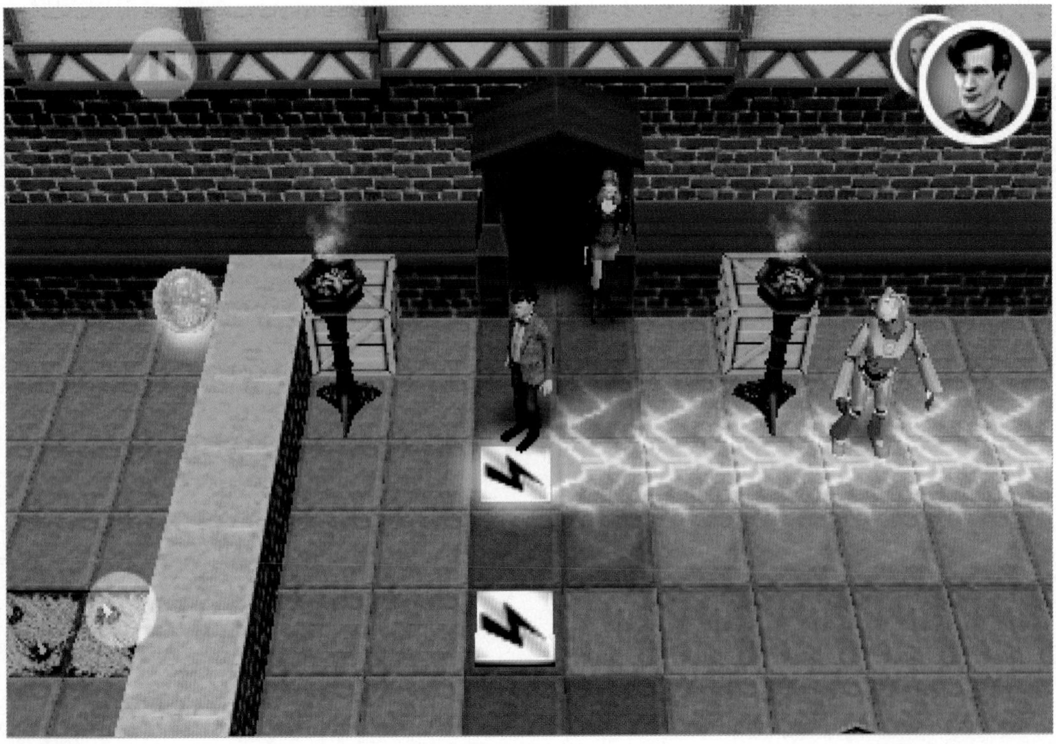

■ There are a huge amount of switches in The Mazes Of Time, and they all have different results when you step on them. This one is great for stopping Cybermen.

■ While the Doctor can die in *The Mazes Of Time*, he never actually regenerates in the game.

■ Being rather lithe, Amy is able to squeeze into lots of tight nooks and crannies in order to reach switches and avoid foes.

Price: £2.99/$4.99 Developer: ElectronicArtsBV

Pictureka! for iPad

Hands-on with the iPad edition of the kids' favourite board game

Based on the popular board game of the same name, Pictureka! presents the player with a screen crammed with images of all different kinds of objects, and then challenges them to identify, locate and tap on a given number of a certain object to complete the task. Instructions can sometimes be very specific – "Find three butterflies", for example. Or it can be more open with its challenges, like finding four things that belong in space. Other stages place no upper limit on the number of specific objects to pick out, instead asking you to find as many as possible within a given time limit.

The vast space available on the iPad screen ensures that Pictureka! can be rammed with tons of objects at once, all competing to distract you from those you're meant to be picking out. Even when you do find one, a different object will instantly pop up to take its place. It never lets up, and is always searching for something new to keep you on your toes. Another advantage of the iPad version is that the extra screen space makes it perfect for multiple people to play together, and Pictureka! takes full advantage of this. There's a fun little 'pass 'n play' mode for up to four players, and there's really nothing to stop two or more people teaming up to finish the main adventure mode together either.

Overall Rating ★★★★★

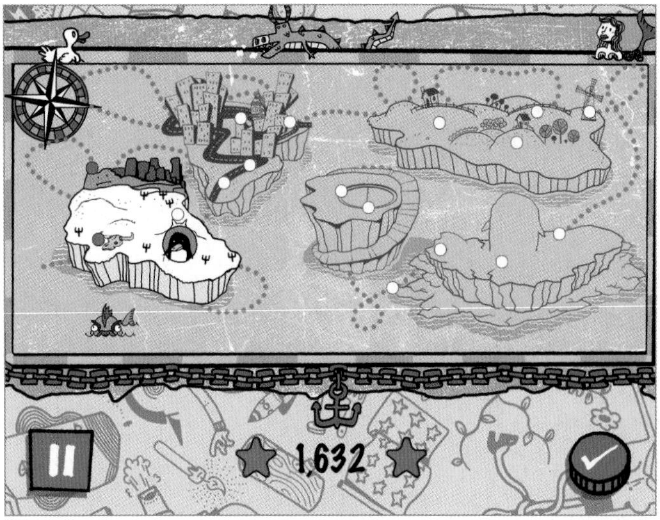

■ The game is packed full of fun little characters, making Pictureka! an ideal game to engage children's imaginations.

■ There is a time limit on each level, but we found it to be very generous. Things get harder the further you progress.

■ Ramp up the challenge. The red card is a slot for another challenge, should one be necessary. You can have a maximum of three types of objects to look out for at any one time.

■ The game does use language quite loosely. Though this challenge is for 'leaves', the game happily accepted the flowers we tapped on. We would have been more strict.

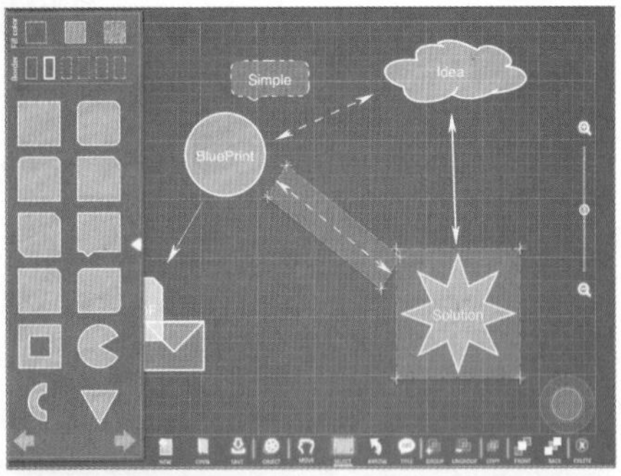

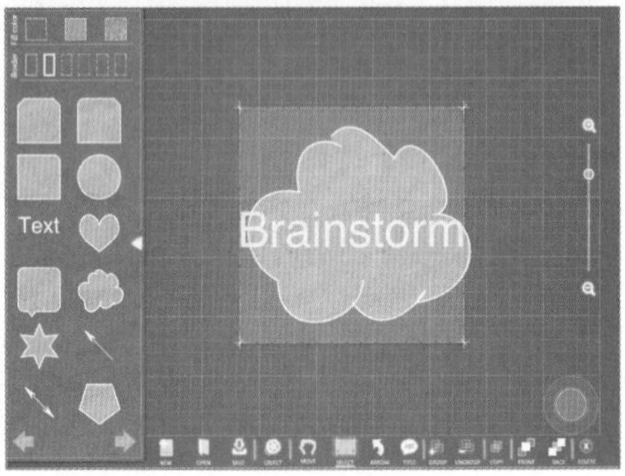

Price: £2.99/$4.99 Developer: ITCreate

BluePrint Sketch

Sketch an idea onto blueprint paper

We have to admit, there's something magical about blueprints. After all, the rockets that took mankind to the moon and back were designed on blueprint paper. Don't raise your hopes too high, however, as this is more of a sketching tool with the ability to create quick drawings and design layouts.

The intuitive interface makes it very easy to manipulate objects. At the bottom of the screen is a tab bar with buttons for adding symbols, signatures and fonts; in total there are 36 objects to be used. With just a simple tap of a finger, objects can be re-sized and edited. It's also possible to edit the fill colour and borders to give objects a unique appearance.

It's easy to whip up a sketch in mere seconds, but by digging further into the interface, more additional features appear. It's possible to group and copy objects, move them via a virtual control stick, and share them with friends via email. Sketches can also be saved to the iPad's gallery for later viewing.

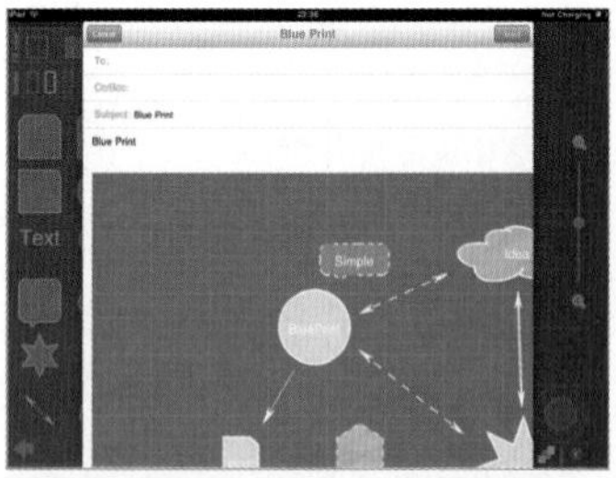

■ The interface allows you to quickly email sketches directly from the app.

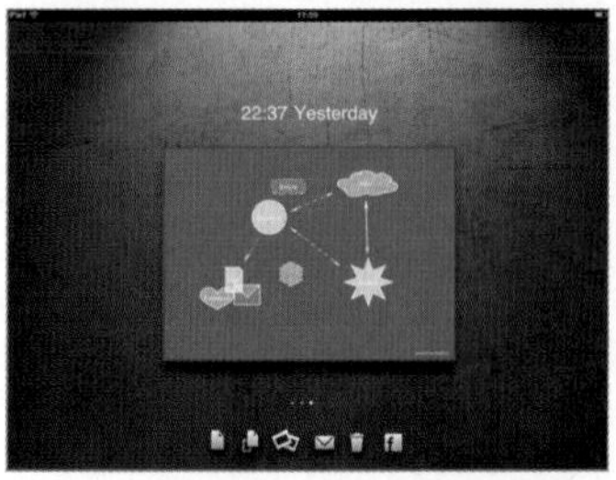

Overall Rating ★★★★☆

Tap Forms HD – database for iPad

Keep your life in order with this forms app

Back in the Eighties, it became fashionable to carry around a pocket organiser known as a Filofax. Like bum bags, they quickly fell out of fashion, and became consigned to the history books, but for a time they nevertheless became essential tools for those with busy lives.

Tap Forms HD is like a 21st Century digital Filofax, enabling users to organise their lives with sections for notes, bank details, contacts, loyalty cards, audio dictation and more. It's an incredibly convenient app for storing masses of personal details, and is a doddle to use. A record tab (called Forms) stories entries, and can be accessed with one tap of a finger. When adding new forms, it's possible to choose from custom templates that include email accounts, insurance details and serial numbers, although it's not possible to add fields from within a template, which has the effect of limiting their usefulness considerably.

As would be expected, the app includes a passcode lock, and the ability to add an encryption key and auto-lock after a set number of minutes. Forms can also be exported via email, Dropbox, Bluetooth, web server or Wi-Fi connection.

Tap Forms HD is the perfect app for anyone with a busy life to juggle. The inability to add entries from within a form is an inconvenience, but look beyond this niggling issue, and you'll find this to be one feature-packed app.

Price: £5.49/$8.99 Developer: ClickSpace Technologies Inc

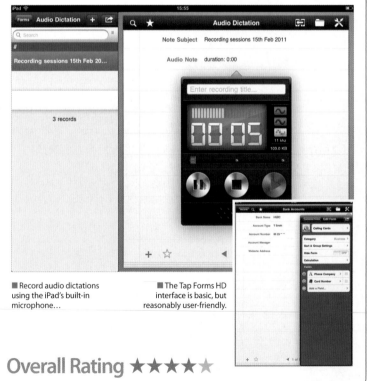

■ Record audio dictations using the iPad's built-in microphone…

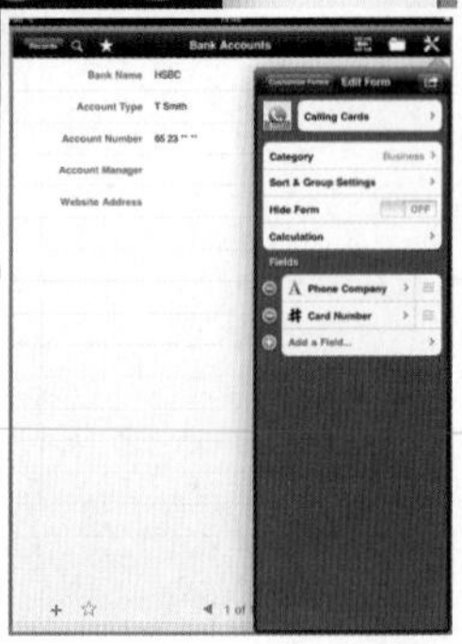

■ The Tap Forms HD interface is basic, but reasonably user-friendly.

Overall Rating ★★★★☆

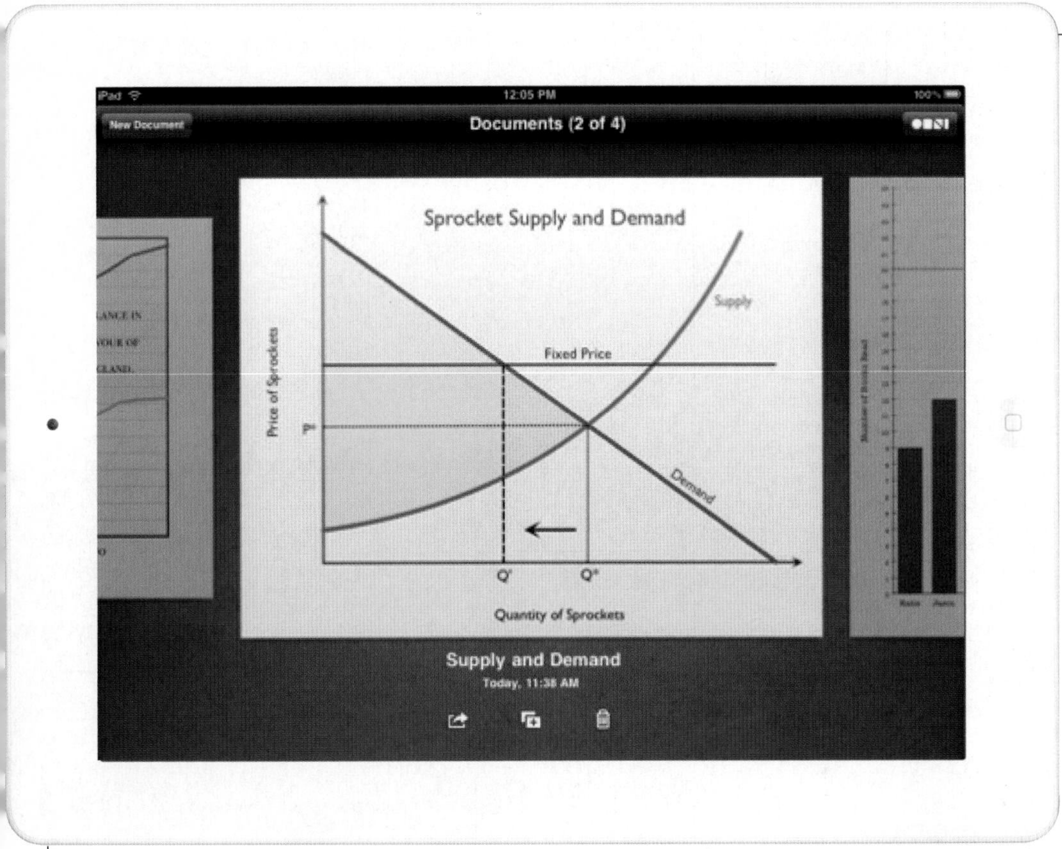

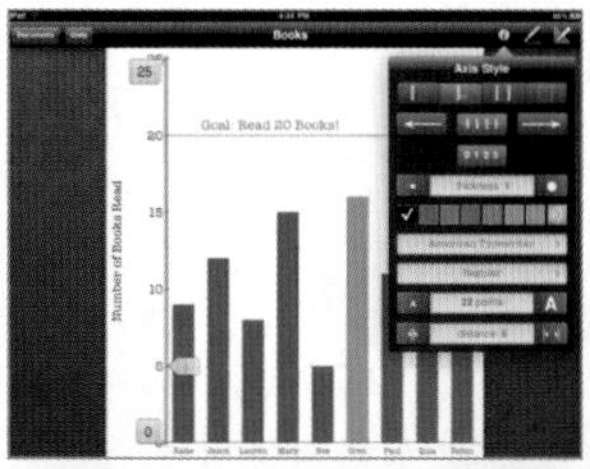

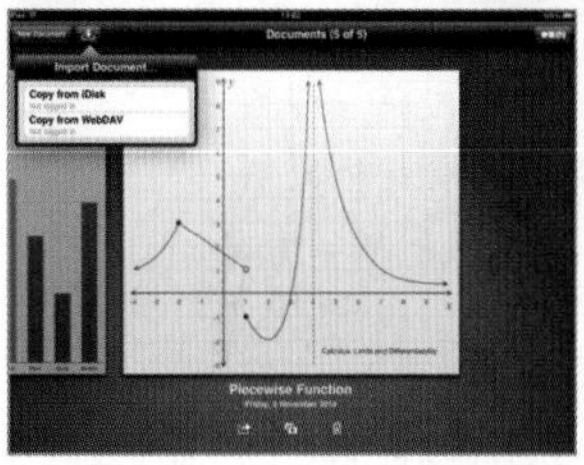

■ Use this drop-down option to import a file. This will be loaded into the app and made editable so you can tap and flick your way to creating a cool graph.

■ As you move a point, you get a heads-up display that shows you the value of the point as it moves. This is an easy way to check it is in the right place.

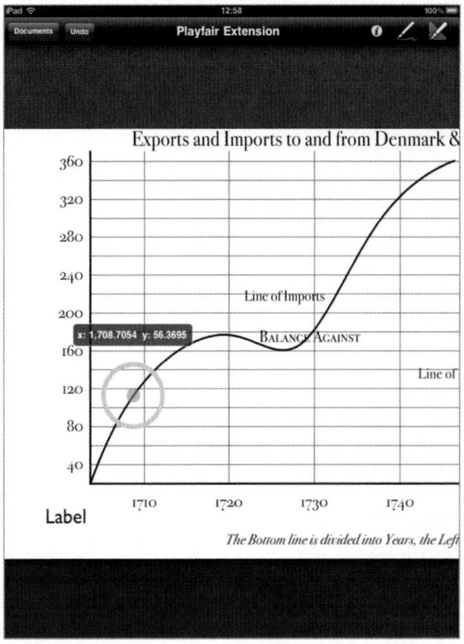

Price: £8.99/$14.99 **Developer:** The Omni Group

OmniGraph Sketcher

Can this app keep you from firing up the laptop?

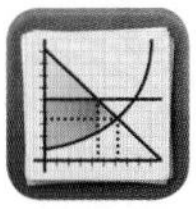

We all know that the iPad has huge potential, and that the allure of touch input has prompted all kinds of innovative ways to do some of the things we've been doing on normal computers for decades. The Omni Group is guilty of getting caught up in this wave of enthusiasm, and has created a very cool graph creation tool called OmniGraphSketcher. The app has a handful of templates and a decent sized toolset, and will let you create all kinds of graphs using your finger to input and draw the details.

The system works well, and in a lot of ways the process makes sense. You can easily draw lines across axis, add text to any area of the screen, and even play around with the colour of the canvass and the thickness of the lines on screen. Despite all this, the big question is whether you can use this to replace your home computer and the software you would normally use? The answer, unfortunately, is no. Without the ability to import figures or automatically generate any part of the graph, life becomes a little more difficult. Not to mention that if you aren't particularly nimble with your finger tips you may struggle to get things moving at any kind of pace, which is a real shame because this app has massive potential.

Overall Rating ★★★★★

Price: £11.99/$19.99 **Developer:** Antecea Inc

Cloud Connect Pro

Manage files, desktop computers and more with this app

If there's one limitation of using an iPad for regular work, it's the file system. To put it simply, there isn't one, so if you were hoping to plug your iPad into a Mac or PC and drag files back and forth between machines, then you'll be disappointed.

Thankfully, Cloud Connect Pro is here to help. It enables you to transfer files from any computer, and access a Dropbox account, iDisk or WebDAV/SFTP/FTP server. Launch the app, and you'll see a sidebar with options for viewing shared documents, accessing bookmarks, connecting to a Gmail account, viewing saved places, and accessing network places. At the bottom is a dock with icons for playing media, settings, file transfers and documents.

So far, so good, but Cloud Connect Pro also has a few aces up its sleeve, the most impressive of which is the ability to remotely log on to your Mac or PC, and interact with it via MultiTouch. As a result, you can log into your home computer over a 3G or Wi-Fi connection, drag files into the Cloud Connect Pro documents folder, and see them appear on your iPad seconds later. Some of the other clever features packed into the app include the ability to play music, watch videos and view photos, open iWork and Office files, zip and unzip files, open files in other apps, transfer multiple files and folders, wake a computer remotely, and many more.

The price is considerable when compared to similar apps. Whether you can justify the price depends on which features you'll use. This app will certainly enable you to easily manage files between your iPad and desktop computer, and it's great being able to remotely access a desktop computer.

If there's one problem we have with this app, it's the custom-built interface. It's not ugly by any means, but the large icons and blue colour scheme feel out of place on an iPad, with a desktop computer feel to them.

Overall Rating ★★★★★

■ Cloud Connect Pro boasts far more features than we could possibly fit into this review.

■ The app gives you access to many ways to manage your files, such as Dropbox, Apple File Sharing and more.

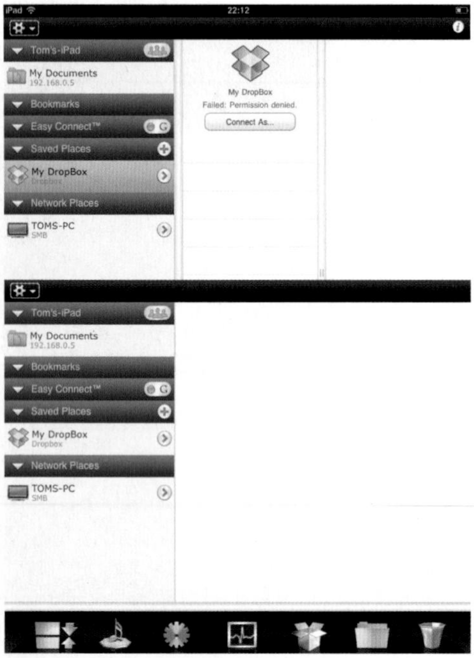

■ Open supported files within other apps.

■ You can access your Mac or PC through the app.

Price: £1.19/$1.99 **Developer:** Lee Heap

Ultimate Browser

Browse the web in style with this superb browser

Preloaded on every iDevice, Safari is a solid internet browsing app that is full of the standard features that you would probably expect from any good web browser. However, it absolutely pales in comparison to the various desktop browsers, specifically Google Chrome and Firefox, both of which offer a wide range of expansive bolt-ons and features.

Enter Ultimate Browser, a web browser that successfully delivers all the features of a high-end browser for your iDevice. While the browser may initially look similar to Safari upon start-up, a quick dabble in the top menu bar will reveal there to be within the app a wealth of features. For starters, you can open multiple tabs for when you want to explore multiple sites in tandem, as well as bookmarking favourites in a clear drop-down menu.

There is also a download tracker, as well as a free service called Ultimate Browser Push, which allows you to send links as push notifications to other users. Or alternatively, if you want to take the social route, pages can be aggregated via Facebook, Twitter and Tumblr in the Action menu. Pages can also be saved and read later in Google Reader and Instapaper.

Underneath the hood lies a plethora of features, such as a cookie tracker, homepage settings, search engine preferences, ad blocking and even privacy options. The asking price is modest given how ultimately superior this app is over Safari, and represents a must-have for any iPad user who wants to surf the web in style.

Overall Rating ★★★★★

■ Ultimate Browser Push is a free service that you can apply for within the app. It lets you send links to users via push notifications, or whole files such as images.

■ It's hard to know where to begin with Ultimate Browser's wide range of settings. The menu is rammed full of search, function and security adjusters.

■ By holding down on an image, Ultimate Browser opens a window that delivers tons of options. You can copy or save images directly, and send them using push. Images can be shared via Facebook or Twitter from within the app.

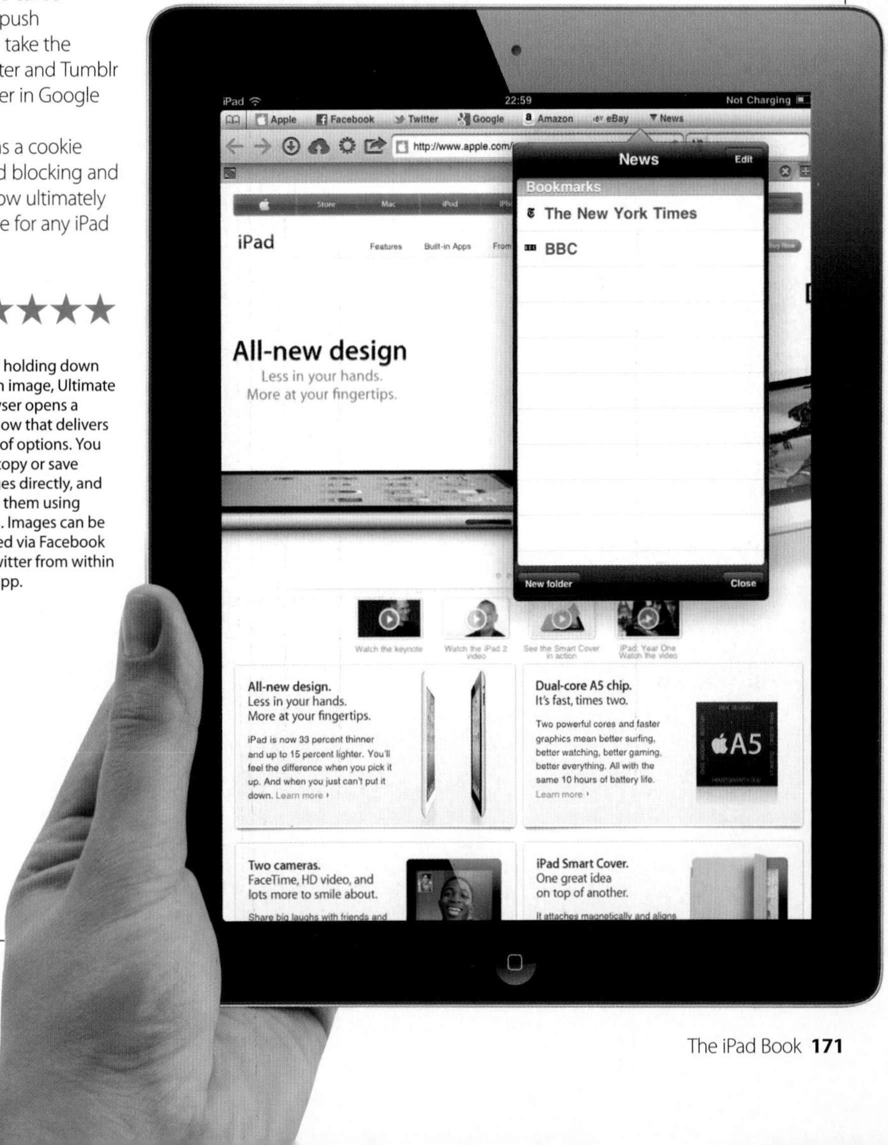

Price: £5.99/$10.99 **Developer:** Avatron Soft

Air Display

Double up your desktop display space with a second screen

Two displays are better than one and the Air Display app is here to make the scenario a reality without the added expense of a second screen. Unfortunately, Air Display did not take off with the instant impact we hoped for. Connection was simple enough: install the software, start the app, connect. But our tests via Windows Vista and XP were drawn out and not completely successful, particularly with Vista. However, this could be down to other factors such as the hardware used and connection issues, and we did have more success via a Mac. Air Display uses the same Wi-Fi network as the desktop so the quality of service can be dependent on the quality of the connection. If the connection does drop out there is the option to connect automatically, but we only had occasional success with this.

Once connected and into action it's all about the moving windows and apps to arrange. The mouse moves right and makes an appearance on the iPad screen, but when dragging a window from desktop to iPad there is a slight delay.

Using the mouse across two screens takes some getting use to and it occasionally disappears when making the transfer. Swapping windows didn't see any auto resize for the different resolutions, meaning the user needs to perform the action. Swapping more dynamic content, ie video, saw a poor frame rate and jerky video. The app is much cheaper than a second screen, and it could prove very useful, but it just doesn't fulfil its potential just yet.

Overall Rating ★★★★★

■ Having that extra bit of screen real estate is a really positive way to use a device you already own.

■ The iPad can be used in both orientations, landscape and portrait. Flipping the iPad will automatically change the orientation allowing users to view the open applications without hindrance. The elements on the iPad screen keep position as is standard for the iPad.

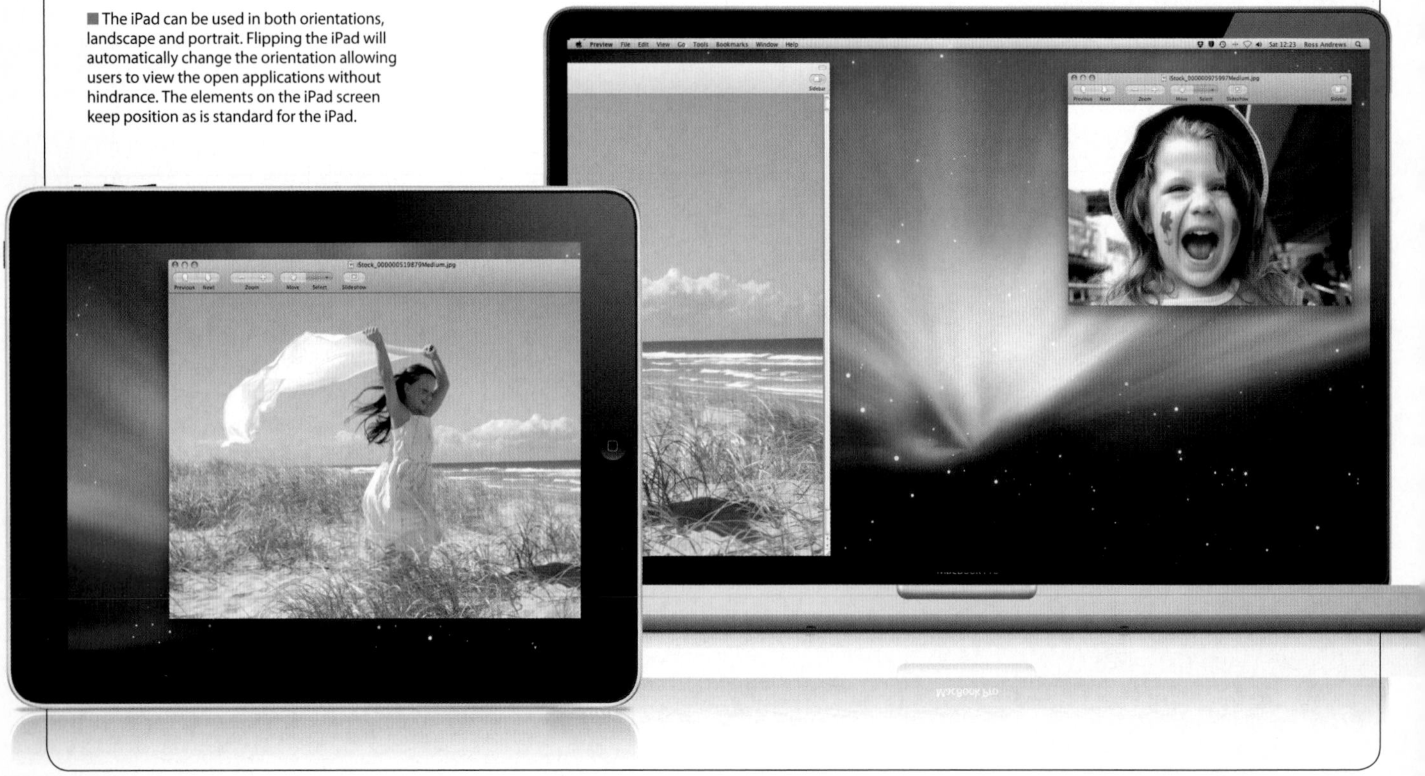

Price: £1.19/$1.99 **Developer:** zheng min Wei

GeoBoard

Shift shapes with the iPad's most popular geometry tool, all at your fingertips

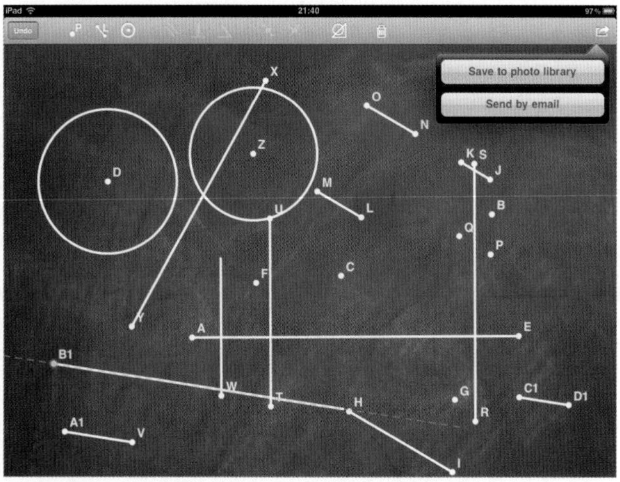

■ 'Save to photo library', and 'send by email'. No app is complete without them.

Being able to draw a perfect circle generally isn't a skill possessed by many people. Regular folk have to use a tool like a compass, but on GeoBoard you just need a single finger. Drag a fingertip across the blackboard-style screen, and it'll make a perfect circle appear precisely to the size you like. Why? Because GeoBoard is a drawing tool that allows you to create all kinds of geometrical illustrations by hand. In addition to circles, they include straight, parallel and perpendicular lines. There's also the ability to draw a line at any angle you like relative to another point, the option to create a point exactly midway between two others, and slightly more complicated things we don't understand, like creating an intersection for lines and circles.

What's the use of all this? As mere intellectual mortals, we're not really sure, but GeoBoard seems to be only suited to geometry students or teachers, and is very popular with said users if the user reviews are anything to go by. Without that specialist knowledge, all we can say is that GeoBoard does exactly what it's supposed to do. Just about the only feature missing is the ability to wipe the slate clean in one go, but with the developer working on frequent updates, we're sure it won't be long before that and a few other features are implemented.

Overall Rating ★★★★★

Wealth Manager

Worried about the future? This might make things better, or worse…

If you want to find this financial planning software In the App Store, then you'll obviously have to search for the words 'Wealth' and 'Manager', but we'd like to think that there are a couple of other search terms that would work just as well. How about 'A way to make you lose all hope for the future'? Or, 'The graph of inevitable depression'? Doesn't sound so tempting a download, does it? But depending on your mood, that's what Wealth Manager is.

In all seriousness, though, Wealth Manager is all about ensuring you can live to a ripe old age (assuming you do), with enough money to keep you going. And it does a fairly good job of this. It allows you to plot your age, how long you intend/expect to live, how much cash you're willing to put away per month, and exactly when you hope to retire. Sprinkle in extra cash vacuums like marriage, cars, holidays and homes, including exactly how expensive you'd like them to be, and the app will then produce a graph showing how long (or not) your cash is likely to last. It's all perfectly simple drag and drop stuff, with some easy to understand pop-up menus. And though there's no tutorial, we got to grips with it within minutes.

Depressing affirmation of life's realities aside, it's really quite a useful application, and at just 59 pence it shouldn't affect your retirement fund too much.

Price: £0.59/$0.99 **Developer:** Prosperity Financial

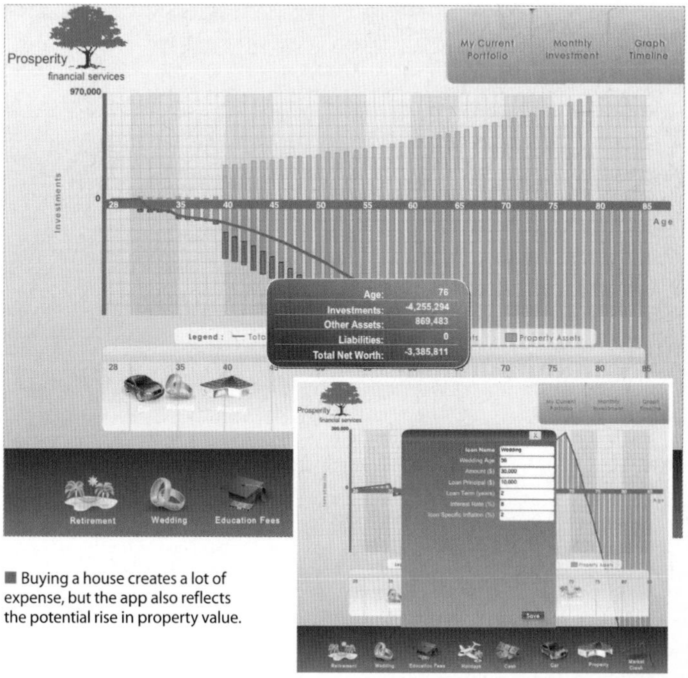

■ Buying a house creates a lot of expense, but the app also reflects the potential rise in property value.

Overall Rating ★★★★★

Go creative with Mac, iPad & iPh

Upskill today with the very best creative bookazines and DVDs

Mac for Beginners vol 3
Starting with the basics, this essential guide will teach you how to get to grips with every aspect of your Mac, from iLife and iWork to iTunes, Safari and Mail.
SRP: £12.99

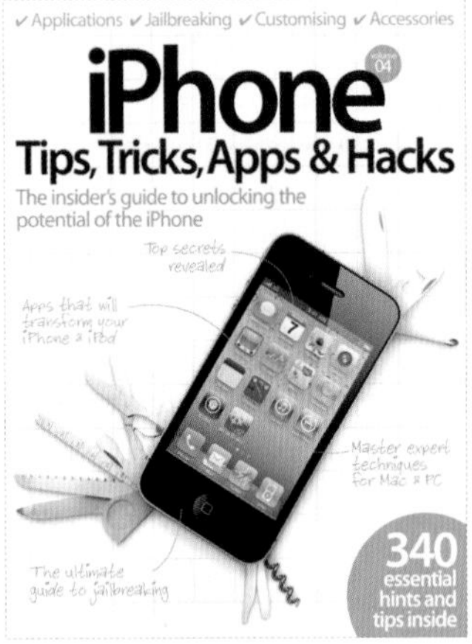

iPhone Tips, Tricks, Apps & Hacks vol 4
Step-by-step tutorials and features covering the secrets of the iPhone and a jailbreaking guide make this a must-own.
SRP: £9.99

iPad App Directory vol 1
Save yourself time and money by using our definitive guide to the best apps on the App Store. Every category is covered and there are over 500 apps reviewed inside.
SRP: £9.99

iPhone App Directory vol 7
The world's best iPhone applications are reviewed right here, including the very best for iPhone 4, with every App Store category featured inside.
SRP: £9.99

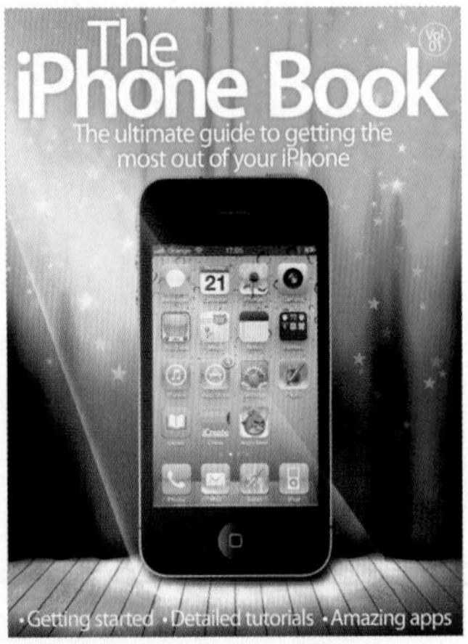

The iPhone Book vol 1
Whether you're brand new to the iPhone or have had one for a while, this book is the ultimate resource for getting the best from your favourite device.
SRP: £9.99

The Mac Book vol 6
256 pages of practical and creative tutorials and in-depth features that will take you through OS X, iLife, iWork and even third-party applications.
SRP: £12.99

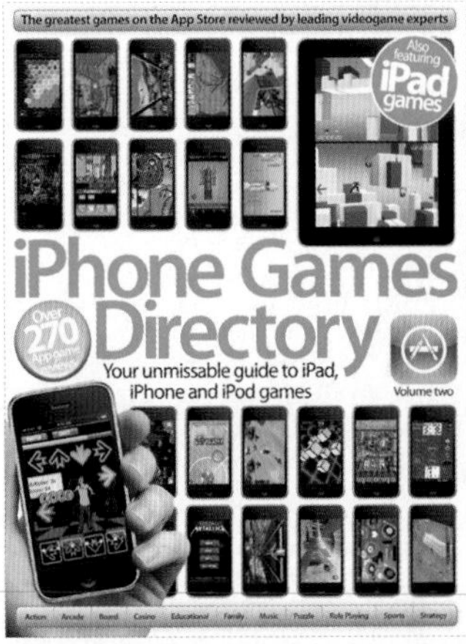

iPhone Games Directory vol 2
The world's most comprehensive guide to iPhone, iPod touch and iPad gaming apps, with all gaming genres reviewed and rated.
SRP: £9.99

iLife Genius Guide vol 2
Easy-to-follow 256-page tutorial guide to the complete suite of Apple iLife apps including iPhoto, iMovie, iDVD, iWeb and GarageBand.
SRP: £12.99

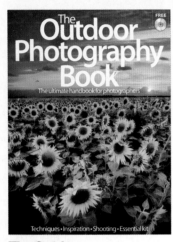

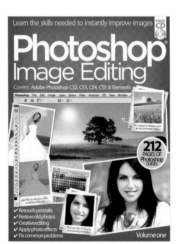

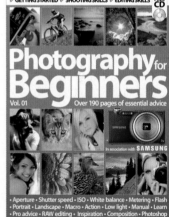